Secret Intelligence in the
Twentieth Century

Books by Constantine FitzGibbon

Fiction
The Arabian Bird
The Iron Hoop
Cousin Emily
The Holiday
Paradise Lost and More
In Love and War
When the Kissing Had to Stop
Going to the River
High Heroic
In the Bunker
The Golden Age

Non-Fiction
Miss Finnegan's Fault
Norman Douglas: A Pictorial Record
The Little Tour (with Giles Playfair)
The Shirt of Nessus
The Blitz
Random Thoughts of a Fascist Hyena
Denazification
Through the Minefield
The Life of Dylan Thomas
Selected Letters of Dylan Thomas
A Concise History of Germany
The Life and Times of Eamon de Valera (with George Morrison)
The Maxims of la Rochefoucauld
Red Hand: the Ulster Colony
Out of the Lion's Paw
Man In Aspic (previously entitled *Music From Far Away*)

Secret Intelligence in the Twentieth Century

Constantine FitzGibbon

𝔰𝔡

STEIN AND DAY/*Publishers*/New York

First published in the United States of America, 1977
Copyright © 1976 by Constantine FitzGibbon
All rights reserved
Printed in the United States of America
Stein and Day/*Publishers*/Scarborough House,
Briarcliff Manor, N.Y. 10510

Library of Congress Cataloging in Publication Data

FitzGibbon, Constantine.
    Secret intelligence in the twentieth century.

    1. Intelligence service–History.   I.   Title.
UB250.F57   327′.12′0904   76-9110
ISBN 0-8128-1937-3

This book is dedicated to
Eric Birley
friend and mentor, then and now

Acknowledgments

Extracts from the following copyrighted material are reproduced by kind permission of the following:

McGraw-Hill Book Company (*The Ordeal of Woodrow Wilson* by Herbert Hoover).

Mrs. H. Yardley (*The American Black Chamber* by Herbert Yardley).

Macmillan Publishing Co., Inc. from *The Great Terror* copyright © 1963 by Robert Conquest.

Michael Joseph, Ltd. (*Panzer Leader* by Heinz Guderian).

Encyclopaedia Britannica, Inc. (*Intelligence Military* in *Encyclopaedia Britannica,* 12th edition [1922]).

Hodder and Stoughton, Ltd. (*The KGB* by John Barron).

Contents

Introduction

If a definitive and final study could be written on this subject, or perhaps on any aspect and period of history, this would have been attempted in the pages that follow. As any such endeavour, particularly when dealing with what is supposed to be secret, would be both pretentious and dishonest, I have limited myself to what I know and to what I regard as reliable sources. Both of these are fragmentary. When I have had recourse to surmise, I say so.

I also give my written sources, on occasion with comment as to my opinion of their reliability. Of the many, many books that I have read over the past few years on differing aspects of this subject, few are entirely trustworthy. Even the captured German state papers are very far from infallible, for a great deal of secret intelligence work cannot be and never has been committed to paper. Therefore I have abstained from including a bibliography. On the other hand the books to which I do refer usually have their own bibliographies, for those interested in specific aspects of the subject. A complete bibliography would lengthen this already long book by at least another hundred pages; a selective one might well be misleading in its very selectivity. So, with apologies to the authors who wrote the hundreds of books, no bibliography.

I should like to express my profound gratitude to three extremely busy men who have somehow found the time, and devoted the trouble, to reading these pages as I wrote them. The first is Professor Eric Birley, to whom I have dedicated this book. The second is the experienced diplomat, chairman of the Joint Intelligence Sub-Committee of the Chiefs of Staff from September 1939 to June 1945, and also Foreign Office Adviser to the Directors of Plans from 1941 to June 1945, Mr V. Cavendish-Bentinck. The third is Brigadier Sir Edgar Williams, who was Field Marshal Montgomery's Chief of Intelligence both in Africa and in Europe. All three have helped me catch the many mistakes that are inherent in such a study. None is responsible for any that remain, nor for my own interpretation of trends and events.

Finally, I should like to express my gratitude to Mrs Robina Quigley who has typed and retyped an excessively difficult manuscript. Of the many persons who have helped me, those who are not mentioned in the book are absent at their own request. And I need hardly say how appreciative I am of my wife's tolerance in listening to so much about a subject so alien to her own real interests.

PART ONE
BACKGROUND

Chapter One

About Intelligence

It is best, when writing about so emotive a topic, to start with an attempt at clarification. Secret intelligence, however, is a field of human activity in which clarity appears to be, and often is, engulfed in obscurity. This is not only intrinsic, but often deliberate and not infrequently self-defeating. Let us take the humble example of the squid which exudes a black fluid in order to disguise its direction of escape from a potential enemy. The squid's enemy will attempt not only to penetrate the cloud of darkness, an attempt which will probably prove a failure, but will also calculate through knowledge of currents, submarine rock formation and so forth, the direction of escape that its enemy or prey is likely to take. Meanwhile the squid itself may become bewildered and lost in its own secret cloud and even have the misfortune to emerge straight into its enemy's jaws.

Let us take another, equally oversimplified, example. Women wear clothes not only, in many climates not even primarily, for warmth, but in order to attract the eye of the male. A man, it is said, having his attention attracted to the girl, will in his mind undress her as he passes her in the street or meets her at a party. And unless the woman is physically of very great beauty, or unless her dress-maker is quite lacking in talent, what the man imagines will almost always be superior to what he actually discovers should he be persuasive enough to induce her to take her clothes off. This sweet form of deception and intelligence will usually have a mutually happy ending, and has made many a *couturier's* fortune and fame. On the other hand the man who, like the Dadaist character in *Annablume*, lacks the intelligence to detect wig, false teeth and padding for breasts, and even mistakes artificial limbs for real legs, has been conquered by a superior intelligence, a secret intelligence.

A third mundane example of secret intelligence is the bluff

12

of a poker player. Any poker player knows the nature of this manoeuvre. Simply, by the way he bets, a player can persuade one or more opponents that he has the better hand. They, having in fact better hands than his, drop out; he never shows his 'secret' hand – and collects the money. A more complex strategy is, through a series of called bluffs, to persuade the opponents that he is bluffing once again when in fact he has a very good hand. The combination of bluffs, non-bluffs and counter-bluffs becomes almost limitless. A skilful poker player can pay for his wife or mistress to patronize a very good dress-maker.

The hoax, whether in the form of a harmless joke, or the emptying of a major rail terminal by an anonymous telephone call about a bomb, is another kind of bluff.

Now, these simple examples taken from ordinary life are merely three among thousands which we encounter frequently though not constantly. And they have one quality in common: the pitting of wits, which implies a relationship based on opposition. This can vary from the competition between friendly gamblers or sportsmen to lethal hostility between states, religions or ideologies. It is with this latter form of intelligence that we are here primarily concerned and, to a lesser extent, with its offshoots, propaganda and sabotage.

Most intelligence, however, is not secret at all. This is particularly true among modern, open societies which may, for the sake of convenience, be here referred to as democracies, states which in peacetime have a more or less free press and open frontiers, which exchange diplomatic missions, trade with one another, and observe similar styles of political morality.

There is no quite satisfactory 'model' but let us take an oversimplified version of Franco-German open intelligence at the beginning of the period which this book covers, that is to say around the end of the last century, at the time of the arrest of Captain Dreyfus (1894), and before the Dreyfus case blew up some four years later. Franco-German relations were then theoretically peaceful but potentially hostile. German victory in 1871, and particularly the partial dismemberment of France by the seizure of Alsace-Lorraine, seemed to many, in both countries, to make another war inevitable. Leaving aside, for the moment, the pacifists and those adherents of the Second International who had persuaded themselves that the solidarity of the international workers' movement had made national wars an impossibility, many Germans and Frenchmen not only regarded a new war as inevitable, but actually desired one: the French for reasons of revenge, the Germans to pre-empt a French offensive. In both countries the general staffs were instructed by their respective governments to make both offensive and defensive plans for such a war. Meanwhile on another level the two governments were manoeuvring for allies. All this was open and obvious.

Other facts were also obvious. The ease with which the Germans had defeated the French a generation before had come as something of a surprise to the world at large. Since then the massive expansion of German industry, particularly of the armaments industry, had greatly outstripped a similar expansion by the French. Few could doubt that in solitary combat the Germans would inflict an even more resounding defeat upon their enemy than they had on the previous occasion. Therefore it was essential for the French to find allies, as the Germans had already done. The Germans, owing largely to the Kaiser's diplomatic ineptitude, gave the French their first important ally in the form of Russia in 1892, and immediately afterwards raised the cry of 'encirclement', with the dreaded prospect of a war on two fronts. At this time massive German naval re-armament had not begun to affect relations with Great Britain, which still relied on its two-fleet navy (i.e., a navy large enough to defeat any combination of two other navies in the world) and on its great wealth to preserve the balance of power in Europe. Much diplomatic manoeuvring was done, by both sides, to influence successive British governments, but with little success until the Kaiser publicly announced that 'Germany's future lay upon the water' and in 1898 the Reichstag publicly voted the credits which enabled him and Admiral Tirpitz speedily to build a great and powerful fleet. The near-uselessness of the 'Russian steam roller' was not fully revealed until Russia's defeat by the Japanese in 1905.

Indeed, to return to Europe, diplomatic manoeuvres were scarcely secret or, if they were intended so to be, did not remain secret for long. Diplomats, it was said, were paid to lie for their countries overseas. But the actions of their governments usually revealed quite quickly the purposes of diplomacy. What was not

14

revealed was the degree of determination, rather than the degree of honesty, of the diplomats' present and future masters. Bluff is infinitely more difficult in the game of foreign affairs than in the game of poker, and strong nerves are essential. A phrase of the period is here perhaps not entirely out of place, though the events of 1914 and after have made its flippancy repulsive: international politics at the highest level were occasionally known as 'the great game'. Many historians, of all political persuasions, have written with contempt and savagery of the men who led Europe, and perhaps the world, to disaster in our century. Yet it must be remembered that most of those men – and women – who bear the responsibility for initiating that disaster were utterly sure of their world. And some of them did treat their awful responsibilities as a game. French eighteenth-century aristocrats who patronized Rousseau and treated Voltaire as an intellectual hero and laughed at Beaumarchais's plays not infrequently died without their heads. The dignified and honoured leaders of Europe in 1900 usually died in their beds, but this, of course, makes them neither more nor less contemptible.

For 'the great game' was not of their invention. It was perhaps inherent in the ideas of Metternich, of Castlereagh and of Canning, intended originally as an antidote to Napoleonic Caesarism and evolving into the so-called Concert of Europe and the balance of power principle. Though for the weaker of the great powers, such as Austria, Spain and Turkey, it gave a welcome respite from violent change, it placed great responsibility, sometimes relished and sometimes not, in the hands of the men who ruled Russia and, above all, Britain. Since both these essentially extra-continental powers were more involved in colonial expansion than in internal European affairs, it was in their direct interest to help keep the peace, by which Metternich meant the *status quo ante* Napoleon Bonaparte. 'The great game' did not, however, allow for the nascent nationalism of Germany, Italy and later of the Balkan nations. It may have been the most durable international political balance of modern times. In its very solidity lay its danger, for it lacked the flexibility essential to any political situation which involves relationships, which is not in fact a total, global tyranny with an immortal tyrant. To phrase this in cruder terms, the fresh pack that had been dealt with such skill at Vienna

15

in 1815 had, by 1870, not only become soiled, with some of the cards marked, others dog-eared, while a few had been lost altogether; but the face values of the cards had also changed. The French emperor's advisers, or at least his public opinion, ascribed far greater value to *la gloire* than did the King of Prussia. Bismarck played a different game altogether, in which German unity was both the stake and the trump card. War, for him, was a means by which at the same time that card might be played and that stake won.

Yet despite the lessons that 1870 might have taught the players the game of international power politics continued, undiminished. What nowadays is called brinkmanship was then almost standard procedure. France and Britain nearly went to war in\1898 over the really unimportant ownership of an otherwise unknown place in Africa, Fashoda. Russia and Austria, friends for so long, were repeatedly close to war as the Turks lost control of the Balkans. The Italians, sensible people, having won their only victory of modern times by at last capturing their own capital city, made an alliance with Germany and their hereditary enemy, Austria. The Kaiser twirled his moustaches, rattled his sabre and redoubled his armed forces. The British fought a war of naked aggression against the Boers; even the distant United States found itself a manifest destiny and fought an equally naked war of aggression against the Spaniards. The great game was, in fact, becoming both pointless and extremely dangerous. Yet despite this the rules, or at least some of the rules, continued to be generally observed. Monarchs made one another admirals and generals of fleets and armies preparing for mutual slaughter; munitions salesmen such as Sir Basil Zaharoff sold weapons openly to the highest bidder and, not infrequently, to his potential enemy as well; smooth statesmen of one country told lies to equally smooth statesmen of other countries, fully aware that both sides knew the truth but were too polite, for the moment, to announce it. The Concert of Europe was a reality. It was, however, more and more a spider's web, or series of webs, good at catching flies (or colonies) but really meant to ensnare other spiders.

And a very important ingredient of this elaborate apparatus was intelligence. As already stated, open intelligence was, and indeed has remained, the most obvious as it is the most easily available source of information about potentially hostile countries in Western Europe. Since Metternich's system had degenerated as described above, this meant in effect that all the European powers required up-to-date information about one another. Provided that an apparatus existed to process and evaluate such information, most of it was readily available in the press, parliamentary reports, trade fairs and general international travel. Army lists were published, naval units 'showed the flag', the great gunsmiths boasted of their latest achievements which were seldom built exclusively and secretly for their own governments.

Only slightly more discreet were the normal activities of military and naval attachés. It was their duty to remain informed concerning the strength, armaments and tactics of the armed forces of the countries in which they served. As guests of honour they were invited to attend manoeuvres. They visited camps and barracks and not infrequently inspected the foreigners' fortifications.

Of course it was all part of the game. A military attaché knew that his hosts wished him to see and report a specific picture of their own strength, just as they wished his ambassador to report the desired view of their intentions. And his hosts knew that he knew, and so on *ad infinitum*. It was his job, and even more the job of his own central intelligence apparatus, to evaluate his reports, to discount what the foreigners had deliberately planted or exaggerated, and thus to create an integrated picture. It is no exaggeration to say that the evaluation of intelligence is at least as important as its collection and collation. However, the intelligence material has to be collected and collated before it can be evaluated. By the beginning of the twentieth century every general staff of any important state contained at least one branch devoted to intelligence. And, as already stated, most of the material sifted and presented to commanders-in-chief and to governments was openly obtained. However, if this mass of material was falsely evaluated it became not useless but worse than useless.

Most intelligence, then, was 'open'. Most, but not all. Two forms of intelligence material are usually secret; for complex and varied reasons that will be discussed later they have tended to become more secret in the course of this century. The first of

17

these concerns the overall strategy of foreign powers; the second can usefully be described by the portmanteau word, technology. At the time, *c.* 1900, of which we here are writing, strategy was perhaps the more important.

Leaving aside high politics – did the French intend to attack the Germans and vice versa, and in what circumstances of alliances? – the two general staffs had to prepare for both a defensive and an offensive war in any of a multitude of circumstances. The classic case of such premeditation was, at this time, about to come to birth in the so-called Schlieffen plan. Politically this involved the highly unorthodox, dangerous and indeed immoral plan of invading France through two countries the neutrality of which Germany had solemnly guaranteed, Belgium and Holland. (The Dutch operation was eventually abandoned and this probably cost the Germans a 1940-type victory in 1914.) The Schlieffen plan essentially involved a huge, strategic outflanking of the French army. It was based increasingly on two political assumptions. The first was that the British were as cynical as the German government itself and would, in fact, not honour its guarantee of Belgian neutrality in order to save France. (And had the Germans not become a naval threat to Britain, it is conceivable that the British might have behaved in 1914 as they had in 1870, despite the Belgian guarantee.) The second assumption on which the Schlieffen plan was based was that even if Britain remained neutral, Germany would have to wage war simultaneously with Russia. Knowing the slowness of Russian mobilization and the comparative lack of communications in that vast country, the Schlieffen plan therefore proposed first to knock out France before Russia could mobilize; then, to turn about and defeat Russia. The whole German mobilization programme, or *Mobilmachung*, was geared to this strategy. The plan became more and more complicated. Indeed in the final crisis of July 1914, pressure was put on the German government by certain elements of the Great General Staff that the plan had passed the point of no return; that if there were to be a European war, the German army *must* immediately attack France through Belgium regardless of all political consequences. Certain modern historians have maintained that even at the eleventh hour the trains could have been turned about and the first, hopefully decisive, battle fought in the

18

east. Had the Germans defeated France and Russia and then been content with those victories, it was possible that Britain, even if it had come to the assistance of Belgium, might have accepted a negotiated peace. But all these highly problematical developments were based on the successful implementation of the Schlieffen plan. Therefore during the period before the First World War this Schlieffen plan (it is not altogether fair that it be linked for ever with his name: he was dead by 1914 and his plan had been much modified) was a matter of supreme strategic secrecy. The German General Staff most certainly did not show its *Mobilmachung* to foreign military attachés. Similar, though far less spectacular, plans by other general staffs were likewise kept closely under lock and key, then as now.

Under the general heading of 'technology' this book means material objects and their application for hostile purposes. This category encompasses a truly enormous variety of things and their use, from the super-heavy siege gun to the infra-mini-camera, from the cloud of mustard gas seeping into a shellhole that shelters coughing men to an aeroplane's bomb-sight, from a hydrogen bomb and its rocket upon a launching pad in a deep silo to a television camera carried by a satellite beyond the earth's atmosphere, from a cipher-breaking computer to a Tiger tank.

Now, 'secret weapons' have long exerted a peculiar fascination over the human imagination, and one that was apparently justified during the two world wars, but that was a concept of comparatively small importance before the First and, to judge by appearances, has diminished greatly since the end of the Second. Most technology is open, though for somewhat different reasons in the conditions of today than in earlier times.

Fighting until modern times was in essence the struggle of one man, multiplied into armies, with another. This was certainly the case before the invention of artillery. It is possible that the inventions of the axe and the spear, and later the sword, by increasing the individual's striking power, were responsible for more major shifts of population and hence of historical change than any technological inventions since; it is even possible that this is why we, rather than the descendants of Neanderthal man, are the lords of the planet. It certainly explains why other mammals are not. Yet these inventions were no more 'secret' than was the later smelting of iron, the building of fortifications, the invention of gunpowder and the creation of chain-mail armour, all of immense military and hence political importance.

Indeed up to very modern times the only 'secret' weapon that remained secret and of great defensive power was the 'Greek fire' of the Byzantine Empire. We are not quite sure what it was, and even less sure how it was kept secret for a matter of centuries. We do know that it was a nautical weapon – it does not appear to have been used on land – which enabled the Byzantine sailors to set fire to enemy fleets, wooden ships of course, a sort of flame-thrower with no doubt a petroleum base. The fact that it was apparently an exclusively naval weapon must have helped the Byzantines to preserve its secrecy, since it was unlikely to fall into enemy hands. In any event it seems to have been extremely effective for a surprisingly long time.

Secret weapons on land were far less successful before this century, principally because they were so tied up with tactics. Before 1870 the French did possess a primitive machine-gun, a multi-barrelled weapon closer to the Gatling gun that was used occasionally in the last stages of the American Civil War than to a modern, single-barrelled machine-gun. This *mitrailleuse* was regarded by the French as so secret a weapon that it was not even issued to their own troops until the outbreak of war, with the evident result that they not only knew nothing about it as a piece of machinery but had had no training in its tactical use. Although it was an effective weapon which caused the Germans very considerable anxiety, it would have been far more effective had it been better integrated into French infantry tactics. Furthermore, there was no reason why the Germans should necessarily have copied it. They had not copied the standard French rifle of the time, the *chassepot*, which was superior to their own. Nor had the French adopted the steel field guns of the Germans, and consequently they lost every artillery engagement and, probably, the war.

Perhaps the only truly decisive use of secret weapons up to very modern times has been purely fortuitous, when the weapon was not really secret at all but was nevertheless totally unknown to the enemy, that is to say when two civilizations first clashed. The classic example is perhaps the appearance, in Mexico, of Spanish

20

horsemen, which the Aztecs regarded at first as a weird and terrifying unit, a sort of armed two-headed, four-legged warrior. The horse, combined with gunpowder, gave Cortés's tiny force his victory over the huge and ferocious armies of Montezuma. But of course neither was in any European sense a secret weapon.

Indeed until very modern times a tactically well-trained army would almost always defeat a vastly superior horde. Hannibal's elephants were not a surprise to the Romans as such. However, their tactical integration into the Carthaginian army was, and so, of course, was the extraordinary feat of transporting them over the Alps.

Is there, then, such a thing as tactical secrecy? The answer is almost certainly that there is not, or at least not for long. Philip of Macedon's phalanx was an infantry formation which any of his enemies could have copied. Had they been sufficiently disciplined, the Teutons could have created legions as tactically effective as those of their Roman enemies. And so on. Guderian's tank-cum-bomber tactics were not secret: they had been formulated and published by Captain Liddell Hart long before 1940, and Charles de Gaulle had accepted and reproduced the Englishman's doctrine. However, it was German, not British or French, generals who applied the theory in practice. Nothing secret here, just better generalship already practised, more or less openly, in peacetime manoeuvres. Tactical surprise, yes; but tactical secrecy is more or less a contradiction in terms. And at times tactical stupidity can be as bewildering, at least briefly, to a professional enemy as tactical brilliance. Non-professional, revolutionary armies have not infrequently won battles simply because they did not know what their enemies regarded as the 'proper' way to fight them. In tactical matters there is very little room for secrecy, and therefore even less for secret intelligence. The methodical capture and skilled interrogation of prisoners, combined at a later date with aerial reconnaissance, will usually suffice, provided as always that these forms of intelligence are properly evaluated.

To return then to the status of Franco-German intelligence a little before 1900, what purpose did secret intelligence serve? At the lowest level it could add to what was openly available concerning such matters as military strength, morale, the quality of officers, perhaps add details concerning the efficiency in war conditions, of road, rail and waterway networks. At a higher level it could obtain or confirm technical information regarding such subjects as the strength of fortifications, the plans for demolitions, the armour and armament of fighting ships, the proposed design of new weapons such as guns, mines and so forth not yet on display. For this purpose it would require the enrolment of spies, who depending on their task could be soldiers or civilians. These were, at that date, usually mercenary spies – ideological spies came later, although a Frenchman in German Alsace-Lorraine, for example, might well spy for patriotic reasons. At the highest level secret intelligence would attempt, almost invariably without success, to discover the secret intentions of the opposite general staff and therefore of its government. At this level the spy could only be so highly placed as to have access to this type of information. In those largely pre-ideological days such traitors were very rare. Indeed history has revealed virtually none of any significance at all in Franco-German relations at that time.

At a slightly lower level, if the military or naval attaché was a spy he was nevertheless an officer and a gentleman, in an age when this word still had a meaning; the mercenary spy was not a gentleman, neither in the eyes of his employers nor in those of their potential enemies. An inherent condition of his employment was that, if caught, his employers would disclaim any knowledge of him whatsoever and certainly would in no way come to his assistance. As for those upon whom he spied, should they catch him at his work they were likely to invoke the most severe penalties, up to and including the death sentence. A professional spy was in fact, and from every point of view, a contemptible fellow, ill-paid, despised and feared, a veritable rat in the bilge of the ship of state, of any state. When communicating with his German, and allied, opposite number in Paris in the '90s, the Italian military attaché, Panizzardi, referred to the spy who had procured for him plans of the French fortifications of Nice as *ce canaille*, 'that guttersnipe', a typical attitude. Yet almost every nation employed them, and was well aware that all the other nations did so too.

This form of hypocrisy was not limited to the varieties of

22

espionage so far touched on. For instance, in theory embassies were physically the territory of the country which the ambassador represented, and diplomatic mail was sacrosanct. In fact, the planting of spies inside embassies, usually in a menial capacity, was common practice: the contents of waste-paper baskets were frequently scrutinized; and great care was needed to safeguard the secrecy of the 'diplomatic pouch' on its way from the foreign capital to the home base and vice versa. Telephones, as they came increasingly into use, were tapped. Telegrams sent in code or cipher were decoded and, when possible, deciphered. Bugging existed in a primitive form, and in general civilized diplomatic conventions were rules made to be broken. Everyone knew this, and it was in everyone's mutual interest to keep quiet about it. Cipher clerks were of particular interest to foreign intelligence services.

In order to frustrate foreign intelligence, countries had evolved counter-intelligence services. These filled two primary functions. The one was to prevent the foreigners from discovering what was hidden; the other was to know precisely how much they *had* discovered. A third, and increasingly important, activity was to feed the foreigners information, false or true, that would pass through the evaluation sieve and be accepted. This form of deception was antithetical to denying the foreigners all secret knowledge. A recognized spy was not automatically arrested. It was soon realized that he was of far more value if he were transmitting misleading information. This apparent paradox was in due course to produce the double agent. However, at the beginning of the century the various counter-intelligence services were almost precisely what their name implies: apparatuses to frustrate the activities of foreign intelligence services.

The work of counter-intelligence was thus inevitably closely intertwined with that of secret intelligence. Indeed in the military and international political fields it became in some ways the senior partner in a joint operation, for it had to supervise the activities of its own secret intelligence too; besides, it also had to supervise itself against infiltration. Counter-intelligence agencies and agents were and are of the greatest possible interest to foreign powers, and their activities and personnel are for all intents entirely secret, or should be.

The activities of the counter-intelligence service, or services, overlapped those of what was usually an entirely different agency of government, namely the police, and especially the secret police. (Every country has its secret police; a country which maintains it has none is simply indulging in the hypocrisy already mentioned.) The task of the police is well-known: to protect the society it serves against that society's enemies. Those enemies fall roughly into two categories. On the one hand there are those who flout the laws – burglars, murderers, embezzlers, arsonists and so on – and the 'open' police are here the arm of the law, though helped by other policemen who are not instantly recognizable as such. They are called in to deal with an identified crime or suspected crime and to arrest the criminal or perhaps to forestall his malpractice. The second, rarer and far more dangerous type of enemy is he who would destroy society as such. The revolutionary will not usually be an ordinary criminal (though the Bolsheviks robbed banks in Imperial Russia, as the illegal Irish Republican Army have done in Ireland, and political murders do not cease to be murder by being called assassination). The primary purpose of the secret police is to deal with organized anti-social activities, including the purely criminal gangs like the Mafia in America or Italy, as well as politically organized groups who may not, and indeed usually do not, regard themselves as criminals at all.

And here a deliberate confusion arises. All governments always claim legality in some form or other. Therefore all governments, though they may accept dismissal by the electorate if there is an electorate with the power to dismiss them, regard themselves as identified with the state that they govern. And the result of this is that the secret police can easily become the agent of a government, not the protector of a society. If the government it serves is itself a largely criminal government, as it was in Nazi Germany, the secret police itself becomes in effect a criminal conspiracy. A government, as in Soviet Russia, that relies on such a secret police force to maintain itself in power governs what is called a police state.

However, when the police is serving a perfectly legal government, such as those of Germany or France c. 1900, it may still be confronted by enemies whose political idealism, misplaced or not, will lead them to desire the overthrow of their society by any means, including co-operation with a real or potential enemy to bring about their country's military defeat. Lenin's co-operation with the Germans in 1917 is perhaps the most spectacular example. And it is in such circumstances, potential or real, that the activities of the secret police inevitably become intertwined with those of secret intelligence and, even more, of secret counter-intelligence. All these machines are usually lumped together in popular parlance as 'the secret service'. This term, though, is a gross oversimplification.

Let us now look at the secret intelligence services of the great powers, as they were at a turning point of historical time, the 1890s. Despite differences of organization, they were all remarkably similar in basic structure. At the turn of the century there were three great powers in Europe – France, Great Britain and Germany (the power of Spain and Turkey had long declined, as had that of Austria, while Italian aspirations to this status have never yet been fulfilled); the great power of Euro-Asia was Russia; in Asia proper, Japan had not yet proved itself, while China was immersed in internal turmoil, and India 'belonged' to Britain; in the western hemisphere only the United States of America had become a great power, recently and almost reluctantly.

Since the middle of this twentieth century the two super-powers, America and Russia, have inevitably possessed, in mutual hostility, the two largest (though not necessarily always the most efficient) intelligence services. At the beginning of the century, however, their respective services were, for very different reasons, internationally almost negligible. Until the Spanish–American War of 1898 and Theodore Roosevelt's 'open door' policy in China of 1907, American policy was virtually confined by the Monroe Doctrine to the American hemisphere. Just as American policy barred the European powers from the American continents, so it barred itself from European and Asian affairs. And over and above that, the very concept of a 'secret service', internal or external, was pungently antipathetic to the political ideals on which the United States as a country was based. The American Civil War and its aftermath had, in general, only reinforced this repugnance. By European standards the Americans had no secret service.

In Russia circumstances were almost completely reversed. Czarist autocracy remained absolute, in theory until the creation

25

of a short-lived and largely bogus parliament, the Duma, after
the abortive revolution of 1905 that followed the war lost against
Japan, in practice until 1917. The Russian Czar controlled, as
do his successors, a reluctant empire, which included and includes
the largest occupied national unit in Europe, the Ukraine, as well
as Finns, Poles and, to the east, a multitude of non-Russian
peoples, Tartars, Turcomen and so on as far east as Vladivostok.
This empire was continually seething with revolt, both in Russia
proper and in the conquered territories, which is hardly surprising
in an ill-run country where the system of government has been
described as tyranny tempered by assassination. Yet Russian
patriotism had proved itself, in Napoleon's time, and had also
proved that with the weapons and methods of war then available
Russia could not be conquered by any foreign nation or combination of nations. The Russian autocrat's enemies, therefore, were
internal and not external. This in turn meant that Russian military
intelligence was, in its co-operation with the secret police, the
junior partner. It was directed inwards, against Russian revolutionaries, while externally its principal targets were Russian
revolutionary *émigrés* and their contacts with potential hostile
powers. In fact, three-quarters of a century ago, Russian international intelligence was scarcely more developed than its
American equivalent, a curious coincidence in view of the situation that was to exist fifty years later.

The purpose of British intelligence in those distant days was
again quite different both from that of its Russian and American
counterparts and from what it later became. The Royal Navy
was the senior service, and it is not accidental that when war
came all British intelligence was centred in the Admiralty, for
naval intelligence was experienced, mature and extremely efficient. It had to be, in a country that not only relied for defence
on its two-fleet navy but also economically on colonies and
dominions around the world with which the only link was by sea.
Since Britain could not feed itself and lacked most raw materials
it had to ascribe primary importance to the safeguarding of
its nautical lifelines. Naval intelligence was flexible, too, and it
was the first secret intelligence service to realize the vast importance of monitoring and deciphering ship-to-ship and ship-to-
shore radio communications. Intelligence work in the colonies

was comparatively simple when dealing with 'natives', less so when fighting the Boers. At the turn of the century even Irish nationalism seemed remarkably tranquil. Nor was there any other revolutionary movement of any significance within the British Isles. Thus internal security was allowed to lapse, or at least to become in some measure ossified. This was to cost the British dear, particularly in Ireland, where the defeat of British intelligence in 1920–1 not only lost Britain most of Ireland but probably led to the loss of empire and, perhaps, eventually to the loss of the country's very status as a first class power. In 1900, however, the great skill of British naval intelligence had made 'the British secret service' legendary. The legend has lingered on, with diminishing verisimilitude.

This very brief summary, this setting of the stage as it were, leaves us once again with the German and French secret intelligence apparatuses face to face at the time of the Dreyfus affair. The Germans were, in this field, efficient. The country was united – separatism from Prussia an aspiration perhaps among some, but scarcely a political reality in the foreseeable future. The country of Karl Marx had then produced few Marxists, and the revolutionaries of 1848 were dead or reconciled to Bismarck's rich prototype of the welfare state – so that despite the growing power of the Social Democrats internal revolution was highly improbable. German intelligence could thus be devoted almost exclusively to Germany's major enemies in the future probable war: France, Britain and to a lesser degree Russia. The history of German secret intelligence will be told later. Meanwhile, and certainly so far as France was concerned, it was both thorough and unscrupulous.

It would be hard to imagine a less impressive star for an historical melodrama than Captain Alfred Dreyfus. Yet upon this dull, correct, intelligent and upright man there converged, like so many searchlights, great rays of violent emotions from the past which, transmuted through his ordeal, through his defenders and his enemies, have cast beams of horror but sometimes of hope into our century. His story is still so well known, though distorted by a multitude of passions, that I shall attempt to recapitulate it as briefly and as objectively as possible, for it is here only of interest in its relevance to quite another subject, secret intelligence as such.

Alfred Dreyfus was born in 1859 at Mulhouse (or, when it became German in 1871, Mülhausen) in Alsace. In 1874, perhaps for reasons of French patriotism, the family moved to Paris. His parents were quite rich, and such a move was no hardship. At the usual age, that is to say in his late teens, Alfred Dreyfus decided to become a professional French army officer. With a private income, in our terms, of some £5,000 or $10,000 a year he was rich by the average standards of junior officers in any army and at any time. He certainly did not need the odd £100, again our valuation, which the Germans paid for information from mercenary spies. He had not, as a boy, joined the French army in order years later to become a spy. He was a clever and hard working officer, with apparently no expensive vices such as gambling, and normal, moderate sexual desires which did not make him susceptible to any form of blackmail. The young artillery officer was chosen to attend the staff college, where he did well though not exceptionally so. He became a staff officer with access, therefore, to very secret information. By all reports he was a clever, hardworking, socially and intellectually rather uninteresting young staff captain. However, he was the first Jew in France, and perhaps in any major European army, to be appointed to the General Staff: certainly there was none in Germany. This must have seemed to him, the totally assimilated Frenchman, as the ultimate justification of his parents' move to Paris a decade and more before. He could hardly have expected that this was to be the cause of so much misery, both to himself and to France, let alone that as late as 1911 the *Encyclopaedia Britannica* would list his wretched story under the heading 'anti-semitism'. Nor for the present writer is this aspect of more than secondary, though still considerable, importance. In 1894 Captain Alfred Dreyfus was a rather gloomy, industrious officer of the staff, one among many.

On 15 October 1894, Dreyfus was arrested, tried by a court martial using 'secret' evidence for selling military secrets to the Germans, condemned, publicly degraded the following January, and two months later transported as far away from France as was feasible, that is to say to Devil's Island. The anti-semitic press was jubilant. So too, no doubt though more discreetly, were

28

the German intelligence officers who knew that the wrong man had been arrested and their access to French military secrets therefore remained undamaged. For Dreyfus was entirely innocent. More important from the German point of view, French counter-intelligence was not simply inefficient, it was corrupt, and that at a rather high level.

There was a considerably greater propaganda bonus that the Germans derived from this gross miscarriage of justice. To understand this it is necessary to refer here to the condition of France at the beginning of the century and in particular to the way this reflected the relationship between the French army and French public opinion. The French economy was booming and well balanced: French culture, from food to furniture, from women's clothes to theatrical production, from the new Eiffel Tower to post-impressionist painting, was generally regarded as second to none, save perhaps to the Germans in the world of music and to the British in political sagacity. From over a century of revolution alternating with reaction France had evolved a political system which was adequate and a civil service that was by then extremely efficient if unloved; it had not inherited a tradition of public happiness, or even of contentment. Politically France was profoundly, and it would seem incurably, divided.

'Divided' is both too weak and too strong a word. Too weak, in that France was in many ways less divided than fragmented. The political clichés 'left' and 'right' derive from the French Revolutionary Assembly's semi-circular seating arrangements, which arrangements have been retained in French parliamentary chambers until today. Unlike the British parliaments and, usually, its heirs elsewhere, government and opposition did not face one another. From the very beginning the French dichotomy was ridiculous.

During the Terror, for instance, as group after group of moderates and less moderates was beheaded, and therefore everybody in the Assembly moved physically into dead men's seats, the point was reached where Danton became, in terms of seating, a man of the right. Even in quieter times the men of the right were very frequently in bitter, mutual opposition: legitimists, Orleanists and Bonapartists were men of equal anathema to the men of the 1871 Paris Commune, but scarcely less so to one another.

The same was to apply, much later, to radicals, Communists and Socialists. Perhaps an indication of the fundamental instability of the French Third Republic is shown by the fact that from its creation, in 1875, to its dissolution, in 1940, the so-called, not infrequently self-styled,. 'left' won every general election; and that within the life of each parliament France was nevertheless being governed by the 'right'. Quite apart from this slithering about on the benches by the elected representatives, France has enjoyed or suffered under some fifteen forms of government, usually equipped with elaborate constitutions, since 1789. Popular French scepticism concerning their politicians is hardly surprising.

The division between rich and poor had long been a reality. The poor disliked the rich; the rich feared the more numerous poor. This simple fact needed no Marxist ideology, and was simply confused by the industrialization of the nineteenth century, which not only made social mobility much easier as class difference became financial rather than territorial, and a quantitative differential replaced what had been, at least in theory, a qualitative lack of egality. The issue of clericalism versus anti-clericalism had been a further divisive factor. The Marxist identification of this factor with their 'class struggle' dialectic is true only in part. Clericals and anti-clericals alike were suspect to large elements of the French population. It is still an issue, in some vague way a class issue, but was ceasing to be of primary relevance by the time of Dreyfus.

In his *Development of Modern France 1870–1939* Sir Denis Brogan saw yet another acutely divisive factor in France, the estrangement between Paris and the countryside.[1] Paris, *la ville lumière*, had indeed little in common with the rural population of, say, the Berri. And every French Revolution was in fact a Paris Revolution, usually carried out by the Parisian proletariat, led by the Parisian bourgeoisie, and crushed by the rural proletariat led by their own bourgeois. According to Sir Denis, when Thiers finally and brutally massacred the supporters of the Paris Commune of 1871 he was quite deliberately completing the work of counter-revolution that took place between 1848 and 1851.

Amid so many divisive forces and cruel memories, one French institution had remained largely untouched by division and bitterness: the army. For a century the French army had, to a quite extraordinary degree, served France rather than the regime in power. When the Austrians and Prussians invaded France to destroy the Revolution in 1793, it was the army of Louis XVI, led by aristocratic officers, that saved France at Valmy. When Napoleon destroyed the Revolution, its army became his army and served him with devotion and despite enormous casualties to the end. Though right-wing in tone, officered in large measure by aristocrats and manned by the stolid peasantry even when a conscript army, it could be wooed though not won by the various pretenders to the empty throne. When its own General Boulanger made his failed bid for a populist dictatorship in 1888, the army did not help him, though it would doubtless have obeyed him had he allowed the Parisian mob in weird, temporary alliance with the Monarchists to put him in power. Like the greater part of the German army from 1918 to the present day, it dutifully obeyed – though many of its officers might despise – its political masters.

The French Third Republic wished to make its army more 'democratic', both by a sensible rationalization of the Conscription system, which had favoured the rich under the Second Empire, and by basing its officer corps more broadly. The first was carried out in stages and successfully: the second was facilitated by a fastidious but surely comprehensible reluctance on the part of the aristocracy to serve its proclaimed enemies. The officers of the army were drawn increasingly from the middle and upper-middle class; its troops from the working class. It was this transition that allowed Alfred Dreyfus to become the first Jewish staff officer. It was this transition that caused the stress and strain within the French officer corps which became crystallized or classicized in the *affaire Dreyfus*. And it was this transition which therefore made the *affaire* a matter not simply of espionage but one which gave to secret intelligence an extremely powerful secondary role, in that it nearly destroyed the confidence of the French people in the French army. In fact it was the first really spectacular example of an intelligence scandal becoming a propaganda victory for the potential enemy.

It is not intended to describe once again the course of the Dreyfus Affair, which lasted until 1906 when Dreyfus was reinstated with full honours. What is relevant is that although to the

Germans French disarray was a most welcome sight, they were clever enough not to intervene in any way. It would seem probable, if not certain, that Lenin had the Dreyfus affair in mind when he wrote: 'The soundest strategy in war is to postpone operations until the moral disintegration of the enemy renders the mortal blow both possible and easy.' And he was showing his usual prescience, when not half-blinded by the blinkers of the Marxist dialectic, for the 'affair' not only revealed the continual bitterness in France but also foreshadowed much that was to come, there and elsewhere.

First there are the motives of the real spy, Major Ferdinand Walsin Esterhazy (1847–1923). This staff officer, of Hungarian antecedents, was a womanizer and a gambler. He was perpetually in need of money in order to live the life that he had chosen. This made him accessible to the German military attaché, Colonel von Schwartzkoppen, who was dealing with French traitors without the knowledge of his ambassador, Count von Münster, who to the best of his knowledge was telling the truth in 1894 when he officially told the French government that no member of his staff was engaged in espionage. The need for money, however, has seldom been enough to make an officer turn traitor. Letters written by Esterhazy to a former mistress showed that he also hated France. These letters included such remarks as, 'Were I told that tomorrow I should die an Uhlan sabring Frenchmen I should be perfectly happy,' and that he would like to see Paris 'under a red sun of battle taken by assault and handed over to be looted by 100,000 drunken soldiers.' Though such sadism can hardly be equated with ideology, it is obvious that many Communist spies drawn from the British and American governing classes have been less attracted by the Soviet system than filled with hatred for their own society in which, like Esterhazy in his, they have often enjoyed confidence, success and even high office.

Secondly, the French counter-intelligence service, under Colonel Sandherr, knew more about Schwartzkoppen's clandestine activities than did the German ambassador. They bugged Schwartzkoppen's office and planted their agents inside the German embassy. The Spanish military attaché, the Marquis de Val Carlos, also worked for Sandherr. In fact the French counter-intelligence had what the British and later the Americans were to call a Department of Dirty Tricks. One of its senior officers was a Major Henry. He was not a German spy, but he was an expert forger or at least controlled forgers. When the 'affair' endangered the French army, and particularly its General Staff, he was ordered to forge the letter incriminating Dreyfus that the Italian military attaché was supposed to have written to Schwartz-koppen. The Italian's denial of its authenticity was not believed. Thus was military counter-intelligence used for internal political purposes, and not for the last time. It is often believed that a Department of Dirty Tricks, being cocooned in secrecy, is immune to normal scrutiny. When this reliance on secrecy failed, when the letter was proved a forgery and Major Henry arrested, he committed suicide.

Finally, Clemenceau's involvement, which became passionate in the campaign to secure justice for Dreyfus, enabled that great patriot to recover from his involvement in the dirty Panama scandal, which appeared to have left his political career in ruins. When he entered into the 'affair' he seemed to his enemies a shabby, political crook. He emerged from it to become one of the great French heroes of this century. And it was Clemenceau, more than any other politician, who led France to victory in the First World War.

Chapter Two

The Okhrana

With brief periods of 'thaw' usually ascribable to internal chaos, a change of regime or both, Russia has been a police state since its creation by Ivan IV, known as 'the Terrible', the first Czar to set up an institutionalized terror apparatus, the Oprichnina, in 1563. This large force of brutal and brutalized men emulated their master's massive, at times exquisite, sadism. They did not merely murder individuals, but whole classes and the inhabitants of whole provinces on a scale not to be outdone before the autocracies of Lenin and Stalin. After the chaos of the seventeenth century, Peter the Great, in his determination to 'Westernize' his empire, employed terrorist methods that foreshadowed Stalin's collectivization of the Ukrainian peasantry. Catherine the Great, patron of Diderot and of Enlightenment anywhere save in Russia, was scarcely less brutal; although not being a Romanov she was neither feeble-minded nor insane nor pathologically cruel. For a study in depth of the Russian police state before 1900, the reader is referred to the early chapters of Ronald Hingley's *The Russian Secret Police*[1] and, for those who desire more, to his excellent, inclusive bibliography. The constant changes of nomenclature and function of the competing secret police forces that controlled Russia throughout the nineteenth century make for complicated and often confusing reading – indeed they frequently confused the policemen themselves – but by the end of that century they had in some measure coalesced; and though the term is not entirely accurate the whole secret apparatus is generally referred to, in one Latin spelling or another, as the *Okhrana*. For purposes of simplicity this word will be used here to describe the Czarist secret police and espionage service as a whole.

Why did the rulers of Czarist Russia need this vast police-cum-terror apparatus? Even the briefest of answers is complex. The first is that from the time of Ivan the Terrible and certainly since

34

the reign of Peter the Great Russia has been a steadily expanding imperial power based on the slavery, serfdom, collectivization, call it what you will, not only of the enormous conquered territories but of the Russian peasantry and proletariat themselves. Unlike the other great empires of history (with the exception of the Chinese and to a lesser extent the Turks) the Russian Empire did not extend overseas nor was it even protected by some natural land frontier such as the Alps. The Muscovite expansion was overland, and thus the revolt of a subject people such as the Ukrainians, the Poles or the Asiatic colonies posed a direct threat to Moscow itself. Since the Russians were themselves only semi-civilized, the only form of administration that they understood was that of the knout, the sword, torture, the gun – and the secret police. To this extent Russian imperialism is one more example of the apothegm that 'geography is history'.

Then the Russian leaders had, and apparently still have, what might be called in Adlerian terms a national inferiority feeling towards Europe and latterly towards the United States. Throughout the eighteenth, nineteenth and well into the present century, the Russians have been heavily reliant on the West for almost every form of technology, from the architects who built St Petersburg to the spies who stole the secrets of atomic fission. Yet they were determined that the importation of Western technology should not be accompanied by Western ideas. Well aware that the basic political philosophy of the West, for which the shorthand if rather unsatisfactory word is democracy, was and is infinitely more attractive to most people than Czarist or Communist autocracy, the Russian leaders have always tried to import only those aspects of Western culture which are practically useful and to keep away from their people the very concept of free thought upon which all that culture is based. When Winston Churchill coined the term 'Iron Curtain' in 1946, he was not referring to something new. In 1815, as in 1945, Russian soldiers who had seen the West, even in the miserable circumstances of war and defeat, were highly suspect on their return to Russia. Foreigners in Russia were spied upon, as were Russians abroad. Before 1914 Russia was the only European major power to insist on passports as a method of guarding its frontiers against persons entering or leaving the country. The dissemination of ideas –

since ideas are international – has always been discouraged. And as writers are the principal purveyors of ideas, there is scarcely a Russian writer of any distinction, from Pushkin to the present day, who has not been harassed, and often hounded to death or simply murdered, no matter how 'Russian' his interpretation of the world about him may be. Only a very small élite around the autocrat is allowed to know the West – knowledge even for such an élite can be dangerous or fatal at times – and even to a larger number of spies and policemen – but these are expendable. The Russian masses, illiterate in the last century, live the life of illiterates in this. For them, Lenin decreed that debased form of one-way, non-thought, the cinema; for their betters the ballet; for all, that non-art called Socialist realism. Even an avowed foreign Communist, such as Pablo Picasso, may not be allowed to show his works to the Russian people, lest they be caused to think or at least to question. And one question may lead to another. Therefore the endemic anti-semitism of the Russians has almost always been encouraged, since the orthodox Jew is the internal target for a xenophobia which should be absolute. Every foreigner is a potential spy in Russia and, abroad, a potential or actual enemy to be conquered, crushed, reduced to mindless slavery. This pathological state of mind existed long before 1917, and its transference into the reality of action was an essential duty of the Czarist police.

Such an unworkable cultural isolation could only become even more unworkable with industrialization, for this implied at least a partial transmogrification of rural peasantry into urban proletariat. The man who works in a factory and therefore lives in a city cannot remain as totally isolated from the rest of the world as the peasant who works on the land. A measure of education becomes essential. But a high degree of industrialization had also become essential in the last century; and it was this, perhaps eventually insoluble, paradox of necessities that confronted the Okhrana during the last twenty years of Czarist autocracy. And the Okhrana tried with considerable ingenuity to find a solution which probably did not exist.

The police, and particularly the secret police, must approximate in some ways to their enemies. A good detective must be able to mix with leading criminals; a good spy must be acceptable to those upon whom he is spying. And it must be repeated that Russian secret intelligence was born internally and its techniques abroad were based upon the exportation of what it was and is doing in Russia. In the age of almost total savagery Ivan the Terrible might dress a recalcitrant bishop in the skin of a bear and have him torn to pieces by hunting dogs, or Peter the Great might have his son whipped to death. By the early nineteenth century a measure of more civilized modes of behaviour had spread to the Russian upper classes, and the threat to the autocracy came from that class, from the officers called the Decembrists who attempted its overthrow in 1825, and later from those students whom Turgenev dubbed 'nihilists' in his masterpiece of 1862, *Fathers and Children*. The top echelon of the secret police, and above all such leaders as General von Benckendorff, Count Ignatyev and Count Dmitry Tolstoy, were ruthless but suave. The last named achieved power in 1882 and set about a drastic reform of the security services which became known as the Okhrana.

Increasingly it became the duty of the Okhrana to control and to foil the revolutionary tendencies of the new proletariat. The time for gentlemen-policemen was passed, but the policy remained the same and may be summed up in the single word: infiltration.

One form that this policy took was the harnessing of the workers to the system by gaining control of the nascent trade unions. For a time this practice was remarkably successful. The unions controlled, often almost openly, by the police were able to obtain for their members benefits not available to the other unions, and were correspondingly attractive to the workers – while, of course, the police could identify and, when necessary, destroy subversive elements within the unions that they ran. It is possible here to see a unique development that might have benefited workers and government alike. However, the scheme, if it was a scheme, collapsed on Bloody Sunday, 1905.

One of the most prominent 'labour leaders', to use an anachronism, was a priest by the name of George Gapon. He led the Assembly of Russian Working Men, some six to eight thousand strong, very large by the Russian standards of the day. And he worked for the police. His union, however, had itself been counter-infiltrated by real revolutionaries. Yet it was he who, in the period of economic and social misery following the loss of the Russo-Japanese War, led some ten or more thousand workers who marched on the Winter Palace with a petition to the Czar containing demands inserted by the real revolutionaries. The army opened fire, thousands were killed and Gapon only just escaped with his life. After being hidden for a while by Maxim Gorki, Father Gapon escaped abroad, almost certainly with the connivance of the Okhrana. He lived high on the hog, a sort of celebrity, notorious for his numerous love affairs and frequently seen in the *salles privées* of the Monte Carlo casino. However, he made the mistake of returning to Russia, and was murdered by the very same revolutionary, Rutenberg, who had saved his life on Bloody Sunday. The police unions never recovered from Bloody Sunday. But the Czar did create a sham parliament, the Duma, in the hope that revolutionary fervour would be directed into this bogus 'democratic' institution. And since a period of economic expansion coincided with this innovation, much of the steam was taken out of the unions. Some union leaders went into the Duma, more into straight revolutionary movements. It was therefore necessary for the police to infiltrate these even more intensely, and for the revolutionaries to do the same inside the police. A *danse macabre* of an extremely weird nature was the result.

Two examples given by Ronald Hingley[2] though spectacular are still characteristic. One is the case of Yezno Azev, born in 1869 the son of a Jewish tailor. At about the age of twenty he became a police spy in Rostov-on-Don. He must have pleased his masters, for in 1893 he was paid to go to Karlsruhe, in Germany, ostensibly to study engineering but actually to infiltrate the émigré revolutionary organizations, in particular the Socialist Revolutionaries, then the most powerful of these with one branch dedicated to assassination and other acts of violence. He soon obtained a leading position among the Socialist Revolutionaries abroad, while passing information to his police bosses which enabled them to carry out successful actions against the revolutionaries inside Russia. Paid by both sides, on an increasing scale, this agent was soon a rich man. And this during a period when the most savage pogroms were being carried out against the Jews. Azev's two most notable characteristics were a total absence of loyalty and a very considerable administrative ability.

In 1901–2, still on foreign soil, Azev reorganized the Socialist Revolutionary Party as a single unit in all Russia, and soon enough was himself head of its Fighting Organization. As he frankly admitted to the police his own views were liberal and perhaps he despised the extremists of both the groups, police and revolutionaries, who paid him. Meanwhile, to prove his value to the revolutionaries, Azev arranged the assassination of the hated Minister of the Interior, Plehve, who was in charge of the police who paid and continued to pay him. He was also concerned with the assassination of the Grand Duke Sergei.

By 1905 he was collaborating closely with Gerasimov, head of the Okhrana in St Petersburg. This enabled him to supply Gerasimov with the names of the St Petersburg Workers' Soviet (or Council) which was planning to become the alternative city government. They were arrested at a meeting; one of them was called Leon Davidovitch Bronstein, whose revolutionary pseudonym was Trotsky.

In the same year of frustrated or premature revolution many members of the Okhrana resigned, fearing the wrath to come. A number of them joined the revolutionary movement, as did a number who did not resign. When the revolution did not materialize, some of those who had resigned rejoined the Okhrana. Thus was confusion worse confounded. Meanwhile Azev soldiered on, under his two flags. Gerasimov encouraged him to spend as much revolutionary money as possible: he did not need much encouragement. The wave of assassinations and reprisals continued. In 1908 Azev was at last exposed by a revolutionary named Burtsev acting in collaboration with a former Director of the Police Department. He fled abroad, with a passport supplied by the Okhrana.

The wave of assassinations died down, although on 1 September 1911 a young man shot dead the Prime Minister who was also the Minister of the Interior. The young man was an Okhrana agent who had infiltrated the revolutionary movement – or, perhaps, vice versa.

No less strange, but eventually far more sinister, was the alliance between the Okhrana and Lenin's Bolsheviks. The Bolsheviks were a wing of the Social Democratic movement and, as such, opposed to terrorism. They were therefore of comparatively little direct interest to the Okhrana. Furthermore, until mid-1917, this small splinter group was of far less importance inside (or outside) the Social Democràt Party than were the Mensheviks. Finally Bolshevik political strategy, which has endured, was to give first priority to the destruction of all other revolutionary movements and only then to seize power for themselves. By these means, in the eyes of the Okhrana, the small group who swore utter fidelity to Lenin were acting as the allies of the Okhrana. There is considerable evidence, though no documentary proof, that before the war a certain Joseph Djugashvili, a bank robber from Georgia and a Bolshevik, was an Okhrana agent; his revolutionary pseudonym was Stalin.

Far more important than he, at the time in question, was a certain Roman Malinovsky. Though the Okhrana did not harass the Bolsheviks to anything like the same extent as it did the other, larger revolutionary movements, it kept them under strict control. Malinovsky, a former burglar, joined the Bolsheviks. He was an Okhrana agent.

So successful was he as a Bolshevik that he was elected to the Duma first as leader of the six Bolshevik delegates, then of all the Social Democrats, where he proceeded to carry out Lenin's policy of splitting the party. His brilliant speeches were edited first by Lenin and then revised by the Director of the Police Department. He became treasurer of the Bolshevik paper, *Pravda*, and kept the Okhrana fully informed of its, and its contributors', activities. In this he was ably assisted by that paper's editor, Chernomazov, who also worked for the Okhrana. When Lenin from abroad sent Stalin and Sverdlov to investigate what was going on, Malinovsky arranged with the Okhrana that they be arrested. They remained in Siberia until 1917. Only in 1918, when Lenin had access to the Okhrana files, did he realize the truth, for which the Russian word is *pravda*, and have Malinovsky shot.

It was in this atmosphere of chaotic double-cross that Bolshevism was born, grew up and came to power. It is really quite extraordinary that any informed person was taken aback by the Hitler–Stalin Pact of 1939.

40

The position of the Russian armed forces was, as is usual in most countries, conditioned by the state of Russia as a whole. In 1905 after the lost war against Japan there had been fairly substantial mutinies among the defeated soldiers and sailors. Military units coming back from the Far East were met by other units travelling eastwards along the Trans-Siberian Railway, and flogged into submission. At Sevastopol and Odessa there were naval mutinies, which included the seizing of the battleship *Potemkin*. These were more exploited than fomented by the revolutionaries, but without any marked success in peacetime. The private soldiers were drawn, in the majority, from the *moujik* class and were scarcely more susceptible to the arguments of the Socialist Revolutionaries or the Social Democrats than their fathers had been when earlier revolutionaries had attempted, with total failure, to rouse the peasants. Although serfdom had been abolished in 1858, in fact the peasants were little better off, their relations to their landlords little changed. Agrarian crime, such as the burning of the landlord's mansion, was spasmodic. Such activities could not be canalized into a revolutionary movement. The peasants wanted land, not theories, neither those of Karl Marx nor even those of Leo Tolstoy. And their wishes have remained unfulfilled, their suspicions justified.

The Okhrana, of course, was active inside the Czar's peacetime army, but was withdrawn in early 1914 on the orders of General Dzhunkovsky, Deputy Minister of the Interior, on the grounds that to have soldiers reporting on the loyalty of their comrades and even of their officers was bad for morale and discipline. He was justified. Although appallingly armed and supplied – in some units many soldiers did not even have a rifle and had to await the death in action of one or more of their comrades before obtaining a weapon – the Russian soldiers fought with their usual, stolid bravery and suffered their usual, enormous casualties until total defeat at the front and revolution in the rear made them give up the struggle. Only then, and only with the promise of land, did they accept the new leadership provided by the Workers' and Soldiers' Councils.

The Imperial Russian General Staff was an appendage of the autocratic regime, the higher commands where possible being reserved for members of the Imperial family. The enormous

Russian army was often compared to a steam roller, and its general staff acted with all the subtlety needed to drive such a machine. Its strategy was of the simplest: to hurl huge bodies of men at the enemy regardless not only of equipment, armaments and supplies but even of terrain and communications. Its intelligence service was so poor as to be almost non-existent: a blind man therefore moved the levers of the steam roller. It is hardly surprising that it lurched from defeat to defeat until at last it broke down totally.

German intelligence was well aware of what was happening in Russia and in the Russian armies. They not only had their own spies, and their own central evaluation agency, but could also use the information supplied by the revolutionaries. As with the Dreyfus case, it was the psychological effect upon the Russians, and particularly the Russian governing class, of the insecurity bred by the perpetual double-cross practised by their own security services that counted. They were able to believe almost anything, to ascribe the basest of motives to the highest in the land. The Czarina herself, being a German, was said to be a German spy. So, of course, and also incorrectly, was her protégé Rasputin. German intelligence was believed to be omnipotent. By 1917 moral disintegration was very nearly complete.

Russian intelligence, as has been seen, was primarily designed to spy on Russian political émigrés, of whom there were some five thousand in the West in 1914. Not all of these were so alienated as to work for a Russian military defeat in order to bring about a revolution. But there were enough, as Lenin proved in 1917. So perhaps the Russian secret service was not altogether mistaken in viewing Russian émigrés as the primary enemy. Russian xenophobia was such that the Russian General Staff was reluctant to accept, even if it had had the ability to apply, intelligence supplied by its French and British allies. And this folly was to be repeated in aggravated form by the new autocracy in the years between 1939 and 1942. Ingrained national characteristics or even modes of thought are seldom, if ever, altered by a mere change of government. Inevitably it was on a Czarist basis that Communist autocracy was built, and Soviet intelligence upon its imperial predecessor.

Chapter Three

The Secret Service

The British, or perhaps one should be more accurate in saying the English, Secret Service enjoyed for a very long time a reputation for almost uncanny efficiency. It is not hard to see how this legend arose, to the delight of the English, to frighten England's real or potential enemies, and thus to be a source of great, additional strength to England, later to Britain, to the United Kingdom and during its historically brief life to the British Empire. The collapse of the legend can be dated quite easily and in two stages. The first was the defeat of British Intelligence in Ireland by Michael Collins and his men (and women) in the Anglo-Irish War of 1918–22. This, the loss of Ireland, led directly to the decline and ultimate dissolution of the British Empire as such. The second stage was the defeat, by Russia and by British Communists, of British intelligence in the period that followed the Second World War. Both these episodes, of the greatest historical significance, will be dealt with later in the book. First, though, it is important to establish the nature and efficiency of the 'Secret Service' during its period of greatest renown.

It was almost certainly the invention of Queen Elizabeth's Mr Secretary Walsingham. For a century the Tudors had created an England at least as united as the France of the Valois and which, since the monarchy together with many of its magnates was a Welsh importation, included the whole of the southern part of the island. Its essential homogeneity was proved by its ability to withstand the social and religious revolution called the Reformation. And by skilful manipulation, in which English intelligence in the widest sense learned the tricks of the trade, Scotland was neutralized and prepared for ultimate absorption. Weaker than France in population and in wealth, England was stronger in that it had no land frontier save that with the Scots. Apart from Ireland, Walsingham's England had no possessions of any importance overseas, and turbulent, almost uncontrollable, Ireland was far closer to England than to any of England's real or potential enemies. England was a tight little island, provided it could control the seas and the Scots. At any time from 1588 to the present day an efficient enemy army, once landed, could have conquered England. It was therefore of supreme importance that no such army be permitted to land; and this in turn meant that the English Government, which could not afford a perpetual full-scale naval alert, must be informed whenever such an invasion was remotely imminent or even planned. At the height of the Counter-Reformation, England stood alone as it did during the French Revolutionary and Napoleonic Wars, as it did in 1940. Few foreign agents, priests or laymen, survived Walsingham's internal counter-intelligence. Externally he had learned much from Scottish affairs. His external intelligence, abetted by semi-official sabotage such as Drake's burning of Cadiz and, more important, the huge stockpiles of Spanish ship-building timber, was without parallel in the Europe of his day.

For three centuries and more the basis of British policy remained unchanged so far as Europe was concerned. Only in extreme circumstances were British armies sent overseas to fight on European battlefields, sometimes with significant effect, as under Marlborough or Wellington, sometimes with almost none, as in the Seven Years' War or the Crimean War, but always on a very small scale compared to the armies of the other great European powers. England preferred to use the 'Cavalry of St George', that is to say the golden sovereign, and to pay others to do the fighting. This of course involved a highly sophisticated intelligence to know not only whom were the best people to pay but also to ensure that England's treasure was not used in interests other than her own. On the whole, the system worked.

The expansion of mercantilism, soon to become an ideological doctrine, combined with the first industrial revolution, created the first British Empire in the eighteenth century. Politically, though not economically, it was a failure. The revolt of the American colonies showed the impossibility of expanding the tight patriotism of the British *outre-mer*. The Indian Mutiny later showed the ineffectiveness of purely economic domination, a lesson that should have been learned in Ireland long before.

Only in the second half of the nineteenth century, with the imposition of direct rule on India and on ever more of Africa, combined with devolution to the 'white' areas which became the Dominions of Canada, Australia and New Zealand and finally South Africa, did the British Empire become a reality for some seventy or eighty years (not a very long life span compared to that of the Spanish or Russian Empires, let alone the Turkish, Chinese or Roman). It was based on the 'two-fleet navy' principle and on minimum entanglement in European affairs. Its sorest point, and because of proximity also its most dangerous, was and remains a minute speck of that Empire, England's oldest colony, Ireland. Great Britain's greatest potential strength, apart from a temporary and almost total command of the oceans, was its growing alliance with the first colony that had broken away, the United States of America, which from the time of its own Civil War was obviously and rapidly fated to become the most powerful state in the world, first economically and then, when challenged, militarily.

Since intelligence reflects, or should reflect, political and military realities, the British variety in the later nineteenth century became increasingly imperialist in external affairs. Canning decided to call in the New World in order to redress the balance of the Old. This pompous, arrogant and much-quoted phrase meant the destruction of the Spanish–American Empire, the acceptance of the Monroe Doctrine by which both American continents became politically though not economically a closed sphere of interest for the United States, while the rest of the seas were to be the highways for the new British Empire. The corollary was British disengagement from Europe where the balance of power was to be left in the first instance in the hands of Metternich's Austro-Hungary backed by the strength of Czar Nicholas I, 'the gendarme of Europe'. It was a good formula for the age. Had it not been for German, Italian, Polish and later Balkan nationalism, had it not been for the revival of revolutionary fervour in France and elsewhere beyond the gendarme's control, it might have worked even longer than it did. For the British, confirmed in their nationalism and scarcely troubled by revolutionaries except in Ireland, it provided a form of political stability that endured throughout the century.

The effect of this, in the subject here under discussion, was twofold. The prestigious British Secret Service continued to enjoy an international esteem which it scarcely warranted. British intelligence was, in fact, almost the precise reverse of the Russian intelligence service described in the previous chapter. Its principal aim, outside the British Isles, was the control of the vast Indian sub-continent, and this it did with a quite extraordinary efficiency, in part because the Indian Civil Service took the cream of the administrative talent then being trained in the new English public schools that Thomas Arnold, of Rugby, had created for the new English upper middle class, in part because the Indian Mutiny had, for the time being, fragmented even further what was left of an already disintegrating or disintegrated multi-religious group of societies. A few thousand clever Englishmen controlled many millions of Indians for some seventy years. In the process, however, they degenerated in large measure to become the 'pukka sahibs' of legend and of farce. Localized in India, glamourized in the pages of Kipling, they were in their time and place extraordinarily efficient. They did not, however, have to compete with any rival force of comparable organization or ability. The result was that in India, British intelligence (perhaps in every sense of that word) suffered from fatty decay.

Internal British security, or counter-intelligence, was less hampered by tradition. It is not without very considerable significance that the Special Branch, which bore the major burden of dealing both with subversion and with foreign espionage, had been originally called the Irish Special Branch. In the last decade of the nineteenth century and the first of this, Ireland was unusually quiescent. Only with the recreation of the Irish Republican Brotherhood, early in the twentieth century, did a really effective anti-English leadership begin to come into existence once again. And this the Irish Special Branch failed, it would seem completely failed, to penetrate. Reporting that Paddy Murphy had expressed anti-English feelings loudly in a pub in the County Clare was hardly the sort of training needed by men who were to deal with the security problems of our century.

As a military force the British home army was so small, and in general so ill-equipped, as to require only the most perfunctory survey. Horseguards and Lifeguards on beautiful horses and

46

dressed in elegant, antiquated uniforms, were of little interest to foreigners, the rest of the army hardly more so. And the internal situation in Britain was extraordinarily placid. Successive Reform Bills, of which Disraeli's in 1867 was the most important, had given the people of Britain at least the illusion of democratic self-government. Though poverty was both grim and widespread, and there were until 1910 no 'welfare' ameliorations comparable to those Bismarck had given to the Germans in the 1880s, extreme poverty was on the decline, even if the huge financial gap between rich and poor was if anything on the increase. However, the class system was generally accepted, palliated by class mobility and the concomitant snobbery, and the ever-growing upper and lower middle class was solidly patriotic and anti-revolutionary. There were no deep-rooted social fissions, as in France let alone in Russia. Even in Ireland conditions were improving as the result of various land reform acts. The policy there was to 'kill Home Rule by kindness' and with the fall of Parnell and the consequent splitting of the Irish nationalists in 1890, even the Irish Special Branch had, for once, comparatively little to do. Finally the policy known as 'splendid isolation' implied no major military commitment, indeed preferably no commitment at all, in the affairs of Europe, and therefore no need for any profound study of military matters beyond Calais 'where niggers begin'. The general picture could be provided quite adequately by the Foreign Office through and from its diplomats.

Only in India, and to a lesser extent in Africa, was there some need of real military intelligence. In India there was not only the problem, quite easily solved since the Mutiny, of ensuring that no new mutiny was brewing: none was. More important there were constant skirmishes with the Afghans and other tribes near the northwest frontier, and more important still was the fact that behind that frontier lay Russia. The pressure of Russian expansionist policy was very real throughout the last third of the nineteenth century and an Anglo-Russian War for the control of the subcontinent was not only feared but also frequently expected. It was therefore in this area, the only one where Britain was confronted on land by a major power, that British military intelligence was most active, and its officers received some measure of practical training. It was probably inevitable that 'the Indians' gained a great measure of control inside the largely amorphous and highly inefficient military contingent in the body known as 'the Secret Service'. The novels of Kipling, and even more those of John Buchan, portray the stereotype: immensely brave, stiff-upper-lipped (the moustache helped here), and making up in patriotic determination what was lacking in brains. When first put to the test outside India, in the Boer War of 1899–1902, British intelligence proved itself hopelessly, one might well say totally, incompetent. No less an authority than Admiral Lord Fisher described British intelligence in that war as 'a wretched failure'. It took the huge British Empire, then at the height of its power, three years to conquer a handful of Dutch farmers. Clearly something had to be done.

Not much was. We have a vignette of Robert Baden Powell, the creator of the Boy Scouts and a keen entomologist as well as an equally amateur spy, taking his butterfly net as camouflage while sketching the fortifications of Cattaro in what is now Yugoslavia.[1] Why, is not clear. There was also a Russian Jew, who took the name of Sidney Reilly and was described by Robin Bruce Lockhart in his biography *Ace of Spies*[2] as just that. He is said to have secured the Persian oilfields for Britain more or less single-handedly, at the turn of the century. Since the value of Persian oil was then scarcely recognized, he was either extraordinarily prescient or as eccentric as the future Chief Scout. In any event the Persian oilfields have remained the property of the Shah of Shahs.

More serious were the creation, following on the fiasco of British Intelligence in the Boer War, of two branches of military intelligence, M.I.(Military Intelligence)1c and M.I.5. Even this seems to have proceeded at snail's, or bureaucrat's, pace. When on 1 July 1911 the German gunboat *Panther* arrived in the Moroccan port of Agadir, with the Kaiser on board and with the apparent intention, or at least the option, of annexing that country, or of preventing the French from so doing, the Secret Service was taken by surprise.[3] Its basic reorganization was expedited. M.I.1c, despite its name which was quite frequently changed as is the habit among espionage organizations, was in fact always headed by a naval officer until late in 1939. M.I.1c later became M.I.6 and, later still, the Secret Intelligence Service or S.I.S.

Very roughly M.I.5 was concerned with counter-espionage, M.I.6 was espionage. This basic division of responsibilities was defined with bureaucratic neatness: M.I.5 functioned 'at home', that is to say within the British Empire, M.I.6 abroad. This should have been an obvious nonsense. A man on the track of an enemy spy was inevitably investigating one tentacle of an octopus whose main body was elsewhere. Yet when he crossed to France or Germany or Russia, he was theoretically acting beyond his competence. Similarly an agent of M.I.6 had to outwit the enemy's or potential enemy's own counter-intelligence service. That service, however, was not neatly confined within the enemy country. This led to a considerable measure of confusion, rivalry and ill-feeling between the two British branches, all the more so since both had in some measure to spy upon the other in order to prevent enemy infiltration. The question *Quis custodiet custodem?* is perhaps unanswerable in any secret intelligence organization.

Furthermore, there was and never could be any hard and fast line between the work of M.I.5 and that of the Special Branch of the police, though here co-operation was easier. Finally there were borderline cases, such as Ireland. Until the creation of the Irish Republic in 1949 Ireland was still (if only technically since 1923) a part of the British Empire and therefore outside the area of operations of M.I.6, while the elaborate if somnolent apparatus of the (originally Irish) Special Branch did not relish M.I.5 poaching on what it regarded as its hereditary preserves. Thus was Easter 1916 as complete a surprise to the army as Agadir had been five years before, and a nastier one. Failing to profit from this lesson, the S.I.S. was not present in Northern Ireland when that province boiled over in 1970, and although M.I.5* was a little more active, its target was originally less the Irish Republican Army as such than the I.R.A.'s relations with Communist secret services. When the I.R.A. split in 1971 into Official (Communist) and Provisional (American-financed) branches, British intelligence failed to grasp the great significance, and British politicians to exploit it, with results that are still incalculable. And the Special Branch of the Royal Ulster Constabulary was, so long as Stormont lasted and perhaps beyond, more interested in

* For the confusion of the nomenclature see p. 54.

serving its anti-Catholic masters in Northern Ireland than in serving the United Kingdom as a whole.

But long before all this happened, the main function of the British Secret Service had been almost completely checkmated. With Russia the principal potential enemy, and recognized as such after 1945, the head of one vital branch of the S.I.S., for ten crucial years was in fact a Russian agent, 'Kim' Philby. For a slightly shorter period the principal link between the British Secret Service and the American Central Intelligence Agency was Philby's friend and protégé, another Russian agent named Donald Maclean. Guy Burgess was the third member of this trio, less dangerous than the others but hardly a credit to British security. And it can be said with reasonable certainty that they were not, and are not, the only Russian agents enjoying high office in the British – and probably also in the American – intelligence services. In fact it is enlarged to global proportions, the old story of the Okhrana and the Revolutionaries all over again, within a new and, in the nuclear age even more frightening framework. And one of the major, if ancillary, functions of any intelligence service is to frighten the real or potential enemy. This is an essential part of what has come to be called psychological warfare.

Secret intelligence shades off into two other activities which have been mentioned already and which will be dealt with in greater detail later in this book: one of these is psychological warfare, the other sabotage. In order to avoid confusion it would be as well to define these, briefly, here.

'Psychological warfare' is a messy phrase, an *olla podrida* of many ingredients. Its basic purpose is to persuade the enemy, soldiers, civilians and even governments, first that they *should* not win or even fight a war (or what is nowadays called a confrontation) and when this is impossible – as is almost always the case – that they *cannot* win the war, that its continuation is a mere waste of life and treasure, and that therefore immediate surrender is desirable. Since nationalism, or what some would still prefer to call patriotism, is even today the most powerful political force in the world, the successful practice of psychological warfare against any foreign power that is not already on the very verge

50

of defeat is extremely difficult if not pointless. This, however, may not always be true.

Its overt form is of course propaganda, to which an exaggerated importance can and has been attached in wartime. It is certainly far more effective in pre-war conditions, provided it is skilfully used; and it is here that it becomes in some measure part of political and military intelligence, for in order to be convincing it must appear to originate in the country against which it is directed. Furthermore it should be based on an emotion or a political attitude that is not only autochthonous but also morally respectable. An obvious example, at least in the Western world, is pacifism. It was obviously in the interests of the Nazis and is now in that of the Communists to encourage such pacifism, but unobtrusively. One method is the infiltration of pacifist organizations with enemy agents. Another, and more successful, is to harness a great reputation to an apparently respectable but in fact a disreputable cause: for example, Bertrand Russell, a distinguished mathematician and philosopher, but a political ignoramus whose 'pacifism' implied surrender to the Nazis ('Let them come here as tourists') and later to the Communists. It was obviously in the interest of England's enemies not to support him directly in his defeatism, but to exaggerate his intellectual brilliance so as to give even his more idiotic utterances an aura of respectability.

Another form of propaganda, and usually a more successful one, is the appeal to an internal patriotism within the enemy state: to the Irish in 1798 or 1914, to the Ukrainians in 1941. This, however, is a very difficult card to play. The Irish did not wish to shake off English rule in order to be ruled by Frenchmen or Germans. The Ukrainians greeted the *Wehrmacht* as liberators, with bread and salt, only to find that behind the soldiers came the murderous S.S. and of course the carpetbaggers. Political intelligence of a more skilful sort than that of the Nazis would have harnessed anti-Russian nationalism within the Soviet Union and won the war for Germany; it could not, however, win it for the Nazis.

A word should be said here about what may be called the fifth column syndrome. It was the Francoist General Mola who said, during the Spanish Civil War in 1936, that he had four columns marching on Madrid and a fifth, awaiting him, inside the Spanish capital. This was in fact untrue, but the words entered the politico-military language. In another form they produced the 'reds under the bed' neurosis of Senator Joe McCarthy's so-called witch-hunt, which found no witches. 'They' – that is to say the enemy – are up to their tricks again. This can often become a sort of paranoia to which a good counter-intelligence service should be immune (but is not always) and to which the general public far more readily succumbs with a consequent loss of confidence in its own security services that can have a damaging, even a crippling, effect upon the whole nation. The French are perhaps particularly sensitive in this area. For many Frenchmen the loss of a battle, a campaign or a war produces an almost knee-jerk reaction: '*Nous sommes trahis!*' or even, '*Nous sommes vendus*', by of course their own allies and their own leaders.

Now there certainly were Spaniards in Madrid who wanted the Nationalists to win the Spanish Civil War. But they were not a 'column'. There were and are Americans in government, the media and so on who, consciously or not, desired and desire to see American society drastically modified if not weakened to the point of destruction. The C.I.A. certainly preferred to see Congolese mineral deposits – the importance of which was perhaps exaggerated at the time – controlled by a Tshombe rather than by a Lumumba. And American business interests in Chile did not like the Allende regime, while the Soviets make the maximum mileage out of American mistakes in Indochina or British mistakes in Northern Ireland or in the so-called Cod War in Icelandic waters. These, however, are more often the exploitation of a situation than the implementation of a plan.

Yet it will sometimes suit one side, or even both, to present the incident as a piece of devilish or skilful chicanery. And the fifth column syndrome is, in moments of crisis, capable of assuming monstrous and even defeatist proportions. When the French were losing the Battle of France in 1940, it became popular belief that the Germans not only knew everything about France but were everywhere, misdirecting military convoys, posing as French officers and so on. All this was quite untrue.

A few months later, when Britain was fighting for her survival, an even more extraordinary myth sprang up. The German radio employed an Irish–American broadcaster by the name of William Joyce, nicknamed because of his la-di-da accent 'Lord Haw Haw' by the *Daily Express*, to broadcast in English. It was said, and for a while believed, that this man knew *everything* that was going on in England. He was supposed to have broadcast, for instance, that a certain town clock was ten minutes slow, that a certain obscure country road was being retarred, that a certain politician had moved house, and so on. Not only was all this totally untrue, but what is more important, no such claim to detailed omniscience of this sort was ever made over the air by Joyce. Yet by word of mouth these stories travelled across England to the extent of causing the British government considerable anxiety. There is no reason to believe that this scare was inspired or even exploited by the Germans in any way. It was simply a manifestation of the sort of hysteria that can arise in a nation when that nation is suddenly made aware that its very existence is threatened. And it is, of course, a quite gratuitous bonus to enemy intelligence. That spies and traitors exist, from time to time and from place to place, goes without saying. Fifth columns, however, do not. Or not yet.

Sabotage, that is to say action within the territory of the actual or potential enemy, is connected with secret intelligence in quite another way. The intelligence service is part of the armed forces. It is also, and inevitably, therefore part of the entire governing apparatus. Sabotage falls roughly into two categories: the physical destruction of enemy installations, and the undermining of enemy organizations such as communication or industrial concerns, trade unions and indeed anything that forms part of the hostile, or potentially hostile, power structure. In the first case the active nation's armed forces are usually involved, in the second often scarcely if at all. The best near-contemporary examples are the Bay of Pigs action, carried out with almost incredible incompetence by the American Central Intelligence Agency – not all their sabotage or quasi-military actions were so ham-fisted – and of the second sort the longer range activities of the Russian K.G.B. in Europe and America. Of all these, more later.

Chapter Four

Behind the Abwehr

One tendency, among others, that national intelligence services have exhibited throughout this century is a frequent and repeated change of name. Since except in revolutionary conditions, and not by any means always then, the newly named apparatus usually consists of most of the same men doing approximately the same job for about the same pay, the change in nomenclature may imply little more than an administrative re-organization at a high level, which can of course be of greater or lesser importance if it brings with it a higher or lower degree of efficiency on the part of the men and women who do the work of collecting, collating and evaluating intelligence material. It may, on the other hand, be a simple mania for secrecy as such. In London, in 1940, everyone who was interested, and quite a few people who were not, knew that the main clerical apparatus of 'M.I.5', the British army's counter-intelligence service, was located in a commandeered prison called Wormwood Scrubs. It would have been easier to change the name of the organization than to move the files, but when the problem was solved by a German bomb that destroyed a large part of the records, M.I.5 did not then have publicly to change its name, simply its location. On the other hand the K.G.B., which before that was essentially the M.V.D., previously the N.K.V.D., the O.G.P.U. and earlier still Lenin's Cheka has functioned, so far as this writer knows, from a permanent base within the Lubyanka Prison, Moscow. You may change the name of their organization, you may move them physically from place to place, but the job of those engaged at the centre upon secret intelligence and counter-intelligence work remains the same, and so in their span of working life do most of the people engaged thereon. Meanwhile, for the convenience of both reader and writer, certain obvious, familiar and not unduly inaccurate terms will be used to cover national intelligence apparatuses: the

54

Secret Service in Britain, the *Deuxième Bureau* in France, later the *Abwehr* in Germany, to give but three European examples.

None is identical with any of the others, let alone with the intelligence services of Russia, Japan or the United States, but all were intended for the same purpose, namely to serve the state by means that apparently could not be openly used. Each was therefore dependent on the state it served not only in its fundamental nature but in the varying needs that the state, or to be more exact its governing élite, was pursuing at any particular time. At the beginning of this century German intelligence served the Imperial Germany of Kaiser Wilhelm II.*

Now, while the nature of any intelligence service is almost inevitably based upon the morality and methods of the masters whom it serves, its importance to those masters will usually be in inverse proportions to their own intrinsic strength. To give a very simple but not altogether misleading parallel, a heavyweight boxer fighting for the Lonsdale Belt may weigh less, have a shorter reach and pack a less powerful punch than his opponent, but may yet win the championship by superior skill as a boxer, which means in these terms a greater intelligence in the use of his more limited means. On the other hand a flyweight, no matter how brilliant his footwork and how quick his reactions, cannot hope to defeat a heavyweight. This means that a state with overwhelming power in relation to its opponent does not really need to bother unduly about intelligence work. A country with fifty armoured divisions need not waste energy and brains – neither of which is ever in adequate supply for all purposes – if its potential enemy merely has five. In the 1939–40 Soviet–Finnish War a stupid Red Army eventually *did* crush its tiny, cleverer enemy. And this applies even when a condition nearer to parity is reached. The stronger power has less need of intelligence than the weaker. History has shown, more than once, that David can defeat Goliath, while if Goliath had been as well trained with a sling as was David there could have been no defeating *him*. When the combatants are closer to parity, technical skill becomes immensely important. It can even be decisive. One direct form of such skill is

* The *Amt Ausland Abwehr* or 'Office of Foreign Defence' was created in 1919. Its officials were in most cases already experienced intelligence officers.

knowledge of the enemy, that is to say intelligence. And an over-whelmingly powerful society is apt to forget this. It is apparent that the Greeks knew more about their enormous Persian enemy than the Persians who stumbled into Thermopylae and Marathon and above all into Salamis had bothered to discover about the Greeks. If your basic policy is one of the knock-out blow, why bother about details? In other terms, when manpower seems overwhelming, brain power is at a discount, as it frequently has been. But the alternative also applies in certain circumstances. The heaviest heavyweight does not always win.

Imperial Germany was indeed a national heavyweight, in any reckoning, at the beginning of this century. It was also, and like most great states at all times, in what is called 'a transitional period of its history'. How, if at all, does one measure the status of an extremely complex society involving scores of millions of persons, all different, against other, similar societies of the same period living in approximately similar circumstances? Then one might try, indeed in the framework of this particular book must try, to measure some aspects and organizations of Imperial Germany against similar aspects and organizations as devolved and created by the British and the French. Or does one compare Germany in 1906, an important year so far as intelligence goes, with Germany forty years before or after? In 1906 the Germans could see the past only. We can, after a fashion distorted by history and our own point of view, glimpse that Germany of 1906, and the 'today' of the people who lived there and then. In the case of this particular country, two major wars have added several extra dimensions to the distortions.

Bismarck had fallen in 1890. Until Hitler came to power in 1933 no Chancellor exercised such power or had any such real and deep influence upon his country and his countrymen's attitudes. Kaiser Wilhelm II, that grandiose, disastrous and slightly ridiculous figure, we see for ever parading in a vast variety of exhibitionist uniforms beneath be-plumed or be-eagled helmets, interfering in complex military and economic matters often quite beyond his comprehension, scribbling comments not infrequently obscene in the margins of state papers, twirling his moustaches and, in the end, leading his country into disaster and his dynasty to oblivion. Yet at the beginning of the century this vulgar *parvenu* among monarchs presided over a country which still bore the mark of an older generation. It took him some time to undo Bismarck's life work.

What Bismarck had left behind him when he retired to his estate of Friedrichsruhe was that rarity among great powers, a new country, proud of recent triumphs in almost every field – including its own unification – and in general without overweening ambitions. Bismarck had taken the quasi-revolutionary nationalism of 1848, had most skilfully removed most of the revolutionary component that had survived the debacle, and had retained the nationalism within bounds by an almost unique combination of aggression and restraint. Building upon the Customs' Union of the various German states, and relying for military purposes upon the Prussian army, he had eschewed pan-Germanism, and had chosen the 'small German' solution to German unification, leaving an Austria defeated but not unfriendly to cope with the Habsburgs' clever, clumsy empire. With France eliminated, at least temporarily, from the European equation after 1871, he had sought to limit his own new emperor's domains to a homogeneous, manageable and, so far as this be possible, happy country. Always conscious of geography, he had sought to ensure – and so long as he held the reins of power did ensure – that this central European power was not encircled by potential enemies. Of equal importance, he relied on the expanding German middle class, the tradesmen, industrialists and bureaucrats, to provide a firm, conservative centre. To the land-owning aristocracy he gave the pomp of the armed forces, and above all of the German army, but under controls and within the limitations of their military profession. To the growing urban proletariat he gave the first rudiments of a welfare state, thus in large measure depriving the proletariat of a revolutionary ardour directed against the state. Despite his contemporary, Karl Marx, German revolutionary extremism remained very limited, particularly by comparison with the Russia of the time and even with France. The German Social Democrats did not wish to destroy the state from which they benefited, but merely to modify it. To the capitalists, on the other hand, he gave great freedom of enterprise, which they used to the utmost and with very considerable skill, perhaps equal to if different from that of their American contemporaries. Education was encouraged as in no other great country, rapidly surpassed English standards for the population as a whole, and was in large measure responsible for an extraordinary increase in productivity, skill and therefore wealth. At a somewhat higher level, the great German universities were second to none. In some fields, such as pure science, they were peerless. And even the French recognized, albeit often reluctantly, the enormous importance of the great German philosophers. The Germany Bismarck created was not limited by a philistine materialism, a ledger mentality which then threatened a vital aspect in the development of the United States.

A high degree of democracy prevailed in Germany, perhaps more in appearance than in reality, but that too was Bismarck's intention. He once remarked that to let the working class run a country was the equivalent of letting the nursery run a household. His policy was paternal, wise and very sane. Perhaps the greatest and most successful statesman of modern times, he quite properly regarded the principal duties of government as two-fold: the safeguarding of the frontiers and the physical and moral well-being of the citizens. To achieve these aims he used all his own great abilities for over twenty years and into them he channelled most of the talents of the people he governed. The Germany that Wilhelm II took over from him was very rich, very powerful, extremely patriotic and (with the exception of those French eager for 'revenge') had no real enemies.

For Bismarck's German Empire was very strongly influenced by the life-style of its 'founding fathers', of the first Kaiser Wilhelm (who is said to have recorked half-empty wine bottles and snuffed candles), of the great Moltke who, in his modest retirement in a small red house, left his tea guests tactfully, to die without complaint in a neighbouring room, of Roon, the creator of the armies that Moltke had led to victory, and of Bismarck himself. This manner of living and dying lingered on in the motto of the German Great General Staff, *mehr sein als scheinen*, which might be translated as 'reality rather than display'. It was the reaction to, and antithesis of, Bonapartist histrionics, whether those of the Great Napoleon or of *Napoléon le Petit*. It was formidable in that it appealed precisely and exactly to the mentality and manners of the north German nineteenth-century middle-class from which the state drew its greatness and its purpose. If it lacked the glamour of French *panache* and elegance, it was very considerably more efficient. Sobriety, responsibility and sustained application are not generally counted among the more attractive virtues, but in Bismarck's middle-class Germans, as among Queen Victoria's middle-class Britons, they can and did produce extremely effective results.

Against all this, elements of Wilhelmine Germany reacted, as did elements in Edwardian England. A generation had grown up which did not know the fatuity of political histrionics, the ultimate tedium of pomp and display. The bourgeoisie might plod along its usual course, 'a proper place for everything and everything in its place'. Such, however, was not the style of the emperor, that knight in shining armour. Unlike his grandfather he did not snuff out the candles before retiring to bed. He did not of course belong in Bismarck's nursery, but Bismarck did despise a quality of frivolity in his new emperor, and made little attempt to conceal it, for he feared quite correctly that Wilhelm II was endangering his and his generation's life work. And indeed though Wilhelm II was far from stupid he did play at politics; for him too, as not for Bismarck, it was the 'great game'. And his favourite toy was his magnificent army. Soon he was to order another, his High Seas Fleet. He aroused fears and he created, almost it would seem deliberately, that encirclement which Bismarck had fought so hard to avoid. And therefore the German army assumed a political, as opposed to a military and social, importance with which it had never been burdened while Bismarck was winning wars and creating Germany. There was a shift in the centre of gravity within government. Its culmination was the implementation of the Schlieffen Plan, whereby military operations in 1914 could not be confined to the Eastern Front but necessitated war with France, the invasion of neutral Belgium and war with England. Military, strategic considerations had become paramount. It would be an exaggeration to say that the General Staff ran the German government in 1914 – that did not happen until 1916 – but one instrument of government, the army, had acquired a disproportionate degree of authority in the making of decisions. The close co-operation between Bismarck and Moltke had been replaced by a state of affairs in which a series of men as

Chief of Staff, men of great efficiency but intellectually Moltke's inferiors and backed by Wilhelm II, were telling a series of chancellors, who were certainly Bismarck's inferiors, what options were open to the German government, which in any case was repeatedly put in awkward and embarrassing positions by the direct interference and adventures of the Kaiser.

And all this was repeated, in miniature but significantly, in the German secret intelligence service. We have already seen Colonel Schwartzkoppen, as military attaché in Paris, carrying out espionage operations with neither the approval nor the knowledge of the German ambassador as early as 1894. This situation was to be aggravated until the army was operating, in this field, purely for itself, not for the government. Since no firm line can be drawn between political and military intelligence, the army was soon dabbling in muddy waters that were not of its own immediate concern and that it was ill-equipped to evaluate. The stresses that thus arose were in some measure resolved by the administrative re-organization of the German intelligence services that took place in 1906. And here, as elsewhere, it was the army's hand that was strengthened to the ultimate disadvantage of the country that that army served most loyally unto death.

The forebear of the whole German intelligence apparatus was a certain Dr Wilhelm Stieber, born in 1818, whose memoirs, *Denkwürdigkeiten des Geheimen Regierungrathes*,[1] seem to be reliable. What is of equal interest to this man's achievements are his own background and the nature of what he took over. He was never a soldier. Born a member of the nascent and solid Prussian bourgeoisie – his father was a civil servant in Merseburg, and he had been himself a civil servant before taking a law degree – he joined the Prussian police, in which he rose rapidly to become head of the Berlin Criminal Police for a decade. He expressed, and no doubt felt, views that were both democratic and liberal. Nevertheless he was sacked, after 1848, for excessive brutality in his interrogation of suspected criminals. These two statements would appear contradictory. He may have been dismissed from his important post for his views or for his methods – possibly for both. As more modern history has shown, men entrusted with the enforcement of democratic law and order are not necessarily very squeamish as to how they perform their duties. In any event, he created a private detective agency and among his clients were the Okhrana. He was clearly in a position both to infiltrate refugee and revolutionary Russian organizations and to evaluate what he there discovered. Obviously the authorities in Berlin kept an eye on Dr Stieber. His anti-revolutionary activities on behalf of the secret police of an allied state would scarcely have displeased them. And if the Russians found his services worth his pay, Stieber also profited greatly from the knowledge he acquired of Russian methods, indeed so much so that by 1863 he was also working for Bismarck, who entrusted him with secret missions outside Germany too, where he created a network of reliable agents. In fact this man laid the foundation stone of a weird relationship between German and Russian secret intelligence that in the past century has survived wars hot and cold, forms of government that have come and gone, and revolutions that have succeeded and failed. The 'historic' hostility between Teuton and Slav has only briefly interrupted a down-to-earth practical collaboration out of the limelights. Arnold Toynbee has remarked upon the qualities some of us not infrequently acquire from our enemies. There can be little doubt that the proven methods of infiltration, the double agent and the double-cross, were of Russian origin and were imported into Germany, probably by Dr Stieber.

In May of 1866 a student attempted to assassinate Bismarck, who then saw that Dr Stieber's talents were perhaps needed nearer home. He was put on the government payroll as head of the new Secret State Police. But that was not all. In the following month Prussia annexed Holstein, Hanover, Saxony and Hesse and was prepared for the war with Austria that took place in July. The Prussian General Staff was then so ill-supplied with intelligence from its own sources, principally military attachés, that it had little idea as to where the Austro-Hungarian Army was nor how it was equipped. The victory at Sadowa was definitely not due to Prussian military intelligence which, according to Field Marshal von Waldersee, provided information that was 'almost exclusively uncertain and inferior'. Dr Stieber's sphere was rapidly expanded to become the Central Intelligence Bureau on 1 August 1866, with headquarters in the Foreign Office and in control both of agents abroad and of political intelligence inside Prussia and the new Prussian dominions. Paragraph 5 of his new commission also ordered him to 'support the military authorities in the collection of intelligence concerning enemy armies'. This in effect put Dr Stieber in charge of all secret intelligence, political and military, at home and abroad.

Needless to say the Prussian General Staff did not appreciate being dependent on the Foreign Office for military intelligence. Early in the following year it created, for the first time, its own intelligence bureau, a negligible affair of three officers, quite incapable of matching Stieber's rapidly expanding organization, now called in its military activities the Secret Field Police. Stieber, who soon had agents all over France, provided the intelligence for the Franco-Prussian War, and when the General Staff objected to his interference in their military affairs they were firmly slapped down by Bismarck.

The reply of the General Staff was to expand its own intelligence apparatus. And a compromise was reached whereby Stieber withdrew into his Central Intelligence Bureau while the army created a new and more efficient organization under a new senior staff appointment, the *Oberquartiermeister III* or Deputy Chief of Staff III. It absorbed the Secret Field Police and created an army military intelligence chain of command eventually down to and including divisional level. These officers, who corresponded to the later G.S.O. (I) or the G-2 (senior intelligence staff officers) of the British and American armies were designated Ic on their respective staffs.

The *Oberquartiermeister III* also had his own secret agents abroad, in 1889 no fewer than seventy-five in Russia alone, for it was against that potential enemy and against France that German military intelligence concentrated its efforts. It was, however, still financed by the Foreign Office, and the inevitable interdepartmental squabbles ensued. Nor was it merely the position of military attachés such as Schwartzkoppen that was ambiguous. Contacts with foreign intelligence services, such as with the experienced Austrian *Evidenz* and even with the British, were confused and therefore more useful to the foreigners than to the Germans. Stieber retired from the Foreign Office in 1882 and his successor allowed the Central Intelligence Bureau to decay until it was disbanded a few years later. The military were winning, and in 1891 the Minister for War, writing to Chancellor Caprivi, claimed that 'only a military organization can guarantee security and achieve something'.

But the Foreign Office fought back, though the power was slipping from between its fingers into the hands of the military. On the other hand there was an insufficient number of staff officers trained in intelligence work, which became increasingly complex in the new century. Finally, the business was rationalized in 1906, as the international situation hardened and the arms race accelerated in preparation for the coming war. All secret intelligence was placed under a comparatively junior staff officer named Walter Nicolai. In 1913 Nicolai was still only a major. But in military intelligence rank is of very little significance. Nowhere is the principle of *mehr sein als scheinen* more important. And Nicolai's staff organization had the very important backing of the head of Section 2 of the Great General Staff, Colonel Erich Ludendorff. He saw to it that Nicolai received not only the funds he needed but, more important, the brains. He also protected this new and growing branch of the General Staff against its enemies: because of its nature, secret intelligence arouses the enmity of the uninitiated. Finally, being himself one of the cleverest soldiers of his generation, he had immediately grasped the vital importance of military intelligence. Indeed, it would be hard to find a really competent commanding general, in any army, who did or does not. Nicolai's military intelligence apparatus was to prove its extreme competence on all the fronts between 1914 and 1918. And for this Ludendorff was in a considerable measure responsible, particularly in the years before the war.

But here a flaw appears for which Ludendorff, both as an individual and as a representative of the very kernel of the German army, its General Staff, was also in some measure responsible. German intelligence was, by the decree of 1906, military intelligence. As the German army assumed greater and greater power before and particularly during the First World War, political intelligence was increasingly ignored. Even naval intelligence suffered and was never able to compete with that of the British enemy. And all this suited Ludendorff's concepts, first of total war, culminating in total victory, and then in a government with an imperial figurehead (though even this might be expendable), founded upon an omnipotent General Staff and an irresistible German army. He might well have said, for he certainly thought: 'What's good for the army is good for Germany.' And this fallacy was to lead him, at least briefly, into Hitler's National Socialist Party, though he did leave it quickly enough after observing how Hitler and his followers behaved during the failed Putsch of 1923.

A higher degree of political as opposed to military intelligence might have avoided several national calamities. It might have averted the war of 1914, or at least postponed it to Germany's advantage; it might have ensured British neutrality, at least until the defeat of France; it might have saved Germany from total defeat by a negotiated peace in 1916; it might have prevented the German government from compelling a reluctant United States to save the Western Allies in 1918; in fact, it might have won Germany the First World War with a free hand in Russia. Of course none of these 'ifs' and 'buts' is anything but gossamer hypothesis, but the fact that whenever a decision had to be taken it was based on military intelligence and carried out for military purposes led to mistake after mistake in the political field. One cannot help feeling that Dr Stieber's organization would never have offered such a one-sided intelligence view. And one can be moderately certain that had he been advising a Prince Bismarck such advice would have been ignored. The very brilliance of German military intelligence led to its omnipotence in that field. And this very omnipotence led to total, national disaster.

After the somewhat grandiose hypothesis of the previous paragraph it is worth examining what, in fact, German secret intelligence was believed to be achieving in the decade or so before 1914. Much literature on the subject, most of it highly inaccurate, was being published, especially in France. In England it tended to assume fictional form, the works of John Buchan for example, or Erskine Childers' *The Riddle of the Sands*. It is not possible nor would it be fruitful to examine here all this mass of semi- or misinformation, but one book which is both characteristic and in some respects better-informed than most deserves attention.

This is entitled *The German Spy System in France*, by Paul

Lanoir, anonymously translated and published in 1910.[2] Internal evidence shows that it was finished in late 1909 or early in the following year, though the translator says it was written in 1908. Monsieur Lanoir was something of an authority on the French railway system, concerning which he had also written at length. He also says that he was an amateur spy-detector, though he obviously had connections with the French police, the French military counter-intelligence apparatus or more probably both. His book is an impassioned plea for a more efficient counter-espionage organization and this, together with the omissions concerning various aspects of German secret intelligence and French counter-measures, indicate strongly that if the book was not inspired by the Deuxième Bureau it was at least vetted there. It too was intended for popular consumption.

Lanoir's politics, though never stated, are clearly revealed. He was most certainly a man of the right, probably the extreme right, and it may be assumed that he had been an anti-Dreyfusard. Furthermore, it was not the Germans of 1918 who invented the 'stab in the back' legend. To a patriotic Frenchman the total defeat of 1870 could not have been solely the fault of a badly equipped and poorly led French army; there must have been more sinister forces at work to nullify the acknowledged bravery of the French soldiers. For the left, the great national humiliation could be ascribed to the fatuous inefficiency of the old imperial regime: for the right, to the disloyalty of the socialist revolutionaries, with their allegedly international class loyalties, culminating in the Commune of 1871; for both to the incredible cunning of Stieber's secret intelligence at all social levels.

Of Dr Stieber's personal activities and those of his principal subordinates in 1870–1 Lanoir has some quite incredible tales to tell. They do not concern us. He does not seem to have known that Stieber had retired for reasons of health in 1882 and sees his guiding hand planning for the forthcoming war many years later. This last is an excusable error. Stieber's espionage organization was inherited and modernized by his successors, nor need Lanoir have been aware of the basic administrative restructuring and shift of emphasis that had taken place in the previous twenty years. The collection of intelligence is ascribed solely to spies, active within France. He does not refer to the activities of military attachés, nor to developments dependent on technological inventions since 1871, such as telephone-tapping, code-breaking, bugging of diplomatic premises, wireless interception and cryptanalysis, all of which were being secretly used in varying degrees by all major intelligence services, including that of France herself, by the time Lanoir put pen to paper.

No, for Paul Lanoir it was all – or almost all – direct espionage. He saw, quite correctly, that the control centres of the spies were not on French soil, but rather in an arc, in part in German territory, in part allied, but perhaps most valuably of all in neutral countries (Belgium and Switzerland), and that these control centres reported to Berlin, where the central files were kept. Indeed he directs much venom against Belgian and Swiss nationals allegedly in the employ of German secret intelligence.

Lanoir distinguishes, with growing disgust, between 'spies', that is to say Germans or the agents of Germany, and 'traitors', that is to say Frenchmen, particularly French officers, prepared to sell military secrets to the past and future foe. He objects strongly to a legal differentiation in France between the law which makes treason a capital offence, and the law of 1886 which makes espionage a less serious crime: he would shoot the lot. For one of the main activities of the more plebeian spy, according to Lanoir, was the creation of traitors within the French army. A card index, he says, was kept in Berlin of all French officers, to which was added the top 25 per cent of all the annual output of St Cyr, the French military academy. (Cards on the other 75 per cent were presumably only added if and when they achieved some promotion or notoriety.) To these cards, which did indeed exist though not to the extent that Lanoir imagines, were added details of the officer's private life by which he could be bribed or blackmailed into betraying military secrets: if he were in debt, unfaithful to his wife, homosexual and so on.

Again, Lanoir is here probably on the right track, though he obviously exaggerates its importance. The persons who produced the material that ultimately reached the Berlin files were usually insignificant residents, shop-keepers, café waiters and so forth, preferably located in fortress or garrison towns, who also had the task of reporting on the strength and armaments of the fortress, garrison troops and communication systems. They should be,

66

Lanoir sternly says, almost immediately recognizable by the fact that they spend more than they can be expected to earn from their 'cover' trade. All such persons, and he estimates their number in 1909 at between 30,000 and 35,000, should be put on the suspect list and arrested as soon as war is imminent. This fantastic figure is ridiculously high when applied to enemy agents, and just as fantastically low if it is supposed to include all those, in any country the size of France, who live beyond their income. However, it is not altogether a bad rule of thumb, though a very crude one, in the detection of spies anywhere and at any time, in so far as a man with a known income who regularly exceeds this without getting into debt must be deriving his funds from some other, probably illegal, source. Espionage can be one such way. For Lanoir it was apparently the only way.*

The petty spy-in-residence was paid, and passed on his information, in a fashion similar to his own employment, semi-bogus commercial travellers being of particular use in this job. At a somewhat higher level persons, particularly ladies, travelling on the great international trains of the day, from Brussels to Genoa, from Calais to Geneva, could meet a man who boarded and left the train while it was in transit through France. He claims actually to have seen such a transaction with his own eyes, and there is no reason to doubt his word. A most reliable friend of this writer once saw a member of the British Labour Party's 'extreme left' in the 1950s being actually handed a large bundle of banknotes in the otherwise empty lounge of a hotel in a Communist-dominated country. After all, as Lanoir remarks, it is not easy to pay your agents by post, and the Germans had by this

* Lanoir's use of statistics is extremely odd. The xenophobia he feels for French-speaking Belgians and Swiss, when extended to the population of metropolitan France as a whole, produces an extraordinary figure. On page 218 he states, without giving any authority: 'In fifteen of the Departments of France the foreign element amounts to between sixty-one and eighty-two per cent of the population; in other Departments it amounts to between fifty-one and sixty-two per cent.' Since in his view all these foreigners are potential, even probable, spies or traitors, a mere twenty-five to thirty-five per cent of the inhabitants of France are, perhaps, reliable patriots. Only one French citizen or resident in three can be trusted to control double their number, if need be by arresting them. In fairness to Lanoir it must be said that this is far and away the most idiotic statement in his book.

time abandoned the system of depositing the agent's pay in banks, the source being too easily traced.

Women, and sexuality in general, were, according to Lanoir, the major levers, those and money; but for people with plenty of money already – that is to say those close to the centre of power – women above all else. Not that the diplomat or senior officer was offered women in exchange for information. Rather were the women expected to extract information of military or political importance in exchange for sexual favours – in particular, Lanoir says, for those of a somewhat eclectic nature, the details of which we are spared. For this purpose, he says, the Germans subsidized a most luxurious brothel in the Dorotheeen-strasse in Berlin. (This story was revived, with how much truth this writer does not know, in the Nazi period.) Now it is hard to believe that amidst the luxuries of the Dorotheeenstrasse any French general of artillery would have been so boorish as to regale the girls with the statistics of the muzzle velocities of heavy howitzers, or that any diplomat would have failed to be surprised if his bedfellow were to ask him about secret clauses in unsigned treaties. For that matter it would not have been easy to blackmail a Frenchman of that period by threatening to reveal his patronage of such an establishment. As for the exported whore, or the French one bought by German money in Paris, her credibility would surely be of a very low order. But the myth still prevails, at least in England, and the reality is still apparently practised by the Soviet K.G.B. English visitor to Moscow, beware that fair guide or chambermaid who between the sheets wishes to be told about the Early Warning System in Yorkshire! American diplomat, watch out if she shows a keen interest in sexual malpractices in Georgetown! Be careful not to drop off to sleep if there is anything in your briefcase or the secret compart-ment of your suitcase that is not intended for the eyes of the K.G.B.

Monsieur Lanoir, like many of his contemporaries including Sigmund Freud, extended this preoccupation with the omnipo-tence of sex to social fields elevated far above the Dorotheeen-strasse or the rue St Denis. Ladies in the very highest society liv-ing irregular private lives and referred to by initials, the Princess S — the Duchesse de T —, were as often as not the cat's paws of other, Prussian lovers and it was in their interest that they extracted from prominent and powerful Frenchmen information of the very greatest value to the enemy. Here, it seems that to a tiny tr ckle of truth – indiscreet remarks dropped in drawing rooms or over dinner tables – was added the far more powerful stream of mutual distrust within the French ruling class. Since Dumouriez in 1793 and Bernadotte in 1810, so many French generals had gone over to the enemy, since Ney in 1815 and Bazaine in 1873 so many a Marshal of France had been tried for treason, when above all there had been such repeated changes of allegiance as one regime succeeded another, it is hardly surprising if what Lanoir and many of his contemporaries regarded as the 'frailer sex' was likely to be led, quite easily, into the betrayal of the nation. In the First World War the more lowly courtesan's role was attributed to Mata Hari; in the Second, and at a more elevated level of political society, to Paul Reynaud's mistress, Madame de Portes. In both cases, almost certainly, with justification.

One form of espionage referred to in this book is the employment, by French military families, of German tutors. These were intended to fulfil a dual role: the rifling of the desk belonging to the *père de famille*, presumably a general who kept his most secret papers at home, and the exercise of positively Jesuitical ingenuity in influencing the political allegiance of future generals while still in the classroom. It is ironic that our author more than once refers to the family of Franchet d'Esperey, who apparently at one time did employ a German tutor. If so, his influence upon the future Marshal of France, one of the two or three greatest French generals of the First World War, must have been minimal, or even enlightening as to the nature of the Germans. In any event, few French military families can have employed German tutors; those who did so were presumably influenced by the acknowledged academic excellence of the Germans and by their well-known attention to discipline.

When dealing with another aspect of national disaffection, Monsieur Lanoir is on slightly firmer ground. The Second International, then the only major non-nationalist Socialist force, laid great emphasis on the word 'international' and on the theory, for it was nothing more, that the workers of one country would never again fight the workers of another. Indeed some of its leaders went so far as to defy any capitalist government to mobilize the workers, for by arming the masses it would be asking for international class war. The Germans did attempt to exploit this fallacy in France, in a rather more cautious fashion than Lanoir realized for they knew it to be a most dangerous weapon, as likely to explode in their own face as in that of the enemy.

While the Kaiser's top Germans were anxious to weaken France, they did not desire yet another French revolution: that of 1792 and its sequel had not done their German forebears any good. So they concentrated on weakening certain vital aspects of French industry, and in particular what happened to be Lanoir's 'special subject', the railways.

Fully aware that the efficiency of the German railway system relative to the French was essential to rapid mobilization, the Germans strengthened their own railways strategically, in part for the same deliberate military purposes that led Hitler to build his *autobahnen*, while at the same time attempting to infiltrate and alienate the workers on the French railways. In 1892 the *Mesmard Pamphlet* was published in French, almost certainly with German secret service financial backing. Its thesis was dual. Any major industrial strike must be backed by the railwaymen, thus effecting at least a partial general strike in French industry. This appealed to the solidarity of the proletariat. But second, and more important, any attempt at mobilization for war would be a threat directed against the French workers, and should therefore also trigger off an immediate railway strike. The two appeals were quite skilfully interwoven. The real enemy were the officers, French officers of course, and on page 80 of the pamphlet its author, who called himself Mesmard, states: 'We know our duty as patriots, and we know when we must become soldiers. But if you gentlemen do not know it, you officers, then leave us alone to manage our own affairs or we shall call in the Prussians.'

It was, of course, too crude. The French government and the railway companies reacted as might be expected. So far as possible the French railways were cleared of subversive, pro-German elements. And they functioned very efficiently in 1914. But here we have, perhaps for the first time though certainly not for the last, a foreign secret service engaged upon large scale internal subversion based upon ideology. French patriotism was ultimately to prove infinitely stronger than Socialist internationalism, and stronger than French mutual self-distrust. But it is significant that our Monsieur Lanoir should have taken the threat so seriously.

And this significance adds yet a third dimension to the conventional espionage activities of a hostile secret service, namely to increase the enemy's self-distrust and to foment an almost irrational fear of one's foe's ability to exploit one's own internal enmities. Monsieur Lanoir's spy-mania was, in itself, a triumph for German secret military intelligence.

Chapter Five

America, the Pacific and Ciphers

In October 1941 the Japanese government led by Prince Konoye was replaced by a purely military government, with General Tojo as premier and Shigenori Togo in charge of Foreign Affairs. The governments of Konoye and his immediate predecessors had scarcely been peacetime regimes – besides being at war in China since 1931, creating the puppet state there of Manchukuo and fighting with some success an undeclared war against the Red Army in Siberia, Japan had been preparing for the expulsion of the Europeans and Americans from all East Asia. But Tojo's government was specifically created to fight the current major war in alliance with the Germans, who were then expecting and expected to defeat Russia within a matter of weeks. One of Shigenori Togo's first actions was to call in his chief of signals, Kazuji Kameyana, and ask him whether the diplomatic ciphers were secure. For Togo had read a book called *The American Black Chamber* by Herbert O. Yardley,[1] in which Yardley told much about American intelligence in the 1920s – and more perhaps than he should have, and this from first-hand knowledge, about code and cipher-breaking before the Black Chamber was wound up in 1929. What Togo wished to know was whether Japanese ciphers were now safe in view of the coming war with the United States. Kameyana replied that this time they were; but Kameyana was wrong.

Yardley was an employee in the State Department, where he first entered the Black Chamber in 1913. It was not what its name implied but, as he says, a 'spacious room with a high ceiling overlooking the southern White House grounds. By lifting my eyes from my work I could see a tennis game in progress where a few years earlier President Roosevelt and his tennis cabinet had played each day.' The job of Yardley and his colleagues was the decoding and deciphering of foreign diplomatic and consular services' communications, and the safeguarding of American ones. Of his colleagues and immediate superiors in those distant days he writes with undisguised contempt.

Indeed the civil servants who worked in the State Department have never enjoyed what might be called 'a good press'. A generation after Yardley's arrival in the Black Chamber President Franklin D. Roosevelt was to refer to the members of the American diplomatic corps collectively as 'cookie-pushers'. The reason for the low status of these men, compared with that of their European equivalents, is not hard to find. In the first place, and until quite recently, government service was not held in high esteem in the United States. 'The business of America,' Calvin Coolidge, perhaps the most 'American' of Presidents in this century until Harry S. Truman, once said, 'is business.' Even army officers were regarded by most of their compatriots, at least in peacetime, as men who had chosen a safe, ill-paid career because of their inability to compete in the market place: officers in the Navy and in the Marines were more respected being on the one hand high-grade technicians and on the other the first line of defence abroad. Secondly, the eighteenth century system of 'place' had in politics persisted, like the Constitution itself, well into the twentieth. The diplomatic plums of office, the embassies and ministries, went not to professionals but to the men who had backed the incoming President, usually financially; in any case they had to be rich men to keep up with the other ambassadors on their own negligible pay, and resigned automatically after each Presidential election. If the head of the other party had won, they were usually replaced. (Relics of this extraordinarily amateurish system remain, but not in the more important posts.) Thus a man who became a servant of the State Department in the years before the First World War had little hope of achieving either financial success or great prestige in a country that was increasingly a plutocracy. On the other hand he was unlikely to be sacked. He therefore tended to be the sort of man who took holy orders in England. There were exceptions, of course, both in the Church of England and in the United States civil service, and of these latter Herbert O. Yardley was certainly one. Finally, contacts between the State Department and the other branches of government, including in peacetime even the armed forces, were kept at a minimum. Yardley says: 'At last I found the American Army pamphlet on the solution of military ciphers.'

In such circumstances it is hardly surprising that American diplomacy was so frequently inept; it was also almost as often adequate for a great nation protected by two huge oceans, a big navy and general global acceptance of the Monroe Doctrine. In fact, diplomatic expertise was scarcely needed, for in Central and South America 'dollar diplomacy' was not yet a pejorative expression: the Panama Canal was bought, as Louisiana and Alaska had been bought in the northern continent. As for Europe, the word 'isolationism' had not yet been coined, for the simple reason that it was so far accepted that no such word was needed. Most Americans, or their immediate forebears, had so recently, so deliberately and at such emotional cost left Europe that there was then little desire to return in any sense. Only the westward momentum that had carried the power of the United States to Hawaii, to the seizure of the Philippines from Spain, and to the open-door policy in China foreshadowed conflicts to come, conflict not with China which appeared to be in a condition of perpetual political chaos but perhaps with the country that Commodore Perry's treaty of 1854 had introduced into the diplomatic equivalent, with Japan that had defeated China and then Russia, with this now major power growing so rapidly and with intentions so difficult to fathom. Here, at least, that form of expertise called intelligence, political, naval and military, was badly needed by the policy makers in Washington. For the popular imagination it might be enough to describe the Japanese as inscrutable: for any administration of a country that was growing to regard most of the vast Pacific as an ocean within its own sphere of influence, it was essential that the new power on the far shore be scrutable. Japan was still a friendly power, but after the Japanese Navy had defeated the Russians at the Battle of Tsuschima in 1905, it became increasingly evident to the other great naval power in the Pacific that it must know what the Japanese were about. Or to put it more bluntly, it was important whether Japanese warships could, if hostilities arose, destroy American battleships, and how, and where, and when.

For Japanese–American relations were, at best, ambiguous. From the Japanese point of view they formed only a part of

74

Euro-Asian racial relationships, always tinged with the potential hostility inherent in great social and religious differences, but until the late nineteenth century a hostility neutralized in part by extreme remoteness. It is said that in outermost space galaxies collide. European, by name at least Christian, civilization did not meet that of the Western hemisphere until 1492, and the collision occurred a few years later when Cortèz and Pizarro conquered and destroyed what are now Mexico and Peru. Since Alexander the Great's expedition into India three hundred years before the birth of Christ, Asia proper too had been left almost entirely alone by Western Europeans, though they fought and ultimately lost enormously protracted wars against the Byzantines and later, the Russians.

By the mid-nineteenth century, however, Western European modes seemed to be dominant in much of Asia. The so-called Indian Mutiny led to Queen Victoria being proclaimed Empress of India; the Dutch had long ago annexed Indonesia; the Western-ized Russians extended their domination to the Pacific; enormous China lost an estimated forty to fifty million lives in the mid-century civil wars called the T'ai Ping rebellion and the ensuing turmoil, from which the Manchu Dynasty never really recovered. The great European colonial powers, in particular France and Britain, descended like greedy vultures upon the enormous moribund, carving out spheres of exploitation for themselves; the Germans joined in the game later, and when the newly in-dustrialized and militarized Japanese won their war against China in 1894–5 and had signed the Treaty of Shimonoseki, they found themselves under the strongest diplomatic pressure not only from Russia, with which country they were now in direct and, from the Japanese point of view, absolutely vital confronta-tion, in the Manchuria–Korean area, but also with the other European colonial powers that had interests in China.

These powers backed Russia and compelled the Japanese to withdraw from the Chinese mainland. The Japanese retained Korea, but the loss of the Tsuschima Strait to Russia would have given distant Moscow dominance in the western Pacific and would have prevented Japan from achieving or maintaining such status. The forced surrender of Chinese territory had greatly offended Japanese national pride, even though they were 'allowed' to retain Taiwan. Euro-Asian relations, already more or less hostile, became catalysed in the Russo-Japanese War, the first great Asiatic victory since the time of Ghengis Khan.

From the moral point of view what happened in the Far East a hundred years ago was and is somewhat disgusting. The importation in vast numbers of high-minded missionaries, principally Protestant and in the majority from the United States, to convert 'the heathen Chinee' was less acceptable to an ancient civilization than had been the arrival, two and a half centuries earlier, of Roman Catholic missionaries sent to convert the far more primitive natives of the Americas. From these Asian activities Japan had remained immune, an island race with a population greatly in excess of Great Britain's and unconquered by foreigners for the better part of three thousand years. Having tasted, and at first accepted, European culture in the form of Portuguese missionaries and traders in the mid-sixteenth century, the Japanese had expelled them less than a century later; the Jesuits were ordered to go, Christianity stamped out, and when the Christians rebelled, Japan was sealed. Such small communities of Christian traders as were permitted to remain were compelled to live in closed ghettoes. Apart from these rigorously controlled, and on occasion persecuted, commercial minorities in their enclaves, Japan had retreated behind its seas, and this for some two centuries. Thus was a Japanese identity, distinct from that of their forebears from continental China, created. And thus did Japan, a nation with its own implosive forces, remain almost totally un-Europeanized both culturally and economically, and above all in its concept of politics, until quite late in the last century. When finally the Japanese in some measure accepted European, by then Americo-European, modes and standards, what they were accepting or modifying was not the Europe of the Renaissance but the methods and morals of high capitalism with its corollary of the time, colonialism. Japan as a world power was born, like Pallas Athene, fully formed. However, its father's forehead was not that of Zeus but what Lenin called colonialist monopoly capitalism, a form of power into which the ancient Japanese system of overlordship slipped far more easily and quickly than had European feudalism. The speed itself, however, was perilous for a country with an intense population density and,

76

apart from manpower and brains, very limited natural resources.

1905 was a climactic year, so far as Japan was concerned. Not only did the Russo-Japanese War and the great Japanese naval victory of Tsushima put a stop for forty years to Russian expansion eastwards, but it also saw a diplomatic démarche, not unconnected with this victory, in the Anglo-Japanese Treaty of Alliance. This was a somewhat cynical treaty based less on any genuine friendship than on obvious mutual self-interest. The building of the German High Seas Fleet and the growing strength of the United States Navy, as proven in the Spanish–American War, had rendered the British concept of 'splendid isolation' backed by a two-fleet Royal Navy out of date. Near-global hostility to the British Empire during the Boer War had underlined Britain's need for a powerful naval ally. The Anglo-French *entente* was tenuous, new and not yet an alliance. Russia was obviously weak, while tension along the Indian northwest frontier had not entirely abated. The Kaiser's Germany was the great potential threat. America was, in theory at least, strongly anti-imperialist, while Anglo-American commercial rivalry was very real and had become overtly political in Venezuela (Lenin misinterpreted this coolness in Anglo-American relations as the inevitable prelude to a war). Only the Japanese alliance offered both a substantial increase in British strength and the protection of the British Empire's distant flank in the Pacific. In the Far East, in 1905, the British and the Japanese had few territorial or maritime areas of potential conflict. Commercial relations were, by the standard of the age, admirable. Britain exported machine tools and technological knowledge; Japan paid in cheap goods produced by rice-eating Asiatics. Therefore it was also in the Japanese interest to renew the Treaty of Alliance in 1911, and to abide by it with impeccable rectitude, immediately, and at very small cost to themselves, when Great Britain declared war on Germany in August 1914.

For, from the Japanese point of view, the enemy was not the north wind that blew from Russia, a gale stilled by Japanese bravery and skill at least for the time being, nor the south wind that blew from Malaysia, Indo-China and Indonesia, but the east wind that blew from the United States, that had engulfed the Philippines and was rapidly turning those islands into the first trans-Pacific American colony. Furthermore these American imperialists were threatening to block the Japanese from what must, eventually, be their main source of raw materials and their first area of Asiatic domination, from enormous China, that huge land-mass with a vast polyglot population, already in obvious political disintegration before Sun Yat-sen gave the old dynasty its *coup de grace* in 1911 and ushered in a new period of war-lord chaos that was to last for a very long time.

Finally in the same year, 1905, that curse of the United States, racialism, had reached the West Coast, and its first victims after the Red Indians were the Chinese and Japanese. In that year racial segregation was introduced into the schools of San Francisco, and it spread rapidly until by 1921 it applied in all the western littoral states. The attempt by President Theodore Roosevelt to stop this obviously dangerous and indeed repulsive populist movement at its earlier legislative appearance had failed. In his State of the Union address to the Congress in 1906 he had urged that an act be passed investing the Japanese who had 'won in a single generation the right to stand abreast of the most intelligent and enlightened people of Europe and America' with the same rights of naturalization that were then reserved for 'free white persons, aliens of African nativity and persons of African descent'. The President was overruled by the Congress. The Japanese already in America became, with a mere handful of exceptions, not just second-class citizens, like American Indians, but aliens. The Congress, representing the American people, had declared itself as anti-Japanese, in opposition to a President who has not been regarded by history as anything other than an extreme patriot. And this was carefully observed, nor was it to be forgotten, in Japan. The Europeans, from Vladivostok to Jakarta, might be resented; but it was henceforth the Americans who were the enemy of the proud and increasingly powerful Japanese.

In 1912 the Japanese Emperor Matsuhito died after a long reign of forty-five years. He was posthumously renamed Meiji Tenno and his reign was called the Era of Meiji (which has been translated as the Era of Enlightened Peace, though it had seen two major Japanese Wars). It was succeeded by the Era of Taisho, of Moral Righteousness (ominous nomenclature: an essentially European, even Christian, concept, in a totally Japanese ideology).

78

And the enemy of this righteousness, once the German outposts in China and the Pacific islands had been rapidly swept aside in 1914, was to be in the first instance American arrogance and American imperialism, and secondly, the European presence in eastern Asia.

This long historical digression is intended to show why Japanese intelligence, at least for most of the first half of the twentieth century, was directed against the United States of America, for America was then the primary enemy in Japanese eyes.

American secret intelligence before the First World War was both neglected and negligible. It has varied, with exceptions, between these two negatives ever since. The great battles of the Civil War were, usually, the head-on collisions of large armies. At the cost of enormous casualties these reciprocal slaughters were won by the army that 'got there firstest with the mostest' and also that had the less inefficient commander. At the beginning of that ghastly war the latter was usually the Confederate general; at the end, and backed by overwhelming strength, the Northern generals. Any civil war should, in theory, be a most fertile field for intelligence of every sort. In fact this seems seldom to have been the case. The explanation may be that on the one hand each side knows too much about the others and the evaluation apparatus therefore becomes swamped and inefficient; on the other, that hatred of 'traitors' distorts judgment. In any event civil wars are notoriously bloody wars, and brute power even more important than in international wars, for defeat must be total, surrender 'unconditional'. Until 1941 at least, the War between the States, was, for Americans, the prototype war. Patriotism at the front, productivity in the rear, such was the war-winning combination. And this suited the ethos of the United States, suspicious of brains and contemptuous of the sly approach. Only very large and powerful states can win wars in this expensive fashion. For a long time the United States could afford the expense, and won wars into which it was, almost always reluctantly, dragged.

Herbert Yardley was, he tells us, employed in a junior capacity by the State Department during the years immediately preceding the entry of the United States into the First World War. He worked in the department engaged upon the encoding and de-coding of communications to and from the Department and its representatives overseas, and soon realized that the American diplomatic cipher system was extraordinarily naïve and most easily broken, even by a quasi-amateur like himself. Since he was, to judge by his book, somewhat anti-British before 1917, he seems to have been incensed by the ease with which the British were reading American material not intended for their eyes. With the American declaration of war upon Germany and Austro-Hungary on 6 April 1917, he and the intelligence section of the U.S. Army General Staff realized that his very considerable talents in code and cipher* matters were better employed in the military than in the diplomatic field. His further activities are described in the second part of this book, which is devoted to Secret Intelligence in the First World War.

As already stated, secret intelligence is the discovery by A of what B would conceal from him, A and B being usually organiza-tions, national, ideological, even religious. To be of any use, the information that A or its agents has acquired about B must be relayed to A's evaluation centre, where the decision can be made whether it is true, false, a deliberate plant or a mixture of two or more of these. Apart from most immediate battlefield intelligence, the discoveries that A may make about B's abilities and intentions are almost entirely dependent on the communications system used by both parties. And it is these that are most vulnerable, in both directions and with an ever-increasing complexity. The three main methods of making and breaking secret communica-tions, whether these be operational or intelligence or both, are agents, variants of what can be called 'invisible inks', and ciphers. The agent can of course be broken, by torture for instance, or

* A code is essentially the substitution of one word for another; a cipher the replacement of one letter by either another letter, a mathe-matical symbol, an ideogram or a jumbling of these, all of which can be carried on, with permutations, *ad infinitum*. Codes are not neces-sarily 'secret', e.g. the Morse code and many commercial codes designed to save time and expense, whereas ciphers are usually intended to be secret. Codes and ciphers can be mixed. Therefore, for the purposes of this book, the word ciphers, encipherment and decipherment will be used to include codes, encoding and decoding. For more detailed definitions the reader is referred to *The Codebreakers* by David Kahn.[2]

turned around, say, by bribery, once he has been identified and caught. Until then, a trained secret agency employing an adequate number of spies is very efficient, but once infiltrated more dangerous to its country than to its country's enemies. The 'secret ink' technique and its successors such as the micro-dot – used in conjunction with apparently innocuous correspondence – assume that A will read B's mail and be misled as to its real meaning. Cipher assumes that he will read the messages but fail to understand them at all. With the introduction of radio the practice of ciphers has taken on a really vast significance in peace and war, but one which may have reached its peak during the Second World War.

It is not possible to invent an unbreakable cipher, for the simple reason that anything which a human mind has knitted together another human mind of equal calibre can eventually unravel. (If beings of a sort from outer space exist, they might have means of communication so far beyond our imagination as to be in-decipherable: on the other hand, they might not be aware that space is filled with our radio and other communications, or even that we were able to communicate with one another at all.) 'Eventually' is here the key word. Ciphers of an almost incredible complexity have been invented, and indeed used. But they usually have one major disadvantage, more in war than in peace, in that their very complexity can make the deciphering by the proper recipient a lengthy business. There is little point in a foreign minister sending an ambassador a communication that the recipient cannot read almost immediately. For if the contents of the secret message are so lacking in urgency that days can be afforded in their deciphering, then it is obviously easier, quicker and safer to send this message verbally or even to summon the ambassador home to the foreign ministry. This of course applies even more in time of war, particularly where immediate military or naval plans are the content. Furthermore, the nearly unbreakable cipher will be broken, eventually. Under the intense pressure of war or impending war, an enemy of equivalent brains, organiza-tion and technological knowledge will break the cipher. Then one of two things happens: either A is not aware that B is reading his top-secret signals and continues to use a broken cipher with disastrous results to himself, or he comes to realize in one way or another that his cipher has been broken, and changes it. However, the more complex the cipher, the more difficult it is to change. Either a whole new system has to be introduced to a whole host of legitimate recipients – itself a most dangerous proceeding – or the cipher has to contain a built-in method of change, involving the mere switching of a button or turning of a notch or two of a wheel. But such a built-in method, being itself an element of the cipher, is certain to be broken in the end. The user of the cipher may change it automatically with a broken periodicity; but even this method of changing an existent cipher will be deciphered, quite quickly, and the more quickly the more often it is done. Increasingly sophisticated computers have, of course, made for the creation of ever more complicated ciphers, but have probably made the breaking of them much easier too. And even a micro-computer is an awkward piece of delicate equipment with which to decipher a message if you are, say, riding a camel or flying a glider in a hurricane zone.

Finally, the nearer to 'unbreakability' your cipher or cipher system becomes, the more reliant will you become upon it. You may even come to assume that it is unbreakable, and this is extremely perilous for, as they say in the higher-class newspaper editorials, you will be lulled into a false sense of security. Even before the First World War constant vigilance was the price of cipher safety. Of this the government and military leaders of the United States were sublimely unaware. Washington had few secrets so far as London or Berlin, Paris or Vienna, Rome or Tokyo were concerned. And when America's intentions were unknown it was almost invariably because such intentions did not exist, beyond the next presidential campaign. This is perhaps the most foolproof form of security imaginable, but one not usually regarded as consistent with statecraft of the highest order.

As will be seen the Americans took this lackadaisical absence of security abroad with their army to France in 1918. And as late as 1941 President Roosevelt still believed the claptrap the British had told him during the First World War about a Danish-based British Secret Service network inside Germany.

PART TWO

1914–18

Chapter Six

Hysteria and Hangover

The outbreak of the First World War in August 1914, though long expected, created almost overnight an atmosphere of mass hysteria such as the world has perhaps never seen before or since. This was the age of high nationalism and it was as though the dam of civilized thought was washed away by the flood waters of an almost mindless patriotism. The British Foreign Secretary might declare sadly in Parliament that the lights were going out all over Europe. But the age of electricity had begun. The candles were not snuffed, one by one; rather was a switch turned, the light was gone, the dam burst. This was also the beginning of mass communications, the popular press raged, and those voices of reason that had prevailed even through the horrors of the French Revolutionary and Napoleonic Wars were rendered inaudible by the howling hatreds of the masses unleashed. It seemed as if almost everybody really wanted this horrible bloodshed.

Among the first to go was the concept of Socialist internationalism. In Berlin the Social Democrats voted overwhelmingly for war credits, and old August Bebel wished he were young enough to shoulder a rifle and march into Russia. The French did the same despite the murder of their leader by an ultra-nationalist; but even 'f Jean Jaurès had lived it is doubtful if he would have wished to o⁻ been able to, oppose a war that soon enough saw German soldiers once again upon French soil. (And note the emotive cliché that should have been meaningless to Socialists.) Lloyd George had been pro-Boer a dozen years earlier; now none beat the drum of British patriotism more fiercely than he. The Russian masses, ill-armed or even unarmed, stolidly marched to their death. It seemed as if 1905 had never been. The American President justified his country's neutrality not on the grounds of common sense or the futility and wickedness of Europe's suicide, but with the peculiar phrase that America was 'too proud to fight'. All the deadly sins, with the possible exception of sloth, were loosed upon the world and indeed not infrequently worshipped.

It was, however, in the matter of spies that the latent hysteria, mostly in England and France where it was in part attributable to the Dreyfus affair, assumed epidemic proportions. There were then no political refugees from Germany. In that atmosphere of hysterical nationalism, therefore, every German no matter how long resident abroad *must* be an extreme nationalist and probably a spy. If he had quietly concealed his nationalism, if he had been outspokenly pro-British or pro-French, if he had even changed his nationality it merely meant that he was all that more clever and dangerous a spy. Shops owned by Germans, or merely with German names, were wrecked.

Spy-mania in Germany was in large measure, and more rationally, directed at the occupied territories of Belgium and northern France, where espionage was indeed to be expected. However, here the Germans over-reacted to a degree that would have been absurd had it not been so bloodthirsty: in 1917, in Ghent alone, the Germans executed fifty-two persons as spies. In Russia the hysteria was easily channelled into the traditional anti-semitism. True, Ludendorff – soon to be one of Hitler's earliest followers – urged the Jews of Poland and Western Russia to remember that their Yiddish language was a bastardized form of German; true, the Russian Jews had no reason to love their Russian rulers and a few did spy for the Germans; but this did not necessitate the wholesale and brutal expulsion of whole Jewish populations from areas near the front.

This sort of hysteria very rapidly vanished among the fighting troops in the West. By Christmas 1914 the British were attempting to fraternize and even to play football with the Germans in the no-man's-land between the freezing trenches, until the scandalized staff threatened to turn the artillery on them.

The stupidest and cruellest forms of super-patriotism did not long outlive the enormous casualty lists, even among civilians, though the gap between the French, British and German fighting men and the flag-wavers safe and sound at home widened. But the spy-mania remained, and in some measure at least was deliberate government policy. The reasons that led the various governments to attach so much public importance to espionage were not always consistent, and varied in emphasis from country to country. There were, however, three major ones.

The first is that, of course, the belligerents did employ spies both in enemy and in neutral countries. None of them had at its disposal in those days the massive and skilled secret police forces of later date. (The Okhrana was massive but neither skilled nor particularly trustworthy. The security forces in Britain, France and Germany were skilled and trustworthy, but far from adequate. This is shown by one fact among many: more British warship tonnage was blown up in harbour, usually British harbours, by German saboteurs than was sunk in the one major sea battle of the war, Jutland. In Austro-Hungary they were skilled and – until faced with defeat – reliable, but primarily concerned with the nationalist movements inside the Empire.) Therefore it was important that the people be used as a sort of auxiliary police and that the danger of spies, loose talk and so on be constantly presented to them. Hence the vast publicity given to such essentially trivial incidents as the Mata Hari case.

Secondly this harping on espionage was a two-edged weapon of psychological warfare. It spread distrust and fear among the enemy to think there were spies in his midst. On the other hand it encouraged 'our' side to think 'we' were spying on the enemy. 'Our spies' are heroes or better still heroines (Nurse Cavell, who was less a spy than a saboteuse) although we can of course say nothing about them until they are caught and executed. 'Their' spies and saboteurs are nasty, slinky fellows or whores.

Thirdly, since spies and spy networks are by definition secret, it is possible to attribute to one's own agents intelligence derived from an utterly different source, as was the case with Franklin D. Roosevelt and the misinformation he was given about the British breaking of German ciphers as described on page 82.

Indeed this whole spy-mania – which has plagued our century, caused immense misery to millions, made huge fortunes for quite a large number of novelists and turned at least a dozen squalid traitors into film star figures – is a deplorable phenomenon worth examination. For with the decline of nationalist, as opposed to ideological, certainties, the black-and-white distinction between their spies and ours has been eroded. Since most human beings are

86

not ideologues, the difference between 'ours' and 'theirs' has become merged with the double agent, and the simultaneous decline of moral values has made the double traitor into a strange sort of anti-hero, a grey figure beyond contempt or admiration.

Before the outbreak of the 1914 war, little importance had been attached to wireless interception by the great land powers. This was due in part to obvious chronology. Guglielmo Marconi (1874–1927) had only invented wireless telegraphy in 1895 and had sent his first, indistinct message across the Atlantic, from Cornwall to Newfoundland, in 1901. A further decade was to pass before wireless telegraphy became big business, and not until 1920, with the creation of commercial radio in Britain and the United States, did it really impinge on the public. As a form of communication between ships, and from ship to shore, its value was realized at an early stage by the great maritime powers. However, very few merchantmen were equipped for radio before 1914, though navies – particularly Britain's Royal Navy – were aware of its enormous potential importance, and so therefore were the naval intelligence services. There were no air forces in 1914, and the few planes attached to the other armed forces did not carry radios. As for the armies, it seems that only the French and Austrians were particularly interested. The French had built a few listening posts on their German frontier to intercept German military radio traffic. Since this was extremely limited before the outbreak of hostilities, for German staffs were talking to one another on land lines, the French seem to have derived little if any advantage from their monitoring of the German air, and their interception installations were rapidly overrun. The Austrians, on the other hand, listened to their Italian allies – their past and future foe – during the Italian–Turkish War of 1911–12, and being already skilled at cipher-breaking they were certainly in this way more advanced than any other land power by July 1914. That they could not make more use of their expertise in the war that then began against Russia was due to the fact that the Russian imperial army had almost no radios and therefore almost no traffic to intercept and decipher.

On the very day that Britain declared war on Germany a British cable ship, the *Telconia*, sailed into the North Sea and on 5 August, off the German coast near Emden, raised and cut a great length off the German transatlantic cable. For the duration of the First World War the Germans were thus dependent either on transatlantic cables under British and French control or on radio, for even if it had been possible for the Germans to repair the broken cable without naval control of the North Sea, the British could quickly have cut it again. This seemed, and indeed was, a great initial triumph for British intelligence, particularly naval and diplomatic intelligence. (In the Second World War the Germans preferred to tap the London–Washington cable, and to listen. When the British Prime Minister spoke to the American President on a 'scrambled' line both thought that the scramble system was unbroken and indeed unbreakable; both were wrong.)

Wireless interception, at all levels, has importance in three major areas of intelligence. The first is in understanding what the enemy, potential enemy or even friend is saying. If what is being said is of any importance cipher-breaking will usually be involved. The enormous value of this intelligence operation, in British and American public usage, generally referred to as X, is obvious.

Secondly, there is the evaluation of the *nature* of wireless transmissions when the content of the message is not, or only partly, understood. This practice can also provide intelligence of the greatest value. In American and British public usage this form of analytical intelligence is usually referred to as Y.

Thirdly, simple triangulation makes it possible to fix immediately the location of a transmitter. In both world wars, and since the creation of the Red Fleet after 1960, this has been of primary importance to every naval intelligence service. It is less so, though by no means negligible, to army intelligence. In time of war it is possible to destroy an accurately located enemy headquarters; this happened, for instance, to Panzer Group West in Normandy, in August of 1944. In time of peace the movement of one or more senior headquarters can reveal a great deal about another power's fears or intentions or both; for example, the appearance in the early 1970s of large Russian army and air force headquarters near the Sino-Soviet borders was highly indicative of Moscow's attitude towards Peking, and hence of Soviet policy throughout the world. And the more precipitate such movements are in peace time, the more will the headquarters have to rely on air links at least until the necessary telephone lines are laid.

At the highest political level, however, such pinpointing of the source of transmission is usually irrelevant, since the source is normally static. But if, shall we say, the U.S. Combined Chiefs of Staff were suddenly to be operating their air traffic from South Dakota or their Russian equivalents from Irkutsk, then this would indeed be intelligence of a startling and probably terrifying importance.

Since every power has long known that every other power, hostile or not, is probably listening, how does it counter this? The most obvious way would be to dispense with radio altogether, but that is not possible, for the time lost would be intolerable. The alternative is to swamp enemy intelligence with X material, real or false. This is also impossible, since the enemy will rapidly distinguish the bogus from the real while the amount of skilled manpower needed to direct and actually transmit the bogus to saturation point would be of prohibitive expense. The answer – apart from the making of increasingly difficult ciphers – has been a mixture of both. Wireless silence is preserved to the maximum, consistent with efficiency and the required speed. And a great deal of bogus material is sent out, usually in the form known as 'cover plans' intended not only to preoccupy the enemy's intelligence service but actually to mislead it. This use of 'cover' will be dealt with later.

Y material can be far more easily concealed by the saturation method. It is possible, quite cheaply, to produce the wireless traffic of, say, a non-existent army group and for a time to keep the enemy's cryptanalysts uselessly occupied in analysing a mass of material that is in fact meaningless; but in due course the deception will be perceived. It was more difficult to carry out this sort of deception with an imaginary fleet. With long-range air reconnaissance and satellites it is probably now impossible, except perhaps in the case of submarines. To give one example: an unmanned sunken buoy could be so equipped as to emit, by remote control, an exact parallel to the radio traffic of a nuclear-missiled sub, while the real and lethal vessel preserved radio silence a hundred miles or more away.

Finally there is no reason, except in very fast-moving land warfare, why a headquarters should not be located at a considerable distance from one or more signals centres through which it receives and transmits its air traffic. This, too, is done.

Battlefield intelligence is essentially but not exclusively tactical intelligence. Its very name indicates that it can only apply in wartime, though a certain amount of its equivalent may be derived across frontiers in peacetime. It is sometimes referred to as 'low level' intelligence, though this somewhat contemptuous phrase is hardly appealing to the soldiers, sailors and airmen whose lives may be dependent on its speed and accuracy. And its enormous importance was recognized by the armies engaged in the static or semi-static trench warfare of the First World War. Patrols are almost as old as armies themselves – one wonders what would have happened at Thermopylae had the Persian patrols, if they existed, been more efficient – and many men of both sides lost their lives on patrol between 1914 and 1918. It was vital that the battalion, even the divisional, commander knew as precisely as possible the nature of the enemy whom he was about to attack, or who was about to attack him, or indeed if no attack were intended. For the navies, and later the air forces, of that war such intelligence was equally important though more difficult to glean. Finally battlefield intelligence, though usually ephemeral, can when quickly and efficiently evaluated contribute a great deal to strategic and hence to political intelligence at the 'highest' level. Any good intelligence organization will always regard its more clandestine sources as subject to instant re-examination if the information they supply is contradicted by the actualities of the battlefield.

There were and are three main sources of battlefield intelligence. The first and most obvious is commonsensical use of the senses: to see where the enemy is and, if possible, how many of him there are, and to note what his guns and transportation are doing, if possible with identification of these. Since the enemy will certainly try to disguise his activities both visually and orally, the I.O. (intelligence officer) in the field must be able to see through any such deception. To know nothing can bring about total tactical, strategic and political disaster, as when Napoleon's staff at Waterloo failed to discover whether the cloud of dust of a distant approaching army was created by Bluecher's or by Grouchy's soldiers.

90

The second source of battlefield intelligence is the interpretation of enemy documents, taken from soldiers dead or alive, or found in captured enemy land installations, ships or crashed aeroplanes. A first glance at these by a trained officer will often reveal matters of immediate tactical importance, such as the arrival of a new enemy unit or formation. Further and more careful scrutiny by specialists far from the battlefield will on occasion give a deeper insight. Evaluation of the mass of such papers frequently captured, particularly by an advancing army, is as tedious as it is time-consuming, but a letter or a Field Post Number may provide the missing clue. The real nugget, though, is rare indeed, as rare as the *coup* by the master spy. Codes and ciphers have been captured, on land as well as on or under the sea. However, all officers of all armies and navies are well aware that such material must be destroyed at all costs; when it is within their power to do so they almost invariably carry out this standing order.

Listening to the enemy's soldiers talk is possible, but extraordinarily unrewarding as well as being excessively dangerous. The apocryphal story of the German who reported that he had overheard a British officer say, 'Send reinforcements, we have our backs to the wall,' when the mythical officer actually remarked; 'Lend me one and fourpence. I am taking a WAAC to a ball,' is not unlike the truth. A soldier creeping through minefields and barbed wire in, say, 1916, in order to hear what the enemy soldiers were saying to one another would only hear what all soldiers of all armies talk about ninety-nine per cent of the time, namely women, sport and grumbling gossip. Since he would have to be a linguist of considerable ability to understand a private soldier from Upper Bavaria, Devon, Kazakstan, Alabama or Provence, it is rarely that his great talents will be risked for so futile a purpose.

The most important source of battlefield intelligence, however, is undoubtedly the successful interrogation of prisoners of war. The information they can supply is fresh, first hand and usually reliable. During the First World War prisoner interrogation became a highly developed skill, scarcely altered or improved upon in the Second. In the series of smaller, undeclared wars that have followed the Korean War, in Indo-China, Black Africa,

Algeria, Northern Ireland and elsewhere, skilled interrogation has deteriorated, principally due to the unofficial nature of the enemy, his brutality and the consequent use of torture by his captors. As will be seen, torture is a most unsatisfactory means of extracting information.

For the basic problem of the trained interrogator is to break the prisoner from his own discipline without destruction of the disciplinary principle and to convert this engendered acceptance of orders into the new discipline inherent in his new status as a prisoner of war. The prisoner has been taught that he need not, and indeed must not, give his captors any information whatsoever save his name, rank and number. A man who abides absolutely by these instructions is impermeable. Few do, for a number of quite simple reasons.

The act of surrender, of holding up your hands and throwing away your weapon, is for most soldiers a most hideous, if not a traumatic, experience. He is likely to be highly disorientated and in a state of mind to accept other disciplines, that is to say other orders, as a surrogate. This state of mind will be of comparatively brief duration, but while it lasts the skilled enemy interrogation officer, who of course speaks his prisoner's own language fluently, will be a substitute for the officers he has known before captivity. The prisoner's reaction will therefore be to remember his instilled obedience above his instructions concerning 'name, rank and number'. He will identify his unit, which is probably already known to the interrogator and which he is merely asked to confirm, and from that point on the interrogator's job is fairly simple. Once a prisoner starts talking any interrogation officer worthy of his somewhat elaborate training can keep him talking and can direct his verbosity, which will increase, into interesting channels. For tactical purposes, all this has to be done with considerable speed. It is of little use to know where a squadron of tanks or even a machine-gun nest was located last week.

Officer prisoners are of course more difficult, being more aware of their knowledge and usually of their responsibility to their own country. This applies particularly to officers in possession of precisely the sort of information most desired by the enemy, usually of a technological nature – artillery, tanks, aircraft techniques – since such officers will be aware that they must on no account give their knowledge to the enemy. This intelligence, which can be quite correctly called secret, will usually be of a strategic rather than a tactical nature. And the interrogation of such officers will normally be carried out at a very considerable length of time and far from the sound of guns. There experts will be available, both in the techniques of interrogation and in the subject of especial interest to the officer's captors – say, the ballistics of a new tank gun, the nature of enemy airborne radio, the pressure resistance of submarine hulls – which would be of little meaning to the field interrogator. Since most technicians derive satisfaction from the discussion of their techniques, a subtle approach by the well-informed interrogator, always implying prior knowledge of the subject and laced with flattery, will very often persuade the prisoner to talk. Bugging his supposedly private conversations with other P.o.W.s of his own or similar expertise is less satisfactory, though sometimes helpful. An officer with the intellectual ability here in question would assume that such conversations are bugged; nonetheless hints useful to the interrogators may be detected.

Deserters, as opposed to genuine prisoners of war, are automatically suspect. They may be deliberately planted, but as such they are likely to be detected very rapidly; or more probably they are men of weak moral fibre, anxious above all to escape the war and therefore to tell their captors whatever they assume those captors might be expected to wish them to say, such as tales of cruelty, inefficiency and poor morale among their former comrades. From the intelligence point of view deserters are usually, though not invariably, a waste of time and of energy.

Torture will, in the end, compel almost any man to talk, but only by reducing him, and consciously, to the degraded status of the deserter. He will then say, first and foremost, what he believes his enemy wishes to hear, in order to obviate the pain; or he will submit to the drugs to which he is being subjected. Whether or not it is justifiable that a captured enemy be tortured in order to save lives or to ensure the victory of a cause or a country, this method of extracting information is far too crude to be acceptable. What a man says under torture has to be re-examined in a much more complex fashion, involving personality, circumstances and background, than whatever he may say voluntarily under the more gentle pressure of skilled interrogation. This axiom is only too frequently forgotten, particularly when dealing with 'terrorists'. The use of torture is only slightly less futile than the shooting of the captured enemy on capture.

Thus battlefield intelligence, applied with increasing skill between 1914 and 1918, was an essential component of the whole scene. It was not secret; it was seldom usefully brutal; but it served to confirm or deny intelligence received from secret sources. For wars in this century are always won on battlefields, on land, on sea or in the air, and perhaps soon in space.

Chapter Seven

Room 40

Admiral William Reginald Hall was an officer of the Royal Navy, that is to say a regular officer trained for the service from the age of fourteen. His father had been a captain, R.N. and, which is relevant but not necessarily indicative, had been the first Director of the Intelligence Division at the Admiralty when that branch of the naval staff was created in 1882.

Born in 1870, Reginald Hall was known as 'Blinker' owing to a slight facial *tic nerveux*. In 1889 he was commissioned sub-lieutenant, R.N., and when not at sea took courses at gunnery and torpedo schools, gaining high honours, which he repeated at the equivalent of a naval staff college. Exceptionally smart, he became a senior staff officer at the age of twenty-seven and was promoted to Commander in 1901. Three years later he commanded his first ship, H.M.S. *Cornwallis*, in the Mediterranean fleet, described by his biographer to whom much of this information is due as 'one of the smartest ships in a very smart fleet'[1] for her captain was a strict but fair disciplinarian. In 1905 he was made a captain, and when war broke out he was in command of the battle-cruiser H.M.S. *Queen Mary*. But almost immediately, and after only a single, comparatively small engagement with the German navy, his health broke. However, he had already been appointed to his father's old chair, as Director of the Intelligence Division, in late November 1914.

A more critical moment for his appointment there could not have been. In less than four months the pre-war plans of all the major belligerents had broken down. The French offensive had failed immediately; the German offensive had been halted and thrown back at the Marne; the Russian steam roller had gone into reverse after the Battle of Tannenberg, fought during the last week of August; the somewhat nebulous British idea of a decisive sea battle was foiled by the decision of the Kaiser to

95

concentrate all possible German energies on an immediate land victory, a decision that was antipathetic both to Admiral Tirpitz and to his Admiral Staff. The major British effort was therefore diverted to supporting the French on land. While each side sought ingenious tactical methods of avoiding it – none of which was to have any lasting effect – the war of attrition in the trenches had begun. There could no longer be any question of getting the boys home by Christmas. Basic strategic rethinking on both sides was imperative, and urgent. And it was of equal importance and urgency to forecast what those thoughts on the other sides of the fronts might be. As with operational plans, so with secret intelligence too, the political and the military soon enough became almost inextricably intertwined.

On land, with the weapons and tactics in use during that war, attrition meant the deployment of vast infantry armies with maximum artillery support. Horse cavalry was virtually useless, and its successor, the armoured formations of the Second World War, did not exist as such, for few of the tanks that appeared in 1916 and after were used by either side as little more than armour-plated mobile artillery. The air forces, too, were primarily a reconnaissance auxiliary engaged in support of these huge infantry armies. The concept of strategic bombing by a massive force of bomber planes was, it is true, being evolved by the British, and would have been put into effect if that war had lasted another year, but as it was the Zeppelin and aeroplane raids on London and the Allied raids on German cities were mere pinpricks with a limited moral and very slight physical effect, comparable to the very long-range German artillery bombardments of Paris. This was an infantry war, with enormously heavy casualties. The god of war was on the side of the big battalions and as these were mown down by enemy machine-gun fire and, soon enough, left 'hanging on the old barbed wire', the call for more and ever more replacements became louder and louder.

Soon the entire male populations of the great powers were beginning to prove inadequate for the slaughter. From the Allied point of view the numerical weight of the Russian masses was, to put it mildly, a disappointment. Those millions of peasants could only in part be spared from the primitive agricultural system, and Russian communications were so inferior that even the mobilization of those who could was slow and inefficient. Even after that it was extremely difficult to keep them supplied with food and ammunition, while their armaments were grossly inferior to those of the Central Powers. Sir Basil Liddell Hart has calculated that in modern war between armies of equivalent military value the offensive needs to outnumber the defensive in battle by between five and seven to one. On the Eastern Front, however, the Germans were able to launch successful offensives and win battles with far smaller superiority of numbers, or sometimes with none, even at the critical point, while the ill-equipped and ill-supplied Russians needed a superiority of perhaps twenty or even fifty to one in order to win a battle and even then were largely incapable of converting a tactical victory into a strategic success. There was no relying on Russian manpower in the war of attrition.

Nor was the entry of Italy into the war in May of 1915 of much help to France and Britain from a military point of view, though from a naval one it was of great value since it secured the Mediterranean. On land, however, the Italians kept losing battles and indeed had to be supported by French and British troops rather than the other way about.

France had of course mobilized at once and at an enormous expense of manpower had held the Germans, with limited British assistance, in 1914. There were thenceforth no major reserves of French manpower on which to draw, and the loss of the industrial north to the Germans for the duration was a major blow to the French war economy.

Britain mobilized more slowly. The idea of huge British armies on the continent had scarcely been envisaged by the British General Staff before 1914, and it was a lengthy process to create such a force, conscription not being introduced until 1916. Much of the then enormous British Empire was for various reasons unsuitable as a reservoir of men to be sent to the Western Front. Large segments of the Indian Army were transported, sometimes escorted by the Japanese Imperial Navy, but it was the so-called white dominions on which the British had principally to rely for forces from overseas, and not even on all of these, for the loyalty of the Boer population in South Africa remained problematical. The Australian and New Zealand Army Corps (the Anzacs) was largely wasted by Winston Churchill's failed attempt at one of those grand operations which he always favoured, on this occasion a huge outflanking operation designed to separate the Central Powers from their Turkish ally by the capture of the Bosporus, an operation known to history as the Gallipoli Campaign of 1915. It was some time before the Anzacs appeared on the Western Front, after this defeat. Only the Canadians played a truly important part on the Western Front and of course it took some time for the Canadians to build up, from scratch, their magnificent army and more time to bring it to Europe.

Beyond that, what? Beyond that, the huge, powerful, rich and peace-loving United States of America. It was even more difficult then than it is now to generalize about 'Americans', though this has not deterred many from so doing. In those days the imponderables were immense. From the Allied point of view there was much in America that was favourable to their cause, if such be the word. America was of course a democracy, its basic political ethos more akin to the French and British models than to the quasi-democracy of the German Empire but utterly remote from the autocracy of Russia. Furthermore this very fact of democracy, of the government having to rely at least periodically on the will of the people, was not altogether advantageous to the Allied cause. In those distant days the attitudes of huge immigrant groups were still largely untested. The German–Americans did not hate Germany. In general the Irish–Americans did hate England, while the Jewish–Americans had often fled the Russian pogroms of the '90s. The Italian–Americans, politically less important, were presumably bewildered by the 'old country's' sudden change of alliance. But one fact applied to all these waves of then recent immigrants: they had turned their backs on Europe. And they all had the vote.

Culturally, linguistically and legally the United States were the offspring of England. The governing class was then primarily of Anglo-Saxon origin. Yet this very real bond, along the eastern seaboard above all, from Maine to South Carolina, also covered a very real breach. The proudest moment in the history of the white Anglo-Saxon Protestants was dated 1776, when British rule was overthrown in battle. Since then there had been one short war against Britain and at least two close shaves. Only the French had preserved a heritage of sentimental friendship in

98

America, dating from Lafayette, but even this was eroded, at least among the highly educated, by the instability of French political systems over the previous century. In American eyes the future lay to the west, not to the east, towards Europe. The Anglo-Japanese alliance was therefore not at all appealing. America, as President Wilson well knew, had no wish to be involved in the European war.

It was this antipathy that the Western Allies, and above all Britain, had to overcome. The Germans were of course equally well aware of the war-winning, or for them war-losing, results of any British success in this matter. German clumsiness, combined with excessive self-confidence, dealt the cards into the hands of British intelligence and particularly of Admiral Hall, the cards that at last brought America into the war, as will be shown later.

The Germans, on the other hand, had no great potential supply of manpower upon which to rely outside their own territory. The Turks might and did eventually tie down a great deal of Allied strength in the Balkans and the Middle East; only thus could they affect the primary Western Front. The Austro-Hungarian Empire, ramshackle and even moribund, could still engage a great part of the Russian army while containing the Italians. But to reinforce their Western Front armies with sufficient strength to defeat France and Britain on land, the Germans could only rely on themselves. And the only way such force could be assembled in Flanders was by moving the German eastern armies to the west, which in turn meant the neutralization or better the elimination of Russia as a belligerent. A Russian revolution was the obvious answer, and as will be shown in a later chapter it was to this end that the more aggressive part of German secret intelligence was devoted. It, too, succeeded. But even this success did not win the war: had it resulted, as it failed to do, in the complete conquest of France, it would no more have ended the war in 1917 than did another such German victory, with a Russia allied to Germany, win another war in 1940. Britain had either to be conquered or forced to surrender before Germany could impose a German peace. This victory had to be achieved before America entered the war. And unless British will broke, which at no time seemed likely, Britain had to be defeated at sea. With his taste for hyperbole Winston Churchill once remarked that Admiral Jellicoe, the Commander-in-Chief of the Grand Fleet, was the only man who could have lost the war in an afternoon. What is certainly true is that the Royal Navy could have lost the war within a matter of months or even weeks, between the time that Reginald Hall became Director of Naval Intelligence and America's entry into the war two and a half awful years later. For the war of attrition was concerned not only with the attrition of manpower but also of supplies. The term 'economic warfare' did not exist in 1914: the reality did.

Much had changed in the methods of blockade and counter-blockade during the century since last the United Kingdom, a maritime super-power, had been at war with a continental super-power. On 21 November 1806, the Emperor Napoleon had pro-nounced the Berlin Decrees which began the so-called 'Continen-tal System' to which he later forced Russia to accede. These de-crees closed all continental ports to British ships and declared all British ports to be in a state of blockade. This was a calculated response to the British interference with French international trade (an interference that much irritated the Americans and led eventually to the Anglo-American War of 1812) but Napoleon's vigorous counter-offensive at sea was a failure. True, it caused the British great expense, reflected in inflation, and some inconveni-ence, but not enough to hinder either supplies or men going to the British armies in the Spanish Peninsula in 1808. It failed for two reasons. From a purely naval point of view Nelson had won the battle of Trafalgar in 1805, and for the rest of that long war Britannia ruled the waves, so that the blockade of British ports was only a phrase. More important, the United Kingdom could still feed itself; and British industry was not totally reliant on the importation of raw materials.

By November 1914 these conditions no longer existed. The British Grand Fleet would be pinned down in British home waters against any sally by the German High Seas Fleet, which it only just outnumbered. Britannia's rule of the sea was precarious, and it is to this that Winston Churchill referred. The fact that no German sally took place until the Battle of Jutland on 31 May 1916, and that the enemy then withdrew, after inflicting heavier casualties than their own upon the Royal Navy, and never emerged from port again, is one of the more curious mysteries of the First World War. It is explicable by the over-emphasis that the German supreme command placed on land victories (the Battle of Verdun was beginning), but is more precisely assigned to a basic change in German naval strategy. The German High Seas Fleet, built so rapidly and at such vast expense before the war, contributed almost nothing to the German war effort. The U-boat fleet, built almost entirely after 1914, very nearly won it for them.

For Britain had become an enormous workshop, after the repeal of the Corn Laws in 1846 increasingly, and soon almost entirely dependent on the importation of cheap food from overseas. The system of empire ensured that the sources of basic raw materials were secure; the existence of an enormous merchant marine, that these could be brought to Britain, there to be transformed in the factories into profitable exports. Only coal, and to a much lesser extent iron ore, existed in adequate quantities in Britain. Almost everything else, including food, had to be brought in from far away. With industrial France largely in German hands since 1871, and particularly since 1914, British factories, aided by imports from American factories, had to supply not only the sinews of war but also the basic necessities of ordinary life. The breaking of the British merchant marine and the interdiction of foreign shipping reaching Britain would rapidly have knocked the United Kingdom out of the war.

German surface raiders secured considerable successes in the early months of the war, but were quite quickly eliminated and German overseas bases overrun. The small U-boat fleet, on the other hand, was extremely effective and almost beyond the reach of British counter-measures when Hall became Director of Naval Intelligence. He realized as rapidly as the German naval staff that the U-boat was likely to be the decisive weapon of naval warfare.

That U-boats torpedoed merchantmen without warning was much trumpeted as another German 'atrocity'. It was, indeed, contrary to the old practice of naval warfare, whereby a warship traditionally allowed the crew of an unarmed cargo vessel time to take to the boats before sinking the ship. But this practice was not possible for a U-boat captain, whose only defence of his highly vulnerable, thin-skinned ship when surfaced was to submerge into secrecy and speed. This was of course understood by

British naval officers, particularly those with any direct experience of submarine warfare. And the Naval Intelligence Division not only understood the U-boat tactics, but realized that it must find a way of detecting the position and if possible the intentions of the U-boat captains. The most obvious and best answer then available was radio intelligence, for there could never be enough ships to scour the oceans for underwater craft. Nevertheless, the atrocity propaganda concerning U-boat tactics brought in rich returns among neutral nations, and particularly in the United States after the sinking of the liner S.S. *Lusitania* off the south Irish coast on 7 May 1915, with many American passengers aboard and, it would seem, an undisclosed war cargo for Britain in the hold.

The two main adversaries were engaged constantly not only in political intelligence but in political subversion on the largest possible scale. As has been remarked, this was the age of nationalism, but it was also the age of empire. The empires of Germany and even of France were comparatively unimportant. Those of Austria and Russia were highly vulnerable. And the Achilles heel of the British Empire was Ireland. Both sides therefore, in the name of nationalism to which the Western powers added the word democracy, encouraged subversion among the enemy empires. Thus the mutual mass murder between the manpower of the great European states was extended, in all cases with ultimate equal success, to the mutual destruction of their empires. As will be seen, the Germans even attempted and failed to apply this technique to the Spanish-speaking population of the southwestern United States, with results disastrous to themselves.

But the forced destruction of the Austro-Hungarian and Turkish Empires was, in the long run, perhaps disastrous to all Europe. And the Wilsonian doctrine of 'self-determination' did not produce linguistically homogeneous nations, but in Europe a hodgepodge of smaller states, such as Czechoslovakia and Yugoslavia, still internally divided, unstable and ruled 'democratically' by the largest national element with a marked tendency to oppress minorities, while even the more homogeneous states contained within their frontiers provinces such as the Banat or Transylvania or Bukovina that were claimed, on Wilsonian principles, by their neighbours. The Irish, again in the name of nationalism, democracy and self-determination, drove an axe into the very foundations of the British Empire. In fact the mutual suicide pact of the European battlefields was extended, deliberately and by both sides, to the state structure of Europe as a whole. And in this suicidal venture the secret intelligence services of all the belligerents were deeply involved.

In November of 1914 the new Director of Naval Intelligence found an enormous and quite unexpected bonus awaiting him at the Admiralty. His superb ability to carry out the new duties assigned him was proved in the first instance by his immediate recognition of its great value, his rapid exploitation and expansion thereof and his grasp of its highly perilous nature.

Sir Alfred Ewing was not a professional naval officer but an academic of the highest quality. In 1902 he had been Professor of Mechanical Engineering in the University of Cambridge. The First Sea Lord, Admiral Fisher, was a revolutionary sailor who realized that the Royal Navy was living on its magnificent traditions and was likely to be technically inferior – he was quite correct – to the new German navy then a-building, above all in engineering, that is to say speed, and in gunnery, both range and accuracy. In the teeth of bitter opposition from the older admirals, often trained in sailships, he set about modernizing the fleet. And he persuaded Professor Ewing to become Director of Naval Education. This introduction of civilians into the centre of the naval establishment was much resented, but was to prove a very happy precedent in two world wars. And Admiral 'Jackie' Fisher's forceful, even brutal, modernization of the Royal Navy may well have given it that marginal superiority over the Germans which neutralized the High Seas Fleet.

With the outbreak of war Sir Alfred Ewing's long-term educational role came to an abrupt end. He did not, however, leave the naval service, but was given a new task. With a small number of carefully selected men, both naval officers and recruited civilians (principally mathematicians and linguists), he was entrusted with the breaking of German naval ciphers. So secret was this form of intelligence that even within the Admiralty only a handful of persons knew of its existence.

The reasons for what might, to an outsider, appear to be an almost excessive degree of security in the matter of cipher-breaking must be explained. To simplify the matter there were, and remain, two main motives behind such intensive secrecy. While a code can be decoded with comparative ease and speed, rather like one of the more abstruse crossword puzzles in the London *Times*, once that code is enciphered it becomes immensely more difficult to break. Furthermore while a code book cannot easily be changed, particularly at vast distances and especially in time of war, methods of alternative encipherment can be, as it were, built in. In the age before computers, each change of cipher required immense, very highly skilled technical ability of many sorts. Obviously it has always been of paramount importance that the enemy should not guess how much of his enciphered communications is in fact being read.

Particularly in wartime, there is no point in deciphering the enemy's operational communications without using the secret intelligence thus supplied for operational purposes. But the enemy will soon enough realize that hostile operations, perhaps naval operations above all, can only be accounted for by a breaking of his own cipher or ciphers and will change these with increasing rapidity even at considerable inconvenience to himself (for he too is busy deciphering). Thus the use that a belligerent power can make of its cipher-breaking apparatus is automatically limited lest the nature of its success be revealed by a too-rapid use of the intelligence provided. When possible this source is therefore camouflaged beneath another form of secret intelligence. Even this does not work for long, for operations must take precedence. The Germans, when Hall took over, were changing their naval cipher once every three months. Within quite a short time they were changing it once a week and then once a day. The pressure upon the men who had to break the new cipher each day in what came to be called Room 40 of the Admiralty was immense. On the whole their success was amazing, and for this Sir Alfred Ewing was largely responsible. For the Germans were not quite so foolish nor arrogant in this matter as the American ambassador to Britain, Walter H. Page, had been led to believe: 'One of the most curious discoveries, and one that casts an illuminating light on the German simplicity, is the confident belief of the German Government that its secret service was in fact secret. The ciphers and codes of other nations might be read, but not the German; its secret methods of communication, like anything else German, were regarded as perfection.' [2]

Perhaps 'Blinker' Hall's greatest psychological attribute as a senior staff officer was his ability to make quick and almost always correct judgments. Slowness, even sloth, may be of value among civil servants – *surtout, pas de zèle* – but will become a horror and indeed a veritable mortal sin when men are being condemned to die by the laziness or tardiness of others, who live in comfort at the expense of the state. Such an accusation could never be levelled against Hall, or Fisher, or Churchill.

The old system of watching an enemy fleet had been a combination of shore-based espionage, in which may be included the evaluation of open intelligence from neutral countries, and patrolling off enemy-held ports as practised since Nelson's time and before. The perils of this latter were revealed unmistakably as early as September 1914 when Cruiser Force C was cruising a patrol line, on Admiralty orders, off the Dutch coast to cover an intended amphibious landing at Dunkirk that in fact did not take place. On 22 September a single U-boat, the U-9, sank three of these cruisers, H.M.S. *Cressy, Hogue* and *Aboukir*, within one hour. Sixty naval officers and 1400 ratings lost their lives. Other methods of watching the enemy were obviously needed.

One was soon to hand. The Imperial Russian Navy had sunk the German light cruiser, *Magdeburg*, in the Gulf of Finland on 20 August. A few days later the corpse of a German was washed ashore. In his arms he was clutching a copy of the German naval signalbook. The Russian admiralty recognized how important this must be to the British, and a copy was sent to London; it arrived on 13 October, and was passed to Ewing. Fleet Paymaster Rotter, the Royal Navy's principal German expert, was assigned to Ewing and rapidly produced the key to the method of encipherment of the groups in the book by a piece of brilliant, deductive reasoning. To this another bonus was soon added.

Interception stations had been set up and also in mid-October reported German naval activity in the Heligoland Bight. British warships were sent in, and on 16 October they sank four German destroyers there. Even more important than this early success of Y, in late December a British trawler fishing the area, brought up in her trawl a large chest containing books and documents jettisoned by one of the German destroyers. These included the one German naval signal book that was needed by Room 40 to complete the picture, though not of course invariably to decipher German naval signals at once. Indeed the occasional, unavoidable errors reinforced the more oldfashioned admirals and politicians in their belief that the Nelsonian tradition remained practical and that this newfangled rubbish was useless.

However, Hall and other more powerful men were convinced of its value, and he proceeded to build up Room 40 – a euphemism or camouflage for his whole deciphering and decoding apparatus – and though not himself in direct charge of its operations, relied more and more on the intelligence that it provided and on its confirmation or denial of information received from more traditional sources. On this level, the Room 40 level, he had soon reached agreement with the Director of Military Intelligence under whose directorate a smaller and simpler cipherbreaking apparatus was more or less merged, for strategic purposes at least, with Room 40. With the mandarins of the Foreign Office it was a slower process. However, it was discovered rather belatedly that the intelligence derived from the trawler's chest also enabled Room 40 to read the signals sent from the German Admiral Staff to the German naval attachés, and this was not only of the very greatest value in itself for both naval and diplomatic purposes but also led at last to the breaking of the German diplomatic cipher, to the reading of the famous Zimmermann telegram in 1917 and thus to the entry of America into the war at the eleventh hour.

But all that lay far ahead in 1914 and early 1915, when Blinker Hall permitted and indeed encouraged his subordinates to use the most unorthodox methods in the creation and expansion of Room 40. Even 'subordinates' is an inaccurate word. Not only were civilians, usually dressed as officers of the R.N.V.R. (the Royal Naval Volunteer Reserve) a strong component of Room 40, and indeed of all Hall's division, but they were also frequently men of great distinction in their own fields of the sciences, academic life and even of the arts. Hall was a disciplinarian, but a very clever one, and he realized that such men could not be subjected to quite the same sort of discipline as regular naval officers. They responded to this, being also very clever men, and did their best to behave as temporary naval officers should. A tradition was thus created which was to be of immense value in two world wars, and one that was hardly emulated by any other power, not even the Americans, let alone the Germans. Many of the best brains in Britain were in fact directed into, and directed, Room 40. Hall went further. He did not insist that these be purely masculine brains. He employed women in positions of very great trust and confidence, but originally with one proviso: that they be closely connected by blood or marriage with the Navy. This requirement was later relaxed. Needless to say the rumours of the establishment in Room 40 quite horrified the stuffier and more oldfashioned naval officers and Foreign Office civil servants. However, the extreme and vital secrecy of the whole operation also ensured that they did not know much.

Hall also established with speed and ease a close relationship with Sir Basil Thomson, who was responsible not only for counterespionage at Scotland Yard but also for the Irish Special Branch; and a collaboration with Spencer Cumming, head of Special Intelligence and known as 'C', which was invaluable to both. Meanwhile he was also engaged in secret activities which did not have to remain secret for long and which incidentally provided the substratum for the fictional espionage thrillers of the next fifty years.

In any attempt to understand what Hall was doing during the winter of 1914–15, what are most impressive are not only the vast scope of his operations combined with his realization of where the 'point of main effort', the *Schwerpunkt*, lay, but also his speed. Here, and in brief, are but a few operational examples of the application of secret intelligence, some a failure, some half a success, one at least a long-range if minor triumph. All lie in what had hitherto been an area of undefined territory between military, naval and political activity, an area jealously and mutually guarded by three bureaucracies against encroachment by the others.

The first will figure later in the book for it is the overture of the breaking of British secret intelligence by the Irish nationalists.

In September 1914, the Irish Republican Brotherhood (inaccurately referred to as *Sinn Fein*, a political and not then a revolutionary movement) despatched one of its members, Sir Roger Casement, to New York, there to mobilize Irish–American and ultimately German support for a rising in Ireland. The cipher with which he and the leaders of the anti-British Irish–Americans, in particular John Devoy and Judge Colahan, communicated with Ireland and Germany was quickly broken; and their and Casement's conversations with the German military and naval attachés in Washington speedily fell into the hands of Thomson, Cumming and of Hall as soon as he became D.N.I. Not only was the name of the Norwegian vessel on which Casement was sailing to Europe, with destination Germany, known, but also that of his homosexual lover, a Norwegian sailor with a New York police record. Casement's purpose was also known: to create an Irish Legion among the prisoners of war, to obtain arms from the Germans and the transportation of these to Ireland, there to start a revolution against British rule. There is an Irish belief that the I.R.B. of the period, a secret society, was impenetrable to British intelligence and in particular to the Irish Special Branch of Scotland Yard. This may have been true on Irish soil: it was most certainly not so once they got on the air.

The cruise of the *Sayonara* was a most secret operation of Hall's, based on the assumption that Casement would sail for Ireland from Germany almost immediately. This yacht was chartered from an American millionaire named Anthony Drexel who allegedly 'sold' it to a bogus German–American. It was crewed by American-speaking bluejackets, no less than forty of them, which in itself aroused the suspicion of British naval officers on and off the Irish coast, none of whom was in the know. The skipper was almost a caricature German of the period, and the leisurely voyage of the *Sayonara* around the ports of the Irish south and west coast, awaiting the arrival of Casement and his German guns and perhaps his Irish Legion, throughout late December 1914 and January 1915, aroused the deepest suspicion. In fact, of course, the Germans realized that they had been misled as to the degree of support such an operation might then expect in Ireland and therefore postponed his departure until the spring of 1916. The whole operation was thus in the first instance a

108

failure, though a certain amount of information useful to the Royal Navy was collected from unsuspecting Irishmen and this certainly contributed to the total failure of Casement's mission when the Germans belatedly allowed him to proceed. This intelligence, however, does not seem to have been passed adequately beyond top-level naval recipients, which contributed to the fact that Easter Week 1916 took the British army and administrators in Dublin by surprise.

More important, perhaps, was Hall's failure to buy the *Goeben* and the *Breslau* from the Grand Vizier of Turkey. These were two German heavy cruisers under the command of the German Admiral Souchon, whose squadron also included Turkish men-o'-war. The Ottoman Empire was in its state of ultimate disintegration in 1914. Technically still ruled by the Sultanate, in fact the most powerful force was the 'Young Turk' movement, which controlled the Turkish armed forces. These in turn were in large measure German-trained, and German industrial and commercial enterprise was well on the way to making of Turkey and its empire a German colony in all but name. Therefore the Western powers supported the decrepit Sultanate of Abdul the Damned, who had the rare distinction of being one of the most repulsive figures ever to appear on the European stage of international affairs.

It was German policy to involve Turkey directly and irrevocably in the war on the side of the Central Powers. Therefore the *Goeben* and the *Breslau*, anchored in Constantinople, hoisted the Turkish ensign and led Souchon's Turko-German fleet into an attack on Russian coastal towns in the Black Sea, with the entirely false excuse that Russian naval forces had attacked its destroyers. This Souchon did without the approval or even knowledge of the Sultan's theoretical government, in order to force their hand, for those officials wished to preserve Turkish neutrality or, to be more precise, their own shadowy power. The attack took place in October 1914, and the *Goeben* and *Breslau* returned to Constantinople. The British and French thereupon presented the Grand Vizier with an ultimatum on the 30th: either he must remove the German crews from the two warships flying the Turkish ensign, or face war with Britain, France and Russia. This the Grand Vizier was most anxious to avoid, but as usual a formula had to be found. And his intentions were thwarted by the Russians, who declared war unilaterally on Turkey two days later. Their objective was what it had always been, and remains to this day, the control of Constantinople and the Straits.

It was in this highly complex situation that Hall now intervened. Through an intermediary, Gerald Fitzmaurice, who knew the Middle East, the Middle Eastern mind and above all the current Turkish situation intimately, he set about buying off the Turks. The haggle, for that is what it was, went on for several months. Without informing either the Cabinet or any other authority, Hall told Fitzmaurice to offer the Turks £3,000,000, with a ceiling of £4,000,000, in exchange for the surrender of the Dardanelles, the removal of all sea-mines and the surrender of the two principal German warships.

This was an arrangement entirely in accord with both the personal and political wishes of the Sultanate's ministers (who, to add to the confusion, were at one time using the Grand Rabbi as their intermediary) but unfortunately they could not carry out their side of the bargain, though this of course they did not admit. A form of bargaining reminiscent of the non-sale of the Sybilline books now took place. The British were preparing for the disastrous Gallipoli operation in which only Churchill, not Fisher, had great confidence. The plans were under way from January 1915, time was running out and the price offered to the Grand Vizier was reduced. On 5 March Hall offered £500,000 for the surrender of the Dardanelles and the removal of the minefields, plus a similar sum for the *Goeben*. Three days later the price for the warship declined to £100,000. It was only now, in mid-March, that Hall informed his First Sea Lord of this bizarre bazaar. Fisher was understandably amazed that his D.N.I. had been engaged in these activities, but he approved them. However, he lowered the bid yet again, for he was now moderately confident the Navy could force the Dardanelles, and only wished to buy the two German warships; price, £200,000 for the *Goeben* and £100,000 for the *Breslau*. Dirt cheap, in fact. But unaccepted. On 18 March the Royal Navy attacked and failed to force the Dardanelles. Britain was at war with Turkey, at a cost very considerably in excess of four million gold sovereigns.

Needless to say Hall was carpeted by the Cabinet for his unauthorized gamble. Oddly he was also criticized by Reginald McKenna, the somewhat obscure Home Secretary whose knowledge of this remote and quite original form of warfare was negligible. Hall had the theoretical backing of the two members of the Cabinet who did know something of war, Churchill and Kitchener, and he was able to convince McKenna that orthodox peacetime standards were no longer automatically advantageous. He held his appointment and continued to apply his own esoteric methods.

There was a rich man who enjoyed the name of Commander Sir Hercules Langrishe, an international playboy, as well as a regular officer. Sir Hercules, an Irish baronet, a great sportsman, a Master of Hounds, as gallant to the ladies as he was good-looking, was provided with a yacht – he was an expert helmsman – named the *Vergemere*, a crew of bluejackets of his own choice and a personal bodyguard, an enormous Irishman, when on shore. Thus equipped Sir Hercules set sail for Spain, ostensibly to enjoy himself, with plenty of very good champagne aboard.

The real mission of this handsome, pleasure-loving man, whose instructions included close attention to Spanish ladies of political influence, was of great importance. The first and easiest task was to show the neutral Spaniards that life in Britain was neither as grey and grim nor as close to defeat as German propaganda made out. The second, and more important, was to ensure as best he could that German U-boats were not refuelled in Spanish ports. At that time the operational U-boat had some thirty days at sea, half of which were spent in getting out of, and back to, German waters. Therefore its operational life on any one cruise was about two weeks, which would be doubled if it could refuel in a Spanish port.

Sir Hercules, being a naval officer and far more than he seemed to be, carried out his task effectively. He was helped in this by the fact that his opposition in neutral Spain was a German vessel, of obvious naval origin, with officers boorish in comparison to himself, and stinted for money, who offered beer to their Spanish guests. Both in psychological war and in espionage Sir Hercules easily over-trumped the enemy. On his return to England he and Hall arranged that A. E. W. Mason, the famous author of many bestsellers including *The Four Feathers*, should establish his residence in Spain. Mason never wrote his memoirs, but certain of his stories concerning naval espionage in Spain are generally believed, probably with justice, to be fictionalized autobiography. (Somerset Maugham was another famous writer then employed by British secret intelligence, in his case in Switzerland. His book, *Ashenden*, is also semi-autobiographical. They were wise to adopt this formula. Compton Mackenzie was prosecuted in court, as late as the 1930s, for publishing certain recollections of his war-time period in Athens and the Aegean Intelligence Service, on the grounds that he had breached the Official Secrets Act; his book *Greek Memoirs* (1932) had to be withdrawn, at great cost to himself. After the Second World War such famous literary figures as Ian Fleming, Graham Greene and Malcolm Muggeridge avoided Sir Compton's mistake.)

Hall's close relationships with 'C' and with Sir Basil Thomson of Scotland Yard led him to be involved, more directly than might appear necessary, in counter-intelligence work and even in direct interrogation, in which form of activity he was by all accounts a master.

Thomson's Special Branch had proved itself to be most efficient. The counter-espionage branch of Military Intelligence, known to this day in the popular press as M.I.5 (or more recently, since the subordination of the three service departments to the Ministry of Defence, as D.I.5) had in fact since 1911 been subordinate to the Foreign Office as a military branch of 'C's Special Intelligence Service.

British counter-espionage had been swift, secret and efficient before even the outbreak of war. The three principal German spies, Parrott, Gould and Graves, were under arrest and, more important, without this fact being known to the Germans. Their interrogation allowed C's men to round up almost the entire German spy network in Britain as soon as war was declared. This again was kept secret, despite the rampant spy-mania earlier described, and false information was thus fed to the Germans.

However, this very important means of misleading the enemy, in the twilight zone where intelligence and counter-intelligence overlap, was suddenly subject to the very arc-lights of publicity by the trial, in public, of the spy Karl Lody. Why did this full-dress court-martial, which caused the British intelligence apparatus to wring its hands at good work wasted, take place? It may have been mere stupidity, an extension into the judicial field of McKenna's foolish and untrue slogan, 'Business as usual'. Or it may have been a deliberate attempt to calm an inflamed public opinion, to show the people that spies were in fact being caught. In any event, from an intelligence point of view the Lody court-martial was a disaster, as Hall immediately realized. Henceforth only quite unimportant spies, such as Mata Hari, were tried in public, more important ones being tried in secret, or better still not at all if they could be turned around.

Naval prisoners, and persons arrested on the high seas under suspicion of being German agents, were handed over to Hall. He himself became a skilled and unorthodox interrogator. The tales are legion. One will suffice. A U-boat had torpedoed a neutral ship off Ireland. Among the survivors was a man who aroused suspicion though he claimed to be an American who knew no German and had never been to Germany. When interrogating this man, in English of course, Hall suddenly barked an order in German: *'Attention!'* The man sprang to attention: his game was up.

More important than such gimmicks were the uses of collaboration between the interrogation service and Room 40. Intercepted wireless messages between Malta and Barcelona, apparently gibberish, were deciphered in London – which cannot have been easy, the cipher used being based on the French dictionary, the *Petit Larousse*. The homes of suspected spies in Malta were clandestinely searched. In the home of one, a Serb named Madame Popovitch, a copy of the dictionary was found, its owner arrested and brought to England by warship. She seems to have been a psychopath – she was certified insane and confined to an asylum – but this had not prevented her from being an effective spy, and her disappearance deprived the Germans, Austrians and Turks of much valuable intelligence concerning the movement of ships to and from Malta.

Finally, there was another form of collaboration, though that is perhaps not quite the correct word, in which Room 40 played the essential role. There were British consulates in most major ports around the world. These were usually local businessmen or shippers who for a small fee carried out, in peacetime, such routine activities as explaining local regulations to the skippers of British freighters, getting drunken seamen out of jail, or simply acting as interpreters. They were seldom trained in even the most rudimentary intelligence nor were they necessarily reliable politically or incorruptible. Therefore in wartime their reports on the movements of enemy shipping were, in many and perhaps most cases, regarded as suspect by the Department of Naval Intelligence. But when such reports could be confirmed by Room 40, then the official source became the local consul and the secrecy of Room 40 was safeguarded. Every ruse of this sort that could be used as 'cover' for X or Y was practised in both world wars and, we may assume, in the Cold War between the Communist powers and the West that has prevailed, at greater and lesser degrees of intensity, since the Second World War.

Chapter Eight

When the Germans were Winning the War

Department IIIb of the German Army High Command was never a very happy organization during the First World War, nor indeed outstandingly successful, though it certainly had its triumphant moments. All this was due, in a way, to its slightly anomalous position, which can be explained by the basically irrational relationship between the German army and the Imperial German government. In a soberly, sensibly run country, as in the Germany of Wilhelm I and of Bismarck, the power of government resides in the ability of that government to control and to direct the vast and complex machineries upon which it must rely and which will not infrequently be in conflict with one another: the civil service, the armed forces, the economic-industrial apparatus, public opinion whether or not expressed through a representative assembly, the educational system, to name but five of the more obvious. When one of these properly constituent forces assumes, even temporarily, an exaggerated importance, then the whole elaborate structure of the state becomes lopsided and is even in peril, for the obviously fallacious cliché that might is right has a false verisimilitude, whether that 'might' be located in Parisian public opinion, in the British Civil Service of the 1930s and perhaps of today, in Wall Street or, in the case of Wilhelmine Germany, in the armed forces. The German people were unfortunate in that during the first two years of the war the Kaiser's own considerable weight tilted the balance in favour of the armed forces and above all of the army – to the comparative neglect of his great naval arm, as already mentioned – whereas during the last two the German army was in direct charge of Germany's political destiny, a role for which it was as ill-conditioned as all armies almost always are.

So far as the subject of this book is concerned the preponderance of the German army in the German state, particularly once war had broken out, severely hampered the German intelligence service. Though from a purely military point of view it was tactically, and by 1917 strategically, at least as efficient as the enemy intelligence services, at the highest level political intelligence was becoming subordinate to its military counterpart. The level of collaboration with the Foreign Ministry and the police was immensely inferior to that achieved by Admiral Hall and his colleagues after (and even before) the Dardanelles disaster.

There were two great contests of brain and skill at the highest level during that war, which might be summarized in two words: Russia and America. Because of Lenin's famous 'sealed train' that took him from Switzerland through Germany to the Finland Station, the Germans claimed that they played a major role in the Russian Revolution, the inaccuracy of which claim has seldom been disputed. That German secret intelligence played an important role in knocking Russia out of the war goes without saying, but it was not a decisive role. This will be discussed later. As for the United States, the final declaration of unrestricted U-boat warfare over-ruled any purely political arguments, and forced a reluctant America into that war as surely as the Japanese attack on Pearl Harbor forced America into the Second World War. Even if German skill had been responsible for the elimination of Imperial Russia in 1917, this was not a decisive war-winning victory, whereas the pressure brought upon the United States at the same time was a decisive, war-losing act of folly. For this the preponderance of military-naval over political thought was directly responsible.

Even within Department IIIb this question of prestige and power worked against the very skilled intelligence officers there employed. In the first place, despite both the reorganization of 1906 and the more important backing of Ludendorff, for the German General Staff there remained something suspect about their own intelligence service. This was certainly in some measure an inheritance from the Dr Stieber period and the long, clandestine struggle that had led to the army's supremacy in the field of intelligence. But perhaps more important, it reflected the German army's attitude towards its own General Staff. In the First World War the soldiers of Britain and France tended to despise their staff officers, not infrequently with some justice, as men of limited

116

efficiency who lived comfortable lives in large *châteaux* far from the sound of the guns and the misery of the trenches. In the German army, on the other hand, an officer who had passed through the War College and could put a crimson strip on his trousers and the letters i.G. (*im Generalstab*) after his name was regarded as belonging to the very cream of the officer corps. German general staff officers were rotated to active commands, and it was from those officers, i.G., that almost all the army generals of both world wars were selected.

But for a long time, despite his proven brilliance, and indeed his own intense ambition, Major, later Colonel, Walter Nicolai did not succeed in having the magical initials added to his rank and name. In the First World War and even in the Second, intelligence officers in the German army were not regarded as the human material from which future Commanding Generals could or should be promoted. There is an obvious argument in favour of this point of view, but the result was that German military intelligence, in which one must include their naval intelligence, was both very powerful and simultaneously the Cinderella of the General and Admiral Staffs. This may have been a minor, contributory element in the later disloyalty of many German intelligence officers, including Admiral Canaris, to the Hitler regime. Even the most disciplined of soldiers and sailors is appreciative of recognition for his talents. This Nicolai did not receive. But here yet another paradox arises. The fact that he was not a 'real' General Staff officer made it easier for Nicolai to play a curious role after 1918.

Another important weakness, at least in the early months of the 1914 War, was one that has been referred to by Ambassador Page and which is mentioned earlier in this book. So efficient was the German *Mobilmachung* and (at least at the very first) so overwhelmingly superior their tactics and strategy on both fronts, that intelligence seemed almost trivial. Did it really matter whether the British Expeditionary Force consisted of three divisions, or five, or even perhaps seven? That 'contemptible little army', as the Kaiser is said to have described it, would be overrun in weeks, if not days. As for the French, all that had been taken care of by careful staff planning before 1 August. And so it seemed, at least until the Battle of Marne and the cracking of the smaller

Moltke's nerve. *Nach Paris* and an even quicker victory than 1870! Why bother about an enemy soon to be eliminated by superior skill and better planning? Only, of course, it did not work out that way, any more than did the bitter French slogan of 1939, *Nous gagnerons parce que nous sommes les plus forts.*

It was about the time when 'Blinker' Hall became D.N.I. that both sides realized that intelligence was not just 'interesting' but might well be vital. The French 75s along the Marne shook the retreating Germans out of their arrogance. It was suddenly of extreme importance to them to know how strong the enemy was, and where, and what his intentions might be. Nicolai might not be considered worthy of those initials, but his opinions were most certainly worth the attention of his superiors.

Nicolai's Department IIIb was divided into four major sub-sections: (1) direct military, naval and political intelligence from all sources; (2) counter-intelligence, which as in Britain included close co-operation with the police forces both civil and military, (3) deception of the enemy, including cover plans and the use of enemy agents and (4) sabotage. In the first and most obvious field of 'straight' intelligence, Nicolai did not attempt to analyse raw material. What was of direct military importance was passed to a branch of the General Staff called 'Foreign Armies', later sub-divided into 'Foreign Armies East' and 'Foreign Armies West'. Much of this material was mutually contradictory: an evaluated report was prepared by 'Foreign Armies' and returned to IIIb. A similar activity was carried out for naval matters by the appropriate office or offices of the Admiral Staff. This material was not then doctored to please the supreme command, as was to be the case in the Second World War, but submitted as it stood, with only the necessary abbreviations and a minimum of factual comment, to the supreme operational command. Thus the German decision-makers in the First World War were usually far better informed about the potential and intentions of their enemies than were their successors in the Second. Even in defeat this had advantages. Ludendorff knew and had no hesitation in saying, in August of 1918, that the war was lost. He and the other German leaders were thus able to save something from the wreckage. Rommel and others knew the same thing in July of 1944. He was forced to kill himself for drawing the obvious conclusions. Until

118

April of 1945 any senior German officer who expressed 'defeatist' views was instantly dismissed or worse. Nothing was saved from the wreckage, and Germany remains divided, perhaps never again to be a major power.

Straight political intelligence was passed to the Foreign Ministry, where the process of evaluation seems to have been inferior. In any event decisions were not made there, and the supreme command remained dominated by the military. Economic and technical intelligence was given to a department within the General Staff for evaluation. This was probably a basic error from the German point of view, and too deeply ingrained in the minds of the General and Admiral Staffs to be put right when Walther Rathenau at last took charge of the German war economy. Total blockade by the British, French and Italians was an obvious and comparatively easy step. And the unrestricted U-boat warfare of 1 February 1917 was the equally obvious response. However, skilfully selective U-boat warfare might have been almost as crippling to the Allies and *might* have preserved American neutrality. Certainly in the Second World War the aerial equivalent, indiscriminate bombing, is believed by many to have failed to produce the military or moral results anticipated; indeed it can easily be argued that its final application – the atomic bombs on Hiroshima and Nagasaki – gave the United States a tactical victory but saddled her with an enormous, long-range strategic defeat.

However, this is anticipating. The point here is that in the First World War the Germans did not grasp, and therefore failed to exploit, the full potential of economic warfare. On the other hand there may well be, to judge by later wars, some doubt about the effectiveness of economic warfare as such, whether it is much more than a meaningless elaboration of the word 'blockade', and whether any 'economic war' between two fairly matched powers is not in reality won or lost long before war between them actually breaks out.

At the beginning of the First World War German counter-intelligence was good, probably as good as that of the British internally, and for much the same reasons. In 1913 the German authorities had arrested, inside Germany, no fewer than 346 persons on charges of espionage or similar offences. This shows a very efficient penetration of the foreign networks, and in particular those of the British and the French, before the war. The gain to the Germans on the Western Front was immediate. Not only were the French quite unaware of German strategic plans but, more importantly, they grossly underestimated German strength. The French reserve divisions were originally a second-line force. It was assumed therefore by the French that the German reserve divisions, like their own, were neither sufficiently well-trained and well-led nor adequately equipped for an immediate offensive role. Thus, according to French reckoning, the initial clash would be between the regular armies of the two countries. Their pre-war intelligence, and particularly its espionage department, should have warned them effectively against this illusion. When it did, it was ignored. Only as one reserve German army corps after another appeared in the offensive of August 1914 did the French learn in the most painful, expensive and brutal fashion that the German reserve formations were far more formidable than the French had expected. They were not, of course, as good as the regular German Army divisions, but nevertheless this huge mass of field grey uniforms very nearly captured Paris and won the war within a matter of weeks. Better French intelligence, or worse German counter-intelligence, should have obviated those errors of judgment and at least have enabled the Western Allies to formulate a more skilful strategy. Curiously enough the French were to make, for different reasons, almost exactly the same, and this time more fatal, error of underestimating the enemy in 1939–40.

Another advantage that the Germans had in 1914, compared this time with their position in 1939, was an almost total sense of national unity. There is no evidence that at the beginning of the First World War any important body of German nationals, let alone any German general, was opposed on moral or political grounds to the government of Kaiser Wilhelm II and did not wish to see Germany emerge victorious from the war. Even the few and politically powerless enemies of the existing regime were almost all prepared to postpone their revolutionary demands until victory should be achieved. With the exception of parts of Alsace-Lorraine – which were ruthlessly and totally controlled –

the western parts of the German Empire were solidly patriotic. So in overwhelming majority were the French, but the nagging memories of the Dreyfus affair, the distinction in the officer class between the *pays réel*, for which they were prepared to fight and die with the utmost gallantry, and the *pays légal*, the authenticity of which they doubted, had no counterparts in the German Empire, as they were to have in Nazi Germany and especially inside the German General Staff in the later war. The Germans did not even have the equivalent of the Britons' 'Irish problem', though this too was shelved, allegedly for 'the duration', by all the prominent Irish leaders. Germany and Britain entered the war with virtually undivided loyalty and patriotism, and this made the task of counter-intelligence in both countries infinitely more simple.

On the Eastern Front German intelligence and counter-intelligence were more complex. The Russians, with their usual passionate interest in this form of activity, had almost flooded Imperial Germany with secret agents, most but not all of them quite useless and quite easily apprehended before the war or shortly after its outbreak. However, German espionage in Russia was not particularly successful, for a number of reasons. The most obvious were simple problems of linguistics, of geography and of communication. Also the Czarist regime, like its successors, regarded all foreigners with the deepest suspicion. Inefficient and corrupt as was the Okhrana in dealing with its internal enemies, it still made life for a foreign spy both difficult and dangerous. Nor had the German authorities of 1914 any real, let alone reliable, contact with Russian revolutionary movements, which indeed the Kaiser regarded with as much distrust and dislike as did his cousin the Czar.

Stories that persons close to the Russian centre of power, such as Rasputin and even the Czarina, were German agents are pure fantasy, in part attributable to the spy-mania of the period, in part to subsequent Bolshevik falsifications of history. The real problem in the East was the cultural, economic and political fluidity of the huge area where German power ceased and Russian power began. Leaving out of the equation, at least for the moment, the Austro-Hungarian Empire, Pan-Slavism and Pan-Germanism as well as the Turko-Balkan heritage, the problem can be limited to Poland and to the large Jewish 'pale' in that then non-existent country and in western Russia, into which the Russians had quite recently expelled almost all of their Jewish citizens who had not managed to emigrate.

To describe this situation as fluid is perhaps an understatement. Not only did the Poles dislike their Russian and German conquerors with an almost equivalent virulence, the Austrians with rather less, they also were, in general, anti-semitic. The Jews who had not emigrated could have no loyalty either to a non-existent Polish state or to an anti-semitic Polish people. Yet those who were not Zionists – and this was a policy with few adherents in those days – or revolutionaries, were in most cases almost pathetically anxious to prove their loyalty to the Russian government, to allow themselves to be assimilated, even to prove in battle their Russian patriotism and thus to obtain the normal civil rights of citizenship. This emotional gesture was brutally rebuffed by the Czarist, as later by the Stalinist and subsequent power apparatus. Since they usually spoke Yiddish, the Jews of Western Russia and Eastern Poland were regarded as potential German agents and treated as such. Some, of course, *were* German agents.

At the cultural level, German–Russian relations were equally confused. The Russian managerial and professional classes had usually been trained at first hand, or at least at second, by Germans. German skills and German knowledge had for two or three generations been poured into the vacuum of Russian savagery. Lawyers, doctors, scientists, factory managers could only respect the Germans and many of them were themselves either German or of German extraction. The Russians might and often did dislike German arrogance, but they could hardly modernize their country without German expertise.[1] This led to a high degree of public schizophrenia towards one of Russia's many 'hereditary enemies', yet it does not appear to have justified the Russian distrust of their naturalized Germans. The part that the German or Russo-Germanized middle class played in the intelligence war between the two countries was almost as negligible as German influence at the Czarist Court. How slight this was is shown by an incident that took place in July 1914.

The dates, though well known, are important if one is to assess the immense historical importance of a single journey by an obscure trader in Kovno named Pinkus Urwicz. An otherwise uninteresting group of youths in Bosnia, that forgotten land, decided to murder the heir to the Austro-Hungarian Empire, and this these students, as they would be styled today, succeeded in doing on 28 June. Nobody minded very much. The students had shot the wrong man, for their victim, Franz-Ferdinand, was in Austro-Hungarian terms a sort of liberal who favoured the nationalism of Bosnians and other minority ethnic groups. As such he was unpopular in the governing circles of Vienna and cordially disliked by his uncle, the aged Emperor. Nevertheless this Archduke was the heir and his assassination therefore seemed to the hawks in Vienna an excellent opportunity for liquidating the new state of Serbia, whence the ignorant fun-assassins had come. The Austrians had their firm alliance with Germany behind them; the Serbs had a form of alliance with Russia, based on the vague concept of pan-Slavism.

Few persons of importance outside of Vienna and Belgrade took this latest Balkan flare-up very seriously. The British Secretary of State for Foreign Affairs, Sir Edward Grey, for instance, retired to his estate at Fallodon, there to watch birds. But with the grinding slowness of imperial bureaucracy, the Austrians set about planning the final destruction of Serbia and thus of anti-imperial nationalism within the Empire. Nor were the members of the Austrian government and of their Foreign Ministry in the *Ballhausplatz* entirely disingenuous in the method and matter of the information that they passed to their colleagues and allies in Berlin's *Wilhelmstrasse*, where in any case many of the shrewdest persons were also on holiday. The Austrian army was partly mobilized for manoeuvres in the southeast of the Empire already – which is why the unfortunate Franz-Ferdinand had been at Sarajevo in late June. And on 23 July Austro-Hungary presented an ultimatum to Serbia. This was, in effect, a declaration of war, which war the Austrians assumed would be so swift as to pass unnoticed until Serbia's destructon was a *fait accompli*. (France's President was on his way to Russia by sea, on a state visit.) The Serbians accepted the main elements of the ultimatum, but queried one or two minor points. The Austrians thereupon mobilized along the Russian frontiers on 26 July – a clear 'hands off' warning to the Russians which took the German government largely by surprise, although they had made certain preparations including a concentration of vessels on the Rhine. Two days later Austro-Hungary declared war on, and invaded, Serbia.

The Germans were ill-pleased. The Kaiser enjoyed rattling his sabre, but had no wish to do more with it than that, and certainly not in the interests of Austria. It was therefore vital that he and his government know whether the Russians would allow Serbia to be crushed, for if not, if Russia were to intervene, the Kaiser and his military advisers could hardly permit the almost certain defeat of Austria by Russia, which would leave Germany totally isolated in Central Europe. Therefore it was essential that Berlin know whether St Petersburg was responding to the hostile Austrian mobilization by a Russian counter-mobilization. In which case Germany too must mobilize, and in such a situation this decision probably meant peace or war on a European scale because of the Schlieffen Plan, while from the point of view of the German Great General Staff the timing of their own *Mobilmachung* was vital: hours, even minutes, counted. It seemed then, that Russia was mobilizing; but to what extent, and above all whether against the Germans as well as against the Austrians to the south, was far from clear. The Kaiser hesitated.

It was now that Pinkus Urwicz made his sole appearance in history and high politics. The German Second Army Corps was located at Allenstein in East Prussia. Its intelligence officer was a Captain von Roeder, and among his agents was Pinkus Urwicz whose business in Kovno led him to cross the border in his little horse-drawn cart. Urwicz saw a notice posted by the Russian government in Kovno, pulled it down, tucked it unread under his blouse and delivered it to his contact on the German side. It was rapidly sent to Allenstein and even more quickly expedited to the Imperial desk in Berlin. The Kaiser now had absolute proof that the Russians were mobilizing on 'his' frontier. The Schlieffen Plan was immediately put into operation: the First World War had begun.[2]

With the outbreak of the German–Russian War the Russian Imperial Army crossed the twilight zone of Poland, helped by their intelligence there planted. Neither their intelligence nor their mobility was adequate. The Battle of Tannenberg, on 26–28 August 1914, not only ended the Russian advance but led directly to the destruction of the Russian intelligence apparatus in the Russo-German frontier zone. When the Russian General Samsonov committed suicide after the defeat of his armies, he knew that he had failed not only as a strategist and tactical commander, but also that that failure was due as much to faulty intelligence as to operational incapacity.[3] Thenceforth the Germans were almost always on the offensive, as were the German intelligence services. Their counter-intelligence very rapidly wiped up Russian intelligence both near the front and in the rear, and at least until 1917 the Russians knew almost nothing about what was happening behind their German front, although they remained slightly better informed concerning their Austrian one.

On the Russo-German front the Jews played an important part. It must be understood at once that when speaking of Russian Jewry at that period, one is talking of whole Jewish communities, not isolated Jews within Russian communities. The Jewish 'pale' was almost a country, almost comparable to the Ukraine. When Ludendorff appealed to them to remember their linguistic connections with Germany, few listened to an appeal that was based on a German, not then a Jewish, concept of 'race'. But what the German propagandists failed to do, the Russian generals did for them. In the military zones, which behind the Russian front were deep, the military commanders had absolute power. And these Russian generals, or at least members of their staffs, were instilled with anti-semitism. They did not wish for Jews to live in their zones, and huge Jewish communities were evacuated or, to be more exact, expelled eastwards (they were seldom massacred) with great speed and not infrequently with extreme brutality. Perhaps a million, perhaps two million Jews, most of whom were simple artisans or labourers, were expelled from their homes, from the enormous ghetto into which they had been often quite recently forced, back into the chaos of wartime Russia. Their sufferings were not to be surpassed until the next generation was dragooned the other way, to death at Auschwitz and the other extermination camps. The Czarist generals' treatment of the

Jews was less drastic than that of the Nazis: it was hardly less cruel, considering the means at their disposal. But in neither case did such brutality create a 'resistance movement' and for the purpose of intelligence the Jews of Eastern Europe were, with of course many individual exceptions, of little use to either of the great belligerents. Yet their brutal expulsion into Russia certainly weakened, if only slightly, the Russia of Nicholas II.[4] The German Jews, on the other hand, had no desire for a Russian victory.

In the West, and particularly in the German-occupied territories of Belgium and northern France, the Germans found themselves in a far weaker position, from an intelligence point of view, than on their Eastern front. There were very few Belgians or Frenchmen who desired a German victory: there were quite a large number in the occupied territories ready to take greater or lesser personal risks in order to help bring about a German defeat. And the area in question being so close to the vital Western Front, the boundary between battlefield and strategic intelligence became somewhat blurred. The recognition, perhaps in conversation, perhaps merely by their insignia, of German formations newly arrived was a matter of the greatest and most important immediacy to the staffs on the other side; a simple counting of troop trains, with, if possible, their destination, was also of inestimable value; the identification of new weapons, such as artillery, gas and aeroplanes and their destination, equally if not more valuable. These forms of direct espionage, whether by a waiter in a café, a stevedore on a canal, a whore, or a train-spotter in a forest, were dangerous but not very difficult. Far more was the speedy transference of the intelligence so gleaned to the Allied forces. Direct communication, by radio, was even more difficult then than in the Second World War, owing to the paucity and cumbersome nature of transmitters. Personal communication by messenger across the front was exceedingly dangerous, over the frontiers with neutral Holland and Switzerland hardly less so. The Germans guarded their frontiers that bordered the neutral countries with extreme thoroughness and skill, besides flooding Switzerland, Holland, Denmark and the Scandinavian neutrals with their own agents, men and women in whom the tasks of intelligence and counter-intelligence were

126

usually unified. As for correspondence and the varieties of 'invisible ink' communications, the German chemical industry was far in advance of its rivals at the beginning of the First World War and retained this supremacy, though to a decreasing extent, throughout.[5] (Which incidentally is one reason why they initiated the use of 'poison gas'.)

They were well aware of the perils that confront an army in a hostile, occupied foreign country. Although it was now more than a century since an enemy army had operated on German soil, the German General Staff had not forgotten the Napoleonic Wars. They remembered how battlefield intelligence had almost entirely dried up when Napoleon was back on French soil, when Bluecher could no longer rely on the intelligence supplied by his compatriots nor Wellington on that of his Spanish allies. It is an historical commonplace that this lack of direct intelligence enabled Napoleon, in 1815, to concentrate his forces almost undetected at and near Waterloo. Had he won that battle, and perhaps the campaign, the failure of intelligence on the part of the Grand Alliance would have been a major, contributory factor. Therefore, in their occupied territories, the Germans of 1914 were determined to avoid the intelligence mistakes that led Soult and Masséna and so many other French marshals to defeat in Spain by numerically inferior forces.

There are two main policies which an occupying power can apply to a conquered or partly conquered population: kindness or brutality. The first is infinitely the more difficult. It implies extreme discipline and tact as well as economic concessions which may well be resented 'at home'. Besides, the mere presence of foreign soldiers giving orders in a foreign tongue arouses instant resentment. The suggestion that the conqueror is thereby a superior person, a member of the *Herrenvolk*, will stamp enemies out of the ground, first as agents and then as warriors in arms.

The second, a policy of *Schrecklichkeit* or deliberate terrorization, is from the superficial, military point of view, and particularly perhaps from that of the arrogant, victorious German soldiers of 1914, far easier to apply. And such was the policy that they then chose. Death sentences were passed and carried out by the thousand. An atmosphere of almost total hatred was created, and not only in the occupied territories. German

Schrecklichkeit turned the Prussian officer into 'the Hun', in previously neutral minds too. Like so many military short-cuts it was self-defeating at any but the least important level.

One of the most interesting and important intelligence actions in the first year of the war, in German-occupied Western territory, is the story of Alexander Szek. It is a characteristic story of secret intelligence in that it involves physical violence, moral pressure, strong emotions; that it is concerned both with espionage and with radio intercepts; and finally that so high was the level of secrecy by the operators on both sides that the fate of the principal individual involved has never been, and now probably never will be, known. Alexander Szek was, briefly, a person of great importance. And like so many who have been in similar situations, he was also expendable as soon as he ceased to be so. Owing to various flukes the young man found himself, unwittingly, of immense value to two huge and mutually hostile power groups. When his value to either ceased, so too did he.[6]

He was, it seems (and although that qualifying verb should probably be applied throughout his brief chronicle, it will be omitted henceforth) there when the German army occupied Brussels on 20 August 1914. They then found that a powerful radio transmitter capable of communication with the Western hemisphere and certainly already known to them was out of order, probably by deliberate action. In view of the cutting of the German transatlantic cable by the S.S. *Telconia* two weeks earlier, such a transmitter – and there were few in Europe of this power in 1914 – was of prime importance. The Germans therefore set about repairing it immediately. Whether Szek had worked in this installation in the rue de la Loi before the war is not known, but is probable. He was a student of engineering aged twenty, whose studies included the engineering of wireless installations, and there were very few if any other practising installations of this sort within the reach of a student at Brussels University. The Germans found his knowledge valuable; the station was rapidly repaired, and he then continued to be employed there, presumably in the capacity of a junior engineer. This was a serious breach of basic, and obvious, security on the part of the Germans.

For young Szek had not only a dual alliance but even a 'dual nationality'. His parents were citizens of the Austro-Hungarian Empire, presumably from what was then called Bohemia and therefore hardly likely to feel any greater loyalty to Vienna than did the good soldier Schweik. By Austro-Hungarian law he was liable to conscription. On the other hand he had been born and brought up in England, which by British law made him a British citizen, and he had only gone to Brussels, with his father, in 1912. These facts of ancestry and birth, combined with his extreme youth and an apparently malleable temperament should have made him a very serious security risk in such a highly sensitive location as the rue de la Loi. For once the transmitter was in order again it was used primarily by the German Foreign Office, as their principal channel for the transmission of enciphered diplomatic messages to German embassies and consulates in the Americas. Szek, it may be assumed, preferred to work in Brussels than to be sent as a private soldier to fight the Russians. The German authorities also felt that he was more usefully employed in the rue de la Loi than on the Eastern Front.

The British Secret Service, which had rapidly strengthened its peacetime base in neutral Holland, became extremely interested in the rue de la Loi, since Ewing, using Y, recognized both the source of origin and the importance of the transmissions, but failed during that critical winter to break the German cipher (and of course with diplomatic communications X is more important than Y, more so even than in military matters). A great emphasis of British and also of French intelligence inside occupied Belgium was placed upon the rue de la Loi. Szek's dual nationality was discovered, and with this discovery the operation passed into British hands. The purpose of this operation was to obtain what we may call, for convenience, the German code-book. However, it was essential that this bulky document be obtained without the knowledge of the Germans, since had they known or even suspected that their enciphered messages were being read in Room 40 they would immediately have changed their cipher.

Young Szek had relations, probably a mother but perhaps a sister, in England, and pressure was put on him, through them, to remember that he was also a British citizen. What precise form this pressure, first on his family and then on himself, took is not known. It was probably a skilful combination of promises and threats. And it worked, immediately but too well. Szek said that he had brief periods of access to the code-book and would steal it, provided he were smuggled into Holland and thence to Britain.

This, however, would have been a self-defeating operation, since the simultaneous disappearance of Szek and the code-book would have alerted the Germans at once. Szek therefore had to be persuaded, at extreme danger to himself, to remain where he was and to copy out the code-book. (Later he would have been equipped with a miniature camera. At that time such a thing hardly existed. And contemporary photographic equipment in the possession of a twenty-year-old engineer in the rue de la Loi would have been detected at once and the appropriate conclusions drawn.) It is not hard to imagine the extreme tensions on the young man as day after day, or night after night, he rapidly copied a few pages of numerals and their meaning, which he passed on to the Allied agent. The promise he had received was that in return for this nerve-racking activity he would, when it was completed, be brought to England and presumably given a suitable reward.

He fulfilled his part of the bargain, by April 1915. The English had the whole code, and Szek vanished from Brussels. He was never seen again. The Germans continued to use the cipher, and Room 40 to read it. What happened to young Szek? The British claimed that the Germans had caught and shot him. This is possible, if he were captured at the border and shot without interrogation by order of some foolish German officer. On the other hand it would seem improbable that he would not have been interrogated, his secret revealed, and even had he not talked – which in view of the little we know of his character seems unlikely – his job alone would have led to a change in the German cipher. After the war his father claimed that the British had murdered him, probably in Belgium. We have no evidence of any sort that this is the truth. But certainly his death, with his job completed, was more in the British than in the German interest. And the lives of men of twenty or twenty-one were not regarded as valuable by any of the belligerents in April of 1915. Had he been conscripted into the Austrian army instead of being employed by the Germans and the British in Brussels his chances of survival would have been little better. But that is not the point.

130

It was Napoleon who won his great battles, not the French corpses left on so many battlefields: Admiral Hall won the battle of the rue de la Loi, a secret victory which was to prove ultimately more important in his war than Ulm or Austerlitz a century before.

Chapter Nine

When Russia was Losing the War

The two great intelligence services – in the widest politico-
military sense – of the First World War became rapidly crystallized with the onset of trench warfare on the Western and
Italian fronts. (The Turkish War was in essence little more than a
very expensive and moderately important sideshow.) The Battle
of the Somme in 1916 and the Battle of Verdun in that same year
should have showed those with eyes to see that the ratio of forces
in the West made a purely military victory – the ultimate defeat
of one army by another – a highly improbable outcome: and both
sides were set on total victory. Therefore other methods had to be
invoked. The military historian senses an undisclosed despair in
the great French and British offensives of 1917 and even in that
of the Germans in 1918. While we have the advantage of hind-
sight, it is hard to believe that either side really thought that any of
these three huge operations, even the Ludendorff offensive of
March 1918, which was the only one to show a great measure of
success, could 'end the war'. Other means beyond shellfire and
slaughter were needed. In the operational field, the Germans
chose U-boats, with almost decisive effect; the British chose
strategic bombing, but too late for it to be tested. On both sides,
however, the closer connection of political activity with intelligence was seen as likely to be a more effective preliminary to a
military victory. For the Western Allies this meant above all the
involvement of the United States in the War. For the Germans it
meant elimination of one or more of their enemies.

The Battle of Verdun, as indecisive as the contemporaneous
Battle of Jutland, resulted in nothing save more huge military
cemeteries. The French have always claimed Verdun as a victory,
which it was in so far as the Germans failed to capture Verdun
and thence perhaps advance on Paris. But it was a purely
defensive victory, and one that in effect weakened the French

132

army even more than it did the Germans. When, a few months later, the French attempted a counter-offensive, under General Nivelle, they suffered a major defeat for which superior German and inferior French battlefield intelligence were largely responsible. The elaborate French preparations for the Nivelle Offensive were known to the Germans, who withdrew to fortified lines. This was not known to, or at least not appreciated by, Nivelle, whose vast *force de frappe* hit a near-vacuum. The complexity of lugging this great infantry-artillery apparatus forward to the real German defensive lines was almost beyond the technical ability of his staff officers, and the French, already weakened almost beyond bearing by nearly three years of slaughter culminating at Verdun, were bloodily defeated. Parts of the French army mutinied, crying for revolution, and peace at any price. However, the presence of a very considerable British army in France, combined with the personality of Marshal Pétain, and reinforced by America's entry into the war, made it difficult, if not impossible, for the French to react in 1917 as they were to do in 1940. The British took the military weight off the French by launching the equally futile, equally bloody Battle of Passchendaele. Pétain shot a few mutineers and exerted his normal, calming prestige. The French remained in the war, a brave but never again a very formidable army. It is, in retrospect, hard to see a method by which the Germans could have knocked France out of the enemy alliance, even after the disastrous Nivelle Offensive of 1917. But it seemed at the time to be almost a case of touch and go. The victory of 1918 was not a 'French' victory, but the Treaty of Versailles in 1919 was most certainly a 'French' revenge, and one that was eventually to be at least as expensive as the Nivelle Offensive.

The attempts of German intelligence officers to undermine French morale were not pursued with any particular enthusiasm or success. During the second half of the war the number of French deserters increased, sometimes across the lines, more usually into neutral Switzerland. IIIb saw that some of these men might be useful in various ways, and an organization was set up, with offices in Geneva and Antwerp among other places and with a headquarters finally established at Freiburg-im-Breisgau, approximately half way between those two cities. French deserters who were regarded as suitable material were extremely well, indeed lavishly, treated, particularly in Antwerp by Dr Elisabeth Schragmüller, known to the French as 'Mademoiselle Docteur'. They were sent back across the front with assignments of varying importance. One was simply to spread defeatism and, where possible, to encourage other French soldiers to desert. More important was to glean order of battle intelligence. For example, when the Germans did not know the location of a French division, a deserter would be sent back, in his old uniform of course, but with false papers assigning him to a unit of the division in question, and leave papers. He would then go to the Rail Transport Officer of the nearest big railway station, say that he was lost, and enquire where 'his division' might be so that he might return to it. Having acquired this item of intelligence he would then desert again, over a prearranged route, and pass it to Mademoiselle Docteur or one of her people, reaping no doubt a suitable reward. The French counter-intelligence soon got on to this trick and by changing the colours of leave documents made the operation far more difficult for German intelligence, and eventually impossible. The returned deserters could then only collect general information, for which they were paid only enough to encourage them in another such dangerous operation. Nevertheless there is said to have been an illiterate flower-seller from Marseilles with an astonishing memory who made no less than fifteen such trips into France for the Germans.[1]

Although the concept of eliminating France by a knockout blow was never entirely abandoned by the German military leadership and was indeed given one last try in 1918, politico-military intelligence was looking for a way round the purely military Western Front confrontation at least as early as 1916. One, as we know, was the elimination of Britain by U-boat warfare. (The Germans of course had as little interest in Irish national aspirations as had the French in 1798 or the Spaniards in 1601; in all three cases the foreigners' motives were the denial of the Irish ports and the entanglement of British forces in Ireland.) The U-boat campaign could, according to the calculations of the German Admiral Staff, not be launched until there were 200 operational U-boats available, that is to say before 1 February 1917. And it had to succeed rapidly after that date, since it was realized by at least the more perspicacious men in Berlin that it would provoke the United States beyond Wilsonian tolerance.

For geographical reasons the elimination of Italy would have proved as expensive in troops, and ultimately of as little value, to the Germany of the First World War as it was to prove to the Anglo-Americans of the Second World War. Austro-German military policy in both wars was simply to tie down the maximum amount of enemy forces in the long peninsula.

There remained Imperial Russia, isolated geographically from Germany's other foes, and here the prospects of success were from the very beginning, and certainly after Tannenberg, far greater. Yet the Germans set about this great endeavour in a curiously halfhearted way. Two myths have come into being. One is that the so-called Kerensky Revolution of February 1917 and its sequel, the Bolshevik November Revolution, were the result of conspiracies between Russian traitors and the German Great General Staff. The other is that both revolutions were 'spontaneous'. The second myth has been propagated by official Soviet propaganda, the first by anti-Communists then and later. George Katkov, writing about the background to the first, the February, revolution, has described in his introduction the 'frequent attacks of despair and despondency' that almost overwhelmed him as he attempted to unravel the mass of lies and contradictions inherent in the subject.[2] The mass of material, mostly false, and the pink spectacles worn by so many Western 'liberal' historians, did not make his labours any easier. And of course our knowledge of the Russian archives of the period is both fragmentary and highly selected to fit the changing theses of Soviet historians. Mr Katkov, on whom this writer has drawn with gratitude, illuminates the extraordinary confusion prevalent in the Imperial Russian war administration. For a more detailed outline of the murky confusion in which German intelligence had to go fishing, the reader is referred to his books.

In her foreign relations the basic source of Russian strength has always been a simple, one might even say a simplistic, patriotism, a peasant patriotism profoundly connected with the land of Russia. So vast is that land mass, so remote its simple farm labourers from all foreign contact, that invasions from East or West, by Mongols or Frenchmen or Germans, have usually evoked emotions of violent resistance only occasionally confused by a desire for 'liberation'. And this basic, rooted patriotism was in large measure instilled into the conquered, subject peoples of the Czarist and Soviet Empires. Only in the Ukraine, and in the border areas of the Baltic states, the Chinese Orient, the Jewish 'pale' and nowadays the occupied Eastern European countries have the Russians had to fear revolt and collaboration with the enemy, and then only marginally. It is almost as though Russian fatalism towards bad government is infectious.

For perhaps no great nation-state or empire under European influence has been, for two centuries and more, so badly, so inefficiently and at times so cruelly governed. Napoleon, bearing no matter how dishonestly the word 'freedom' on his banner, was accepted as the liberator in Germany and Italy. He had every reason to expect an even more enthusiastic welcome in Spain and Russia and indeed in those countries he received it, but only from a tiny minority among the governing class which had some knowledge of the ideals called 'the Enlightenment'. From the vast majority, the peasants in arms, he met brute resistance and defeat. For it did not occur to any but a minute number of Russian serfs, or their Spanish equivalents, that any rulers could have any interest whatsoever in the well-being of those over whom they ruled.

Throughout the nineteenth and twentieth centuries ripples of liberalism – in the real sense of that word – had affected the Russian centre of power, only to be greeted with dumb apathy by the masses, and the tide has repeatedly ebbed more rapidly than ever it flowed, from the Czar Alexander to First Secretary Krushchev, and with an almost audible relief. Heads rolled, and all was once again as it always had been.

After the demise of a bogus parliament in 1914, Russia remained, as in 1814 and 1944, an autocracy, but unlike both its predecessor and its successor an extraordinarily inefficient one. The liberal ripples had, at the centre, undermined the sands upon which the autocrat sat enthroned. Furthermore the Czar Nicholas II was a quite remarkably weak despot, the weakest perhaps who has ever ruled the Russian Empire. And that empire was governed with a quite remarkable ineptitude. The corruption and indeed near-disintegration of its secret police has already been described. It was paralleled in these by the other organs of government. The Russia that went to war in 1914 could neither arm nor even

136

pay its soldiers. To the German mind of the period it seemed that this was the inefficient enemy that could most easily be eliminated. Their German logic was impeccable, but as usual their German methods were fallacious when dealing with Mother Russia.

The Russian state apparatus that lurched into a war situation in July of 1914 was so cumbersome and inadequate even in peace that it could not, logically, deal with the problems of a major war. Even the enormous problems of mobilization were almost irreversible. That is to say that for the Russian autocracy to mobilize meant to go to war, just as for the German General Staff going to war meant the implementation of the Schlieffen Plan, the invasion of Belgium and so on. If Imperial Germany's destiny was sealed by an excess of skilful planning, Imperial Russia's may be ascribed to a contrary weakness. Russia's war was improvised.

In part this can be ascribed to the little waves of liberalization that had undermined the sand-castle for well over a century; in part to the weak character of the Czar, no doubt in some measure a Romanov inheritance but one shared to a certain extent by all the famous monarchical families of that age, blinded by diamonds and decorations which they had not themselves won and seldom deserved; in part to the defective administration on which the autocracy had to rely in time of peace and *a fortiori* once the fatal order for mobilization had been pinned to the walls of public buildings from Kovno to Vladivostok, from Murmansk to Sebastopol.

The autocrat and his immediate advisers, who enjoyed the status of government, were at the centre politically. Around this soft centre, with its shell the corrupt Okhrana, revolved many forces, but usually in elliptical motion, liable not only to mutual collision but also, after such collision, to the destruction of the centre itself or, more exactly, to its replacement. From the point of view of German military and political intelligence in 1915, there were four such comets that might destroy Russian ability to wage war at all, for to the German mind a war waged without a central control was an impossibility. Apart from the Imperial Russian Army itself, these centrifugal – but what was even more important for German aims, centripetal – forces were of two sorts, the constitutional or reformist movements and the

137

revolutionaries. These were again divided, both in function and intent, and further sub-divided.

The constitutional reformists were, politically, the heirs to the almost defunct Duma, the last of the Czarist-style liberals, who clung to the belief that Russian autocracy could be modified into a Western, even a British, type of representative, elected parliamentary form of government with a constitutional monarchy. Their 'right wing' or more conservative leader was A. I. Guchkov who led the Octobrist Party, was a member of the State Council (roughly the equivalent of a senate) and was always close to the centre of power. He represented the rich and the landowners. The president of the Duma's *Lower Chamber*, M. V. Rodzianko, was to prove of greater, if ephemeral, importance. He might be said to have represented the small, indeed nascent, Russian middle class. Both these men and their followers were patriots who desired a Russian victory over the German and Turkish foreign, indeed any foreign, enemy. Nor did they regard the overthrow of the Czarist regime as essential.

More vulnerable in retrospect than the 'liberal' politicians was the administrative and economic structure of Czarist Russia at war. And here the Voluntary Associations were of the greatest importance.

Even the great centralized Western European powers soon found that the demands of 'total war' exceeded the capacities of government. Relying on patriotism, the help of voluntary, non-governmental organizations was invoked by the authorities in Britain, France and Germany in such matters as ambulance and hospital work (which appealed to the women) and to the co-operation, usually granted, of the trade unions. Indeed in Britain, at least until 1916, the new, vast armies and the enormously expanded navy depended for its manpower entirely on volunteers. Labour was attracted, not directed, into the war industries by inflated pay. The control of all these forces, voluntary or otherwise, remained in the hands of the central governments. This was far less so in Russia, where the Voluntary Organizations were of an entirely different character from their namesakes in the West and were also of considerable political importance.

Their growing importance was based not only on the inefficiency of the Russian central power, which stemmed in turn from

138

the weakness of any autocratic system facing the magnitude of a major war and in this case aggravated by the lethargy and stupidity of the autocrat himself, but also on the enormous geography of the Russian Empire. A more efficient emperor might have been able to gather the strings, many of them decrepit, entangled and liable to snap, into reins with which to control his huge country through a competent and obedient secretariat: Nicholas II was no Napoleon. He listened above all to his wife, whose mind was in her son's nursery. The Czar turned out to be above all the junior partner in a marriage and the *materfamilias* an admirable wife and mother devoted above all else to the preservation of their son and thus of the Romanov dynasty. It is touching and indeed pathetic that it was the Czar's friends, not his enemies, who were opposed to his assumption of supreme control of the armies – surely an essential role for an autocrat in time of war – since they feared lest defeat further tarnish his tawdry reputation as a leader.

Thus was the enormous front not only divided for normal operational purposes, but each of the three commanders was given a huge rear area in which he had complete authority of every sort. Theoretically these huge satrapies were to be assigned to members of the Imperial family and thus, by a sort of cousinage, to the autocracy. This was attempted at first, but there were not enough Romanov generals. Soon enough the excellent Brusilov was in command against the Austrians, while senior staff officers were in fact in charge further north. It was these people who lost battles and who carried out the forced removal of the Jews, among other follies – the Czar was not to blame. He never was, except perhaps for sins of omission.

It would be wrong to suggest that the Voluntary Organizations 'filled a gap': the gaps in the Russian administration were never filled, but at least these essentially capitalist and patriotic associations helped keep the Russian army going, even in some cases to the provision not merely of food but also of weapons to the soldiers. So great were the distances, so poor the communications in Russia – during the extreme crisis of late January/early February 1917 the Czar himself was *incommunicado* for some forty-eight vital hours aboard a train that had been obliged to take an alternative route from G.H.Q., Mogilev, to Petrograd – that the various Voluntary Organizations, in their increasingly important role of auxiliary quartermasters or even supply ministries, became linked with the groups of armies in front of them, particularly as those higher commands became more and more autochthonous. Thus Brusilov would deal directly with the Voluntary Organizations in Kiev and elsewhere behind his front, his colleagues to the north with Moscow or Petrograd. That the autocracy did not fully control its fighting forces nor even the supply services along the German, Austrian and Turkish fronts was a sure indication of weakness that any enemy must try to exploit.

There were of course also centralized Voluntary Organizations. There were even Jewish organizations such as the *Jewish Committee for the Aid of War Victims*, created as early as August 1914 in Petrograd and reproduced elsewhere: a unified Jewish Committee contributed 31 million roubles to the Russian war effort, some 12 per cent from Russian Jews, some 32 per cent from international Jewry and the balance from government funds for war victims.[3] It is almost impossible to translate First World War currencies into our own, equally fluctuating, values, but this figure can be compared with a contemporary one.[4] In December 1915, in a despatch to the German Chancellor, the German Minister in Copenhagen, Brockdorff-Rantzau, estimated the total cost of overthrowing the Imperial Russian system at 20 million roubles.

There were other centres of the Voluntary Organization movement or apparatus (neither word is satisfactory for so amorphous a force) and these were generally in a loose political alliance with the constitutionalist, or anti-absolutist, politicians whose party (again too exact a word in the circumstances) has gone down in history as the Kadets. It was to these people that German intelligence at first devoted most of its attention. The Voluntary Organizations appeared to the Germans vulnerable, even corruptible, and of course opposed to the system of government; they were, however, generally patriotic and seldom of a revolutionary temperament. The forces, political, economic and emotional, represented by this loose conglomeration were probably the best that the Germans could have chosen to win the war and preserve their society. Still, there was a quicker, and therefore to the military mind, more attractive, immediate alternative.

140

The revolutionary parties were basically three. On the one hand were the anarchists, with roots deep in one part of the Russian ethos, men often of extreme intellectual brilliance and emotional honesty. By definition, however, they could not form a political force that was either cohesive or durable. An anarchist revolution, even an anarchist state, is a philosophical possibility but a political impossibility in our age, at least in any country even as moderately complex as was Russia sixty years ago. The anarchists were to play their part in the elimination of Czarism; they were then to be liquidated by the succeeding autocracy. They fought and died with the utmost bravery and integrity, physical and mental, against two tyrannies. Only their emotions and their morality linger on in Russia, and perhaps elsewhere. Save as potential assassins they were certainly of no use to *Abteilung IIIb* of the German Great General Staff.

When the Germans came to examine the other Russian revolutionary movements, both inside and outside Russia, they were confronted with problems for which the staff officer's methodology was and remains quite unsuited: it would be impossible to establish an order of battle among the Okhrana-infiltrated and highly fissiparous movements that regarded the overthrow of the Czarist regime and its society as their primary objective. The mass of lies that have accumulated about events and motives before, during and after 1917 have not made this maze of personalities, feuds and treacheries any easier to traverse. Nor is it this writer's intention to attempt that labour, save in so far as to aim at a brief panorama of what was perhaps seen from Berlin in 1916.

Undoubtedly the largest revolutionary party, if such a word can be used when dealing with a highly amorphous group of persons, was the Socialist Revolutionaries. Briefly, they represented the peasants. And, again briefly, what the peasants wanted was the ownership of the land they worked. The end of serfdom had not meant the end of the landlords. Russian mobilization had meant, among other matters, the donning of military uniform by millions of peasants. But they remained peasants, and their officers were in large measure their old landlords, also now in uniform. Therefore when the Revolution came, and the soldiers shot their officers and deserted to go home, this 'voting with their feet', in Lenin's much-quoted phrase, was not a vote for Lenin or

Communism or even any sort of Marxist Socialism, but a desire to see the land returned to the people by the elimination of the land-lords. In so far as any intellectual scheme can be applied, it has been described as a desire for a return to the ancient communal ownership known in Russia as the *mir* system, qualified by the imposed concept of ownership. (A similar emotion, based on the vaguest historic memories and traditions, lay behind the Land War in nineteenth-century Ireland: to get rid of the landlords and go back to something like pre-Norman or at least pre-Elizabethan conditions of life.) It was to this deep-seated but inchoate emotional force that the Russian Socialist Revolution-aries appealed above all, both in the army and in the vast stretches of the steppes. This was not a force that could be manipulated by a foreign hostile power, though it could perhaps be encouraged. However, the destruction of landlordism, even in Russia, was hardly a crusade in which the German and Austrian governing class, themselves largely landlords, would wish to be involved.

This applied even more to internal patriotism. Much as the Ukrainians, Finns, Poles, Baltic peoples and others might hate their Russian imperial overlords, this hatred too was a weapon that the Central European powers had to use very gingerly – which is precisely what they did, both in the British Empire, par-ticularly Ireland, and in Russia. In effect this psychological weapon was to be of far greater use to the Western Allies, par-ticularly once America was in the war. The nationalism of the subject peoples within the Austro-Hungarian Empire was far better organized and far more inflammable than that of their equivalents in the Russian Empire. The proof is that despite defeat, revolution and civil war the Russian Empire has remained intact and indeed been enlarged; the other has vanished for ever.

There remained, then, one major, potential revolutionary force in Russia, the Social Democrats. They were Marxists; they had had their representatives in the Duma; and they were in theory a political party, with an organizational apparatus. These three advantages, however, were from the point of view of Department IIIb, the Foreign Office and the Kaiser only mitigated assets. The Social Democrats in Russia, as elsewhere, represented above all the new urban proletariat, new in Russia that is, where it has been estimated that genuine industrialization (as opposed to the mere manufacture of weapons and explosives) had proceeded at a greater rate in the decade just before the First World War than in any decade before or since. However, the industrial proletariat was still a small minority save in the Petrograd area, in Viborg (Finland) and to a lesser extent in Moscow and some other growing cities. Marxism could not expect to command the support that its creator had anticipated for Germany. Indeed his ideology, his interpretation of past and future history, had categorically ruled out primitive, peasant Russia as the powerhouse of revolution, had specifically assigned that role to Germany. It is hardly surprising therefore that Marxism was in German governing circles at least as unpopular as were the theories of national self-determination in Austria, or peasant revolt in both countries.

Nor was the transitory representation of the Social Democrats in the Duma regarded as an impressive performance. First of all the delegation was very small, secondly it had been thoroughly infiltrated by the Okhrana, and finally it had no internal cohesion. The split of the party into Bolsheviks and Mensheviks after the failed revolution of 1905 had, in 1912, become apparently total.

The leader of the Bolshevik faction was of course Lenin. He lived in exile in Zurich, frequenting a café that was also patronized by another 'revolutionary' of a very different sort, cultural not political, named James Joyce. Lenin's principal lieutenants in Russia, such as Stalin and Sverdlov, were incarcerated in Siberia. He was almost penniless, and had the greatest difficulty in meeting his printers' bills. His followers inside and outside Russia have been estimated as being, in 1916, between five and ten thousand. His definition of Bolshevism can be summed up in two phrases: the absolute acceptance of Lenin's interpretation of *Das Kapital*, and the absolute acceptance of Lenin's personal authority. This second enabled him to become the first totalitarian dictator, but few, if any, apart perhaps from himself, foresaw this. He seemed, in effect, too unimportant for the well-informed Okhrana to bother even to murder him, which would have been extremely simple in Zurich in 1916. He himself, indeed, then foresaw no Russian revolution in his lifetime.

The Menshevik wing of the Social Democrat Party was more solidly grounded among the industrialized Russian proletariat.

(It has been estimated that in the small Bolshevik Party, two-thirds of the members were, like Lenin himself, middle-class intellectuals.) It was gaining strength in the crude trade union movement, though the most successful trade unions were run by the Okhrana. The Menshevik leaders were not subject to quite the same degree of persecution as the Bolsheviks. And the most important of the Mensheviks, Lev Davidovitch Bronstein, alias Trotsky, who had played an important part in 1905, although himself usually in exile, had some of his own people at large, particularly in the Petrograd area. His own two autobiographical books are as mendacious about this as they are about so much else. In particular he is totally dishonest about the funds provided for revolutionary purposes by the German government.[5]

The key figure in this murky business was a certain Alexander Israel Helphand, whose pseudonyms included that of Parvus (which indeed may have been his real name). He was, like Trotsky, a Russian Jew. Trotsky was born in 1879, Helphand twelve years earlier. There is some doubt as to the date when Helphand and Trotsky became friends and, inevitably with any friend of Trotsky's, accomplices in revolutionary activities. Indeed it is suggested by Mr Carmichael that they collaborated on *Permanent Revolution*, a most important re-interpretation of the Marxian thesis which did not deny the possibility of a pre-capitalist revolution and which has therefore been of the greatest value to Chinese Communists. This thesis put Trotsky to the 'left' of Lenin and made him the principal enemy of Stalin when that dictator produced the equally un-Marxist policy of 'socialism in one country'. But any attempt, and there have been many, to see Trotsky as more 'liberal' in the Western sense than Stalin or Lenin is the purest nonsense. To none of these people did the Western concept of liberalism or freedom have any political meaning whatsoever. It would seem probable that Trotsky's first encounter with Helphand took place around 1905.[6]

Helphand was perhaps the first, but certainly not the last, millionaire to be a Communist. His psychological motivation is easy to fathom despite its apparent contradictions. As a Jew in pogrom-ridden Russia the most obvious escape from his predicament was to make a fortune; the next stage was to destroy the corrupt and evil society that used anti-semitism for political and

144

social ends. For the first, to quote Carmichael, 'one gets the impression that attractive blondes and torrents of champagne in posh hotel suites surged back and forth against a background of vast business deals'. His enormous wealth was not acquired by direct production but in the fringes of capitalism, the shrewd purchase of commodity 'futures' and what is loosely called 'import–export'. It is not hard to see that he came to despise an economic system to which he contributed so little and from which he derived so much. It is also not hard to see that he must have become so self-assured as to assume that he would do equally well for himself in a more meaningful, socialist society. By 1914 his financial enterprises reached from Stockholm to Constantinople, which was his headquarters if such a word can be ascribe to so international a financier. It is probably exact to describe him as the perfect profiteer. Despite the state of war between Russia and Germany some expensive trade between the two countries continued via Turkey, at least until 1915, and later via Sweden. Helphand was a prime operator, with contacts of the greatest value to IIIb, and also, of course, with prime profits to himself.

Helphand had been involved before the war with the German Social Democrats, who viewed him with a certain comprehensible distrust. It was in about 1910 that he established himself in Constantinople. It will be recalled that in 1914 the German Social Democrats were, with a very few exceptions, unanimous in their patriotism; therefore Helphand's impeccable, German, Marxist orthodoxy had small appeal for Trotsky. Helphand's argument was that the victory of Imperial Germany over backward, peasant Russia was the preliminary to revolution in both countries. It was a theory that appealed more to Bolshevik Lenin than to Menshevik Trotsky. This, however, did not prevent Trotsky and Martov, who edited a Menshevik publication in Paris, from accepting money from a very rich Rumanian socialist, by the name of Christo Rakovsky, who was himself on the payroll of the German Foreign Office.

It was in January of 1915 that Helphand met the German ambassador in Constantinople (Istanbul). Turkey was then still neutral. A month or two later Helphand drafted a memorandum for the ambassador, which was passed to Berlin. It is of great historical interest. In the memorandum Helphand maintained that he could close the breach between Mensheviks and Bolsheviks; that it was possible thus to organize a Russian revolution; and that furthermore he could organize rebellion against the Petrograd government, in the Ukraine and elsewhere. For all this he needed German money. This memorandum was read both by the German Foreign Office and of course by Abteilung IIIb of the German Great General Staff. Its recommendations were not, however, put into immediate operation, for the Kaiser and his circle continued to believe that a more effective, and to them more attractive, lever of corruption could be applied at higher social levels in Russia. Nor, it seems, was Lenin informed at this time.

However, the bribing of the court, the powerful and the rich did not prove successful. Indeed after its defeats of 1914 and 1915 the Russian military machine was showing signs of an unexpected recovery in 1916. The Imperial Russian soldiers were better equipped and better led than they had been two years earlier. To German intelligence the Brusilov Offensive of that year, though a failure, was ominous in view of Verdun and Jutland and the general stalemate on the Western Front, while the effects of the economic blockade were beginning to be felt in the Fatherland. Only a major *coup*, Berlin realized, could prevent defeat. Desperate times required desperate measures. A political offensive in the East, combined with a U-boat offensive in the West, seemed an ever more attractive road to victory. From German documents captured after 1945 we know that this policy was studied and finally endorsed by the Kaiser himself; we have his marginal comments to Foreign Office and General Staff documents concerning Russian affairs.

For the Russian Communists it has been a point of ideological as well as of patriotic pride to maintain that the two-stage Russian Revolution, the so-called Kerensky Revolution of January–February and the Bolshevik takeover of October–November 1917, were of purely Russian origin. Ideologically, this misinterpretation fits, just, into the Procrustean bed of Marxist historical materialism, if the public is prepared to accept the somewhat idiotic idea that the transitory, capitalist period between feudalism and socialism can be squeezed into eight months of wartime. While from the patriotic point of view, much emphasized by Stalin and his successors, the fact that Soviet Russia had, as its

146

midwife, a German moneyman is highly bad publicity at least.

Even Trotsky in exile lied about the financing of Lenin's takeover, with more effrontery than his lies about the February Revolution. Nor did Kerensky tell all the truth, perhaps in his case from ignorance, in his *Memoirs*. Fortunately Joel Carmichael, George Katkov and others who have had access to the German archives have established the facts. The first or February revolution was a chaotic spontaneity, caused by the lock-out at the Putilov factory in Petrograd. When this turned out not to be of immediate military advantage to the Germans, they stirred the pot by the importation of Lenin. When Lenin and his closest colleagues ran away to Finland in July, the Germans pumped a huge sum of money into Russia – probably by our currency about half a billion dollars. These gold marks cemented the weak Bolshevik–Menshevik realliance. Most of this enormous sum passed via Helphand through Trotsky into newspapers. The second revolution took place, and in January of 1918 the Russians denounced their French and British alliances; two months later the Soviets signed an ignominious peace of defeat at Brest-Litovsk. The German Great General Staff was already moving divisions from the Eastern to the Western Fronts in preparation for their last, the March, offensive.

This failed. And many of the German divisions from the East were themselves tainted with revolutionary motives, after contact with the Russians. The operations of Abteilung IIIb had secured their most spectacular victory, but like so many victories it was a Pyrrhic one, and yet another example of the truism that wars are not won, but lost.

To ascribe a measure of perspective to this tale of brains, skills and lies, it is as well to recall the background. On the battlefields, the rough statistics known to us show that throughout the First World War the casualties, among all the armies and navies involved, were somewhere in the nature of ten millions dead. This can be broken down: one young or not-so-young corpse every six seconds, for some four years. It was against this backcloth that Hall, Nicolai, Helphand, Trotsky performed their parts upon the stage of Europe's first attempt at continental suicide.

Chapter Ten

To Make America Win the War

The early weeks of 1917 were critical to the outcome of the First World War and therefore to the history of this century. Indeed the crisis can be pinpointed, in retrospect, to a very few days at the end of January and the beginning of February, when the United States moved, or to be more exact was moved with considerable reluctance, to replace Russia as the principal ally of Britain and France. It was a period of comparative calm along the land fronts, as the belligerent armies froze in the icy mud of the trenches or skirmished, more or less ineffectually, in the Arabian deserts. The turning point lay not on the battlefields nor even in the oceans, but in the highest government offices, where decisions were in large measure guided by politico-military intelligence. We think of the First World War as lasting from mid-1914 to late 1918, but it would not be untrue to say that two world wars overlapped, and that though the guns never fell silent to mark an armistice, as was to happen between 1918 and 1939, another war began on 1 February 1917.

Events in Russia marked then, albeit unknowingly, the beginning of ideological as opposed to national wars. The decisions taken in Washington, in large measure under the influence of London's Room 40, and in the implementation under the Atlantic of decisions taken earlier in Germany, marked the birth of what we have come to call 'total war'. Since then all wars of any global significance have been both ideological and total. It was indeed a turning point, and without doubt one for the worse, in mankind's history.

So far as America was concerned, the question was not merely one of nationalism but also of morality, particularly the moral values of President Woodrow Wilson, though these two primary subjects are inextricably intertwined.

Down the ever-lengthening corridors of history, Woodrow

148

Wilson must appear an increasingly strange figure. Even to his contemporaries, at least to the minute minority who understood was what happening as their concept of total war was born, he seemed a strange, Gladstonian anachronism. A perfect example of the white Anglo-Saxon Protestant ascendancy within the still partly unassimilated immigrant population of the United States, the ex-president of Princeton remained, when elected to a greater Presidency, a teacher, above all a teacher of righteousness. He believed, and therefore he expected to be believed, and indeed he was believed both at home and by honest people on both sides of the murderous, suicidal, European fronts. He did not wish America to be involved in that war. He did wish America, the western hemisphere, to remain inviolate to the vast and mindless emotions of war. This attitude was in tune with the wishes of what was later called 'middle America', although distasteful to a strong economic, political and cultural element resident largely in the Atlantic-bordering states and their immediate hinterland. They did not want Germany to win the war; they did want France and Britain to be victorious, in particular after the *Lusitania* incident of 1915. But numerically they were in the minority, and Wilson was re-elected President in 1916 on a peace platform.

Yet though the American President might find refuge from European entanglements in the Monroe Doctrine in reverse, that Doctrine, probably the very cornerstone of all American foreign policy from its formulation in 1823 until the Marshall Plan of 1948, gave the American government almost a free hand, in American eyes, in the western hemisphere. Dollars might do the job in the southern continent. But when Mexico, or Cuba, was a nuisance, Theodore Roosevelt's 'big stick' – that is to say military intervention – might be invoked and employed. It was used by Woodrow Wilson, ineffectually as might be expected by a man of his high pacifist principles, against Generals Villa, Huerta and later General Carrahza of Mexico in 1916.

American intervention, and not for the first time, in Mexico could no more be justified from the high moral ground where Wilson chose to stand, than could Russian intervention in Czechoslovakia fifty-two years later, on the ground of Marxist-Leninist theory. The Russian act had to be explained, *post facto*, by the declaration of the Brezhnev Doctrine; the Americans could hardly invoke the Monroe Doctrine in backing one set of Mexican political gangsters against another. Instead they had to beat the old patriotic drum and talk about the illegality of a Mexican government ·seizing or threatening to seize American assets. It was alleged that the Mexicans desired to conquer, or regain, New Mexico, Arizona, Texas, maybe even California. The improbable idea that America would somehow impose the form of government practised in Washington on Mexico City was also put forward as justification. But few could swallow this, even in the United States. Almost the only result of the stupid, bungled American military operation was to reinforce Mexican dislike of the Yankee *gringos* and to stimulate in American minds a quite unjustified fear of Mexican irredentism. Woodrow Wilson might act as if Mexico were in reality an internal American problem, as do the Russians in Eastern Europe today, but the United States did not conquer and occupy Mexico. And for Wilson the country south of the border became almost an obsession. We can on occasion forgive those who have wronged us: it is far more difficult to forget our animosity to those whom we have wronged, in particular if we have failed and they remain, obstinately, in control of their own destinies.

The political and military aspects of the Mexican operation seem to have been based upon a grossly inadequate, perhaps total, lack of intelligence. General Pershing's soldiers marched about Mexico in pursuit of an enemy they could not find, with allies they should not have trusted, for ends that were unobtainable even if they so much as existed.

If Wilson's morality was in abeyance in the affairs of the North American continent, it was at full stretch in European affairs, and increasingly so. Unlike his successor in a later war, Wilson was entirely genuine in his desire to preserve American neutrality. Unlike, too, that predecessor also called Roosevelt, a pragmatist who saw that an Allied victory was essential to America, Wilson believed that the great republic, as represented by its President, was cast in the role of peacemaker in Europe. This was above all a moral attitude but still one which in the 1916 election appealed to the electoral majority for numerous reasons. From the point of view of the business community, which may be inaccurately but conveniently described as Wall Street, it was even then becoming out of date. Great Britain and France, but not for naval reasons Germany, were buying armaments, food and much else on a massive scale from the United States. However, the enormous wealth of the Allies was running out, as was their manpower. At an increasing rate the United States was becoming a creditor, where before Wall Street had been not infrequently in debt to the City of London. This trend was obviously going to continue until the end of the Great War, as it was called. Therefore, to Wall Street, it became essential in the somewhat simple capitalist ethos of the time, that the Allies emerge victorious and able to pay their debts. There were no Central Powers' debts, nor would a victorious Germany be likely to repay the money owed by France and Britain, while these countries if defeated might be scarcely able to repay them either. (The possibility that the Allies, when victorious, might refuse to repay their own debts was hardly considered; it was a contingency which the capitalist morality could scarcely take into account.) The result of all this was that even while the American Government talked of morality, neutrality and its role of peacemaker, the real power apparatus within the United States became increasingly convinced that American intervention in Europe was inevitable.

Well aware of the pressure to which his policy of neutrality was being subjected by extremely important domestic interests, increasingly attacked by ex-President Theodore Roosevelt and the Republican Party, Wilson almost fell backwards in his attempt to prove that his neutrality was genuine. More and more did he equate the moral values and political aims of the Central Powers with those of the Western Allies. In effect what he said, with increasing, desperate vehemence until February 1917, was that the First World War was about nothing; that the issues involved were contemptible and irrelevant to himself, the President of the United States; that he knew better than the belligerents; that six men per minute were dying for nothing; that every statesman was misguided, save only himself; that only he, the elected leader of the Great Democracy, could make peace between the ill-informed and immoral belligerents, who must therefore and by definition be of equal moral turpitude. Wilson's was indeed a hard furrow to plough, but from his point of view all the more

151

worth ploughing in consequence. The Mexicans, whom he hated, molested and often killed, dubbed him 'the schoolmaster'. It was not an unjust personification.

The educational furrow he had chosen to plough with moral lectures, blood and iron was not made easier by German operational and intelligence activities. Not only were the Germans, by 1915, torpedoing liners without warning on the high seas, they were carrying out acts of sabotage against ships in American ports. The German military attaché, Baron Franz von Papen, and the naval attaché with the curious name of Captain Boy-Ed were further incriminated in the stirring up of Mexican troubles. (One of Papen's closest contacts left his briefcase in the Sixth Avenue El; it was stuffed with evidence; Papen and Boy-Ed were expelled.) A more powerful figure, Captain Franz von Rintelen, had already arrived in America. The Department of Justice, which was then responsible for security, watched him and his bank account most carefully and successfully. He too was deeply embroiled both in sabotage and in the Mexican affair.

A great deal of this got into the newspapers. To reinforce his stance and that of his country as neutral, President Wilson then and therefore made a most extraordinary concession to the Germans. The Swedes were, in the First World War as they were to be in the Second, essentially pro-German, Germany's non-belligerent friends. They allowed the German government to use their Stockholm cable to the New World. The cable went from Stockholm to Buenos Aires, whence the messages were passed to Washington, Mexico or elsewhere – including China. This route was known as the Swedish Roundabout. The Swedes would add a few words in Swedish cipher, but the main message would be in a German cipher which the Swedish diplomats would hand un-read to their German colleagues in the foreign capital of destination. However, it did not take an agent of Admiral Hall's very long to realize that the Swedish *chargé d'affaires* in Mexico City, a certain Folke Cronheim, was also acting as a German messenger boy. And since the Swedish cable touched England, Room 40 was soon reading the German signals. A direct radio link to Say-ville, Long Island, from Nauen, the most powerful German transmitter, was not only of course subject to British interception but also to American naval censorship. Nor were the Germans supposed by their neutral, American hosts to be using it for military or naval purposes though of course they did so, by camouflaging their signals as commercial messages. Three principal German ciphers were used, two of them diplomatic and one naval. Admiral Hall in Room 40 of the London Admiralty was by 1916 reading two and probably all three of these ciphers, from which the British learned as much about Wilson's thinking as they did about German–Mexican plans, almost all of which passed over the desk of the German Ambassador in Washington, Count Bernstorff, and thus over Admiral Hall's.

The Germans becoming, as was in the end inevitable, suspicious, requested that they be allowed to use the American diplomatic cipher; that their enciphered communications be transmitted, as by the Swedes, from the U.S. Embassy in Berlin, via Copenhagen, to the State Department, there to be passed in the original German cipher to Bernstorff for rendition into clear German. Incredibly, Wilson agreed to this most un-neutral procedure, presumably from a fundamental ignorance of intelligence and its importance, and in order to prove his own neutrality in an ever less 'neutral' America. This German intelligence operation was based upon a subtle flattery of the President, and on the assumption, quite correct at the time, that American intelligence was both incapable of, and more important, unwilling to, break German ciphers even when enciphered messages were sent through State Department channels. To justify this strange request, the Germans alleged that to help Wilson pursue his major ambition, a compromise peace, Germany could only cooperate if Berlin were certain of an absolutely secure means of communication between Berlin and the German embassy in Washington, their messages unread either by their European enemies or their American friends.

To President Wilson's peripatetic emissary, Colonel House, the Germans made their simple request in late 1916. He passed it to the President who, to the lasting horror of Secretary of State Lansing, agreed that American diplomatic cable facilities be placed at the disposal of the Germans. However, this cable, too, touched England. Although this strange German–American arrangement caused Room 40 a brief inconvenience, the American diplomatic ciphers were rudimentary and had long ago been broken. Berlin's communications with its people in America continued to be read in London. The British did not feel any need to inform President Wilson that they knew of his odd gesture in allowing one of the belligerents the use of American signal facilities (nor had they informed the Swedes). The Germans were delighted, and the British were extremely judicious in the use of the intelligence received. It would in due course produce the trump card and they played it only when it was absolutely essential to avoid losing the game and, as history shows, to win the match.

For any premature release to the Americans of such 'raw' intelligence would have been dangerous or even disastrous for two reasons. When 'cooked' such intelligence might be given the cover of espionage or counter-espionage. The British Secret Service kept a close watch on German agents in the neutral United States, and was able to pass intelligence concerning their activities to the agents of the Department of Justice, for action. At this level a good relationship was established and as has been shown the American police co-operated with the British in such matters as Irish plans for rebellion. Into this two-way traffic the British could and did slip material derived from cipher breaking, but with the source well disguised. This enabled the Americans to deal with quite a few German spies and saboteurs within the United States, to the mutual advantage of both countries so far as trans-Atlantic shipping was concerned and, to a much lesser extent, primarily to America so far as Mexico was concerned.

To reveal the source of such intelligence would have been dangerous. In the first place American security was, as it has almost always been, a very leaky bulkhead. The danger of the German enemy discovering or even suspecting through such a leak that his own ciphers were not secure need not be mentioned again here. It was not a risk worth taking except for the highest prize, that is to say the involvement of the United States in the war on the side of the Western Allies.

And here one is again confronted with the strange morality of President Wilson and, indeed, of the mass of the American people. Victorian morality was concerned with the relationships of man to God, of man to woman, and less effectively of man to man. It was taken even more seriously by white Anglo-Saxon

154

Protestants, that is to say by the governing class, in America than in Britain; and its enforcement officers, in internal American affairs, were the lawyers and judges. It is not for nothing that American lawyers have been predominant in the government of the country, nor that a legal document – the Constitution and its amendments as interpreted by the Supreme Court – has filled the role of theoretical, absolute authority which most other nations in their hours of greatness have given to a monarch, constitutional or absolute, or to a dictator. Since the end of the Civil War America has been what the Germans called a *Rechtsstaat*, a state based squarely upon laws supposedly equal for all. That is why it was accepted by many outside America too as the 'last, best hope on earth'; that is one very important reason why the immigrants flocked there from Europe. However, this basic concept of personal and commercial relationships founded on law does not and did not translate easily into foreign policy and the relationships between sovereign states. Gladstone had long ago learned most painfully that high personal morality is a poor guide when dealing with Turks or Sudanese. It might be invoked, but it was seldom applied for national ends. The British have frequently, often correctly, been accused of hypocrisy in foreign affairs. Albion, mouthing sentiments of altruism and moral purpose, has steadily pursued British, or to be more exact English, interests. The Victorian governing class saw little personal harm in hypocrisy: it was as well that vice pay its tribute to virtue. However, such an arrangement, applicable perhaps to the atheist who goes to matins every Sunday, since it would be even more scandalous did he not, will hardly appear attractive to foreigners when their own national interests are at stake.

Now Woodrow Wilson, who was the very opposite of a stupid man, had no wish to be a hypocrite either publicly or privately. That the Mexican venture had in some ways pushed his country into such a situation can only have served to harden his dislike and contempt for moral compromise. But in order that American foreign policy might continue to be based on moral certainties, one major factor was lacking. There was, and indeed is, no such thing as 'international law', since not only is there no body of law, save a handful of agreements between some states, but above all there is no way save war whereby such agreements can be

155

enforced. Wilson was determined to put this right. He failed twice. He failed to use America's might to stop the war and impose a 'peace without victory' as he announced to Congress as late as 22 January 1917 in his State of the Union address. And he failed to create a powerful League of Nations or even to take America into the one of which he was the spiritual father. As for his first ambition, two world wars produced results precisely the opposite of what he had wished: victory without peace. It is hardly surprising that he became too sick to be an effective President in 1920, a broken man, a failure, he who in 1919 thought himself summoned to recreate the world which he then appeared to hold in the palm of his hand.

Moreover, he created a strange dual standard in foreign affairs which, substituting Russians for Germans, has endured longer than his dream of an international morality. The moral enemy, being damned, did not need to be further condemned. The Germans in 1914 had violated their oath and invaded neutral Belgium; they had broken the usages if not the rules of war by such hideous innovations as poison gas and the sinking of merchantmen without warning; they had behaved abominably in occupied France and elsewhere; they had even abused American neutrality in violent fashion. What else could one expect of the damned?

The British and French, however, were not damned. They were America's natural allies and therefore they must observe American, that is to say Wilsonian, standards of moral rectitude. It follows that it was the duty of the American government to chide London and Paris most sternly for any step off the steep and narrow path. And this at a time when Britain and France were fighting for their lives! He mouthed platitudes even more stunning in their insolent certainty than those of Franklin D. Roosevelt. It was to be a war to end war, to make the world safe for democracy, by which word he meant the U.S. Constitution feebly foreshadowed in Britain and sometimes in France. And these fatuous slogans, embodied only to be later dishonoured in his famous Fourteen Points, worked – once. Even the starving Germans and Austrians believed that Wilson would be able to carry out his promises and for them America still remained, in 1918, 'the last, best hope on earth'. Wilson, with his absolute

156

certainty in his own rectitude, was perhaps the greatest propagand-
ist and unwittingly the most dishonest the world has ever produced. Unlike Joseph Goebbels his words reached far beyond his
country's borders and had an immense impact, for a few critical
months. Few foreigners have ever given implicit belief to the
words of any American President since.

Yet it would be very unfair and indeed untrue to accuse President Wilson of dishonesty. He was quite simply ill-informed.
The Great War had changed the nature of foreign policy among
the belligerents rapidly and drastically. And, it seems, Woodrow
Wilson was quite uninterested in creating an intelligence service
that would tell him what was going on. Indeed his whole attitude,
conditioned by the age and environment in which he had spent
his earlier years, made the very idea of secret intelligence unattractive to him. Open covenants openly arrived at, this was to
be one of his slogans, one of the cornerstones of the imaginary
future, and this at a time when all the other powers were most
busily engaged in making secret covenants behind locked doors.
For Wilson intelligence was something sneaky, underhand,
shady and disreputable. It was certainly, at that time, and
in many Congressional minds to this day 'un-American'.

Herbert Yardley's account of how he attempted to reinforce
American intelligence during and after the First World War
reveals much, even sixty years later, about American methods.
It is a nice problem whether the revelations contained in his book[1]
were of more value to America's enemies in a future war or to
the United States, which had then sunk back into a posture of
isolationism buttressed by ignorance. Since Yardley's story was
heeded more by America's future enemies than by the American
political and military authorities, it would seem probable that
his book led to the killing of more Americans than of Japanese or
Germans in the Second World War. Such, needless to say, was
not Yardley's intention: he was a patriotic American. Still,
his very explicit warnings, or rather their application, remain a
double-edged caution: whereas the importance of secret intelligence cannot be over-emphasized, a description of precisely how
such intelligence has been garnered can be extremely dangerous
to the state in future, unforeseen contingencies.

Yardley wrote his book in disgust at the destruction of American

157

intelligence when Secretary of State Stimson, a most honour-able man, closed Yardley's cipher-breaking Black Chamber in 1929 with the remark: 'Gentlemen do not read one another's mail.' The American pendulum between personal morality and political expediency had once again – and not for the last time – gone in a direction that a man with a career such as Yardley's could only regard as fatuous. This swing had not only destroyed his life's work, but had left him penniless and almost totally unthanked. There was no reason, in American law or in current morality, why he should not make capital out of his experiences. He was not a very good writer or historian – his book has no index and contains few dates – but he knew a very great deal about codes, ciphers, how to construct and how to break them. Well aware of how important this had all been, he yet tempers his account of his achievements with an agreeable personal modesty. He does not seem to have understood why the French and the British, even when allied to the United States, refused to let him penetrate their own most carefully guarded secrets. His very book is in itself the answer.

Born in 1889 in Indiana, he was a good mathematician and, from an early age, a very enthusiastic poker player. The transi-tion to and interest in codes and ciphers is not hard to follow, though as he says the mind of a cryptanalyst is both peculiar and rare. In 1913, that is to say at the age of 23 or 24, he became a civil servant and worked in the Code Room of the State Depart-ment. He rapidly amused himself by breaking safe combinations and then American ciphers which were supposed to be the prerogative of his seniors. When he showed those seniors that even the most secret American diplomatic ciphers – such as that used by Colonel House in his communications from the capitals of the belligerents in Europe to President Wilson – could be deciphered by a young man in his spare time, those superiors had the sense not to fire but to promote him. It is not possible here to describe his almost meteoric rise. The Army took him over. He created M.I.-8 within a year of America's entry into the war, and this unit was rapidly expanded to include foreign diplomatic codes and ciphers. The United States Navy was stuffy and in-credibly secure. At last Naval Intelligence asked, with surprising humility, to be allowed to participate. Yardley then discovered why naval signals security had been so impeccable: they had nothing to hide, since they had not broken a single enemy code. Collaboration with the British and French was good, in so far as they told the Americans what they had discovered about the common enemy, poor in so far as they did not divulge their methods. Unlike the politically eschatological American President, Lloyd George and Clemenceau hardly believed that this was a war to end wars, but a war for immediate survival and, if possible, to end Germany's might. The British and the French were not prepared to give even to the Americans secrets that might well be needed after victory. Yardley's growing disillusionment during the Versailles Treaty negotiations and after will be described later. They paralleled those of his country as a whole. Meanwhile he had built, virtually from nothing, a very good intelligence service in M.I.-8, though inferior to that of Admiral Hall in Room 40. His despair at its destruction is comprehensible, and his book well worth reading, particularly by those interested in cryptanalysis as it then existed.

It was during the First World War that radio intercepts and decipherment overtook espionage as the prime source of intelligence and this for obvious technological reasons. The spy has to communicate with his centre. As noted earlier, the Germans had developed various 'invisible ink' techniques to a higher degree than anyone else, but wartime mails are slow and in any case cannot reach ships. When the espionage apparatus went on the air it became, to experts, highly vulnerable.

What is also of historical interest is that a special type of mind was needed in code-breaking. Admiral Hall had already realized this. So did Yardley. Perhaps the most important man who worked in M.I.-8, and with the most success during its best period, was Dr Manly of Chicago University. By a protracted and immensely detailed analysis of all existent, early texts, he produced what is still the authoritative version of the works of Chaucer. His mind had thus been trained to examine evidence in a way of which few lawyers are capable. Such minds are quite invaluable in any attempt to see through enemy signals in the fog of war, and were even more so in the age before computers, when the possible errors of mathematicians had to be taken into account (even as the erroneous programming of computers must be today).

Yardley and Manly, in themselves, exemplified twentieth-century intelligence. The British and French intelligence services were certainly more expert, but have remained less accessible to the historian. Yardley's book is therefore of extreme interest to the student of this subject, in that it shows a vital element in the relationship between states at a critical moment of change.

The Germans had two plans for outflanking the Western Front stalemate, the one military, the other diplomatic. The military solution was unrestricted U-boat warfare and the near-total isolation of Britain. This strategy, ardently desired by the Imperial German Navy, won increasing support from the army leaders, in particular from the dynamic Ludendorff who, in his capacity as Field Marshal von Hindenburg's chief of staff on the Western Front, was in 1916 becoming the most powerful man in Germany. However, the civilian government, as represented by Chancellor Bethmann-Hollweg and his Foreign Minister, von Jagow, was deeply opposed to this. Until November 1916, th civilians retained control, though a weakening control, of German policy. They were convinced that unrestricted U-boat warfare, that is to say the sinking of American merchant ships on a massive scale, must bring America into the war against Germany. Woodrow Wilson's pacifism, expressed both in words and deeds, helped erode their position. Indeed, in retrospect it is by no means certain that unrestricted U-boat warfare alone would have caused the American President to change his mind, though the German ambassador, Bernstorff, assured his government repeatedly that American public opinion would almost certainly force him to do so.

Very well, said the military, let us assume that America comes in. We can, they said, still starve out Britain before American troops sail for Europe in any numbers, and furthermore, we will sink their troop-ships. But as a further precaution it was the duty of the Foreign Ministry to arrange that even if America did declare war, it would be America herself who was encircled. Four-fifths of America's tiny army was tied up in Mexico. Her navy must be similarly preoccupied in the Pacific.

Feelers were already out to the Japanese, who had taken little part in the fighting since November 1914, when they had overrun German colonies and bases both in the Pacific and on the Chinese mainland. Their war aims were very simple, to keep and expand their Asian conquests. This meant that they must be on the winning side. Their alliance with Britain was one of expediency; their hostility towards America was growing as one after another of the Western States legislated or prepared to legislate against Japanese immigrants. If the Germans looked like defeating both Britain and America, then did the future look rich indeed to a Japan allied to the victors. The Germans made the most tempting offers to Tokyo, including the renunciation of Germany's pre-war Asian and Pacific possessions, a free hand in China and Eastern Siberia and perhaps along the American Pacific Coast. To Mexico, which was already on excellent terms with Japan – a small Japanese naval squadron was in Mexican waters for months in 1915 with the ridiculous explanation that a Japanese cruiser was stuck on a mudbank there – the Germans promised the southwestern states which had once been Mexican. The Mexicans were positively enthusiastic, and they were Germany's principal intermediaries with Tokyo. The Japanese did not say yes, but they also did not say no. They kept their options open, and one option was a *renversement d'alliance* if a German victory were assured.

While this diplomatic activity was going on, not unperceived by Room 40, throughout 1916, the U-boats were a-building. Wilson continued to talk of peace, and Pershing's army, lacking intelligence, to muddle about in Mexico (a performance not dissimilar, in its effect on German estimates of a future enemy's strength, to that of the Red Army in Finland in the winter of 1939–40). But it became increasingly obvious to those who knew the facts that the first battle that the German General and Admiral Staffs had to win was against Bethmann-Hollweg and von Jagow. It was won in November when Alfred Zimmermann succeeded von Jagow as Foreign Minister.

Another failure of American intelligence was a complete misappraisal of Zimmermann's character. He was of lower-middle-class origin in a country where it was then virtually unheard of for a man who was not an aristocrat to hold so high an office. He was a jolly sort of fellow, it seems, and these two facts led Americans, even the United States ambassador, to believe he

161

would be more reasonable, less arrogant than the *Junkers*. It was believed that he would hold the same mercantile, and therefore basically pacifist, views as so many Americans with a similar background. Nothing could have been further from the truth. Barbara Tuchman[2] suggests that it was precisely this background which led him to be even more of a militarist than the Prussian officers themselves, for he had to prove himself. And this should have been perceived even before his elevation to his new office, for he made little attempt to keep quiet his views concerning America, acquired many years before during a single journey from San Francisco to New York on his way home from a consular appointment in China. He was firmly convinced, and his conviction was supported by the German consul in New York despite Bernstorff's contrary views, that the German–Americans would 'rise' if America were so foolish as to declare war, in any circumstances, on the Fatherland. He said this repeatedly, not only to the generals and the Kaiser but also to Americans. Thus did he not only embrace Ludendorff's policy but further it. Even without Japanese and Mexican help, America was a feeble giant, a pushover. In view of Wilson's behaviour and gullibility, Zimmermann's false appraisal was, admittedly, slightly more excusable than was Hitler's in 1941. Zimmermann became Foreign Minister on 22 November 1916, and almost immediately the word was sent out to selected German officials abroad to prepare for the contingency of unrestricted U-boat warfare. This message was intercepted in Room 40, and the Americans were told, somewhat vaguely so as not to reveal the source. President Wilson interpreted this as yet another British attempt to undermine American neutrality and to deprive him of his cherished mission as the peacemaker.

Dates now become important. In early December 1916, the German Supreme High Command had accepted the strategy of unrestricted U-boat warfare, even if this should bring America into the war. The Admiral Staff thereupon fixed the date, 1 February, by which time there should be two hundred U-boats, most of them new, at sea. The Chancellor, Bethmann-Hollweg, was summoned to the Kaiser's headquarters at Pless on 9 January. On the following day he, the head of the government, was informed of the decision taken by the Supreme Command.

162

He suspected what was going on, as did Zimmermann. It would be an exaggeration to say that the Chancellor was distressed. He attempted to have the decision reversed, but was informed, just as he had been told in 1914, that military and naval plans could brook no interference from civilians: the U-boats were already at sea and could not be recalled. Bethmann-Hollweg is said to have murmured *Finis Germaniae*. With even less real power than he retained once the 'irreversible' Schlieffen Plan was rammed through by the Great General Staff in 1914, he continued to serve his Emperor as titular head of government for a few more months. He did not govern, and indeed had scarcely been doing so for some time. Though their characters, motives and much else were utterly disparate, the men of the belligerent powers who had held control at its outset all lost the reality of power within a matter of weeks during the winter of 1916–17, to be replaced by Lloyd George, Clemenceau, Ludendorff, Russian revolutionaries, Young Turks, weak men anxious but unable to obtain peace in Vienna. If the judgment given earlier is correct, a new World War was beginning among the ruins of the First, with the Americans as the primary power, the Japanese holding their hand. And the pointless slaughter continued along the Western and Italian fronts.

Few people, no matter how well informed, can have had any idea that a cosmic change was underway, and so speedily, in the affairs of man. If such existed, Zimmermann was not among them. On 16 January he sent the telegram that, alone, has made his name famous. It would appear that it was sent in a spirit of elation, in the belief that he was helping to end one war victoriously for his country, not that he was helping to start another that was to culminate not only in the defeat of his country but also in the destruction of the society into the higher reaches of which he had been accepted. He sent his 'telegram' over all four of the networks available to him, unaware of course that Room 40 was reading his most secret cipher.

Nor was this easy for Room 40. The Germans were altering their ciphers daily by then, though not changing their basic method. Admiral James[3] has described how the new shift of cryptanalysts, coming on duty in Room 40 early in the morning, could immediately tell by the expressions upon the faces of the night shift whether the day's cipher had been broken already. In an age that had not heard the word 'computer' it was a matter of brain power alone, so exhausting and performed under such pressure that nervous breakdown was not the exception but more usually the ultimate rule. Nor was the breaking of a cipher a simple achievement, comparable to turning a key in a lock. A cipher could be half-broken, its significance recognized. That was what the Rev. William Montgomery, a scholar of the early Church and employed in Room 40, had achieved with the Zimmermann telegram at 10.30 a.m. on 17 January 1917, that is to say a few hours after its despatch. What he submitted to Admiral Hall at that hour was the following:

> Most secret for your Excellency's personal information and to be handed on to the Imperial Minister in (? Mexico) with Telegram No. 1 (. . .) by a safe route.
> We propose to begin on the 1st February unrestricted submarine warfare. In doing so, however, we shall endeavour to keep America neutral. (?) If we should not (succeed in doing so) we propose to (? Mexico) an alliance upon the following basis:
> (joint) conduct of the war.
> (joint) conclusion of peace.
> (. . .)
> Your Excellency should for the present inform the President (of Mexico) secretly (? that we expect) war with the U.S.A. (possibly) (. . .) (Japan) and at the same time to negotiate between us and Japan. (Please tell the President) that (. . .) or submarines (. . .) will compel England to peace in a few months. Acknowledge receipt.
>
> Zimmermann.[4]

The major effort of Room 40 was now devoted to discovering the full text. It was soon established. President Wilson's State of the Union address to the Congress, five days later, his 'peace without victory', must have struck ironic chords among those in London who now knew that in nine days, and one day after a German ultimatum, the United States was not only to see her merchantmen sunk without warning on the high seas but also to be threat-

164

ened by a German–Mexican–Japanese military alliance and invasion.

Yet London had to hold its hand, to hold its trump card. And this for two reasons. The first and most obvious was to conceal, from the Germans, that Room 40 had broken the German cipher. Even more important, though, was the need to persuade President Wilson and the American public that the Zimmermann telegram was genuine. The British knew that the unrestricted U-boat part would soon be justified by the U-boats themselves. As they feared, however, this would not necessarily involve the United States in the war. A bill for the arming of American merchant-men was already before the Congress, though in danger of a filibuster from Senator La Follette and other pacifists, with the backing of 'middle America'. Alternatively, and this was to happen, the shipping lines of a neutral America might simply refuse to sail their ships, unconvoyed, across the Atlantic. This would have been, indeed for some weeks was, a most severe blow to Britain and France. Therefore the innately insane German policy of involving Mexico and Japan must be used to convince both the American President and his people that a real threat to the terri-torial integrity of the United States existed. And, from the British point of view, this had to be achieved without a mortal blow to Room 40.

By now, that is to say mid-February, the slaughter of neutral, particularly Dutch, ships had persuaded the President that at least part of the famous telegram was genuine, but American ships were not moving from American ports. A British act of applied genius in Mexico obtained a copy of the telegram from the German Embassy, Washington, to the German Ministry, Mexico City. It contained minor modifications to the texts originally intercepted between Berlin and Washington and there-fore did not compromise the primary link, and with it Room 40. Finally, the American government, now convinced by Ambassa-dor Page, among others, that the Zimmermann Telegram was genuine, needed – themselves to convince the die-hard pacifists – evidence that it had been deciphered by Americans on American soil, in a word that it was not a British plant. This requirement was met, ingeniously and somewhat disingenuously, by allowing the American attaché in London responsible for intelligence, a

Mr Edward Bell, to 'borrow' the German code-book from Room 40 and, with British assistance, to decipher once again the full and already deciphered text inside the U.S. Embassy, Grosvenor Square, that is to say on what was technically and in international law American territory.

The result, if slow, was exactly what the British had hoped for. On 6 April 1917, the United States declared war upon the German Empire. War against the Austro-Hungarian Empire was delayed until December, in the mistaken hope that the Dual Empire might be persuaded to sue for peace on its own. This misappreciation by President Wilson, was, however, more than compensated for by Zimmermann's earlier folly: the United States was fully committed to the defeat of Germany, while Japan remained an inactive ally of Britain, and Mexico stayed neutral. The 'ifs and buts' of history are misleading. It is possible, however, that the skill with which the Zimmermann telegram was deciphered, and above all the way in which it was used, saved Britain and France from defeat in 1917. It was, in fact, perhaps the most perfect large-scale politico-military action based on secret intelligence of the century, combining as it did collection, evaluation and exploitation, each of an extreme complexity, all used in this case for a single purpose, with secrecy at all stages kept as inviolate as was wished, and above all crowned with final success.

It would be a gross, an obviously gross, exaggeration to say that Room 40 'won the war'. It would, however, be no overstatement to suggest that without the existence of Room 40, and its very high level of efficiency, America's entry into the war might have been delayed intolerably, and that the Western Allies might therefore have lost it. If it were possible to weigh imponderables the one against the other, which of course it is not, it might be maintained that Room 40, in such a fanciful pair of scales, outweighed two hundred ocean going U-boats. Such imponderables are what secret intelligence is really all about.

Chapter Eleven

... To End Wars

If it is correct to say that the early days of 1917 were the occasion of a very important shift in political forces in this century, the effect of this change only became apparent – and then not to all – after the defeat of the Central Powers. Few people realized that the great European nation-states and empires had inflicted upon one another and upon themselves a sort of suicide, a *felo da se*, from which the Concert of Europe could never recover. Few Europeans, that is, though many realized that the vast slaughter of Europe's young men had grossly exceeded any reasonable purpose, and that therefore the entire political structure was discredited. So, at least, it seemed to English, French, Germans and Italians. Among the more percipient young survivors a premature scepticism became the dominant emotion. Hedonism, that is to say a denial of values in favour of pleasure, rapidly replaced the search for purpose. However, since this search for purpose in life is almost as fundamental a wish as is the satisfaction of personal desires, the inherent longing of man for a reason soon reasserted itself as either a rationalization of hedonism, or a search for a cause. Nor are the two quite contradictory in a negative sense. The dismissal of Victorian morality, on the grounds that it had failed politically and ended in a slaughter of the innocents, led to some strange, subjective alliances. The concept of 'youth' became the linking ideal: the totalitarian ideologies became the *Weltanschauung*, the socialist realism, of youth; their slogan, *nous avons changé tout cela, Georges Dandin*. Half a century later it is easier to be sour than to achieve comprehension.

Yet for the basic theme of this book some measure of speculation as to the motives of those who were prepared to work actively against their society is inevitable. Throughout the past three or so centuries many a man – and woman – who has enjoyed all the benefits of privilege has yet rebelled against our Western society

167

that bestowed these upon him, sometimes due to his own endeavour, more frequently in earlier generations by a mere accident of birth. It is these people, not at all the *sans-culottes*, who have been, at best, a form of yeast seething for justice based upon a religion that they have quite frequently abandoned. At worst, and particularly in the more feeble or enfeebled societies of Europe and Asia, they become quite simply wreckers, arrogant manipulators of anti-social forces that they have never understood, revolutionaries eaten by their supporters. A Marat murdered by an enemy is rare; a Danton guillotined by those whom he has believed he led, far more common. The spectacle of French bourgeois revolutionaries trooping up the ladder in the place de la Révolution is, perhaps, saddening, as was the ultimate fate of the Bolshevik leaders in the 1930s – saddening but yet inevitable. They had lived by the sword, and thus did they perish. They were part of the evil society that they destroyed, and so they died with it, in the ignominy and humiliation that they had inflicted upon others. In the real sense of a much-abused word, they were reactionaries. And their brave new world reacted in its turn against its saviours, not once but over and over again.

Intelligent, educated people born in Western Europe or the United States just before or just after the beginning of the twentieth century grew up into a suicidal society. Many of those who survived the First World War wished either to play no part in so hopeless a social arrangement or to change it utterly; some, less logically but certainly with no less intelligence, desired both ends at once. In retrospect the great thinkers of fifty years ago, Gide, Spengler, Russell – to name but three among so many brilliant men – have a strange tarnish, hit an unmelodious, cracked gong. And their *epigoni*, their less lucid successors who knew the depression years of the 1930s and Nazi-Fascism and the Stalinist Terror, had not even the reactionary certitudes of their teachers. Many, Nazis or Communists, had no longer any wish to remodel their societies, but merely to betray them. For many Western intellectuals it was no longer Alfred Dreyfus who was the heroic, ill-treated figure, it was his enemy, Count Esterhazy, whose sadistic nihilism struck a chord in Berlin, Paris, London, New York. In 1919, those future traitors were very young indeed, although those who had fought throughout the First World War were aged beyond their years.

But the men who decided, or to be more exact failed to decide, how the First World War should be terminated – the men of Versailles and its ephemeral treaty – were not the young. Georges Clemenceau has remarked that a million and a half young, dead Frenchmen gave him and his colleagues a right to decide the future of Europe.[1] His mathematics misled him. He weighed his compatriots' corpses against the mere fifty thousand American dead. But his beastly little sum makes no sense. Putrefying brains and bodies do not count, for the dead divisions cannot fight, nor make money, nor formulate ideas, nor control history in a century that has little respect for respect.

Yet it was, and inevitably, this older, usually much older, generation of men who made the peace in which the young had to live. These old men, from the Allied and Associated powers, who met and squabbled in Paris, had seldom met before, and when they did confer to decide upon the future they rapidly found that they shared very few concepts as to what that future should be. The resultant fiasco is well known, and served to alienate the young men even more perhaps than had the war itself. Among the very first gestures that these old men, Clemenceau, Wilson and to a lesser extent Lloyd George, made to the young who so hated their war, was a minor return to the *status quo ante* 1914, the virtual abolition of their intelligence services. Thus might the old men quarrel with one another in the dark, just as they or their predecessors had done a dozen years before. The war was to be demolished. High level intelligence had been invented as part of that war. Since so few people were involved, it could be quickly scrapped. Admiral Hall, probably after the Prime Minister the most powerful man in Britain, was not allowed to go to Versailles, and his Room 40 was handed over to charwomen. The American story, as will be shown, was even more deplorable. The expensive stupidity of Versailles was firmly rooted in an ignorance of what was going on, for intelligence was then regarded, by many of the old as it was by many of the young, as something militaristic, even disgusting, an aspect of the horrible years that were gone and best buried beneath the countless war memorials.

The war was over. The very clever men who had worked for the Royal Navy in Room 40 knew that they had served their

169

country to the best of their abilities, and wished for a speedy return to what they regarded as normal life: the Rev. Mr Montgomery no doubt to the study of the early Church, his colleague who had also helped decipher the Zimmermann telegram, Mr de Grey, to his publishing business and his Medici Society, A. E. W. Mason to the writing of successful novels; the linguists to their philology, and the numerous mathematicians to their universities and, in some cases, to their nuclear physics; the archivists and librarians to archives and libraries of another sort. The extraordinary concentration of intellectual power that had been Room 40 disappeared, in silence, as silently as it had come into being. For many years it was not discussed, in public, at all. It was almost as if it had never been.

That this complex, successful, indeed perhaps war-winning, apparatus was allowed to disappear so rapidly is explicable in at least two ways, apart from the desire of the wartime soldiers and sailors to leave. These can be described, in the British case, as both a hubris and a nemesis. The hubris[2] echoes the arrogance that Walter H. Page had detected in German intelligence, an arrogance that would appear to be a built-in hazard to any very successful intelligence apparatus, which can seldom measure its successes or its failures against those of other secret organizations. According to Donald McLachlan, the British authorities were so confident of their achievements in the creation of Room 40 that they assumed it could be safely dismantled because, if need be, it could be rebuilt with equal speed. Nor would it have been possible to keep so complex a mechanism functioning and secret in peacetime. And the Naval Intelligence Division did not allow, could not allow, for unforeseen and unforeseeable technological developments. N.I.D. became more or less what it had been in 1912, with a largely theoretical knowledge of the whole cipher complex added, though even this was permitted to fall into desuetude between 1920 and 1937. Admiral Hall lived on as a rather obscure political figure. His past was not made public by himself, nor recalled by many public men. Winston Churchill was one of the exceptions, but he had little power during the locust years between the wars. The Germans, on the other hand, did not forget Room 40.

Its nemesis, in the years between 1918 and 1922, lay in the fact that secret intelligence of its quality was not in demand or at least only peripherally so. Based on global wireless intercepts, reinforced and covered by the work of secret agents, it was hardly equipped to deal with the problems that faced Britain immediately after the First World War, save perhaps at the highest levels of international diplomacy. And the senior officials of the Foreign Office were as anxious to return to the methods of their youth as were the senior officers of the Army and the Navy.

In the immediate post-war years the British found themselves engaged, and usually floundering, in various fields of politico-military activity the relative importance of which was not always understood at the time and is equally hard to evaluate today.

In the first place there was 'high diplomacy', a phrase almost out of date by 1919, concerned with the place of the British Empire in a Concert of Nations now far greater than the old Concert of Europe, yet seen by many as a mere extension of that older system, with the United States, Japan and perhaps eventually Russia to be added, the whole to be justified and underpinned by Wilson's League of Nations. Clemenceau accused Lloyd George of attempting to resuscitate the old British 'balance of power' concept: nor did Lloyd George deny this. The Anglo-French wartime alliance was falling apart.

Secondly, the margin of victory over the Central Powers had been so narrow that German military and political impotence seemed essential to the French, slightly less so to the British; but it was almost irrelevant to the Americans.

Thirdly, the Russian Revolution, which by all the established precedents should have made the Bolsheviks unimportant, was not working out that way. The last 'Allied' attempt to crush the Revolution by half-hearted invasion of Russia had failed. Only the French, by supporting the Poles, achieved a success in confining Bolshevism to Soviet lands. Had this not happened, a Communist Germany would have been a very real threat to the entire world which was being elaborately and not very successfully re-built. British intelligence in Russia during the Archangel and Crimean campaigns seems to have been inadequate, its evaluation in London even more so. The same judgment may be passed on Lloyd George's attitude to the Greco-Turkish crisis, which led to the ignominious defeat of the Greeks and the final fall of Lloyd George's then ramshackle coalition government. It is fair to assume that in none of these crises would the type of secret intelligence that Room 40 had provided been of much use.

Nearer to home the Irish were in rebellion against British rule. Once again the highly sophisticated methods of Admiral Hall's organization were of little value. When the Anglo-Irish War began in early 1918, Irish strategy was simple: first to blind the British, then to make British administration an impossibility, and finally to obtain maximum support, moral, financial and political, from the United States.

This was in effect the first of the twentieth-century-style guerrilla wars. Encouraged by the slogan of 'self-determination' first penned by Lenin and later trumpeted by Wilson, a small number of Irish nationalists tried to organize a rebellion against the British rule. They failed in 1916, but in 1918 they were led by men of genius, in particular by Michael Collins. He and his few armed followers first neutralized the rural police, then the legal system, then the administrative apparatus and in particular the collection of taxes. He also organized a large bond issue, in the name of the future Republic of Ireland, as well as a comparatively effective clandestine press. In this field much of his work was done for him by his enemies. The British reacted, at first, clumsily and with a brutality reminiscent of the Germans so recently attempting to control Belgium. This, far more than the few guns of the Irish Republican Army, united almost all the people of Ireland against the might of Britain. But the British soldiered on, importing more and more Black-and-Tans, ex-soldiers of an increasingly brutal nature recruited to replace the old Royal Irish Constabulary which had been neutralized or had defected. As is usual where there is a guerrilla force with the backing of the native population, the Black-and-Tans had really no control beyond the range of a ·303 rifle. They might outnumber the I.R.A. by ten or a hundred to one, but such strength is not preponderant unless the ten or one hundred men are in the right place to fight a battle. Because of the destruction of the Royal Irish Constabulary, the Black-and-Tans were rarely, in the right numbers, where needed. They seem to have preferred to drive about, shooting up villages, looting pubs, and thus stamping new I.R.A. men out of the ground.

Thus did the Anglo-Irish War become what was even then an old-fashioned intelligence war. The British knew that they could crush the minuscule, ill-armed I.R.A., if only they could find it and force it to fight. Failing this, and their failure quite quickly became apparent, they could decapitate it by arresting or killing its leaders. And this involved intelligence work of an exceptionally difficult nature in a largely hostile country. Nor was this task made easier by the almost perpetual misapprehension of the English concerning the Irish, the concept then more prevalent than it is now that an Irishman is a quasi-Englishman, and not a foreigner with different mental processes and even more different allegiances.

Collins realized long before his British enemies that intelligence must provide his answer to their power; the weaker power, if it is to survive, has always realized this. Collins had few men at his disposal, but those whom he employed were utterly reliable; they had to be, since there was a price on his own head that rose to £10,000 dead or alive. His dealings with his agents were verbal, frequently in public places. Not for him conferences and minutes, which would have made his opponents' work much easier. For this was not an exercise, let alone a game. Collins was a threat, and as it turned out a lethal threat, to the whole British concept of an Empire just saved from German attack. His life, in 1920, was worth considerably more to the British imperialists than £10,000, and at least as much as what they had been prepared to pay for the *Breslau* and the *Goeben* five years before.

The British had three secret intelligence services operating in Ireland in early 1920, and as always in such circumstances there was rivalry and usually poor co-ordination of effort. There was the Irish Special Branch, under Scotland Yard; there was Military Intelligence, taking its order from the Commander-in-Chief but also from the War Office; and there was G Division of the Dublin Metropolitan Police.[3] The Dublin Metropolitan Police was not, and never had been, a part of the Royal Irish Constabulary, and therefore continued to function when the larger body had been eliminated or confined, by its enemies, to its provincial barracks. The first four divisions of the D.M.P. were engaged in patrolling the metropolis, Divisions E and F the suburbs, while G was the detective unit. Like the London Metropolitan Police, on which this force was modelled, all branches were usually unarmed. The G-men (it seems that the Americans later adopted this term) were more likely to carry pistols. They were almost invariably Irishmen, and few came from the Protestant Unionist North.

Colonel David Neligan estimates that Collins had perhaps half a dozen men working for him within the D.M.P. The most sensitive area was, of course, G Division. Collins relied very heavily on his men inside that division to report upon the build-up of British personnel, mostly military intelligence, who arrived, usually in civilian clothes and with false names, in 1920. Collins had his 'squad', a dozen or so men who were trained assassins. Through Neligan and his other spies inside Dublin Castle he usually knew with great speed what the British plans were. When he realized that British Military Intelligence was becoming very dangerous, he acted with ruthless brutality. Early one Sunday morning, 'Bloody Sunday', 21 November 1920, his squad murdered most of these intelligence officers in their beds, sometimes before the eyes of their wives. The British response ran sadly true to form: an Irish crowd, attending a sporting event, was machine-gunned that afternoon. Collins had in large measure killed British intelligence in Ireland; the British had themselves almost exonerated his crime by a stupid, pointless revenge. Six months later the British, not the Irish, were suing for peace.

Despite all Lloyd George's bluster, this was the nemesis of British intelligence. If the 'Zimmermann telegram' saved the British Empire in 1917, a problematical assertion, it is not unfair to say that 'Bloody Sunday' may have set about its destruction three and a half years later. For India and Africa studied the Irish experience most carefully.

The story of American intelligence during the immediate post-war period is very different from that of its British counterpart. And again it cannot be viewed as acting in the abstract – a fallacy to which persons engaged on most secret intelligence tend on occasion to fall victim in their isolation – but as an instrument primarily of the military in wartime, of the foreign policy officials in time of peace, and of the government that these huge and powerful organizations are intended to serve both in peace

174

and war. This is perhaps particularly true in a democracy, and above all in that created by the Founding Fathers in America two centuries ago. However, since secret intelligence must be what this implies, its practitioners have almost always found themselves in an anomalous position. The situation may be summed up in a single paradox. The more efficient a secret intelligence service may be to its political masters, the more essential secrecy will be both in the service and to those masters who either do not know, or cannot understand, why it must be preserved. This paradox applies even more to a free press, above all the American press except in times of extreme national crisis, which will usually complain, often simultaneously, about the 'undemocratic' nature of the government's secret service and about its inefficiency. By definition, no American secret service can complain about the inefficiency, or on occasion the undemocratic and even unpatriotic nature, of the American press. But then the elaborate checks and balances within the whole American apparatus, which so frequently astound foreigners, are often equally amazing to Americans themselves. Those inside the circus tent, as well as those outside, are often on the edge of their seats as they gape at the daring young man on the flying trapeze whizzing between the Congress and the White House, the Supreme Court and the important editorial offices or television boardrooms, the Pentagon and the State Department, while the klieg lights switch from one section of the apparatus to the next.

For some thirty years after its real birth in 1918, American intelligence was not allowed its share of the lights, in part because its essentially secret nature was understood by its principal operatives, in part because the great ringmasters of American public spectacles had, and were encouraged to have, crassly misleading views about the methods and purposes of such intelligence agencies. It would have been hard to cast Errol Flynn or Clark Gable to play the Rev. Mr Montgomery, even harder to fit the obligatory, happy-ending love story into Room 40 or Yardley's M.I.-8.

One of the minor, occupational hazards of any secret intelligence service is that only its failures hit the headlines. When it establishes itself in huge, glittering headquarters, publicizes its bosses, and holds press conferences (no matter how misleading:

every psychologist knows that deliberate lies are as revealing as believed truth) then it ceases to be a secret intelligence agency in any meaningful sense and merely becomes another facet of the American way of government. Assimilation, too, can be a betrayal.

This did not happen to Yardley's M.I.-8. If anything it was the contrary that occurred. The American army played only a very small active part in the First World War. The American military victories at St Mihiel, in the Argonne and elsewhere were almost supererogatory, for by the summer of 1918 the Germans were being defeated by the French and British. But the presence in France of some two million American soldiers was very far from supererogatory, was indeed almost certainly decisive, for their very existence in Europe meant that the Germans could not hope to win the war with a 1919 campaign. The huge and growing American army in Europe was brave, young, healthy and on the way to being extremely well-equipped. It paid for its training in the usual, brutal fashion: by casualties. For the American government refused to accept the Anglo-French suggestion that American troops be sent into action, immediately and when most needed in the spring of 1918, as the components of British or French formations and even of units. The Americans insisted on the creation of an independent American army, under the supreme command of Marshal Foch after March 1918, but in no way under the command of the British or French governments. The creation of Pershing's army, virtually from scratch, was a lengthy, cumbersome and expensive business. Its independence was, however, essential to Wilson's policy and it directly affected the new American Military Intelligence service. (The United States Navy rapidly realized that it had almost everything to learn from the British; it did so, and played a major part in the transfer of American troops to Europe, while simultaneously helping to destroy the U-boats. But then the U.S. Navy did not start from scratch – or Mexico.)

Technically the French and the British were prepared to give the Americans almost every form of assistance in the creation of efficient military, naval and air forces. Experienced officers were withdrawn from the front during the critical battles of 1918 to be sent across the Atlantic there to train American officers who

176

would eventually train American soldiers. The French watched, sardonically one may be sure, the growing American armies on French soil which remained almost entirely inactive throughout the early summer of 1918, while the Germans advanced closer to Paris, and more French soldiers died than at any time since 1914. They realized how essential was American involvement, and they understood that Wilsonian policy was far from that of Clemenceau or even of Lloyd George. Since the American government was obviously reticent the French and British decided that they too must preserve some secrets. The Wilsonian slogan that, since America's entry, this was a 'war to end war' was regarded in London and Paris as an admirable slogan with which to encourage the Western populace and to discourage the populace on the other side; however the Allied leaders could hardly regard it as more than a naïve cliché. They knew too much about economic, cultural and demographic forces to believe in any 'final' war. Only some Marxists and some Americans believed that history might stop, the Marxists through total power to themselves, the Americans by means of an American global morality. The rulers of the ancient states of Europe shrugged their shoulders, smiled agreement to their American saviours and prepared for the world that must exist after the war. And though the Americans might have, for the foreseeable future, the big battalions with which to smash the Germans, the French (even less than the British) saw no reason why they should give to the Americans all their secrets. Perhaps the most important of these was the collection, evaluation and use of most secret intelligence. Battlefield intelligence, by all means, since the more efficient the future American army, when at last it became operational, the better for the Allies. But secret intelligence – who knows? – might perhaps be needed against even the Americans themselves.

For America was not an ally of France and Britain, as were Belgium, Italy, Romania, Japan. America had declared war on the German Empire in April 1917, and on the Austro-Hungarian Empire some eight months later. On this point President Wilson was and remained entirely adamant. Never has a great Western statesman adhered more rigidly to Clausewitz's much quoted apothegm. He declared war in order to continue his policy by other means; and that policy was the dictation, by American might, of a peace without victory between belligerents of roughly equivalent moral turpitude, a peace to be enforced forever by his democratic League of Nations. To men of a pragmatic frame of mind ideologues can sometimes appear remarkably blind to realities; however, the pragmatists can themselves be so blinded by their own experience as to confuse blindness with stupidity.

Wilson's famous Fourteen Points were foreshadowed on the day that he declared a state of war to exist between the United States of America and the German Empire, that is to say on 2 April 1917. He said: 'We have no quarrel with the German people. We have no feeling towards them but one of sympathy and friendship.' He then proceeded to conscript the male young people of America and arrange that they be trained to shoot and gas the young German males in, no doubt, a spirit of sympathy and friendship.

The Fourteen Points were first adumbrated in December of 1917, and defined a few weeks later. In three further speeches he increased their number to a total of thirty-eight 'points', 'principles', 'ends', 'particulars' and 'declarations', some of them repetitive but comprising a corpus of moral law upon which he intended the peace to be based. Compared with what they might expect from their original enemies, this corpus was a strong inducement to the war-weary Germans and Austrians to sue for peace. For this reason the leaders of France and Britain found the Points of use while the war went on, expendable as soon as it was over.

Perhaps the most important of Woodrow Wilson's legalistic formulae during the period 1917–19 was his determination to preserve his image of ultimate peacemaker by the denial of an obvious fact. The United States, he said repeatedly and insistently, was not allied to France, Britain and the other belligerents, but was an 'associated power'. He put this perhaps most clearly in a letter to Herbert Hoover, with a very early date.

The White House, December 10, 1917

My Dear Mr Hoover.

I have noticed on one or two of the posters of the Food Administration the words, 'Our Allies'. I would be very much obliged if you would issue instructions that 'Our Associates in

178

the War' is to be substituted. I have been very careful about this myself, because we have no allies and I think I am right in believing that the people of the country are very jealous of any intimation that there are formal alliances.

You will understand, of course, that I am implying no criticism. I am only thinking it important that we should all use the same language.

Woodrow Wilson [4]

This insistence on 'association' rather than alliance, frequently repeated, is far more than a matter of terminology. Wilson made it plain to the soldiers that America was fighting her own war, at her own time, for her own ends. The logical outcome could only be that America must sign her own peace treaty. This in turn implied that American policy must be based on American intelligence. Such intelligence could be derived from any source, from the enemy, from neutrals or from the Associated Powers. And the Associated Powers, in return, did not regard it as their duty to help American secret intelligence – which was virtually non-existent outside the Monroe Doctrine area – beyond the needs and ends of the Associated Powers themselves. With British naval intelligence, the exchange was inevitably very frank. Two navies fighting a common hostile navy had to be very open with one another for obvious reasons of mutual self-ii.terest. The land battle was rather different. Of course the French wished the Americans to defeat the German enemy, but they were not going to endanger their own rather fragile secret intelligence apparatus, and thus risk yet further French casualties, in order to save American lives. Since the Americans were far the weaker partner in this field, it may be fairly assumed that Pershing's army would have made less blunders, and therefore suffered fewer casualties, if Wilson had committed his nation wholeheartedly to the Allied cause. There was little such Anglo-American reticence in the Second World War. On the other hand, as will be seen, relations in this field with the Soviets were far more acutely distrustful, particularly on the Russian side, and gave the Nazis a lever which they quite failed to use but which might have been decisive.

The weakness of American intelligence in 1918, and its consequent relations with British and French intelligence during the last period of the war, is admirably portrayed in Herbert Yardley's book. And Woodrow Wilson's well nigh complete failure to grasp its importance is shown not only in that book but in almost every study of him, his policy and his government known to this writer. He never seems to have realized that he need know what was going on in the minds, or implied in the policies and actions, either of his country's enemies or of its associates. The very first of his Fourteen Points, with its rejection of all 'secrecy', shows that he must have regarded secret intelligence as a relic from an evil age and evil methods that he would 'crusade' to abolish once and for all.

With a fantastic speed and efficiency only to be surpassed in 1942, the hugely powerful American economy was geared to war. Skilled brains and great resources were given to the specialized agencies, among them M.I.-8 which expanded rapidly in manpower (from Yardley and two civilian assistants in June 1917, to close on two hundred men and women a year later), essential in those days when deciphering was done by men almost unaided by machines. With a great deal of help from Room 40 the American intelligence service rapidly became very effective. And yet the more it learned about techniques, the more its controllers realized how far behind the Associated Powers, and therefore behind the enemy, it still must be. In 1918 Yardley was sent to Europe, with letters from almost the highest levels within government, to close this gap.

He left in July 1918, but his own account of his odyssey makes it far from clear who sent him to Europe, or why. He was apparently close to a nervous breakdown due to overwork. This was one very good reason to take him away from his sensitive post as head of M.I.-8, and indeed he says that he recovered his health completely during the two weeks' voyage to Liverpool. On the other hand, and immediately before his departure, he had been engaged by the head of U.S. Military Intelligence, General Churchill, in drawing up plans 'for a Cipher Bureau for the Expeditionary Forces to Siberia which was then being formed. Papers were drawn up ordering me to Siberia with a selected personnel, when a cable came from General Pershing, asking that I be sent to France.' [5] He goes on to say: 'Although I felt some pride in General Pershing's request for my services in France,

I was too ill to take a great deal of interest in what was going on.'

This rather confused, and on the face of it improbable, competition for the services of Yardley may be interpreted in several ways, apart from his recollections as to why he was wanted where (he would scarcely have been told) during a period of mental exhaustion. In view of his past and future career as head of a cryptanalyst bureau, the Siberian assignment makes sense, but not anti-Bolshevik sense.

For Wilson's ideology of neutrality, fair play, call it what you will, extended to the Russian situation too. For simplistic minds, not necessarily simple ones, the United States was itself created by revolution. Indeed revolution implied to Americans a sort of legitimacy, by choice, which found few echoes within the chancelleries of Europe where it meant, as it was then meaning for the Russians, mass-murder, civil war, chaos and terror. From all this, Wilson stood as grandly aloof as he did from so much else that did not directly affect the biennial American elections. Therefore America was neutral, though hostile to an anti-capitalist regime that had also deprived the United States of an 'associated power' in America's war against Germany.

The collapse and chaos in Russia were viewed with far less equanimity not only in Europe but also in Japan, though from quite different motives. Once America was in the war, the men who held power in Tokyo were in no doubt which would be the winning side, and within a few weeks the Japanese–British Treaty of Alliance was renewed. At the same time the Japanese were promised, by the British, a free hand in post-war Shantung, a most important littoral province of Northern China. Japan thus became, at long last and as the Japanese leaders wished, a continental power upon the mainland of Asia.

With the collapse of Czarist Russia and the virtual isolation of Siberia – by the summer of 1918 the Czech legion of ex-prisoners held several hundred miles of the unique and vital Trans-Siberian Railway, their armed enemies being in large measure other ex-prisoners, now converted to Communism, of German and Austrian origin – the Japanese rather cautiously moved in. It was their first major military operation of the war, and so chaotic were the circumstances that its extent was, and remains, problematical. Nevertheless it was a matter of concern to the

Western Allies and particularly to the United States. The British and French moved small forces into the Siberian and North Chinese ports, to safeguard their interests. The Americans sent some U.S. Marines to safeguard their own interests, including a policing of railways.

This U.S. Force hardly needed an intelligence unit of such sophistication as to include a cipher-breaking group if it were merely to inform the force commander concerning internal Siberian affairs. On the other hand, the Japanese presence was of a very different importance. In view of what had not happened in the immediate past and of what was to happen in the immediate future, it would seem that had Yardley gone to Siberia it would have been to watch the Japanese, not the Russians of various political beliefs nor their polyglot ex-prisoners, none of whom had an intelligence service so advanced as to require supervision at Yardley's level. This conclusion is in itself an intelligence appreciation, based on a minimum of facts.

On the other hand it seems unlikely, though not impossible, that General Pershing would have asked for Yardley by name. There is no particular reason why so elevated an officer as was Pershing should ever have heard of Yardley. That he found himself unduly dependent – as commander of an entirely independent army fighting an independent war – upon French and British military intelligence must have become very obvious to him by the summer of 1918. He would therefore, and logically, have asked the War Department for a high-level intelligence unit to complement his own inadequate Army G-2. Yardley's immediate bosses, Colonel van Deman and General Churchill, would presumably have considered Yardley for the job, would have discussed it with him in a more or less oblique way, and may have decided that his mental exhaustion did not qualify him for so important an assignment with the first large American army ever to serve overseas. On the other hand they knew his value and his experience and they therefore sent him on what might be described as a fact-finding mission to London and Paris.

Yardley's account of his protracted and repeated visits to Europe in 1918 and 1919 is of great interest at several levels, the most obvious being the least important. He was sent to London and thence to Paris in order to find out as much as he could

182

about British and French secret intelligence. In London he was, as he says, treated with the greatest friendliness. This cannot have been a hardship, for Yardley was evidently a man of considerable charm. On the other hand it was not solely for his amiable qualities that the men of British intelligence entertained him with whiskys-and-sodas in their clubs and dinners in their homes. Those highly experienced British intelligence officers were already committed to two Americans in London: to Edward Bell who had been shown how the Zimmermann telegram was deciphered and had been allowed to repeat the operation, and to Ambassador Page. Apart from what the British knew Page and Bell must be passing to Washington, apart from a distant interchange at another level with General Churchill and Colonel van Deman, and apart from the operational interchange between the two naval commands in the Atlantic, there was no reason why the British should reveal any more of their secrets to the Americans. America was, after all, in the war, and could hardly now get out again. Hence the whiskys-and-sodas for Herbert Yardley. However, there are certain indications, of so vague a sort as scarcely to be called evidence, that the British helped him with his anti-Japanese intelligence operations. This would have been a small price for the British to pay in order to keep the Americans sweet. Also, it makes sense.

Yardley, having as he says failed in London, moved on to Paris. There he was also treated with the greatest social courtesy. Unfortunately, though, the French told him obvious lies, which he recognized as such. He was interested in the breaking of diplomatic ciphers, but was told by the appropriate person at the French Foreign Ministry that such activities were exclusively carried out by the military, and at the Ministry for War that diplomatic cipher-breaking was handled entirely by Foreign Affairs. He went to higher and higher levels, eventually to the Prime Minister Clemenceau himself, who gave instructions in his usual vivid fashion. They were of no avail either in the Ministry of War or in that of Foreign Affairs, and this despite Yardley's seeing a diplomatic cable on the desk of a military intelligence officer. Yardley continued to be blandly pinged and ponged between the one ministry and the other. He may have learned nothing about French intelligence but he certainly left Paris with little doubt as to where French loyalty lay, and that this was not to the future wellbeing of that 'associated power', the United States of America. Many Americans, patriots and loyal to their fellow-combatants, were making similar discoveries in other, not dissimilar, fields of action. And as the ghastly war approached its end, an end to which the United States contributed little by way of force, but an incalculable amount in the way of moral persuasion and potential power, the leaders of the great countries set about deciding how each wished the future to be. The negotiations before the Treaty of Versailles, and indeed the treaty itself, became a strange two-headed animal. Intended to conclude one war, Wilson's 'war to end wars', it was also the first manoeuvre for the Second World War. Of this all the major powers, except perhaps the United States but not excluding the supposedly 'eliminated' powers, Germany, Russia, Turkey, were well aware. And among the weaker powers, intelligence was not forgotten, for that is always the weapon of the weak against the strong. The weakest of all, with the disappearance of Austro-Hungary, were the two pariahs of Europe, the German Republic and the U.S.S.R.

PART THREE
1919–45

Chapter Twelve

The Horizon

The diplomats have a phrase to describe certain occasions when they or their employers meet to discuss the global situation and its future: a *tour d'horizon*. These exercises of frank interchange laced with competitive mendacity can seldom have been more necessary, or more difficult, than in the years immediately after the First World War. The globe may have looked as round and solid as ever, large parts coloured British Imperial red, other great areas a French green, or a Dutch yellow; Russia filled most of the frozen, uninteresting north; the only large, politically ambiguous area, as the globe was spun, remained China, and even here an attempt was manfully made, at least among the European and American diplomats, to maintain that a form of government existed comparable to their own, a point of view not shared by the Japanese government who continued quietly to strengthen their position in northeast Asia despite the 'loss' of Shantung at Versailles.

However, if we rotate the globe, as it appeared in the early '20s, rather slowly, the horizons are far less gently curved. Before examining the very disparate intelligence purposes of the great powers, it would be as well to try and gauge briefly what were the national and indeed personal ambitions of the men who controlled those powers. And to evaluate these it is necessary to revert, in some cases at least, to the manner in which the First World War came to an end: 'not with a bang but a whimper'.

On 11 February 1918, when the Central Powers had certainly not yet lost the war, Wilson said: 'Self-determination is not a mere phrase; peoples may now be dominated and governed only by their consent.'

And in order to weaken Austria he proceeded to instruct his subordinates to open negotiations with at least four peoples, paired off as Czecho-Slovaks and Serbo-Croats. Other historical peoples such as the Bretons, the Irish, the Ukrainians, to name but three among many, hardly existed in Princeton's practical geography.

On 4 July 1918, at Mount Vernon, a further collection of clichés was announced: 'What we seek is the reign of law, based upon the consent of the governed and sustained by the organized opinion of mankind.'

If the ghost of George Washington still haunted Mount Vernon he might well have refrained from comment. On the other hand yet a third President from that once slave-owning state of the Union, Thomas Jefferson, would probably have raised an eyebrow even if he had bitten back a pungent aside. Leagues of nations were not for the Founding Fathers, for the concept is not at all an extrapolation of the idea upon which their United States had been based.

Throughout that summer of slaughter Wilson continued to issue his moral pronouncements, with considerable effect upon the enemy. As late as 12 October 1918, when the new German government of Prince Max von Baden was preparing to negotiate peace, Wilson promised the Germans 'a permanent peace of justice'.

The French, and to a lesser extent the British, were not very impressed. The French in particular were less interested in justice for Germans than in reparations for themselves, and on a scale as massive as their past sufferings. Pressure was brought to bear on Wilson. The Germans must not merely evacuate the occupied territories but also be rendered militarily impotent *before* a peace treaty would be imposed upon them.

And now, with the war nearing its end, President Wilson made two major mistakes, the one domestic, the other foreign. It may be that Colonel House, who was travelling to Paris from 17 October to 26 October to make the necessary diplomatic preparations for the end of hostilities, might have restrained him, but Herbert Hoover, who was very close to Wilson at the time, maintains that the President was becoming less and less amenable to advice, let alone phraseology. He had already rebuffed his loyal old friend, Walter Page, who had indeed resigned from his London embassy in consequence.

The domestic error was this. The United States government

had been bipartisan for a year and a half, Republicans serving beside Democrats in the highest offices, in patriotic unity. But in October 1918, the Congressional Campaign was taking place. And on 24 October, when Colonel House was at sea, Wilson made a truly extraordinary speech. Suddenly ceasing to be Head of State and becoming the head of a great political party, he asked the American people to elect a Democratic Congress without which, as he said, it would be difficult for him to arrange a peace in the best interests of the United States. He went further. He attacked Republican members of the Congress by name, even some who were his loyal and patriotic servants. The consternation that ensued is evident. It was compounded by the failure of this party-political exercise. A Republican Congress was elected. And only the Congress can ratify an American treaty of peace. Domestically, therefore, Wilson had isolated the Presidency. Next year he, and for a generation perhaps the world, were to suffer the consequences.

On the previous day, that is to say 23 October, he had committed a major international blunder. After all the high liberal talk about justice for the Germans, he had allowed the French and British to throw him into reverse. America, he had said, 'must demand, not peace negotiations, but surrender'. The German army had almost ceased to fight, but Hindenburg succinctly and correctly defined this demand as 'unconditional surrender', ominous words indeed, and ordered the German armies to resume full hostilities. True, he and Ludendorff were rapidly dismissed, and within three weeks the armistice was signed; true this total change of American policy was not immediately understood by the exhausted and often revolutionary peoples of Central Europe; but American moral values became and remained increasingly suspect among the educated.

When Wilson arrived in Europe early in the following year, and more or less installed the White House in the Hotel Crillon, Paris, he was greeted by the populace as perhaps no hero has ever been acclaimed. However, those who knew, whether French, British, Germans or Italians, adopted a considerably more sceptical attitude towards the great liberator and his plans for the future of their continent.

Yet more serious than these grave political sins of commission

188

was an even more significant sin of intelligence omission. When the President of the United States at last and reluctantly declared that the country of which he was head was henceforth to be associated with the Allied Powers in their war against the Central Powers, he had almost no picture of the secret world of high, or low, international politics as it then existed.

We now know, thanks to the capture of the German archives in 1945 and to their brilliant interpretation by Professor Fritz Fischer,[1] how the men of power in Berlin then wished the future of the world to be. As brutal as it was unattractive, it could have had little interest for President Wilson, not even such elements as may have reached him through his intelligence services. When the decision was taken to commit the United States to the war, German war aims automatically ceased to be relevant.

On the other hand, since American intervention was intended to ensure the victory of those Allied Powers with which the United States was associated after 6 April 1917, the war aims of the Allies were clearly of the greatest importance to the President, busily drafting his Fourteen Points of which, it will be recalled, the very first deplored secret covenants. It would be assumed, therefore, that he would have had the greatest possible interest in what 'secret covenants' had been reached between the Allies in the years of American neutrality. Indeed had there been a United States intelligence service of any ability whatsoever, such discoveries would surely have been among its very primary aims before and during April 1917.

In fact the following arrangements had been made before that date between the powers who became 'associated' with the United States.

March 1915. Russia, Britain, France. Russia to get Constantinople, the Dardanelles, Northern Persia and control over Southern Persia. The British and French to divide between themselves control of Mesopotamia, to include what are now Iraq, Jordan and Syria.
April 1915. The Pact of London, between Britain, France and Italy. In exchange for a betrayal of her Central Powers allies and entry into the war against them, Italy to receive the Trentino, South Tyrol, Istria, Trieste, part of Dalmatia and some Adriatic

189

islands, a share of Anatolia (part of Turkey). Fiume, however, was reserved for the Serbs.

May 1916. The Sykes–Picot Treaty between Britain and France, giving more detail to the Russian–British–French Treaty of the previous year. Apart from Russian territorial claims, the Middle East to be subdivided much as it eventually was in 1919 upon the abolition of the old Ottoman Empire. However the Italians got wind of this in the following year, and were promised their slice of Turkey, namely Smyrna and a large 'zone of influence' to the north of that city.

August 1916. France, Britain and Russia enticed Romania into the war with the promise of Transylvania (from Austria) and the Dubruja (from Bulgaria).

February 1917. Britain and Japan agree that Japan acquire Shantung and all German islands north of the equator, Britain all to the south.

February–March 1917. A new Franco-Russian treaty, after the fall of the Czarist autocracy and clearly intended to keep the so-called Kerensky government in the war. The Russians were confirmed in their claims to Constantinople and the Dardanelles. To these were added Poland and a 'free hand', whatever that may mean, in the other eastern territories of the German and Austro-Hungarian Empires. The French were to get Alsace-Lorraine, which was obvious anyhow, the Saar, which was a little less so, and a new 'neutral country' on the German left bank of the Rhine. When the Bolsheviks published and denounced this treaty in November 1917, the British Foreign Secretary, the amiable Mr Balfour, denied all knowledge of it. Mr (later Lord) Balfour's charm was legendary. Charm, however, is not incompatible with disingenuity.

March 1917. The French signed a new agreement with Kerensky's Russia. The Russians were to get a further 60,000 square miles between Persia and the Black Sea, the French a slice of Turkey's Mediterranean coast, the details of this to be worked out with the British. Again, Mr Balfour knew nothing about this deal, which seems odd.

(After the Bolshevik Revolution of November 1917, the French unilaterally denounced their promises to previous Russian regimes, while maintaining the validity of the Russian promises

190

to France. The Soviets must have very soon regretted the impetuosity of their diplomats who had published the secret agreements; no doubt the diplomats rapidly regretted this even more.)

Such, then, was the spiderweb of international intrigue into which Wilson led his country. His reaction was quite extraordinarily astonishing. He seems to have believed that the first of his Fourteen Points quite simply cancelled all these secret agreements, when the Allies accepted those Fourteen Points as the basis of a peace treaty. However, before the Allies accepted Wilsonian dogma, and immediately after Wilson's declaration of war, the President did make, through Colonel House, a somewhat feeble effort to correct his grossly misleading intelligence, if such it can be called, and to acquire some appreciation of the international diplomatic and military situation. On 28 April 1917, Colonel House wrote in his diary that he had asked Mr Balfour:

> . . . what treaties were out between the Allies as to the division of spoils after the war. He [Balfour] said they had treaties with one another, and that when Italy came in they made one with her in which they had promised pretty much what she demanded.
>   Balfour spoke with regret at the spectacle of great nations sitting down and dividing the spoils of war, or as he termed it, 'dividing up the bearskin before the bear was killed'. I asked him if he did not think it proper for the Allies to give copies of these treaties to the President for his confidential information. He thought such a request entirely reasonable and said he would have copies made for that purpose . . .[2]

It seems, however, that Mr Balfour only sent the President the text of four of the secret treaties listed above, and Ray Stannard Baker adds, curiously: 'The President did not answer this letter in writing, nor refer to it in writing at any time, so far as the author has been able to discover, nor did he [Wilson], apparently, give the treaties themselves any study.'[3]

Thus when President Wilson first arrived in Paris on 16 December 1918, he seems to be amazing in his ignorance of what he was entering: he had left a politically divided America behind him, and the fantastic popular applause that he received, as he made speech after speech in France, England, Italy, combined with the knowledge that the Germans and Austrians, the new minority states and even the neutrals also greeted him as a saviour, must have given that somewhat chilly man a sense of confidence such as few can ever have enjoyed and probably none for long. Wilson's hour of glory was to be of a quite pathetic duration. So, too, was Europe's moment of relief.

For Wilson's Fourteen Points, even with their numerous elaborations, had not brought history to an end. When he arrived in Paris in December of 1918 the guns along the Western, Italian and Turkish fronts may have already fallen silent. In Russia they had not, nor had they in much of eastern and southeastern Europe. The Bolsheviks controlled most of Russia between the Urals and the Pripet marshes with the exception of the Arctic and the Black Sea ports. The Red Army was fighting a civil war against the Russian White Army while simultaneously engaged in mass extermination of the 'class enemy'.[4] And despite this bitter war against their fellow-Russians, the Red Army was also at war with almost all the neighbouring states who had no wish to exchange Czarist whips for Leninist scorpions. Finns, Letts, Estonians, Latvians, Poles, Ukrainians, Caucasians, Turkomen and indeed the whole circumference of the old Russian Empire formed an unorganized but real alliance in arms. Weird situations arose. German units fought both Russians and Poles, who were also fighting one another. A Bolshevik takeover in Hungary was crushed with some Austrian support as the Austro-Hungarian Empire ceased to exist. The British, with French and American support, helped the White Russians hold Archangel and Murmansk; the French, British and Greeks held the Russian and Bulgarian Black Sea Ports. The concept of 'national self-determination' was even more murky than the principle of 'open covenants', and the murk was the blood of massacre amounting at times to attempted but postponed genocide. The national frontiers of post-war Europe were not easy to draw, even upon the maps.

Lenin, and to a lesser extent Trotsky, had accepted and indeed reinforced Marxist theory that Russia was not ripe for a meaningful

192

Communist revolution. Lenin's programme can be expressed with extreme simplicity. First, all power to the Soviets, that is to say to his own minute political party; second, the ingurgitation to be followed by the excretion of all other revolutionaries or democratic parties, once these had been used to conquer Russia for the Soviets and to kill any who might disagree; third, the use of an absolutely autocratic Bolshevik power-base in Russia for the purpose, by conquest or by propaganda, of seizing the great bastions of capitalism. The ultimate centre of Communist world power, as Lenin saw it in 1918, must be Berlin or London. The welfare of the British, German or Russian peoples, indeed of all peoples, was entirely irrelevant, since systematic terror would rule out any danger of a counter-revolution or, as some might say, a real revolution in the interests of the people. Morality was redefined as whatever served Lenin's bid for global omnipotence. All strategy was permissible. London and Paris, as he said, might be conquered on the banks of the Yangtse, or they might be captured by mendacious propaganda and deliberate economic misery.

In the immediate circumstances of 1918–19, with the Red Army scarcely capable of defeating its numerous enemies inside Russia, propaganda was really the only vein for Lenin to exploit. He cannot have failed to see how successful Wilsonian propaganda had been so recently; he now watched it crumble, as the British continued their blockade of Germany, causing countless casualties among an exhausted, starving population in a Europe suffering from the most lethal influenza epidemic in modern history. The Fourteen Points withered. In Germany the Communists gained much support as the representatives of the workers who had 'ended the war'. However, they were not much use to Lenin, being in general ill-disciplined bands of marauding brigands who aroused much antipathy. Furthermore, apart from those soldiers who had been directly influenced by contact with Russian rebels and mutineers, the German army, and above all its officers, remained almost entirely opposed to the Leninists. Indeed they came to believe, against all evidence, that the German revolutionaries had stabbed them in the back. Quite rapidly the danger of a Communist revolution in Germany receded and in 1918 Winston Churchill, the Minister for War and Air, was advocating, as he was to do again in 1945, that the German army be used to repel the Russian threat to Eastern Europe.[5] As on other very important questions, he was politically premature.

But his motive was not, or at least not primarily, ideological. The danger of Bolshevization was not limited to defeated Germany. In early 1919 British troops in control of Archangel were threatening to mutiny. And even before the end of the war, on 30 October 1918, Colonel House had written to President Wilson of a conversation he had just held with Lloyd George and Clemenceau: 'I pointed out the danger of bringing about a state of Bolshevism in Germany if terms of armistice were made too stiff, and the consequent danger to England, France and Italy. Clemenceau refused to recognize that there was any danger of Bolshevism in France. George admitted it was possible to create such a state of affairs in England and both agreed that anything might happen in Italy.'

Such was the atmosphere, out of sight of the tumultuous crowds in London, Paris and Rome where Wilson received his unprecedented acclaim. Only a few men of knowledge and experience can have realized that Lenin was on his way to perfecting a new form of politico-military intelligence. And as Woodrow Wilson ploughed ahead, with increasing lack of success, to see his Fourteen Points made into a solid edifice for peace, what had he to rely upon in the form of intelligence? Lenin had sympathizers, usually vocal though seldom then in high office, throughout a world exhausted and disgusted by war and old-fashioned *Machtpolitik* and whom he could use for his new-fashioned ideological *Machtpolitik*. Wilson, that is to say the United States government, had the information derived from its increasingly tepid Allies and from the American intelligence service. When to this is added the fact that the Western Allies handed over half a million Russian prisoners held in Germany to the Red, not the White, Russian army, it is not surprising that many intelligent people foresaw a speedy Communization of Western Europe and perhaps of the world. And here Marx was probably right, as he not infrequently was: a country less backward than the Russia of the time might have pulled it off then, despite the chaos, cruelty and horrors of its civil war. After all, Bonaparte's situation had not been so very different in 1795.

194

Lenin, like Wilson, was engaged in dual combat. The Third Communist International was formally created only in 1919, although by then international Communism had been an active force for over a year. Lenin, however, unlike Wilson, had been compelled by circumstances first to master his Russian base. The result of this was that his Comintern was built on foundations utterly different from those of the League of Nations. It was in fact modelled on the Russian experience, that is to say the Czarist tyranny as embodied in the Okhrana (now of course dissolved) modified by Leninist rather than by Marxist theories of revolutionary practice. Russian intelligence abroad remained, and has remained ever since, a branch of the Russian imperial police force, its primary purpose being the safeguarding and to a lesser degree the extension of Russia's internal security into foreign lands. This is endemic in any great modern imperialist system (i.e., the Irish Special Branch, the intelligence apparatus of Britain's Indian Civil Service, and so on, though never institutionalized to such an extent as in the short-lived empire of Napoleon I) and therefore in the Czarist and Soviet Empires. In fact the foreign branches of the Comintern were, from the beginning, modelled on the Bolshevik faction of the Russian socialist movement. Their purpose was to serve Russian Soviet interests, their methods to be Lenin's own, the elimination of all enemies, starting with alternative revolutionary parties. Any form of 'left wing' democracy was and has remained the prime enemy. It was upon this rather insecure basis that the Soviet intelligence service, an extension of the Russian internal police, was created. Its strength lay and lies in its tight central control, but therein also lay and lies its weakness. Russian xenophobia has not decreased – rather the contrary – and the Soviet intelligence service is by reason of its foreign contacts always and inevitably most suspect to its masters. As Robert Conquest has remarked, for some forty years the disgraced heads of the Soviet Secret Service were invariably accused, before or after their murder (judicial or otherwise), of having spied for one or more foreign intelligence services. And since all such heads until and including Beria died violent deaths, Conquest remarks drily that it is hard to envisage a great state which *invariably* appointed foreign spies to head its own secret service.[6]

This apparently ridiculous paradox was not in fact ridiculous at all. It was indeed probably inevitable in view both of Russian history and of what came to be called Marxism–Leninism. As has been suggested in an earlier chapter, the Czarist secret service had been essentially a security service, designed to thwart Russian anti-Czarist revolutionaries whether living in Russia or in exile. Its principal method was the infiltrator, the *agent provocateur*, who can so easily become the double agent of today. Its methods were influenced by a minimum of morality; its successes were few, culminating in utter, incompetent failure; and most, though not all, of the men who had worked for the Okhrana publicly or secretly were swept into the proper garbage can of history when Lenin read its archives in November 1917. Lenin, it would seem, was aware of the inherent dangers. He appointed the Pole, Dzerzhinsky, to run the new, Bolshevik secret police. He presented Dzerzhinsky as the Communist ideal, a latter day St Just, to complement his own role of a 'sea-green incorruptible', a man of such moral purity as to be incomparable with his Okhrana predecessors. Perhaps Lenin was jesting. Dzerzhinsky was the first in a series of monsters, torturers, mass-murderers, diabolical police chiefs. There is no evidence that he was taken aback, or indeed disagreed, when Stalin allegedly said to him and Kamenev, when Lenin was dying: 'To choose one's victims, to prepare one's plans minutely, to slake an implacable vengeance, and then to go to bed . . . there is nothing sweeter in the world.' [7]

The first and principal job of Dzerzhinsky's Cheka was of course the destruction of the internal enemy – those people dubbed 'the enemies of the people' – which proceeded throughout and continued after the Russian Civil War. By then, however, many Russians had fled abroad, and once again the Cheka found itself in the same role as the Okhrana. There were scores if not hundreds of thousands of the latter-day émigrés, now called 'White Russians', from Harbin to Paris and beyond. Among them activist, counter-revolutionary organizations existed, with a diminishing hope that history might yet be reversed and they be permitted a homecoming. These organizations abroad the Soviet police infiltrated, as had the Okhrana. They surpassed the Okhrana, though, in the methodical use of assassination. This writer, a child in Paris in 1927, was staying with Russians in Passy when the Grand

196

Duke Cyril was assassinated in the flat below; or so I have since been told, for the atrocity was of course kept from me at the time.

In Lenin's time the Cheka was marked by one important policy variant from its Czarist predecessor. It served an autocrat, as before, and its prime targets were that autocrat's Russian enemies, but Lenin's autocracy had no basis in patriotism or religion. Trotsky, too, believed in global, not national, revolution. Only after Lenin's death, and the defeat of Trotsky, was Stalin able to create National Socialism in Russia, so soon to be successfully copied by Hitler in Germany. Nevertheless the Comintern continued to exercise maximum control over foreign Communists and, as best it could, all other 'left-wing' parties, its main instrument still being the Russian secret service and its foreign agents.

A second evolution, or perhaps an exaggeration of the old Okhrana's intelligence function, lay in the area of Russian security. Fear of foreign spies had always been acute. It very rapidly assumed paranoiac proportions. This was in some measure explicable in terms of the Russian Civil War with its atrocities and the multitude of enemies thus created; in some ways by the hatred engendered by the internal and external methods of Russia's new rulers, social, political and economic, and by their repeated and loudly proclaimed intention to conquer or subvert the world to their own generally unattractive ideology. But perhaps more important than this was the theory that *everything* in Russia now belonged to the state, which meant in practice that all Russian activity of every sort, from the writing of symphonies to the rolling of cigarettes, was to be centrally controlled by the growing apparatus of bureaucrats whose leaders had conquered the Russian people and whose principal weapon of consolidation was and has remained the secret police, both at home and abroad.

Thus everything in Russia became a state secret. Since the new system was grotesquely incompetent, all information about anything was potentially dangerous. It was not just the huge slave labour complexes that had to be hidden, nor the breakdown of communications, of agriculture, of medicine. The production of a sock factory in Kamenetsk-Podolsk, the photograph of a horse-drawn plough near Kharkhov, all this was potential propaganda for 'the enemy', that is to say for everyone outside the apparatus.

All contact with foreigners became, and increasingly, classified as espionage. With the Stalinist terror this grew. Had the results not been so atrocious, the illogicality of it all would have been almost comical. For the workers on the railways there can have been little humour in the situation described by Robert Conquest; the quotation he gives is from a speech by N. M. Shvernik at the Twenty-second Party Congress, in October of 1961.

The railways were subjected to particularly Draconic laws. The Criminal Codex of the R.S.F.S.R. in its Article 59 covered 'crimes against the system of government', including various offences on the railways which 'lead, or might lead, to the breakdown of State transport plans' and of which some examples given are the accumulation of empty trucks and the dispatch of trains off schedule. The prescribed punishment was up to ten years or, if done with malicious intent, the death sentence.

Kaganovich also devised the so-called 'theory of counter-revolutionary limit-setting on output', with the help of which he organized the mass destruction of engineering and technical cadres. 'In a short period of time most of the directors of railroads and of the railroads' political departments and many executive officials of the central apparatus and lines were dismissed from their jobs and later arrested.'

As to 'sabotage' itself, on the Russian railways at this time there was an accident of some sort about every five minutes. This led to the slaughter of the railway cadres. Kaganovich had made a tour of the railways of the Far East early in 1936. Following this, the Military Collegium went on tour and handed down five death sentences and ten long jail terms in Krasnoyarsk and Tomsk in March, for wrecking for 'foreign intelligence services'. This was only a beginning.

In his speech at a meeting of railway activists on 10 March 1937, Kaganovich said: 'I cannot name a single road or a single system where there has not been Trotskyite–Japanese sabotage. Not only that, there is not a single branch of railway transport in which these saboteurs have not turned up . . .' Under Kaganovich arrests of railway officials were made by lists. His deputies, nearly all road chiefs and political-section chiefs, and other executive officials in transport were arrested without any grounds whatever.

On 10 August 1937 Kaganovich wrote to the N.K.V.D. demanding the arrest of ten responsible officials in the People's Commissariat of Transport. The only grounds were that he thought their behaviour suspicious. They were arrested as spies and saboteurs and shot. He wrote in all thirty-two personal letters to Yezhov, demanding the arrest of eighty-three transport executives.

The North Donets railway was the only line not involved in these sweeping arrests of early 1937. In August, the heads of the line were called to Moscow and instructed to find saboteurs. An estimate by the Director of Locomotive Service of the line is that about 1,700 out of the 45,000 employees were arrested within months. In mid-November he himself was called to the N.K.V.D. and asked how he proposed to end sabotage. As he was unable to think of any cases of sabotage – the line being an exceptionally efficient one – he was bitterly harangued and during the next wave of arrests was pulled in, on 2 December 1937, without a warrant or charge.

His wife and six-year-old son were thrown out of their house two days after his arrest, and he was subjected to severe interrogation, with beatings, together with a number of other prisoners, including several station-masters and the deputy head of the line.

Special railwaymen's prisons were set up, in small towns like Poltava. Arrested railwaymen were kept in coaches in unused sidings. Special military courts travelled about the country dealing with them. They were almost invariably Japanese spies. The reason for this was that the Soviet Union had in 1935 handed over the Chinese Eastern Railway to the Japanese. The Russian railwaymen who had operated it and who now returned to the Soviet Union were almost the only non-diplomatic Soviet personnel who had been living abroad, and on their return they were automatically high-grade suspects. (With their families, they are said to have numbered about 40,000.) And they had meanwhile worked on all the railway systems and recruited all their colleagues.[8]

The miserable experience of the railroadmen was and is repeated at every level on which the Russians had contact with the outside world. It also became the fate of those foreign Communists who accepted the Soviet leaders as allies and even as friends. But at diplomatic, military and commercial levels the Soviets found themselves faced with a dilemma which has not yet been resolved.

The position of the Soviet diplomat was from the beginning, and has remained, both anomalous and dangerous. At first they were few in number, since most of the world, civilized or not, failed to recognize the Leninists as the government of Russia. During the immediate post-surrender years, just before and after Brest-Litovsk, Lenin's and Trotsky's emissaries dealt with the representatives of various foreign countries, such as Germany, Poland, Finland, the emergent Baltic states and so on, but despite their occasional claims they could not, and usually did not, pretend to represent 'Russia', for most of the past and future Russian Empire was loosely controlled by the enemies of the new revolutionary regime or by those who were hostile to both. Therefore a Soviet Russian, as opposed to a Leninist or Comintern, diplomatic service did not really appear upon the scene until nearly the mid-1920s. And when at last it did, it was of a most peculiar sort. Old-style diplomats were of course unacceptable class enemies. Turncoats from this class were suspect, though used. Real power, therefore, was usually vested in an apparently menial subordinate of proven loyalty to the Bolshevik 'ideology', the ambassador's chauffeur, shall we say, or maybe his cook's potboy. These people, members of the secret police, did not of course deal with the foreigners, but they reported on what their allegedly superior diplomats were doing. With the repeated alterations to the Party line in Moscow, which were not always communicated to the 'official' Soviet diplomats, this meant that those diplomats enjoyed a short and precarious career, and few of them have died a natural death. On the other hand, the 'secret' diplomats were also suspect both because of their inside knowledge and because of their inevitable contact with foreigners. They might be secret policemen, but the secret police became increasingly subject to purges as one or another group of autocrats seized power, openly or secretly, within the Kremlin. So the chauffeur's life insurance was also not an attractive proposition. Nor need it be. One wing of Moscow's largest pre-revolutionary insurance company now filled a new role: it was called the Lubyanka prison, and this is where most Soviet diplomats, official or otherwise, found themselves at one time or another. As the wheel spun, some emerged, usually in a battered condition. Finally, and in quite recent times, the secret police took over the entire Soviet diplomatic service. This of course meant the interminable Russian proliferation of internal informants, which is one reason why Soviet embassies, trade missions and so on require such fantastically large staffs. But only when the Soviet diplomatic service became an intrinsic part of the K.G.B. (ex-N.K.V.D.) during the post-Stalinist period could it devote itself seriously to espionage and other forms of secret intelligence. And even so, foreign service with the K.G.B. may be a passport to relative comfort but hardly to longevity.

In industry and commerce the managers and technicians suffered from similar though less acute dangers. In the first place, the fact that they were educated made them suspect, and as 'class enemies' a high proportion had been eliminated in the initial Leninist terror. On the other hand they inherited a tradition of copying, or indeed stealing, the methods of the more advanced Western societies. In order to continue this age-old practice, contact with the foreigners was inevitable but now very dangerous. Finally, an efficient manager cannot invariably know what lie his superiors may wish to hear. The fate of the manager of the Upper Donets Railway was far from unique. The very fact that a man had achieved a managerial situation, unless he were also so shrewd a politician as to anticipate the zig-zags of the 'ideological' scenic railway, made him automatically suspect. It was only with the invasion of Russia during the Second World War, and the acceptance of the Soviets as allies by London and Washington, that Soviet industrial and scientific espionage began to achieve any real success.

All superficial Soviet Russian or Comintern propaganda, whether in word or deed, whether of official inspiration or gullible repetition, was like all intelligence work merely a weapon at the service of the Russian Soviet Empire and of its aspirations to global power. And despite the zig-zags of that country's policy over the past half century and more, those aspirations have never been denied. While the policy has veered, internally and externally, between Lenin's class slaughter and his New Economic Policy, between Stalin's massacre of the peasantry and the wartime acceptance of their religion, between alliances with Weimar Germany, isolationism, alliance with Nazi Germany, then with Britain and America, with and against China, this one propaganda theme has remained unaltered and seldom unsung. From Czarist days there was inherited, among much else, the farcical idea that there had been two Romes and that Moscow would be the third and last. The Roman legions, the diplomatic and military skills of the Byzantines, these were now to be reinforced by the Marxist doctrine of world revolution. All Soviet propaganda, all that vast element of global intelligence, with its lies and its so frequently successful deceptions, had this end in view. Little attempt was ever made to conceal this simple-minded ambition, but only to disguise it, abroad, in the simplicities of economic egalitarianism. It had, nevertheless, great appeal to those who yet regarded themselves as democrats as well as to those who were motivated by envy, or by guilt, or sometimes in the case of many middle-class intellectuals by both. Apparently, and despite all that has happened, this appeal still exists.

Men with practical knowledge of what power politics are all about were less easily convinced than liberal writers brought up on Shelley, Morris and Wilde. As early as 10 August 1920 Woodrow Wilson had approved, paragraph by paragraph, a communication from the Secretary of State, Bainbridge Colby, to the Italian ambassador. The abbreviated quotation is from Herbert Hoover and it is the clearest indication of the American government's attitude not only at that time but for several years to come.

[The] Bolsheviki . . . an inconsiderable minority of the people, by force and cunning seized the powers and machinery of government and have continued to use them with savage oppression to maintain themselves in power . . .

It is not possible for the Government of the United States to recognize the present rulers of Russia . . . This conviction . . . rest[s] upon . . . facts, which none dispute . . . that the existing regime in Russia is based upon the negation of every principle of honour and good faith, and every usage and convention, underlying the . . . structure of international law . . . The responsible leaders of the regime have frequently and openly boasted that they are willing to sign agreements and undertakings with foreign Powers while not having the slightest intention of observing such undertakings . . . They have not only avowed this as a doctrine, but have exemplified it in practice . . . Responsible spokesmen of this Power . . . have declared . . . that the very existence of Bolshevism in Russia . . . must . . . depend upon . . . revolutions in all other great civilized nations, including the United States, which . . . overthrow . . . their governments and set up Bolshevist rule in their stead . . .

. . . the Bolshevist Government [has] . . . extensive international ramifications through the Third Internationale . . . which is heavily subsidized by the Bolshevist Government . . . [and has] for its openly avowed aim the promotion of Bolshevist revolutions throughout the world . . . There is no room for reasonable doubt that such agents would receive the support and protection of any diplomatic agencies the Bolsheviki might have in other countries. Inevitably, therefore, the diplomatic service of the Bolshevist Government would become a channel for intrigues and the propaganda of revolt . . .

. . . There can be no mutual confidence . . . if pledges are to be given and agreements made with a cynical repudiation of their obligations already in the mind of one of the parties. We cannot recognize . . . the agents of a government which is determined and bound to conspire against our institutions; whose diplomats will be the agitators of dangerous revolt; whose spokesmen say that they sign agreements with no intention of keeping them . . .[9]

And this overt political activity produced an inevitable reaction among politicians in the West. The Great Red Scare in the United States effectively castrated the Comintern in that country. Efforts to ascribe this to induced hysteria were ineffective in a country well aware of its own democracy. Soviet intelligence tried to blow up the Sacco–Vanzetti trial into a major crisis, a latter-day Dreyfus affair. A lot of hot air was created, particularly in

Europe, but the American working class was not interested, despite the obvious inefficiency of the American judicial system in dealing with this complex case.* A repetition in the Rosenberg case, a quarter of a century later, was equally ineffective and led to quite a strong reaction that has gone down in history as 'McCarthyism'.

In Britain the anti-Socialists were able to win an election on a forgery, the Zinoviev Letter, which was believed by the public to be a Soviet instruction to the British Labour Party.

In Italy the Socialist Benito Mussolini turned his country against Soviet Communism, and violently.

The Germans never quite accepted Marxism, and in extreme crisis preferred their national version of Socialism to the Russian model.

In France a strong Communist Party tried to gain power through the back-door of a Popular Front, but failed.

In Spain the Communists fought two wars simultaneously and lost them both.

In fact no country has ever deliberately gone Communist, on the Soviet model, without the presence of the Red Army and under the most dire compulsion.

Thus it may be said that nowhere has that aspect of Russian intelligence which may be called propaganda succeeded in causing any but minimal damages to any of its enemies abroad save the Social Democrats. Since in fact the prime enemy is democracy this is hardly surprising.

The essentially defensive nature of Russian intelligence, before and for a generation after the Revolution, was externally self-defeating. If the endless trumpetings about world revolution and so forth only served to alert foreign intelligence services, attempts at technological improvement were likewise frustrated by Soviet policy. Had the Russian educated, managerial and administrative class not been eliminated twice – first by Lenin and again by Stalin, in the '30s – it seems probable that Russia would in its own fashion have produced the brains and talents that were needed, that already were active, to achieve at least a measure of parity

* The 'liberal' assumption that Sacco and Vanzetti were executed innocents has been adequately refuted. See Manes Sperber, *The Achilles Heel*, Andre Deutsch, London, 1959.

in material achievement with America, Japan, Germany and the other so-called developed countries. But the head was lopped, at least twice. Political toadies replaced managerial experts, wrote lies about their failures to produce, were in due course and quite properly, according to Soviet morality, shot. Their survivors and successors usually suffered the same fate. If, therefore, the Soviet Union were not to become a permanent economic morass, it was necessary to rely on the feared and hated foreigners. The foreigners obliged.

The basic problem that faced this Soviet society, the rulers of which were bent on world conquest, was first of all how to make 'things' and then how to make them work. The brutal elimination of those men who were competent to do either the one or the other, based upon an almost Byzantine scrutiny (*theology*) of subtle and shifting interpretations of minute nuances that had become part of orthodox Marxism–Leninism, led to an enormous reliance upon the foreigner, who was of course himself destined for liquidation as soon as possible, not merely because he was not a Russian but also because, by reason of his superior knowledge, he was a class enemy too.

The knowledge that the Russians required from their enemies may be roughly subdivided into two kinds, industrial and military, though these of course always overlap. The military (including air and naval) will be dealt with principally in the next chapter. The industrial can be quite rapidly dismissed in this.

Technological espionage abroad was an almost total failure, for three reasons. By their propaganda the Russians, at least until 1941, had made themselves highly suspect among those in the West who might have helped them. Secondly such elements within the Okhrana who had worked in this field had been almost entirely eliminated, usually by death, and their Communist replacements were either incapable or, if they were not stupid, saw the dangers inherent in their jobs, more so in Russia than abroad. Finally all such intelligence was centralized, at times to a ridiculous extent, in Moscow, where a vast complex of 'classified' intelligence was established at the *Institut Nauchnoi Informatsii*, or Institute of Scientific Information, just outside the city, where it still exists and constantly grows. Much of this huge amount of material was not classified at all in its countries of origin, was indeed easily available at book stalls, but as soon as it reached Moscow it became 'secret'. And because of the inefficiency of the men who were supposed to process and distribute this intelligence, it often accumulated unused. To give but one example, Leninist–Stalinist Russia never succeeded in producing an aeroplane, civilian or military, of any value, though they produced scores of thousands that were of no value. (It is a general estimate that in June 1941, the Red Air Force outnumbered the Luftwaffe by five to one. It was immediately almost wiped out and even when partly re-equipped with American and British-built planes played no part of any significance in the Second World War. This most certainly does not mean that the Russian aircraft industry and the Red Air Force have remained contemptible, though they may well be overrated through the usual propaganda methods.)

The importation of foreign experts was also in large measure shipwrecked on the uncharted reefs of Marxist–Leninist dogma and Russian xenophobia. Lenin, it is true, was highly cynical about, perhaps contemptuous of, both the ideology that bears his name and of the only nation that he had conquered. His New Economic Policy (March 1921) restored a little freedom to the individual trader, without whom recovery from the war, revolution and civil war would probably have been impossible. To the foreign capitalists, or at least to some of them, it seemed to show that Soviet Communism was not irreversible, in a word that there was still money to be made in Russia. Lenin would certainly have foreseen this appeal to doctrinaire, colonialist capitalism and both he and his successors did and do their best to exploit the Western free-enterprise ideology with ultimate aim the destruction of that ideology by any and all means. Thus it was American engineering experts who opened up the gold and other mines at Kolyma and elsewhere, later to be manned almost entirely by Russian slave labour. The British, French and Germans also hired out their expertise to their declared enemies, and the Soviets were most punctilious in paying their own financial debts to the foreigners, though disclaiming all responsibility for those of their predecessors in government.

However so great was the chaos in the centralized administration, that while one branch of government might wish desperately to use foreign brains, another regarded these foreigners, inevitably, as spies. Among the more spectacular of these failures by Soviet intelligence was the arrest, in 1933, of the British engineers sent to Russia by Metro-Vickers, the great armaments combine. Another, described by Alexander Weissberg who was one himself, was the treatment of Russian physicists.[10] With enormous difficulty, and relying almost entirely on foreigners or to a much lesser extent on Russians trained abroad, the Soviets were creating a competent group of physicists. Suddenly almost all these highly skilled men were arrested as spies and sent to work in the mines of Kolyma or as lumberjacks in the far north. Whether they were Communists, like Weissberg himself, was irrelevant. The foreigners were therefore spies. Thus was the almost totally defensive nature of Soviet intelligence, inherited from the Okhrana, self-defeating.

It went further. All Soviet citizens abroad were and are spies, simply because of their enforced contact with the dread foreigners. This perhaps explains why, at least until the 1940s, Soviet intelligence was so poor and the Soviet authorities so crassly ill-informed about the world which they would dominate.

Not that the Americans were much better at the game in the immediate post-First World War period. Yardley recounts, with some bitterness, how the reports of his skilled intelligence agents in Europe were ignored by President Wilson in favour of those obtained by Herbert Hoover's Relief and Reconstruction organization, men whose interest in intelligence was of course peripheral. Hoover confirms this. Wilson, at loggerheads with the Allies by early 1919, could seldom trust information given him by Lloyd George or Clemenceau. After his first sickness early in that year, he came also to distrust House and Lansing, who had been his closest advisers, while his relations with the United States government and the Congress rapidly deteriorated. It would hardly be an exaggeration to say that he went down to defeat, and death, in the dark.

Yardley's M.I.-8 was not immediately wound up, but it soon ceased to be recognized as an official organization. Paid now out of secret funds, and much reduced in strength, it was hidden away in New York. There it enjoyed its final, perhaps really its only, major triumph.

The Anglo-American–Japanese naval treaty of 1922 was the last major American effort to limit if not to prevent a Second World War. An agreement as to naval strength was to be reached which was intended to ensure a peace-keeping parity. The navies of the United States and of the British Empire were to be of equal strength, that of the Japanese to be either 60 or 70 per cent in relation to each of the two larger forces. Yardley, reading the Japanese cipher, was able to keep his government informed as to the exact instructions the Japanese delegates were receiving from Tokyo and how low they were allowed to go in limiting their naval strength. This knowledge was of course of the greatest value to the American negotiators. The intelligence victory did not, however, help much at Pearl Harbor, nineteen years later. On the other hand the fact that the Japanese accepted a 6:10 as opposed to a 7:10 ratio of strength (which they did not honour for long) may have contributed to their inability to build a larger navy in the 1930s and '40s, and thus have given the Americans a marginal supremacy at a most critical moment. Despite his extreme indiscretion in writing his book, Yardley may yet have served his country to which his dedication was transparently sincere.

After which, while Soviet intelligence assumed the posture of a dog biting its own tail, American intelligence simply faded away.

French intelligence was for years totally preoccupied with Germany and French imperial affairs, though in neither field does it seem to have influenced the successively fatuous governments of the Third Republic. The British, again for imperial reasons, watched Russia quite closely,[11] their own subject peoples, and of course the naval situation. The Japanese watched Asia and America. In fact the preparations for the Second World War got off – to a slow start at first – in the negotiations that were intended to terminate the First. The German situation will be dealt with in the next chapter.

Chapter Thirteen

The Rebirth of the German Intelligence Service

The failure of the negotiations and treaties at Versailles in the 1919–20 period is hardly surprising, unless the comparative success of the Congress of Vienna be regarded as normal. It was not normal. The allied signatories to that earlier peace treaty were of course far from unanimous in their morals and even less so in their national aspirations. They, too, had endured a war, of equal horror to that of 1914–18 and of five times its duration. They too, even such 'liberals' as Canning who was not there, desired something like a return to the *status quo ante* revolution and slaughter, and none more so than the leaders of a defeated France. They did not, however, envisage a new world, bound by huge, amorphic, abstract ideas. Talleyrand and Metternich, Wellington and the less spectacular representatives of Prussia, had at least a certain amount in common, a shared attitude to what they regarded as the natural order, to the Concert of Europe in which national aspirations played a major, but not ā suicidal and invariably dominant part. Little such community of interest existed in 1919, even within Europe, and what remained was largely battered to bits by the ideologies of the two soon-to-be-dominant, quasi-European powers, Soviet Russia and the United States of America.

The failure of Wilsonian morality, the obsessive though comprehensible preoccupation of the French with German *revanchisme*, the clear symptoms of declining British imperial might to be discerned equally in the City of London, the Royal Navy, and in Black-and-Tans rampaging through obscure Irish country towns, sporadic civil war in Germany and its threat in Italy: such was the world into which the Soviet Union sprang, armed but exhausted, generally feared and hated by its neighbours and, because of the massive atrocities committed in the name of 'liberty', by those further afield. It was the general wish, then, to bottle up the Soviets in Russia, to create a *cordon sanitaire* of anti-Communist states along her European border, above all to prevent her, or her agents of the Comintern, acquiring power in Germany – which was and for many years remained the prime Soviet objective.

Even the French, though, admitted that Germany must not be allowed to go Communist. This necessitated the retention by the German government of some measure of military power. The alternative was total German disarmament and total Allied occupation, as was attempted in very different circumstances in 1945. But since the Western leaders in 1919 did not wish to give the Bolsheviks a third of Germany, nor pay the expense of occupying the entire country for an indefinite period, a compromise was reached. The Germans were to be permitted defensive forces sufficient to put down internal revolution but not to defend their country against foreign, particularly French, attack. Indeed, in 1920 the 100,000-man army, the *Reichswehr*, smothered Communist attempts to seize power in Munich and elsewhere. And when the vast Red Army was defeated by the small Polish army in the summer of 1920, Germany was largely safeguarded against a Russian, though not against a Polish, invasion. Illegal German auxiliaries, the volunteer *Freikorps* sometimes called the Black Reichswehr, fought an irregular war, with tacit support from the Reichswehr proper, against the Poles, the Hungarians, and the irregulars of other newly created states. These gradually petered out. In effect by late in 1920 the geography of Europe was set for some fifteen years. The geographical changes since 1914 were far less drastic, and above all far less durable, than they appeared at the time. Precisely the contrary was true of power ratios and ideologies,* both those of recent birth and those in a state of gestation.

And as many realized, particularly among the more percipient members of the Soviet upper class, Germany must be the fulcrum or perhaps the cockpit. In the middle of the nineteenth century Karl Marx had begun his famous polemic with the statement that

* This writer dislikes that hackneyed word at least as much as the discriminating reader, who is reluctantly asked to accept it as an amalgam of ideas concerning such utterly diverse matters as political and economic administration, patriotism, religion, even sexual mores, among much else.

210

a spectre haunts Europe, the spectre of revolution: the memories of the Paris Terror (though this he did not add, for he disapproved of the Terror). From 1919 and for the better part of half a century at least it has been the spectre of counter-revolution, Stalinist, Hitlerian, call it what you wish, that has not merely haunted Europe but in very material form has almost destroyed that ancient, resilient continent, and may yet succeed in so doing before this century is out.

The Treaty of Versailles, which the Germans were compelled to sign while the blockade ticked away its hourly starvation death toll on 28 June 1919, must be counted among the least felicitous documents that any politicians representing victorious powers have ever thrust upon a defeated enemy. In their attempts to compensate for German numerical superiority, the French, with British agreement, handed over millions of Germans to the new states, intended to be French client states, of Poland, Czechoslovakia and so on, thus ensuring the instability and ultimate destruction of potentially stable countries. Schleswig-Holstein was given to the Danes, even Eupen-Malmédy to the Belgians. German-speaking Austria, shorn of its great empire, was forbidden for ever to amalgamate with the German Republic and one of Europe's very greatest capital cities was supposed to preside over a new country comparable in size to Switzerland but penniless and starving. The French strutted into Frankfurt and quarrelled with the British about Germany and the Middle East, after having driven America out of Europe. If a ghost ruled France, it was certainly not that of *Napoléon le Grand*, nor even of *Napoléon le Petit*, but perhaps that of some gibbering incarnation of a yet more conceited, incompetent and non-existent Bonaparte.

For that was not the sum of the folly. In the compromise to save Europe, and above all Germany, from Bolshevism, the German army was not liquidated. At Versailles the military adviser to the German Peace Commission was a certain General Hans von Seeckt, a staff officer of the greatest brilliance by any standards, German or foreign, who, as Field Marshal Mackensen's Chief of Staff, had more than any single man won the 1915 Eastern Campaign and hence the war against Imperial Russia. According to Sir John Wheeler-Bennett his was a military mind comparable to those of Roon, the great Moltke and Schlieffen. He was not just a soldier, Prussian monocle notwithstanding, but a man of great culture in literature and the arts who again according to Wheeler-Bennett, quoting two very different but equally shrewd men, King Ferdinand of Bulgaria and Count Bernstorff, 'alone among German Generals . . . had a clear and precise appreciation of the political aspects of the war.[1] It did not take Seeckt long to realize that the peace of 1919 was no peace but an armistice. Meanwhile he had to accept the terms laid down by the victors, and to rebuild the German army accordingly. If there was a Napoleonic figure (in smallness of stature too) at Versailles in 1919, it was he, not Pershing or Haig, or even Foch.

Deprived of all heavy weapons, tanks, military aircraft and any but the lightest of coastal naval vessels, the 100,000-man army was supposed to have no general staff at all. This order must have seemed grotesque to the staff officers of the victorious armies, since an army without a general staff is about as useful as a motor car without a steering wheel, but the German Great General Staff had been built up as one of the great dangers – which it was – and its assumption of near-total power in 1916 had made its destruction politically desirable in the popular press of London and Paris. It was abolished. It was replaced by something called the *Truppenamt* (literally: troops' office) attached in theory to the Defence Ministry. Just as the 100,000-man army contained the very cream of the volunteers from the huge old Imperial Army, so the Truppenamt was staffed by the very finest general staff officers available. It was soon enough headed by Seeckt himself. And the Socialist quasi-revolutionary government, welcomed and then rapidly humiliated by the Western Allies, knew that without the army it would be rapidly and immediately crushed between the Reds and the Reactionaries. Seeckt knew this too, but he also knew how narrow was his room for manoeuvre.

The pot boiled over when the Allies demanded of the German Socialist government that they hand over some eight hundred Germans for trial as war criminals, early in 1920. They also demanded that Erhardt's Marine Brigade, part of the Iron Division sporadically fighting the Poles, and consisting of extreme nationalists, be disbanded. The German government tried to oblige, but

212

in Germany counter-revolutionary sentiment was rising, and the eight hundred included almost all those men whom the Germans had been led to revere as war heroes. Captain Erhardt, a naval officer who might be described without too much inaccuracy as a proto-Nazi (Hitler was still unheard of, but the Marine Brigade wore swastikas on their steel helmets), did not disband but marched on Berlin and kicked out the government, which fled. When ordered to open fire on the Erhardt Brigade, Seeckt refused; his men would not fire on their comrades, he said.

This was the so-called Kapp Putsch of 13 March 1920, technically led by a rather obscure civil servant named Wolfgang Kapp, a front man for more important forces still in a somewhat inchoate form. Seeckt refused to back him; and when the embattled government called a general strike and the soldiers in the provinces observed total neutrality, the Kapp Putsch collapsed within four days. Kapp had had powerful backers, inside and outside the army, but was short on administrative talent. His actions – he disappears from history – had only three achievements, one negligible, the other two not. He gave the word 'putsch' a universal significance, to define in modern terms a *coup de main* or takeover by force but without revolution. His putsch established that the German army was above sectional politics, purely the servant and therefore ultimately the master of an otherwise unarmed state. And finally, the spectre of counter-revolution had come to life in Germany, within less than three years of its counterpart being triumphant in Russia.

Nor was the position of the German High Command (which of course did not exist according to Versailles, and was officially called the *Heeresleitung* or 'Army Control', a euphemism which, together with Truppenamt, will hence forth be discarded in this book) as anodyne as Clemenceau would have wished. This was so in political, as well as military, terms from the very beginning.

In the sphere of international politics Seeckt was fully prepared to use Anglo-French and American fears of the Bolsheviks for German national purposes, though himself at least was opposed to the Bolsheviks as was any prominent Englishman, Frenchman or American. As early as 9 February 1920, in response to the Allied demand for the eight hundred alleged war criminals, Seeckt had called a staff conference, the contents of which were intended to be leaked. In the event of an Allied entry further into Germany to seize the eight hundred, the new Reichswehr was to withdraw eastwards, establish contact with Poles and Russians and, presumably after the installation of a Polish Communist government within the Russian Empire then being so rapidly reconstituted, to make a joint attack westwards. Thus was the horrid prospect of a Red Army on the Rhine given a little, but not much, plausibility.

The staff conference was from a military point of view an illogical anachronism, harking back to the 'interior railway lines' of the Schlieffen Plan and the Imperial German Army in all its might, while ignoring Trenchard's untried Bomber Command. From a political view it was of the greatest significance, foreshadowing much that was to come. How much it affected Allied strategy and policy towards Germany it is hard to say. Probably very little, since the Dutch refused to surrender the refugee Kaiser, the Americans had gone home, and the British were weakening in their hatred of the Hun. With the Russo-Polish War the whole fantasy faded away. The Germans dissolved their Freikorps, incorporating the best into the new Reichswehr, there to be 'above politics' after the Kapp Putsch, while many of the worst went to Bavaria, there to become the *Alte Frontkaempfer* or 'old front fighters' of the nascent German National Socialist Workers' Party, led by Adolf Hitler. By the time Hitler came to mount his unsuccessful putsch in 1923, he could no longer rely on the support of any, even insignificant, element of the army. Seeckt's Reichswehr had pulled on its kid gloves and pronounced itself above all squalid party politics, loyal only to itself, the Fatherland and to that last symbol of its pristine loyalties, that titanic if wooden relic of Imperial Germany and its class structure, Field Marshal von Hindenburg.

Since German secret intelligence had been run by a branch of the old General Staff, it was of course dissolved. Its new name was the Abwehr, which simply means 'defence', and it got off to a very shaky start in 1919. Its first head was a certain Winiker, or such was the name he used. Like Dzerdzinski, he was a Pole, but unlike his compatriot in Moscow he also worked for the new Polish government. He alleged, probably incorrectly, that he had a teaching doctorate from the Berlin Technological High School.

He had worked, as a civilian it seems, in the cryptanalytical section of Abteilung IIIb. He called himself, perhaps correctly, Dr Winiker. His employment in the most sensitive centre of German intelligence, both during and after the war, was not likely to encourage any German general staff to rely on brilliant civilians. He quite rapidly vanished into Poland and the Abwehr was taken over by a more traditional type, a Major Gempp, late of Abteilung IIIb and, in those days before defeat, a Major General. Such was the new Reichswehr, even in its intelligence apparatus.

Abwehr was indeed a term of considerable technical subtlety. No aspect of any foreign general staff is more disliked by others than its secret intelligence service. In the conditions prevailing in the 1920s, with Seeckt, his staff and his commanding generals using every peaceful means to distort the Treaty of Versailles and re-create the German army, the Abwehr was indeed essentially defensive, for Germany was heavily infiltrated by French, Polish, Russian and to a lesser extent British and other spies. The creation of the 100,000-man Reichswehr was legal; much else was not. It was for the protection of that which was *not* that the Abwehr was created. Yet even this was not all. Cryptanalysis, and hence cipher-breaking as well as cipher-creation, had been resumed, as early as 1919, under Winiker. Such an activity can hardly be described as 'defensive', at least not from the point of view of the Versailles French. But the fact that Winiker was involved at this very early stage may have had some future importance.

Seeckt's Reichswehr was to be one hundred per cent, or indeed one hundred plus, professional: internally devoid of party commitments, externally as solid as a phalanx of interlocked shields. Its generals, staff and officer corps were poorly paid in money, abundantly so in power, pride, arrogance and national respect. They could no longer serve the Kaiser, but no more did they serve the populist parties, whether the Communists or (later) the Nazis. They, and this includes privates as well as generals, were professionals, professional soldiers. As the world was to discover they have, as such, seldom been equalled. And they learned from the past, even as their Prussian ancestors had done after the disaster of Jena.

So far as the Abwehr was concerned, this meant learning the

lessons of the last war, and quickly. Neither Abteilung IIIb (Gempp) nor of course Winiker was what Seeckt required. The naval captain Patzig therefore succeeded Gempp, to deprive the Abwehr of a pure military bias, and when he turned out to be over-inclined politically, he was replaced in 1935 by another but most unusual naval officer, Admiral Canaris. Much has been written about this enigmatic figure but before discussing his character (the Nazis murdered him in 1945) it might be as well to see what Seeckt's Reichswehr was, in fact, doing in the 1920s. What it was doing was above all collaboration with the Red Army.

Ostensibly its intelligence service was devoted to precisely what its name implied, defence, in the first instance against the internal political enemies of the German Republic, whether Communists, Monarchists or Populist Anti-democrats, in the second against foreign, and particularly French or Polish, espionage agencies active inside Germany. This was a role for which the heirs of IIIb and its traditions were scarcely well cast. Once Winiker was gone, and perhaps even before, the Abwehr was the nucleus of a future German secret intelligence service to serve the future German armed forces in a future war. It was above politics in so far as it refused to identify with any party-political group. This did not prevent the Abwehr from keeping the High Command informed about political developments within Germany. Indeed, Adolf Hitler was first sent to a meeting of the German Workers' Party in Munich as an army spy, on army orders, though these like his part-time pay came from the Munich military and not from the embryonic Abwehr.

Thus there arose another, hereditary paradox. The heirs of Abteilung IIIb were supposed to be engaged in internal counter-espionage, not at all their role; though with Karl Radek and his international Communist apparatus firmly and openly ensconced in Berlin the role was perhaps not all that remote from a subsidiary one of Nicolai's people. Meanwhile the Cheka, heirs to the Okhrana, were supposed to serve a political party but in fact had two masters, the Kremlin and the Comintern, the interests of which were not always identical. Thus Radek was also suspect in Russia, which eventually cost him his neck. In the 1920s, though, he rode high in Moscow and above all in Berlin. Russo-German intelligence was playing a complicated, and not altogether inelegant, game, with a morality quotient of zero.

The place is Rapallo, the date 16 April 1922, but of course all the preliminary arrangements had been made elsewhere and at an earlier date. The Versailles powers, the victors among whom now included Fascist Italy, were still attempting to salvage something from the wreckage of Versailles. Yet another European economic conference – heaven knows how many of these international, useless, over-publicized and extremely expensive jamborees have taken place since 1918 – was convened at Genoa. The two pariahs of Europe, Germany and Russia, were invited. Their delegates repaired to Rapallo, leaving the economists to their junkets of words, statistics, folly and cuttlefish in Genoa, and got down to business. The Germans recognized the Soviet Union as a great power (the Vatican, rapidly followed by Mussolini's government, also did this within a matter of weeks), and the Republic of Germany established full diplomatic and commercial relations with the government of the U.S.S.R.

F. E. Smith, later created Lord Birkenhead, once advocated 'enlightened self-interest' as the principal guideline of national policy. What was agreed, or rather what was formally signed, at Rapallo was clearly a matter of mutual self-interest to Russia and Germany, and no doubt appeared 'enlightened' to the signatories, as it did to 'liberals' like J. M. Keynes.* But behind this European attempt, both at Genoa and at Rapallo, to re-create what President Harding in America was to call 'normalcy' there were other forces at work, of lesser enlightenment.

The Russians needed, as usual, Western technological expertise. The new German army had the French upon its neck. The commercial deal between the German and Russian governments was perfectly cynical. The Germans would train the decrepit Red Army; the Russians would give the Reichswehr facilities for tank and aircraft production and practice denied them in their own country; each would spy upon the other, since each intended eventually to defeat the other. Colonel Nicolai disappeared from

* Keynes had been the principal British economic adviser during the Versailles conference. His most important book, *The Economic Consequences of the Peace*, had appeared as early as 1919. Its influence remained enormous, and for half a century.

the German public scene. We glimpse him in what was certainly a key position, arranging this most sinister deal. He reappears, in a flickering light, later. Meanwhile, for the Reichswehr Russia became the great training area, for the Red Army German technology became the basis. Stalingrad was a victory of Western technological skill over numerically inferior German manpower, whereas the prototypes of the planes that destroyed the Red Air Force a year earlier had been built, and the crews who became instructors trained, in Russian factories and on Russian bases. By 1942, most of the Russian officers had been executed by Stalin as 'spies'. A few of their German counterparts suffered a similar fate; more survived, in Russian captivity, to work for their enemy-ally during and after the Second World War. And by the laws of geography they, or their heirs, have not seen the last of one another in peace or war, or in intelligence.

Seeckt's Reichswehr based its traditions, as best it could, on the old Imperial Army, but technically and tactically it had the immense advantage of starting afresh. Unlike the staffs of the victorious armies, or even of the decrepit Red Army, it looked back on defeat. It had won, by 1922, its internal victory, but only just. Externally the whole military dogma had to be re-examined in the light of the next war. Little was done to alter naval tactics or strategy, save that the U-boat weapon was slowly improved, the 'High Seas Fleet' concept more or less abandoned. In the air, a future Luftwaffe was envisaged as a supporting force to aid a mechanized and fast-moving army, or at least an armoured spearhead that would break the trench warfare strategy that had failed. However, intelligence was not, under Patzig and Canaris, to be merely a branch of the General Staff. It was to have extreme technical expertise and this to be used at the highest level.

A very thorough re-examination of secret intelligence was carried out in Germany in the early 1920s. Germany was of course extremely weak, though far from powerless, and as already stated it is to the weak rather than to the strong that intelligence is a particularly valuable weapon or technique. The new German army, created to fight and of course to win the next war, was not to reproduce the failures of its predecessors. The whole question of intelligence and counter-intelligence was therefore examined with the utmost thoroughness by a handful of professionals under

218

what were supposed to be conditions appropriate to a laboratory. Captain Patzig was the man responsible; Admiral Canaris took over an intelligence apparatus in being. As naval officers both men were unimpressed by Abteilung IIIb of the old Great General Staff, but they were extremely interested in technical matters rather than traditional methods. Espionage based on sexuality was, for example, abandoned almost entirely, on the grounds that it was unreliable: the blonde might, after all, fall in love with the foreign diplomat or soldier. This ancient form of espionage, and even its male equivalent, remained in existence, but principally as cover. The only spies of real interest were those in comparatively high places who had already achieved security clearance from the real or potential enemy. By the mid-1930s the Soviets were employing, and blackmailing, such men. The Germans learned a little, though not much, from such sources, for the Weimar or Nazi ideology was of far more limited appeal to educated foreigners likely to hold high office than was that of the Comintern.

In effect the whole 'business' of secret intelligence needed to be revised as drastically as did the tactics that had developed in the First World War, and it was of course the defeated powers, Russia and Germany, which realized this before the victors.

Even before Stimson had dissolved Yardley's deciphering apparatus, Yardley had realized how hopeless it was to persuade the United States government that security was essential to his country's survival. He had also seen that cipher security, and of course cipher-breaking, were the key. I quote from his book; the jaunty style is suited to the old *Saturday Evening Post*, the content is of the greatest international importance. He does not name the senior State Department official. The conversation must have taken place in 1926 or perhaps 1927.

'Yardley,' he finally began, 'I have wondered for a long time whether our own codes are safe.' Another long pause. 'It may be possible for me to get copies of some of our coded messages, so that your office can see whether you can decipher them.' He would not, of course, tell me that there was a report that the Mexican Government had already broken the code.

'I should be very glad to look at them, but that isn't necessary.'

'Why not?'

'I am familiar with the Department's codes. I can give you my opinion without your sending me the coded telegrams for analysis.'

He looked at me for a long time. 'What do you know about our codes?'

'I know all there is to know.' And I went on to describe their construction and all the intimate details of the Department's secret means of communication.

'How do you know these things?' he asked.

'Well,' I said, smiling inwardly, 'cryptography is my business. Does it seem odd to you that I take an interest in not only the codes of foreign governments, but also in those of our own?'

'You mean that State Department employees discuss these matters with you?'

I said nothing, while he eyed me in silence.

At last he said, 'Suppose you give me a memorandum showing how you could solve our codes.'

I dreaded this request, for any recommendation I would make would require the Department to revolutionize its entire system of secret communication, and as everyone knows, departmental procedure is too cumbersome to permit revolutionary changes.

'I don't think it would do any good,' I replied.

'Why not?'

'Well, the question of secret codes goes deeper than you imagine. It isn't a question of a slight change. You see, during recent years cryptography has grown into a definite science. And during this growth the Department of State has remained stationary. As you are aware, no one in the Department has had any experience, and therefore no one can know anything about the science of cryptography. Its position is hopeless, and I do not see how I can help any.'

'Why not?'

'You oblige me to be frank.'

'Go on.'

'Well, to begin with, let us see who is responsible for the Department of State codes. What does he know about the

220

subject? Nothing. Why was he appointed to his present position? Because he is an experienced cryptographer? No. He was appointed because he is an expert on archives and indices. The construction of codes and ciphers is only incidental to his present position.

'You might point out that since he was appointed he has compiled a number of codes. That is true. But one learns nothing about cryptography by compiling codes. One learns by tearing them apart. Now if you will call him in here he will tell you that he couldn't decipher the simplest types of codes and ciphers. He doesn't pretend – at least not to me – that he understands the science of cryptography. How could he? He has had no opportunity for experience. This is not his fault. It is the fault of the Department of State. Though you employ experts for every other conceivable subject, you leave the very basis of successful diplomacy, which is safe communication, in the hands of an amateur cryptographer.

'You and I have been closely allied in the game of solution of government codes. It is needless to point out to you that the Great Powers all maintain staffs of experienced cryptographers to solve our, as well as other governments', codes. Isn't it a rather pitiful spectacle to see the Department of State require an amateur cryptographer to compile codes and ciphers that will be torn apart by the best cipher brains in the world?'

'That is exactly why I am asking your advice,' he interrupted.

'If the Department of State expects to keep up with the growing science of cryptography, it will require more than my advice,' I replied. 'Now you ask for a memorandum that will point out just how I would go about solving your diplomatic codes. To what purpose? The memorandum reaches the employee who compiles your codes, and he says, "Oh, yes, I see how you do it now. I'll make a code that doesn't have this weakness." But he doesn't see at all. He only knows how this particular problem is solved. No amount of exposition can ever make him realize, simply because he is not a professional cryptographer, that the skilled cipher expert solves a problem by the first weakness he discovers. This doesn't mean that there are no other weaknesses in the system, and it does not mean that his solution is the most rapid one.

'Now he corrects this weakness, and what then? The skilled cryptographer searches for another. To illustrate, I was the first person in the United States to write an exposition on the solution of our own diplomatic codes. What did the Department do? Just what I have already said. It made a few improvements, corrected the weakness by which I solved these codes, but your basic method of communication is the same as it was when I was a youngster in the Code Room.'

He was intensely interested and stared at me for a while, then said:

'Instead of preparing a memorandum outlining how you would solve our codes, why don't you prepare one telling us what changes we should make?'

I smiled at this, for I knew the situation hopeless.

'I can't do it. I would not care to have the job of trying to make your present methods indecipherable. And if I can't do it, I don't see how an amateur can. As a matter of fact the Department is so far behind in the science of cryptography that its position is hopeless. Your codes, your point of view, belong to the sixteenth century.'

'Sixteenth-century codes!'

'Yes. You have made a few improvements, but basically the codes in use are the same as those of the sixteenth century. Aside from this, your codes are just as cumbersome, just as antiquated as the sixteenth-century methods of communication. Though we now have instantaneous communication by telegraph and telephone, and the Department takes advantage of these, you still require your code clerks to fumble around for hours encoding and decoding dispatches when you should have not only instantaneous transmission, but also instantaneous encipherment and decipherment. Aside from this, the State Department should have an indecipherable means of communication.'

'Aren't any codes indecipherable?'

'No. Not as the Department understands a code or cipher. *But there is one indecipherable means of communication.* To adopt such a system, however, the Department would be obliged to discard all its antiquated ideas. The means I refer to revolutionizes communications. You could discharge ninety per cent of your code clerks; and your telegrams would be absolutely indecipherable.'

'You mean a cipher machine?'

'Yes, but not the type of machine you have in mind. During the war the American Telephone and Telegraph Company invented a machine that automatically enciphered and transmitted a message over the wire by merely striking the letters of the message on a typewriter keyboard, while the machine at the other end of the wire automatically deciphered the message and at the same instant typed it. Had the enemy at any point between these two machines tapped the wire he would have intercepted nothing but a jumble of letters. In cases where instantaneous transmission and deciphered was not practicable the operator first enciphered the message by striking the letters on the keyboard and turned the resultant cipher message over to the cable company. When the cipher telegram reached the addressee, he adjusted his machine, struck the cipher letters on the keyboard, and the original telegram appeared before him.

'This machine filled every requirement of simplicity of operation, speed and accuracy. *But it was not indecipherable.*

'There have been many cipher machines invented. One in particular was so ingeniously contrived that there is no repetition for four billion letters. Or at least that is what the inventor thinks; for you see, there again you have the amateur attempting to escape repetitions by a series of discs, tapes, electric impulses, etc. These machines fill your needs in simplicity, speed and accuracy, and if you adopted them, you could discharge ninety per cent of your code clerks, but all these machines are invented by people who haven't as yet grasped the fact that there is no method of avoiding repetitions. To the eye these machines, as well as innumerable other ciphers and types of codes, do escape repetitions, but mathematical formulae will reveal them.'

'If this is true, and I am ready to admit anything you tell me, how is it possible to construct any practicable means of secret communication that is indecipherable?'

'There is no way as long as the attempt is made to avoid repetitions. *The only indecipherable cipher is one in which there*

223

are no repetitions to conceal. Therefore no need to attempt to escape them.'

'There is such a method?'

'Yes.'

'It can be made practicable by some such machine as the American Telephone and Telegraph machine that you described?'

'Yes, though for small offices the machine need be no larger than a typewriter. If and when the Government of the United States adopts such a system, and not until then, may they have absolute certainty that their messages will never be read by a cryptographer. Sooner or later all governments, all wireless companies, will adopt some such system. And when they do, cryptography, as a profession, will die.

'I hope you now understand why I prefer not to write a memorandum for your Code Bureau. Even with all my experience, I wouldn't know how to go about compiling an indecipherable code or cipher along the conventional lines. There is only one indecipherable means of communication, and its adoption would require the Department to revolutionize its antiquated methods. I'm afraid there is nothing that either you or I can do about it.

'What I have said might have seemed disrespectful to the Department, but I'm sure you appreciate my position. I am not a State Department employee and feel free to say what I believe.'

He looked worried.

'I fully understand your position,' he interrupted, 'and I am grateful for what you have said. This matter must be given serious consideration, but you know as well as I how slowly the Department acts.'

I agreed with this and the conference ended. I rather regretted having gone off on such a tangent, for the situation I knew was hopeless.

Nothing less than an international scandal would wake up the Government to the fact that the very basis of all successful diplomacy is safe and secret lines of communication. But my whole life had been devoted to destruction. I should like to leave a monument to constructive cryptography.

224

As I walked through the wide high corridors on my way to the entrance, I mused how proud one might be to leave to the United States Government a method of communication that would insure the secrecy of her dispatches throughout the ages. Aside from this, of course, was professional pride. Then, too, it would be fun to laugh at foreign cryptographers as in my mind I saw them puzzling over our secret telegrams striving in vain for a solution.

But why dream? After all, weren't all diplomatic representatives just funny little characters, on a stage, whispering, whispering, then yelling their secrets to the heavens as they put them on the cables![2]

In fact the 'defensive' little German army, with its technical expertise, had 'invented' precisely the machine to which Yardley referred, and of which it seems improbable that he had any direct knowledge. It was called the Enigma Machine. Its failure changed the history of this century.

Chapter Fourteen

Past, Present and Future Enemies

While Mr Yardley was writing his angry report in the mid-twenties, America's two future, major enemies were in fact working intensively on the creation of machines very similar to the one he had envisaged. The Germans were building the Enigma Machine and the Japanese, quite separately, what came to be called in America the Purple Machine. It is just possible, but highly improbable, that Herbert Yardley knew of these inventions: simple deduction by an experienced intelligence officer would have led him to his conclusions that such machines were then inevitable. There is no reason to believe that competent authorities in the United States, Great Britain or France were interested in any basic change to what was then believed to be their absolutely secure cipher mechanism; having quite recently won the Great War, they were satisfied with their methods, nor did they foresee a Second Great War.

The attitude within the allegedly non-existent German General Staff, and encouraged by its chief, von Seeckt, was very different. Germany, that great power, had lost the Great War. The question that was asked in Berlin, but far less so in London, Washington or Paris was: why? And this in turn led to two far more important questions: first of all, how had the war been lost and how could such a defeat be avoided in another? This entailed a most detailed examination of tactical and technical matters. The first of these are only marginally of concern to the subject of this book, though the development and use of German tank and tactical air power in close support won the *Wehrmacht* its great *Blitzkrieg* victories of 1939–42. The German naval technicians likewise studied with the greatest attention the lessons of the U-boat warfare that only just failed them in 1917–18. The German armed forces were, of course, limited drastically by the Versailles Treaty – submarine, tanks and military aircraft being 'illegal' –

226

and this is yet another example of the importance which must inevitably be attached to brains when brawn is of limited availability.

The Reichswehr in fact fulfilled a dual function. It was to be, within its limited scope and apparent observation of the Treaty obligations, as effective a fighting force as possible. It was also to provide the cadres for a future and vastly expanded Wehrmacht with which to reverse the defeat of 1918. The victorious Allies may well have hoped that this new German army would be the equivalent of those, say, of Denmark or Holland. Such, however, was not at all the intention of the greatly reduced German officer corps. Some of its less intelligent members may have accepted, and some of the more intelligent may for politico-military reasons of morale have pretended to accept the 'undefeated in the field' myth; the men in charge knew that the next German army, while preserving the traditions of the last, must be technically far its superior. And one field in which this applied was secret intelligence, above all cipher intelligence and counter-intelligence. Although the British and French remained remarkably secretive, it did not take the German post-war analysts long to realize that they had been outwitted by Room 40 and by its French military equivalent. They therefore invented the Enigma Machine, attempted to perfect their espionage apparatus (particularly in the Soviet Union where they had more or less a free hand so far as the Western powers were concerned), and set about breaking the somewhat obsolescent British and French security systems.

The position of the Japanese was similar. Though theoretically among the victors, their participation in the Great War had been limited, and they felt, not unjustly, that they had been deprived of victory's fruits. In their case this meant the domination of East Asia, and great naval power in the western Pacific. The former was stultified by Western, particularly American, domination in decrepit China, the latter by the limitations imposed upon the Japanese Imperial Navy in the treaty of 1921. Only in eastern Siberia did the Japanese have, again with tacit Western approval, a more or less free hand against the Soviet Union. Therefore the Japanese, too, soon decided to ignore in clandestine fashion the agreements of the Naval Treaty, and to prepare technically against another war. These measures involved not only air strength, in their case perfectly legitimate, but also a restructuring of their secret intelligence apparatus. Since for obvious reasons of physiognomy Japanese espionage was largely limited to Asia and to maritime matters, they too concentrated on a supposedly foolproof encipherment and decipherment system. There is no evidence that during this period there was any collusion, save perhaps in espionage matters concerning the Soviet Union, between Germany and Japan, yet the Japanese Purple Machine was not unlike the German Enigma Machine, though in some respects more vulnerable.

The essence of these machines was much as Yardley had predicted. A form of typewriter enciphered a message; a machine at the other end deciphered it; and a mechanism at both ends could change the cipher used either at fixed regular or irregular times or whenever so desired, provided of course that the recipient was informed. Without the physical possession of such a machine by the enemy or potential enemy, this form of conveying secret intelligence as well as operational orders did indeed appear to be both quick and foolproof. It is not intended here to describe in any detail the mechanism of these machines. They are, in any event, quite out of date, largely due to the subsequent invention of high-speed computers, but for those interested in such matters the reader is referred to David Kahn[1] and to *The Ultra Secret* by F. W. Winterbotham.[2]

This matter of cipher-breaking was, and is, a most secret business. Those of us who were engaged in it during the Second World War swore a sort of oath never to divulge what had been done, nor how. The code word for the operation was 'Ultra Top Secret', the central place of activity a rather dreary provincial English town named Bletchley. Some of us made this promise personally to Group Captain Winterbotham; neither the word 'Ultra' nor the name of Bletchley was ever to be mentioned in our lifetimes. Although there is no Official Secrets Act in force in the United States, and despite a Congressional investigation in 1946 into the Japanese attack on Pearl Harbor which already revealed too much, the Americans have remained remarkably reticent. So indeed had the British, until the publication of Group Captain Winterbotham's book in 1974. This took place against the wishes of the British security services, which were overruled by the Prime Minister, Mr (later Sir) Harold Wilson, who decided that the serving of a D-notice (a preliminary to a prosecution under the Official Secrets Act) was not warranted in the circumstances. Many former, and presumably some active, intelligence officers question this decision. It is therefore possible for me to write something about the subject, though not using personal knowledge. Group Captain Winterbotham's statement, doubtless accepted by Mr Wilson, is that the whole subject is by now totally out of date, but this is only in part true. And the law by which British governmental files are allegedly 'open' after thirty years is one that does not apply to certain sensitive matters which happened far longer ago, as many a research historian can testify.

First of all, how did we get the Purple and Enigma Machines? In the case of the Japanese one, the story is almost but not quite incredible. When, in the mid-thirties, the Americans decided that it was not so ungentlemanly to read other people's mail, a mass of filed but undeciphered Japanese messages was collated by experts. They then proceeded to work *backwards* and to *build* a Purple Machine in Washington. Such a feat of expertise is, to this writer, almost incomprehensible. Nor need it necessarily be the truth. Nonetheless, by 1940, the Americans were reading at least some of the Japanese ciphers. The Japanese may have been aware of this, for the great fleet that sailed towards the Aleutians before turning south to destroy the U.S. fleet at Pearl Harbor kept radio silence. From then on, however, American intelligence improved greatly, in large measure thanks to British advice, and the decisive battle of the Pacific war, Midway in 1942, was won not merely by the extreme valour of the sailors and aviators but also by the superiority of American naval intelligence over that of the enemy, and this in turn was due not only to air reconnaissance but above all to cipher-breaking. In an ocean the size of the Pacific you can hardly hope to find the enemy's ships unless you have some previous ideas where they are, whither and whence they are headed. Subsequent American victories followed the same pattern.

How the German Enigma Machine was obtained is an even more complicated matter, since several versions have been given. It seems that at least one was taken from a sunken U-boat, but this cannot have been before the outbreak of war. Another story is that the Poles captured one in the brief campaign of September 1939 and transported it to the West. Since the Poles captured virtually no German equipment in their retreat and defeat, and had only the most limited means for transferring anything to the West, this would seem improbable. A third explanation is that the Germans employed Polish labour in their pre-war eastern factories, that one such man realized the nature of what was being built, memorized the parts, and passed the information to the Polish government or to the French, presumably through the Polish authorities. This, too, seems an implausible tale.* In any event it does appear that the French possessed the Enigma Machine quite some time before the outbreak of the Second World War, and certainly before their own defeat in 1940.

Until the collapse of the western Front, Franco-British land intelligence was largely controlled by the French, particularly at the *Front Nord-Est* which was facing, together with part of the British Expeditionary Force, the coming German offensive. It was remarkably inefficient. The total German order of battle was estimated in March of 1940 at some ninety divisions, whereas German documents captured two months later revealed that it had then consisted of 130 (including two S.S. divisions), a truly remarkable discrepancy. The attack through the Ardennes was deemed topographically impossible and therefore no serious counter-measures were prepared. Nor does the revived Schlieffen Plan of an attack through Holland and Belgium seem to have been expected: at least no effective plans were in existence to counter this. The historical outcome of this gross failure in intelligence, and hence of operational preparations, is only too well known.

That the French had the Enigma Machine, and were therefore reading German top secret plans, is attested by Gustave Bertrand,[3] who was personally involved. That little of it was used at higher levels is obvious. This is a subject which will be dealt with later.

* Yet another version, and from a generally reliable source, is given in *A Man Called Intrepid*, Macmillan, London, 1976, published since the above was written. If this version be true, then others are not. Alternatively, of course, the British intelligence apparatus may have obtained more than one Enigma Machine from various sources. How they got it is not really relevant: the fact that they did get it most certainly is.

The presence of a Naval Intelligence officer at Bletchley, in April 1940, indicates that the Royal Navy were at least partly informed. It must be said, to the credit of the French intelligence officers, that when their country was defeated they understood the value of Enigma, that they arranged the physical transportation of the machine or machines to Britain, and that they did not divulge this to the German conqueror. This, even more than the bravery of the Maquis, was probably France's greatest contribution to ultimate victory. For Ultra was, as will be shown, a war-winning technique, and the Germans' ignorance of this weapon's mere existence a major contribution to their defeat.

Meanwhile the Germans, in the pre-war years, had been far from idle in this field, particularly in its naval aspect. The British naval ciphers were more primitive than the newer German ones, but they were still not easy to crack. However, in 1935, when the Italians invaded Abyssinia, the British involved themselves in a quasi-naval operation intended to impose League of Nations sanctions on the Italian aggressor. No shots were fired, but a great deal of information was passed by British ships, both naval and mercantile, from ship to ship and from ship to shore. Since these communications were frequently carried out by inexperienced clerks, and since the volume of traffic was so great, it was not very difficult for the Italian intelligence service to crack the British naval cipher, which information they passed to their German allies, certainly after their declaration of war in the summer of 1940 and probably well before. In any event German intelligence had already infiltrated Italian intelligence and would have had little difficulty in obtaining these vital figures and methods. British naval intelligence, on the other hand, does not appear to have realized that its own security was breached much before it obtained Enigma from the French, or if it so realized it was careless and lackadaisical. The result was the destruction of many British ships and the loss of the naval battle for Norway in the spring of 1940. It must here be stressed that the entire British attitude towards secret intelligence was drastically changed once Winston Churchill became Prime Minister in May of 1940. Not only did he, both as an historian and as a former Lord of the Admiralty in the First War, realize the immense potential of the intelligence weapon, but a weak, exposed and solitary Britain had to rely very much on British brains. The situation was thus, in 1940, an almost exact equivalent to that which had prevailed in Weimar Germany twenty years earlier. The British response, however, was to be very different and far more sophisticated.

While the Americans were ineffectively reading some of the Japanese ciphers, the Japanese were certainly reading American naval ciphers and, perhaps via their German friends, other United States ciphers too. Thus a curious and perhaps unique situation arose in 1940-1, that all the belligerent or pre-belligerent powers save one knew a very great deal about the plans and dispositions of the other. The major exception was the Soviet Union.[4] The Soviet leaders were entirely taken aback when the Wehrmacht invaded their country in June of 1941, had taken no dispositions against this act of aggression, saw their air force destroyed within a matter of hours, and very nearly suffered total military defeat in their huge country within six months. Why?

In Communist and 'extreme left-wing' circles it has long been policy to blame all Soviet crimes and failures not on the dictatorship of Stalin but on Stalin personally. This is of course a gross exaggeration and an abnegation of responsibility. Stalin did not invent Bolshevik terrorism, though he approved and exacerbated it. Single-handed he could no more have run the evil system, which he inherited and passed on to his successors, than could Hitler have single-handedly run his own equivalent tyranny and murder apparatus. Yet Stalin has been blamed even for the total failure of Soviet intelligence to anticipate the Nazi attack. That he felt a considerable empathy for his fellow-tyrant was only a contributory factor. He and his advisers saw the crude logicality of the Nazi–Soviet alliance of 1939–41 – indeed Stalin had been aiming at just such an alliance for some three years before the Ribbentrop–Molotov Pact was signed – and once it was signed he and his fellows must have assumed that the Nazi leaders were equally logical. Their systems of government were both threatened so long as the concept of personal freedom to choose was permitted to exist anywhere in the world. The destruction of all democratic power everywhere was clearly of immediate, mutual benefit. Only then would the time come to decide where the centre of totalitarian power be located, perhaps by negotiation, perhaps by some version of what has come to be called polycentrism, per-

232

haps and most probably by war. But this was a distant problem.

Pragmatically the Soviet leaders were undoubtedly correct. However, Hitler was not much of a pragmatist, his ideology considerably less cynical than Stalin's. And we know from Whaley[5] that within a year of the signing of the Nazi–Soviet pact Hitler was beginning to plan the invasion of Russia. A captured document dated July 1940, obtained in a British commando raid on Vaagsö, Norway, revealed this intention of Hitler. The Nazi regime had a weakness for disseminating information unduly and to unnecessry recipients.* This vast operation escaped the attention of the enormous Soviet intelligence apparatus. Again one must ask the question: why?

The answer is moderately complex. No tyrant cares to be told that his preconceptions may be wrong, may even be disproved by the facts: indeed so to tell him may be excessively dangerous and nowhere more so than in Stalin's Soviet Union. The rigidity of Marxist–Leninist doctrine reinforced Stalin in his belief that any information emanating from Western sources was suspect, hostile and provocative. If such intelligence bore some evidence of factual truth, this was only inserted to mislead the Soviets and was further proof of the diabolical duplicity practised by the capitalist or religious enemy. Thus did the Soviet leadership ignore all warnings of the Nazi wrath to come when these emanated from Churchill, Roosevelt, the Pope, even from their double agent in Tokyo, Dr Richard Sorge. Sorge was ostensibly the Tokyo correspondent of the *Frankfurter Zeitung*, and was belived by the Ribbentrop organization to be a reliable source, which up to a point he was; but he was also an agent of the Soviet G.R.U., to whom he passed exact and accurate dates of Operation Barbarossa about a month before it began. He was arrested in October 1941 by the Japanese, and later beheaded. His grandfather had been Secretary-General to Karl Marx's *First International*, a fact which the Germans ignored.[6]

* The capture of the official truck belonging to the German 90th Light Division by the British in North Africa was of extreme importance in 1942. It contained a mass of information concerning German order of battle, of the greatest strategic importance. Operationally, *Ultra* was predominant as an intelligence source; strategically, the evaluation of captured documents was at least as important.

Secondly, since the October Revolution the Soviet Union had become increasingly backward in most technological fields. (This is explicable not only because of the massacre of the managerial class and later of the scientists, but also because such as remained were frightened, particularly during the Great Purge, of attracting attention by expertise, preferring to let all decisions be made by ill-educated bureaucrats in Moscow and the provincial capitals.) It would, in the 1930s, have been wellnigh impossible for the Soviets either to invent an Enigma Machine or to have broken German and Japanese ciphers. Nor were the British or, later, the Americans prepared to give the main source of their own secret intelligence to a government which might, once again, as speedily 'change the Party line' as it had done in 1936, 1939 and 1941. Therefore the intelligence which the Russians did receive was largely and inevitably supplied without true authentication. How this was in some measure overcome during the second half of the war will be mentioned later.

Thirdly, the vast and often conflicting nature of the Soviet espionage organizations led to confusion and inefficiency. There were more than three of these, but the most important were what was at one time called the N.K.V.D., direct heirs of the Okhrana and responsible for intelligence both at home and abroad (it is, or until recently was, called the K.G.B.); the second was the military intelligence service, to include the Red Navy and Air Force, and is, or at least until recently was, called the G.R.U.; the third was the somewhat looser Agitprop organization, controlled by the Comintern (which also likes to change its name) and which was then run by the brilliant Willie Muenzenberg, its purpose being to obtain intelligence and to achieve Communist revolutions outside the Soviet Union, its primary objective the destruction, by infiltration or other means, of alternative Socialist parties and trade unions.

The immense complexity, and indeed inherent contradictions, of the tasks assigned to Soviet secret intelligence in its very different branches led, inevitably, to the most ruthless varieties of infighting.

In Stalin's vain search for absolute power, the massacre by Lenin, himself and others of the old governing class left him with only one group of political rivals, the old Bolsheviks. Trotsky,

234

the most powerful of these, was outmanoeuvred, exiled and eventually murdered in Mexico. More important, the other old Bolsheviks were incriminated in the campaign of lies directed against Trotsky and thus in his downfall. One by one they were in their turn eliminated in the Great Purge trials that resulted from the murder of Kirov by the N.K.V.D. on 1 December 1934.[7] That the assassins belonged to a subordinate branch of the N.K.V.D. (which was the G.P.U. recently abolished and re-created under this new name) is irrelevant. One after another of the old Bolsheviks was handed over to the N.K.V.D. and under pressure, usually involving mental and physical torture and increasingly the use of hallucinatory drugs, confessed involvement in the murder of Kirov, the famous machinations of Leon Trotsky, and espionage activities for the Japanese, Germans, Americans, French and British. By 1937 Stalin had nothing left to fear from the Bolshevik Party, either in Moscow, Leningrad, Kiev or the other provincial centres – nor in Spain, where the Soviet intelligence apparatuses were involved in the Civil War there, to the great detriment of the Republican cause. Politically Stalin was surrounded henceforth by murderous toadies such as Molotov or Vishinsky, Malenkov and Krushchev, and the indestructibly twisting Mikoyan. This had been a triumph for his N.K.V.D.

The next task entrusted to these increasingly non-political state criminals was the elimination of the one remaining 'managerial' group with access to power and therefore constituting a threat, no matter how remote, to Stalin's autarchy, namely the leaders and staff officers of the Red Army. This was carried out with the now customary pantomime of open trials for some of the leaders and the disappearance *en masse* of their subordinates. In the summer of 1937 Marshal Tukhachevsky and eight other generals were arrested, tried in secret, and executed. Many more followed, including Marshal Blyukher, commander of the Far Eastern armies which had just defeated the Japanese in an undeclared war. It has been estimated that two-thirds of the trained staff officers were eliminated at this time, though some of these were recalled from the Gulag Archipelago when the Germans invaded.

This meant that the huge Red Army was so enfeebled in its leadership that it suffered initial, severe defeats when Finland

235

was invaded in December 1939. One of the reasons for this fiasco was that with the decimation of the Red General Staff, the army's intelligence, the G.R.U., had suffered even more heavily than the other branches owing to its inevitable foreign contacts. (Radek, the spectacular Comintern boss, attempted in 1937 to 'enlist' Captain Liddell Hart as an adviser to the Red Army on tank warfare.[8] Sir Basil told this writer that having declined the offer, he was visited by the Soviet military attaché, after Radek's arrest and perhaps before his execution. The Russian military attaché in London was recalled and executed.) Nor was the N.K.V.D., being a semi-secret police service with responsibilities that were essentially internal, capable of replacing the trained intelligence officers with any speed.

The *Yezhovshchina*, as the purges were named after Yezhov, one-time head of the N.K.V.D., thus led to the laming and indeed near-destruction of one of the most important arms of Soviet intelligence. Furthermore the G.R.U. officers who survived, or who replaced those who had been liquidated, were more reluctant than ever to submit any intelligence reports, no matter how true, that might annoy their political masters.

The Comintern's agents soon suffered a similar fate. It was not easy, in Paris or Madrid, for Communists in the late thirties to follow the zigzags of the 'Party line as laid down in Moscow'. From being the prime enemy, the Social Democrats, long referred to as Social-Fascists, suddenly became the allies of the Communists with the creation of the Popular Front movement in 1935. Yet with the outbreak of the Spanish Civil War in 1936, the Russian-dominated Spanish Communist Party set about methodically undermining and destroying its allies, whether these were Basque or Catalonian nationalists, the anarchists who were the most representative of the Spanish revolutionary movements, or Social Democrats. Indeed they devoted far more effort to these fratricidal efforts than to fighting Franco and the Falange. And when the war in Spain was lost, those Spanish refugees who sought an expected haven in the Soviet Union were, almost without exception, thrown into the concentration camps to perish. But by then, early 1939, the popular front concept was in ruins almost everywhere.

Hitler had of course done his best to eliminate the German

236

Communist Party but had not been entirely successful. In 1939 a secret, skeleton organization still existed inside Germany and was controlled, allegedly by the Comintern, from Moscow. Numerous German Communists had also fled to Russia. These were subjected to the *Yezhovshchina* as rigorously as their Russian comrades, indeed rather more so, being foreigners.[9] Tried and true Stalinists, such as Walter Ulbricht who had masterminded N.K.V.D. policy in Spain, survived – if they were lucky. When Stalin signed his pact with Hitler the majority of the German Communists were handed over by the N.K.V.D. to the Gestapo who, by subjecting them to torture in the Nazi camps, found it not difficult to uncover the remnants of the internal German Communist Party organization.

Much the same was to happen to Communists in France, Scandinavia and the Low Countries after the German victories of 1940. Willie Muenzenberg himself was murdered, almost certainly by the N.K.V.D. Other Communists, such as the French Déat and Doriot, promptly became 100 per cent collaborators, in obedience to the party line, as well as in their own self-interest. Thus the second arm of Soviet secret intelligence, the network of the Comintern, was also destroyed by the N.K.V.D. Only in the United States, and to a lesser extent in Britain and in Switzerland, did it continue to function after a fashion. But it was not listened to in Moscow being, by contagion, suspect.

The N.K.V.D. might thus appear, by the time Russia was invaded, omnipotent in the field of intelligence, but this is misleading. In the first place, as its power grew its leaders became potential rivals to Stalin and his toadies. Yagoda and Yezhev were in turn arrested and executed for the crime of having carried out their master's orders. Beria was, we are told, shot out of hand by Krushchev at one of the meetings of the Politburo, the only functions at which he appeared without the armed protection of his own people. On each occasion many other heads rolled. At the time of writing, June 1975, a similar fate seems to have befallen another K.G.B. leader, Shelepin, at the hands of Brezhnev.

If the life expectancy of the men in charge of the N.K.V.D./ K.G.B. is low, the quality of the rank and file was deliberately lowered by Stalin. Better fifty stupid but committed policemen than one brilliant detective has always been Russian policy.

Under Stalin the N.K.V.D. man became an accomplice in murder and torture, a concentration camp guard, often trained since childhood in such a camp to which he had been committed for the 'sins' of his parents. Such a force of criminals in or out of uniform does not spontaneously rise in protest against the criminal regime that has created it. On whose behalf could it rise? Hardly on that of the people it has systematically mal-treated for years. And the Leninists had stamped out, as best they could, all vestiges of morality. (There is good reason to believe that attempts have been made since Stalin's death to improve the quality of at least some members of the K.G.B. This will be considered later.)

Nazi Germany's secret intelligence services did not suffer from the same disabilities as those of the Soviet Union, but from similar weaknesses which are probably inherent in any form of totalitarian government, namely a multiplicity of often competing organizations and a comprehensible reluctance to tell the omni-potent dictator anything that he does not wish to hear.

So far as pure military intelligence and counter-intelligence went, the Germans had a fine organization in the Amt Ausland Abwehr. Built up during the Weimar period, it was of course expanded with the rest of the German armed forces after 1933, and particularly after the reintroduction of conscription and the tearing up of the Versailles Treaty in 1935. On 1 January of that year Admiral Wilhelm Canaris had succeeded Conrad Patzig as head of the Abwehr. The Abwehr came under the direct control of the O.K.W. (the Armed Forces High Command), while straight military intelligence, in the form of Foreign Armies East and Foreign Armies West, was subordinated to the O.K.H. (the Army High Command). Similar organizations concerning enemy air and sea forces were controlled by their appropriate commands, though all these were also subordinate to the O.K.W., which was in effect Hitler's personal command with the obsequious future Field Marshal Keitel as his chief of staff. In view of the clan-destine nature of its activities, the Abwehr still preserved a considerable measure of independence and was less subject to Nazi supervision than any other legal organization in Germany.

This state of affairs did not appeal to the Nazi Party leadership and particularly little to its own security service, the *Reichssicher-*

238

heitshauptdienst, or Main National Security Service, a branch of the S.S. directly under Heinrich Himmler, later in charge of all German police forces. It was run by Reinhard Heydrich from its earliest days in 1931 until his assassination in May 1942. For most of this decade he was among the most powerful men in Germany and certainly among the most ruthless. However neither his nor Himmler's power can be equated with that of a Yezhev or a Beria, owing to the different origins of the two great National Socialist revolutions of our centuries. (Mussolini's fascism can be dismissed as a brief attempt to restructure the Italian economy without any serious attempt to re-engineer Italian society, while Japanese Imperialism was little more than an aping of British and French modes in a traditional and oriental context.)

Nazism was based upon a compromise, arrived at in the summer of 1934, though foreshadowed by Hitler's appointment as Chancellor of a Coalition Government in January of the previous year. Once he had disposed of his bedfellows in the coalition, and created the one-party state he desired, he still had two non-political power groups with which to deal: his left-wing element, Roehm's S.A., the street fighters of the past who aspired to military power but lacked strength of leadership and organization, and the army, which lacked neither, but was deliberately deficient in political ambition. Hitler sensibly chose an alliance with the army, which stood by, its kidskin gloves unbloodied, while Hitler's personal bodyguard, the S.S., murdered the leaders of the S.A. (together with a few others for good measure). For some years the revolutionary wing of the Nazi Party was at a discount. And for some years Hitler more or less kept his part of the bargain that he had made with the leaders of the armed forces on board the cruiser *Deutschland* in April of 1934, which bargain had given him a free hand to massacre his own most turbulent supporters. The Wehrmacht was to be the only armed force in the state: in return it was to continue its policy of avowed abstention from politics.*

It was this that gave the armed forces, and its Abwehr, an

* In fact this abstention had been directed against the Weimar regime, but only honoured at a low level. See John Wheeler-Bennett, op. cit.

apparently almost free hand to rearm and then to win its great victories of 1939–42. Despite the resignation of the army Chief of Staff, General Beck, who saw only disaster in Nazi policy in 1938; despite the shameful and dishonest dismissal of its leaders, Fritsch and Blomberg, earlier in that year, the Wehrmacht stuck to its side of the bargain. Repeated German successes, such as the reoccupation of the Rhineland in 1936 and the invasion of Austria in 1938 – the first of which had been carried out against the advice of the German High Command which believed that the French would react, the second being simply an order concerning the nature of which the Wehrmacht was not consulted – weakened the position of the army in so far as it was opposed to Hitler's policy of powerful aggression. Many, probably most, of the German generals disliked Nazi policy; but they were not usually averse to military victory and national glory. Few generals ever are, anywhere or at any time.

The S.S. were less interested in keeping to their side of the compact. Its organization was modelled in military matters on that of the Wehrmacht.[10] Heydrich controlled its intelligence services, the most important of which was the *Sicherheitsdienst* (security service) or S.D., the armed force of which was the S.I.P.O., or security police. And he immediately came into confrontation with the Abwehr. (The actual fighting strength of the Waffen, or armed S.S., only amounted to two divisions in 1940, but even this was a vast expansion of Hitler's personal bodyguard of some 10,000 since 1934, many of whom had gone to form other branches of the S.S., such as the concentration camp guards.)

Heydrich's S.D. formed an alternative secret service to that of the Abwehr. In due course it was to conquer its rival, as will be seen. Meanwhile it was lacking in expertise. Nor were its pre-war triumphs as spectacular as some would have made them out to be. There is, for example, the Tukhachevsky case, about which we know a great deal from German archives but nothing reliable from those of the Soviet Union. It was a typically flamboyant and – if such a word can be used in such a context – dishonourable action.

As everyone who was not blinded by Communist propaganda was well aware of the *Yezhovshchina*, it was obvious by early 1937 that the Red Army, unless it reacted, was next for the Stalinist

240

chopper. Since the Red Army, like all Russian armies, including that of General Vlassov at a later date, was inbred with a stubborn patriotism, it was clearly impractical for the Nazis to weaken it by the same methods that the Communists were to use in the French army in 1939–40 and, later, among some American units in the Asian wars. Therefore in clever minds such as that of Reinhard Heydrich the accusation of treason, with evidence, against the leaders of the Red Army could only encourage Stalin to decapitate his own defenders. The greatest Russian soldier, Marshal Tukhachevsky, became the prime target. During the period of anti-Versailles, that is to say from the Soviet viewpoint anti-Western, collaboration between the old Reichswehr and the then new Red Army, some documents had passed from the one to the other, so Tukhachevksy's signature was available for forgery. What was forged was intended to prove that the Russian marshal was working for the Nazis. This Heydrich proceeded to do.

The operation was carried out with a certain *finesse*. A direct German plant into the hands of the Soviet espionage organization must arouse immediate Muscovite suspicions. On the other hand Edouard Beneš, somewhat pathetically as usual, was hoping for Russian backing against inevitable future German aggression.[11] Therefore the forged documents were passed to the Czechs. The Czechs believed that these were genuine, or at least said so when they passed them to Moscow in their attempt to woo the Soviets. Since we have no transcript of the secret trial of the Russian generals, we have no certainty that the N.K.V.D. either accepted their authenticity or used them. Nor is the fact that Tukhachevsky was posthumously accused of being a German spy of much relevance. Similar, meaningless accusations of spying for the Japanese, British and so on were levelled at other dead generals without even the basis of forged documents and certainly with no element of truth. Nevertheless Tukhachevsky died. We have a description of this brilliant soldier walking away from Red Square, in civilian clothes, his hands in his trouser pockets, on 1 May 1937, to face certain arrest and death. His strategic plan, as perfected by General Shaposhnikov (another accused in the Purge but who survived) and later carried out by General Vlassov, was in large measure responsible for the saving of Moscow in

December 1941. Yet Stalin was determined to kill him in 1937, and would have done so, forgeries or no forgeries, for Trotsky in exile had written that Tukhachevsky would be the Bonaparte who would overthrow Stalin. Perhaps the *Sicherheitsdienst* saved the N.K.V.D. from the trouble of forging such documents themselves, though by then they probably hardly troubled to expend the effort.

Still, Tukhachevsky's death was regarded as a triumph by Heydrich and his S.D. and was accepted as such by the Nazi leaders. This, following upon their detection and smashing of a genuine Polish espionage network led by Colonel Sosnowski, gave the S.D. a considerable measure of prestige. It became the potential rival of the Abwehr, which it was to conquer in 1943 and 1944. For bit by bit the S.S. became even more revolutionary than the old S.A., which it had smashed in 1934 with tacit army support. Before the end of the war that revolutionary element was to control the S.S. far more effectively, hold far more power than had ever belonged to the street-fighters of the S.A. Its hatred of the old officer corps as a remnant of an earlier social system increased, steadily. Had the Germans won the war, the S.S. would have become the might of the 1,000-Year Reich and held a power not dissimilar to that of certain Roman generals or indeed of today's K.G.B.

If the S.D. was overtly political, the Abwehr, or some elements thereof, were covertly so. History has shown us that Heydrich was quite correct in his distrust of the Abwehr. Although Admiral Canaris remained deliberately ambiguous, he was no Nazi. He must have known that several of his senior officers were actively anti-Nazi, though he apparently preferred not to be involved. General Moravec, for instance, tells of an Abwehr officer whom he does not identify save as A54 but whose name is known, who offered his services to Czech intelligence, for money, in 1937. The money was simply good cover, for he went on supplying the Czech intelligence service with accurate information long after its government was in penniless exile. He was small fry, though. The deputy chief of the Abwehr, Colonel Oster, was a confirmed anti-Nazi, who would have preferred to see Germany lose the war rather than that Hitler should win it. He, and several like him, deliberately betrayed German operational secrets to the Western

Allies, and to a much lesser extent to the Soviets, both before and during the war. They were engaged upon what in any country and at any time would be called high treason.

Furthermore Oster concealed beneath the Abwehr's cloak an active resistance group to Hitlerism. Being an intelligence organization with very limited reliable armed support it was in no position to act, to mount a *coup d'état*. Yet without the organizational support of the Abwehr, and its secrecy, it is fair to say that Colonel Stauffenberg and his friends inside and outside the army could never have obtained such real military support as they managed to muster on 20 July 1944. Had their attempt succeeded much of the credit would have rightly gone to some members of the Abwehr. Indeed the Abwehr supplied the very explosive, captured from British agents, with which Stauffenberg attempted and just failed to kill Hitler on that day.[12] But it must be emphasized that only a very small number of soldiers and others serving in the Abwehr were involved in anti-Nazi activities, the great majority being intelligence officers or agents engaged upon their normal duties.

Nor were these extramural activities known to Heydrich's S.D. until well into the war, for otherwise the anti-Nazis would certainly have been arrested. Nevertheless in the eyes of the Nazi leaders there was something suspicious about the Abwehr, and they were setting about its overthrow as the intelligence service of the State long before 20 July 1944, Admiral Canaris having been dismissed though not arrested in February. Still, the net was closing. They would have liked to see German intelligence firmly in Nazi hands, but until Germany began to lose the war even the most powerful Nazi leaders could not force the victorious General Staff to hand over one of any staff's principal and indeed essential branches. The temporary reprieve was difficult to maintain. Nor was it maintained. Even without the events of 20 July, the S.D. would soon have completed its victory over the Abwehr.

Ribbentrop's diplomatic intelligence, once he had become Foreign Minister in February of 1938, was amateurish compared to that of contemporary Russia, and was scarcely on a par with that of the British, Italians, French or Americans. But he attached the greatest importance to this branch of his Ministry's activities, and what was perhaps more important he had Hitler's ear, principally because he told the Führer what the Führer wished to hear

He had previously been German ambassador in London, where he had associated almost exclusively with anti-Communists, pro-Germans and what were later to be called 'appeasers'. He had also gleefully culled the pacifist press, and the Peace Pledge Union was very active. The British, he informed his leader, would not again go to war against Germany. In this view he was supported by Sir Nevile Henderson, who had been sent to Berlin as British ambassador in 1937 to replace Sir Horace Rumbold, whose well-informed warnings about Nazi Germany and its intentions had become unpalatable to the Baldwin–Chamberlain governments, bent on appeasement or *détente*, and on the winning of the British pacifist vote. What is more, Ribbentrop's thesis was proved right in 1936, when the Germans reoccupied the Rhineland, and France's preparations for war were held back by the British government. The Anglo-French alliance was already weak. It survived, but as little more than a formula. And Hitler, in his cynicism, discounted the validity of the British guarantees to Poland and Romania in the spring of 1939. He was somewhat taken aback when one of these was honoured in the following September.

Such ineptitude was not confined to British and German ambassadors in their respective countries. Joseph Kennedy, when American ambassador in London, believed in 1940 that Britain was about to surrender, and Churchill was compelled to ask that he be recalled. President Roosevelt's other sources of political intelligence, a year or two later, led him to believe that Stalin was a faithful ally, while Britain remained the old, imperialist ogre and France was forever henceforth negligible.

Similarly Mussolini, and his son-in-law and Foreign Minister, Count Ciano, made such drastic miscalculations both before and during the war concerning British, later Greek, and later still American intentions that Mussolini eventually had his son-in-law executed, shortly before being hanged himself.

The Japanese and German underestimation of America's patriotism probably lost them the war. In fact none of the great powers exhibited much skill in the procurement, and even less in the evaluation, of political intelligence either before or during the

244

Second World War. There is little evidence that their expertise has increased since 1945. It may be that this is an activity bound to usual failure, since the elements both of personality and of time are decisive. Which is perhaps why history, unfortunately, does not and will not stop. Who could have guessed, twenty years ago, that the Soviet and Red Chinese armies would be facing one another in massive strength? Political prophecy can, like its military equivalent, only be based upon the facts. Where there are no facts, the prophecies become the product of a roulette wheel equipped with quite unimaginable permutations. Some people, however, do have the skill and the luck to win at roulette.

Technological and industrial espionage is a field that overlaps both the military and the politico-economic, and one that has assumed an ever-growing importance in the past three-quarters of a century. It will be discussed later, particularly in connection with nuclear weapons, satellites and computers. Meanwhile an early example of the grinding wheels of multiple, overlapping intelligence services is well provided by General Guderian, probably the greatest tank general of the Second World War, who would almost certainly have captured Moscow in the autumn of 1941 had his army not been diverted, by Hitler, to capture the Ukrainian wheatfields and the industrial area to their east on 4 August 1941. On that day, when German strategy was in the balance, Hitler had said to him:

'If I had known that the figures for Russian tank strength which you gave in your book were in fact the true ones, I would not – I believe – ever have started this war.' He was referring to my book *Achtung! Panzer!* published in 1937, in which I had estimated Russian tank strength at that time as 10,000; both the Chief of the Army General Staff, Beck, and the censor had disagreed with this statement. It had cost me a lot of trouble to get that figure printed; but I had been able to show that intelligence reports at the time spoke of 17,000 Russian tanks and that my estimate was therefore, if anything, a very conservative one. To imitate the ostrich in political matters has never been a satisfactory method of avoiding danger; yet this is what Hitler, as well as his more important political, economic and even military advisers, chose to do over and over again. The

245

consequences of this deliberate blindness in the face of hard facts were devastating; and it was we who now had to bear them.[13]

Long before this, while the campaign called Operation Barbarossa was still being planned, Guderian states:

A consequence of the Balkan campaign was that the Russian offensive could not be launched until late in the summer.

Far more significant, however, than either of these facts was the underestimate of the Russian as an enemy. Our outstanding military attaché in Mosow, General Köstring, had reported on the military strength of that gigantic country: Hitler attached as little importance to these reports as he did to others concerning the production capacity of Russian industry or the stability of the Russian political system. On the contrary, he had succeeded in infecting his immediate military entourage with his own baseless optimism. The O.K.W. and O.K.H. were so serenely confident of victory before winter set in that winter clothing had only been prepared for every fifth man in the army.[14]

Finally, the technicians were well aware that the Russian T34 tank was superior to anything available in 1941 to the Germans, was already in massive production, and that the new Russian heavy tank, the T51 or Stalin tank, was to prove the best heavy armoured fighting vehicle of any army of the period, with the possible exception of the German King-Tiger, which came too late.

Yet Hitler's view of Red Army feebleness prevailed, supported by the evidence of the *Yezhovshchina*, of Finland, the political intelligence supplied by Ribbentrop and by the S.D., and also by the Abwehr. He thought, in effect, that the Russian campaign would be a walk-over. Here he was wrong, but it was, as Wellington is said to have remarked about Waterloo, a damned close-run thing. German technological intelligence was good. Had it, and Hitler's strategy, been only a little better, Russia might have been conquered before the winter set in. The Russians have learned from the German error. It is to be hoped, for our sakes, that they have not learned too much and that we too may have learned a little.

246

Chapter Fifteen

The Dogs of War

Even before the outbreak of the Second World War, both the British and the Russians had begun the creation of double agent systems. They were quite dissimilar being directed against different enemies, but both were in effect based upon a similar premise: that it had become possible to penetrate the enemy's intelligence apparatus, particularly in a free society and more in a totalitarian society where a contrary tradition lingers on. To this must be added the fact that the use of radio ciphers and their vulnerability had not been fully understood – if they have been today or ever will – and that this provided an additional means of misleading the enemy through his own intelligence apparatus. If a distinction has hitherto been drawn between 'traditional' espionage (the stealing or photographing of documents, the reporting of conversations, by straightforward listening or by bugging, and so on) and cipher-breaking, in the context of what follows any such distinction becomes very blurred. Nevertheless, though purely for reasons of convenience, it will be for the moment pursued, since the balance varied from country to country. The reader must be reminded that secret intelligence was and is checked against open intelligence – the monitoring of the press and ordinary radio, the censorship of letters – and by battlefield intelligence, aerial reconnaissance, prisoner interrogation and plain visual observation, to name but a few. But the provision of open intelligence to the enemy can also be used secretly to mislead him.

The ideal spy is not one who is introduced – an extraordinarily difficult task – but one who is, as it were, already *in situ*, who has already obtained the security clearance of those for whom ostensibly he works. These may be 'sleepers', to be activated only in a period of crisis; if they have in appearance loyally served their ostensible masters for several years they will have become increasingly valuable as they obtain access to increasingly secret information. The ideal location of such an agent is at a high level of the enemy's own intelligence service. (A divisional intelligence officer will seldom have anything more to divulge than any other officer on his staff, though on occasion and usually for ideological reasons, he may defect with some vital piece of battlefield intelligence. But this is not what he will have been trained for.) The Russians have proved particularly adept at this form of long-term infiltration. In this they have been greatly helped by their allegedly international ideology and the Agitprop organization referred to earlier. Thus Dr Richard Sorge joined the N.S.D.A.P., the Nazi Party, in order to spy for the G.R.U., in 1934. At approximately the same time Kim Philby, Donald Maclean, Guy Burgess and others whose names have not yet been disclosed, were recruited as undergraduates and instructed to obtain jobs in British intelligence or in the Foreign Office, though they were not to be used for a decade or more. At about the same time others were being recruited in America, principally it seems from the Harvard Law School. In due course it will be established who were the 'recruiting agents', almost certainly fairly senior academics, at Harvard and Cambridge. Well-informed rumours are not, at present, acceptable. This same sort of activity was going on in other countries, but the purges and the smashing of the Comintern and then the war seem to have led to its temporary suspension.

The British use of agents at this level was far more direct, at least so far as has been revealed. This applies even more so to the Americans in pre-war years. Immediately after the war Sir John Masterman, who became Provost of Worcester College, Oxford, after he left the army in 1946, wrote at that date a study of his wartime activities in the recruiting and employment of double agents to act against Nazi Germany. This was subsequently edited for general publication.[1] It does not, or only in a very tangential fashion, deal with political intelligence, but with the turning around of the German espionage apparatus inside Britain. This was started in a small way in 1936, with an agent whom Sir John calls SNOW, for he sticks to code names throughout. The system employed by Double-Cross became increasingly elaborate and quite quickly entirely effective: by 1942 or 1943 the whole of the German spy system in Britain was effectively controlled by XX, but this of course the British could never know for sure, since there was always the possibility of an unknown, parallel spy organization in existence. There was in fact none, and during the critical build-up period before D-day, 6 June 1944, all the information that the Germans were receiving from their spies was what the British, or to be more exact the Anglo-American Command, wished them to hear.

There is no need to stress the extreme importance of this. Since by then the Allied air forces had virtually complete control of the skies above Britain, German reconnaissance aircraft had the greatest difficulty in photographing any areas other than those which the Anglo-American High Command (C.O.S.S.A.C., later S.H.A.E.F., which is the name that will henceforth be used) wished to have photographed, for camouflage or deceptive purpose. From the purely military, naval and air points of view, the operations of XX seem to have had that extreme rarity in military history, a complete success, at least until the summer of 1944, when its methods became much less effective with the occupation of France and later of Belgium and a part of Holland. So far as is known the Russians had no such sophisticated a system for dealing with spies, preferring to execute them rather than turn them around against the enemy.

In the political intelligence field, however, the British and Americans lagged behind the Russians, and this for various reasons. On the outbreak of war, the British government announced that it was fighting Nazism, not the German people, and during the 'phoney war' of September to May 1940 dropped a mass of leaflets (but no bombs) on the German cities explaining this to the citizens who were urged to overthrow their government. How they were supposed to do this was not made plain. When this feeble appeal failed, British and later American might was directed against the German people as a whole. The British had no source that they regarded as reliable either high in the German Armed Forces or in the government. When, therefore, a real resistance movement to Nazism became active, the British discounted its very existence. The Foreign Office is particularly stubborn even now in revealing why the information it was receiving via Bishop Bell and others was blocked.* The Joint Intelligence Sub-Committee of the Chiefs of Staff passed on the information received. The political leadership, however, seems to have had no contingency plan prepared for immediate implementation, should Stauffenberg and his friends have succeeded in their attempt to kill Hitler and overthrow the Nazi regime. One plausible explanation is that the Foreign Office overestimated the Gestapo. Those files are not open. Perhaps it was a policy designed to please the Soviet ally, which of course it did. In any event it prevented a unilateral German surrender to the West in the summer of 1944, and thus allowed the Soviets to occupy Eastern Europe a year later. Or, incredible as it may seem, it may have been based upon loyalty towards the reluctant, hostile ally. In any event this misinformation or false evaluation deliberate or otherwise, and sealed at Yalta, was a disaster, the full cost of which is far from paid even now.

Later in the war, when the British espionage organization was operating inside German-occupied Europe and collaborating with various nationalist groups, the Germans were to emulate, though never to surpass, their British enemy. In Holland, however, they did turn around a British intelligence group and for some time succeed in persuading the receiving end in London that the radio signals were genuine. The difficulty of so doing was, to both sides, immense. The style of a man working a transmitter is, after a time, as distinctive as handwriting. Furthermore the bogus intelligence so passed must be credible to experts. One slip, and the system is blown. From the German point of view, their Dutch operation was the one of most protracted success: others were of briefer duration; none compared with the British success in

* Bishop Bell, the Bishop of Chichester at the time, had attended a theologians' conference in Stockholm in 1943. Among those present was the famous theologian Dietrich Bonhoeffer who, together with his brother Claus, was deeply involved in the anti-Nazi conspiracy inside Germany. Both were later executed, after the failed uprising of 20 July 1944. Bonhoeffer had asked Bishop Bell to convey to the British government that an anti-Nazi movement did exist, and at a high level, within the German armed forces. Bishop Bell has said in print that he conveyed this message personally to the Foreign Minister, who showed no interest.

250

this field before D-day. So far as this writer knows, no similar operation (for the purely tactical *ruse de guerre* is not such) was mounted and sustained either in the Pacific War or on the Eastern Front, by either side. The explanation might be the comparatively very static nature of the Western Front, at least so far as land forces were concerned, together with the geographical isolation of the British Isles until the summer of 1944, which provided the perfect conditions for intelligence and counter-intelligence operations of a strategic nature in wartime, the strategy being limited to military matters.

As has been already said, the British intelligence services were immensely reinforced during the First World War, and even more so in the Second, by men and women who had had little or nothing to do with such activities either before or after. The extraordinary homogeneity of British society, which the Tudors had first forged and which had survived nearly four centuries of social change, resulted in a country united in crisis, as were the Maltese and the Knights of Malta during their great siege of 1565. The parallel is not fortuitous. The Maltese had no reason to love their foreign Knights, nor did they, but both elements of the population knew what to expect from the Turks. The people of Britain had been engaged in internal class and ideological warfare during the thirties, which was to be resumed after the destruction of Nazism. Yet for a while this was forgotten, and though help from outside – particularly from the United States – was hoped for, the British like the Maltese at that earlier date dared not rely on this. They closed ranks and fought, alone. There were virtually no pro-Nazis in Britain. The Communists might have as their ultimate objective a Communist Britain, but for the time being, after June 1941, they were prepared to fight bravely against Nazism, with their muscles or their brains. Such activity, even such ultimate ambitions, were not then regarded as incipient treason. The British, with their two-party political system and perhaps even their games system involving two sides, had for centuries believed that 'my enemy's enemy is my friend'. This is not a simplification into which the Russians – whose game is chess and who therefore understand the importance of the knight's eccentric move and of the occasional need to sacrifice men in order to achieve a stronger position and ultimate victory – have ever fallen. In a word, the Russians are adept at triangular warfare, while to the British and Americans it is a matter of 'us' and 'them', our side against theirs. During the period 1939–45 neither the British nor the Americans were preparing for a post-war confrontation with their wartime Soviet ally. Indeed they fell over almost backwards in their determination to prove their loyalty to Stalin's Soviet Union. Arthur Koestler, a Hungarian by origin and a one-time Communist with a profound knowledge of Soviet methods learned both in Russia and Spain, correctly estimated the situation when he later said, of the war against National Socialism, that it was fought against an absolute lie in the interest of a half-truth.

This almost repetitive digression is not as irrelevant as it may appear. For in this twentieth century the temporal objective of secret intelligence can be as relevant as the spatial, the ultimate aims beyond the winning of a war, as important as winning the war itself. The Leninist–Marxist concept of inevitable, ultimate victory, although it has no historical or logical base, was directly confronted by the Anglo-American concept that what mattered was 'who wins the war' and, at a lesser but still not negligible level, 'who wins the next election'. It was this backbone of ultimate intent that permitted, if only just, the zigzags of the Communist party line. It was the contrary conception of freedom, restrained in wartime but the immediate objective once war was won, that limited Western ambitions, in the strategic field and therefore in their intelligence activities. This is most clearly seen in one of the by-products, one might say spin-offs, of the double agent syndrome: the cover plan. This was copied in part from the Comintern's Agitprop system, which in any short-term scale had proved ineffective, being repeatedly frustrated by changes of Soviet policy, though its long-term effects still remain to be proved. In part it was an attempt to duplicate the propaganda successes of the First World War, and in particular of Wilson's Fourteen Points. The fact that most of the Fourteen Points had been disavowed by the victorious powers at Versailles in 1919, and that therefore all enemy propaganda was automatically distrusted in central Europe, was originally overlooked. Hence the dropping of leaflets in the winter of 1939–40 urging the Germans to choose democracy, and the total failure of this operation. More sophisticated, or at least more cunning, methods were chosen. These may be roughly divided into 'agitation' and 'propaganda', though the second – which will be briefly considered first – was intended to be ancillary to the other. In both, radio, radio-intercepts and the methods used by double agents were implicit. Both were, inevitably, connected with the margins of intelligence, secret and not.

Some of those conscripted from civilian distinction into British intelligence were journalists. Since their previous occupational training had been the dissemination of information, usually true, occasionally false, but in general designed to attract the maximum public interest, they were almost without exception barred from most secret intelligence, and particularly from Ultra. This writer, when serving on the staff of General Bradley's Army Group was firmly ordered to divulge nothing to any other staff officer on this subject, and in particular warned against a certain, very famous, American journalist who was also employed by G-2. Inevitably, he published after the war his first-hand report on 12th Army Group G-2. Inevitably, it was grossly misleading, since he had been screened from knowledge of the reality. Similarly a journalist was employed at G-2 of Patton's Third Army in 1944; his principal ambition seemed to be the discrediting of American political and military leadership in the powerful yellow-press columns of his Washington colleague. He was an acute and sensitive journalist but a very poor intelligence officer. However, he realized that he was not getting at the truth and indeed once attempted to bribe this writer with a case of brandy. It was an ineffectual operation, though the brandy was delicious. He, too, wrote a misleading book.

Journalists were seldom employed by the British in highly sensitive intelligence organizations or operations. They had, however, been scooped into the whole, vast business, along with the humanist academics and the scientists and others. Being mainly go-go men they did not care to be shunted into obscurity; being publicists, their obvious field was propaganda. The most prominent of these journalists was Mr Sefton Delmer, known to his friends as 'Tom'.[2] As his book shows he was also, marginally, involved in the Agitation as opposed to Propaganda element, and also connected with elaborate cover plans, some of which will be discussed later in this chapter.

Throughout the winter of the 'phoney war' and during the real campaigns of 1940 in the West the British listened, more out of curiosity than for any other reason, to the English-language broadcasts from the *Grossdeutsche Rundfunk*, particularly to those of the Irishman William Joyce, dubbed 'Lord Haw-haw' by the *Daily Express* because of his affected Oxford accent. Once the war became serious, however, and was being fought over Britain for survival, the British quickly realized not only that Dr Goebbels' propaganda machine was a lie-generator but also and to a lesser extent that it was unpatriotic to listen to such stuff. From then on German radio propaganda became, and remained, negligible, except to a section of the intelligence service interested in finding out what it was that the Germans wished us to believe. In fact German propaganda became, in the West, counter-productive. Since in those days the citizens of the Soviet Union did not own many private receivers, it was equally ineffective in the East.

The British, and later the Americans, had one huge handicap, their own remembered propaganda lies of the First World War. The British, at least, had one very powerful antidote in the form of Sir John (later Lord) Reith's B.B.C. That most remarkable Scotsman, a puritan to the extent that some called him a prig, had a great moral and intellectual hatred of dishonesty. So firmly was his personality stamped upon the British Broadcasting Corporation that it was able to withstand pressure from the very highest political levels against mendacity. The news broadcasts were censored, of course, lest they provide the enemy with operational intelligence material, but this censorship was negative. The B.B.C. did not tell lies, though it used its wave lengths to pass operational messages in simple code to the resistance movements in occupied Europe. Its reports of military, naval and air operations were, within the limits of security, accurate and as such increasingly accepted by the German people, as they came to realize the deliberate mendacity of the *Grossdeutsche Rundfunk*. Indeed it soon became necessary for the German government to impose severe punishment, including incarceration in a concentration camp, on those who listened to the B.B.C. at all. A higher tribute to Lord Reith and the senior staff he had chosen and trained would be hard to envisage.

This dour, Scots atmosphere was no place for Sefton Delmer and his people. Their invention was far more spectacular. It was, essentially, the creation of bogus radio broadcasts, allegedly German in origin (*Soldatensender Calais* was the prototype), modelled on Lord Haw-haw and almost totally ineffective. They came under the heading of psychological warfare – in itself a completely ridiculous combination of words – and were intended to make the German private soldier distrust his officers' statements and his own political leaders. These radio broadcasts from bogus stations were, on occasion, supplemented by the dropping of leaflets and by rumour campaigns, for German ears, in occupied Europe. This writer, in 1945, asked the head of the Psychological Warfare department at the Pentagon, an officer who had recently returned from defeated Germany, whether he believed that such expensive activities had shortened the war. The answer was: 'Perhaps by five minutes.' The same would probably be true of organized, external spy-war against the Soviet Union in the years that have passed since then.

The various cover plans used throughout the war were far more elaborate and usually, though in the opinion of this writer incorrectly, believed to have been far more effective. A cover plan was more than a mere *ruse de guerre*, such as the Japanese fleet pretending to go for Alaska when in fact it was destined for Pearl Harbor* or Midway. It was a major deception of the enemy, involving all possible enemy sources from a controlled enemy espionage service, through false wireless links and even networks, as well as 'dirty tricks' that were, or were believed to be, quite

* Mr Cavendish-Bentinck has informed this writer privately that the British at least knew when the Japanese fleet changed course. His statement is so important that I quote him directly. Referring to a Joint Intelligence Sub-Committee meeting held on the Friday before Pearl Harbor, he writes: 'We knew that they changed course. I remember presiding over a J.I.C. meeting and being told that a Japanese fleet was sailing in the direction of Hawaii, asking "Have we informed our transatlantic brethren?" and receiving an affirmative reply.' Why did the U.S. authorities not act on this warning, which would have given the U.S. Navy ample time at least to send most of the fleet out of Pearl Harbor? Bureaucratic inefficiency, rather than a Wilsonian fear of British provocation would seem the more obvious answer. Treachery, or political skulduggery on the part of President Roosevelt, can in this writer's opinion be ruled out.

new. There are two much publicized classic examples from the Second World War. The first preceded the invasion of Sicily in 1943, the second that of France a year later. Both were based on what might be described as journalist-intelligence, that is to say 'selling' the wrong news to the enemy. The first was a failure; the second, at best, a partial success. The first might be termed 'the man who was not', though its operational code name was 'Mincemeat'; the second was called F.U.S.A.G. Both were intelligence-operational efforts with heavy journalistic overtones.

The story of the dead 'marine' officer has been twice told, once in quasi-fictional form by A. Duff Cooper (later Lord Norwich), in direct breach of the then observed security regulations, and later by the Hon. Ewen Montagu who in fact was directly involved in the technical and tactical planning of Operation Mincemeat.[3] The story is so well known that it can be recapitulated briefly.

After the final expulsion of the German–Italian forces from North Africa in the spring of 1943 there was some divergence of opinion as to where the powerful Anglo-American armies should strike next. Initially the Americans wished to strike at France, from Britain, that summer, but they were soon convinced by their own Chiefs of Staff as well as by the British that this was not logistically feasible in the time available to the navies before autumn set in, quite apart from the shortage of landing craft, airborne and other specially trained troops, and tactical intelligence. The British and Canadians had learned the lesson of the previous year's disastrous attack on the beaches of Dieppe. Therefore these large armies, which could not be kept indefinitely cooling their heels in Africa, must be used in the Mediterranean. It was decided to invade Italy via Sicily and knock Mussolini off his perch: Churchill spoke of the 'soft underbelly of the axis'. It would have been possible to invade neutral, though quasi-fascist, Spain, or Sardinia, or Greece, where there was a very active resistance to Nazi rule. The Allies could then have linked up with Tito's even more active partisans in Yugoslavia, thus occupying the Balkans, covering the left flank of the Red Army which was attempting to begin a major westward advance, and depriving the Germans of Romanian oil. For obvious reasons such a plan would have been highly unpopular in Moscow. (Even then the Russians were putting out peace feelers to the Nazis,

256

via Mme Kollontai, the Soviet ambassador in Stockholm.) No plans were made for the immediate seizure of Rome or points north, should the Italian government capitulate. In January Roosevelt had pronounced 'unconditional surrender', and Churchill had not demurred. Italy, therefore, must be conquered and occupied physically. Churchill would have preferred to invade the 'underbelly' by way of Yugoslavia, but was overruled by Roosevelt, who curiously was backed in this decision by the Joint Chiefs of Staff. The highest policy-makers seem to have preferred to ignore, for resumably non-military reasons, that there are a lot of mountain ranges between Calabria and the Po Valley, culminating in the Alps. The Italians may by then have been soft, but to describe their country as an 'underbelly' is odd.

In any event, such was the plan, and Operation Mincemeat was designed to persuade the enemy otherwise. The most spectacular part of this was the floating ashore, off Huelva in Spain, of a corpse dressed as an officer in the Royal Marines carrying all the appropriate documents plus top secret operational plans which indicated that Sardinia and/or Greece were the invasion targets. The rest of the cover plan operations were concentrated on Greece, where the resistance fighters were encouraged to believe in rapid liberation from their German conquerors. They reacted valiantly, but since part of the cover plan implied German knowledge, they suffered heavily. Indeed, trust among the Greeks in Anglo-American promises waned, and many joined the Communist Resistance. This was not unconnected with the Greek Civil War of 1945–8 and thus to much subsequent Greek history. Although the Communists lost that Civil War, the decision to invade Italy rather than the Balkans suited them admirably: it gave them the Balkans.

It has been claimed by the two authors cited that Mincemeat, the dead marine gimmick, was a success because the Germans moved the 1st Panzer Division and other forces into Greece and not into Italy. That the overstretched Wehrmacht was nevertheless able to tie down vastly more powerful Allied forces in Italy until the end of the war would seem to invalidate this argument. Furthermore Operation Mincemeat had nothing whatsoever to do with the increase of German strength in Greece.

What about the elaborate and expensive Mincemeat operation

257

itself?[4] The Spaniards who found the corpse, and who permitted a full military funeral for this bogus non-officer, handed over his secret papers, supposedly but improbably unread, to the German Abwehr. The head of the Abwehr, Admiral Canaris, was himself in Madrid at the time and immediately recognized them to be a plant. They were forwarded on, as such, to the O.K.W. At that time Jodl's Chief of Bureau or deputy was General Warlimont, an extremely clever and essentially non-political professional soldier. He has told this writer that in view of Canaris's judgment and of his own subordinates' agreement with this, the elaborately planted papers were ignored and were indeed never even mentioned at any supreme council presided over by Hitler. They had thus absolutely no connection with the move of the 1st Panzer Division and other German forces at this time. Nor was Sardinia strongly reinforced. Meanwhile the extremely formidable Hermann Goering Panzer Division was moved into Sicily. This Luftwaffe organization was to reinforce and protect the German air force formations already there, to parry any assault on Greece.

For it was not Mincemeat which diverted the eyes of the German Supreme Command from Sicily and Italy to Greece, but simple military logic. Distrustful as they rightly were of their Italian ally, they were also well aware that the Italian peninsula is almost perfect defensive territory if attacked from the south and that the German army could there tie up maximum enemy forces almost indefinitely. Furthermore – and here I may be asked to excuse the earlier digression about triangular warfare – General Warlimont has told me that while he and his staff may have at times doubted the sanity of Adolf Hitler, they had considerably more respect for the political acumen of Winston Churchill and of Franklin D. Roosevelt. They knew that the Soviets were not true allies of the Western powers. They assumed the Western leaders knew the same. And from this it followed that the Western Allies would not hand over the Balkans to Russia, that they therefore must land in Greece in 1943, and, in his own words, that they were not solely interested in winning the war but also in what the map of the world would look like once it had been won. By the summer of 1943 few intelligent Germans with access to the facts doubted what the outcome of the war would be. In any event, Operation Mincemeat was an expensive flop in pursuit of a poor policy.

Far more elaborate was the cover plan to disguise Operation Overlord, that is the invasion landings in Normandy on 6 June 1944, and the subsequent plans to defeat Germany and end the war. Although Overlord was always regarded as the major effort by the Western Allies, its ultimate objective was not defined during the planning phase save in such vague terms as those quoted above – the defeat of Germany, the end of the war. This is comprehensible, in that an over-remote objective is pointless, and indeed even the limited time-table of the operation was not kept, since the British were too slow and the Americans, once they got moving, went too fast. The plan itself was crude: it involved the landing of huge forces in Normandy, an advance across France and into the Low Countries, and then an advance into Germany to achieve the famous formula of 'unconditional surrender'. What was to be the ultimate arrangement with the Soviets was left undecided for the moment, though the details of future military boundaries and zones of occupation were later worked out in London between an Anglo-American team of diplomats and soldiers, led by Lord Strang, and their Russian equivalents. These arrangements could not be legally binding, nor were they made at the very highest level, for the situation was fluid. Such open options would have admirably suited Napoleon in his prime; General Marshall or General MacArthur might have had the courage to stand up to the heavy and not infrequently foetid breath of the politicians at his back. General Eisenhower was of a different calibre, although a man of very great charm and an obedient servant, as he had shown in Africa. This no doubt is why he was chosen to command the greatest Western operation of the Second World War.

If all was left vague for the future, the actual landings were prepared with the greatest possible care and attention by the Western forces both in the operational and in the intelligence fields. By early 1944 British intelligence was reaching an expertise which had perhaps never been equalled before and may well never be again. The Germans could scarcely build a machine gun emplacement before it was photographed by an R.A.F. or U.S.A.A.F. reconnaissance plane. The navies tested the quality of the sand on the beaches and submariners watched and reported on the creation of underwater obstacles. Our knowledge of the German Order of Battle, derived in small part from the French Resistance, strengthened somewhat by parachutists of the S.O.E. (Special Operations Executive) and the O.S.S. (Office of Strategic Survey), but principally dependent on Ultra and above all on Polish intelligence and the interpretation of captured German documents, was well nigh impeccable. Meanwhile our total control of the German espionage network in Britain enabled us to give them a very misleading picture of the Anglo-American Order of Battle, of our intentions, and even of our time and place of landing. The civilian brains of Britain, recruited in defensive haste some four years earlier, had been trained, or more exactly tuned into playing this most complex intelligence symphony in near-perfect harmony and with seldom a false note. Polish intelligence was also very reliable indeed.

To this was now added the cover plan. This was designed to disguise the place, rather than the approximate date, of the landings. The admirals and their staffs knew how dependent they were on tides, wind and weather. The tides of course concerned the rising and setting of the moon, as well as the hour of daybreak in order that darkness give cover to the invasion fleet and landing craft. They knew that the German admiralty was only too well aware of the facts in the Channel, from their own failed attempt to mount Operation Sealion in 1940. To some of the soldiers the sailors seemed to be almost obstructive in this insistence on nautical considerations. (Hitler had found the same in 1940. General Buhle has described, to this writer, standing on Cap Gris Nez with Hitler that summer, and quoted Hitler's remark as he gazed across the water at Dover: 'If only I could leave it to my army combat engineers – *die Pioniere* – and not to those saboteurs dressed up as naval officers!') Furthermore the air forces, on whom almost everything depended during the transportation, landing and consolidation of a strong beach-head, were dependent in those days on the weather. This made the date of the landing reduced to a very few days within a very few summer months. Finally, the great influx of troops and landing craft from the United States and the Mediterranean could not be concealed from the U-boats and from sources in Spain and elsewhere.

260

Secrecy could not be kept indefinitely, with these huge army, maritime and air forces poised in Britain. The meteorologists suddenly became of vast importance, but theirs is a most inaccurate science, as everyone who pays any attention to long-range weather forecasts knows. The fact that the weather was foul on 5 June almost necessitated a postponement, and the German meteorologist assumed that it must, and German tension relaxed, expecting a month's delay. It was then that General Eisenhower made his one, vital decision, and he was lucky, for the weather improved. Had he been unlucky, the invasion might well have failed.

Since the men responsible could hardly juggle with time they had to devote themselves to place. And this they did with the greatest enthusiasm, reinforced by what they regarded as the success of 'Mincemeat'. Some of their manoeuvres were trivial. For example an actor was dressed up as General Montgomery and made prominent in Gibraltar. Nobody seems to have been impressed or led to believe that Spain was the target. The Germans were nudged into thinking that Norway was the objective. The German General Staff could not easily be persuaded that the route to Berlin led through Oslo, though they rightly feared raids up there. Even the Greek story was given another run, with no success. The German General Staff knew that the enormous invasion force – the strength of which was exaggerated to them – must come in the west, roughly between Cherbourg and Ostende, but that is, in itself, a long coastline. An attempt in 1943, named Operation Sledgehammer, to make them believe that Brittany was to be the Western objective made no sense to the Germans unless the Western generals were still happy with their Italian folly. Since this was unlikely Operation Sledgehammer was a non-starter.

One (to this writer still somewhat mysterious) aspect of this cover plan business (if such it was) took place far away in Ankara. This is the story of the Albanian spy, 'Cicero,' written by a former S.S. officer, a member of the S.D., translated and slightly edited by myself.[5] The longer I worked on this job, the more sceptical did I become, not about the authenticity of Moyzisch's story but about what lay behind it. This scepticism has increased and, since

261

'Cicero' is dead, cannot be verified, though such verification would probably have been impossible even in his lifetime. Briefly, I became convinced that 'Cicero' was a rather obvious double agent at a time before that word had become a commonplace in novels and on the television screen.

The 'Cicero' story is very well-known. The British ambassador, a most experienced diplomat named Sir Hughe Knatchbull-Hugessen, had been appointed to this most sensitive post; the German ambassador in Ankara was Franz von Papen, the former Chancellor. Sir Hughe engaged, as valet, the Albanian known as 'Cicero' in October 1943. It was Sir Hughe's habit to lock away the most secret of his papers in the safe in his bedroom. The valet had access to his master's bedroom, and when Sir Hughe was asleep would take his keys from his bedside table, open the safe, rapidly photograph the papers, and then replace them and the keys in their proper place. The negatives he would then sell to Moyzisch, who passed them to Kaltenbrunner, Heydrich's successor at the S.D. For this he was paid, by Moyzisch, in high-denominational forged British banknotes. He gave the Germans the code name, Operation Overlord, and the approximate date, but not it would seem the intended beach-head. Meanwhile two Abwehr agents in Turkey, who had nothing to do with 'Cicero', were planning to desert to the British. This they did early in 1944, with the result that the S.D. were in a position to discredit the Abwehr, to arrange the dismissal of Admiral Canaris, and eventually to take over German secret intelligence. In April 1944, after their defection, 'Cicero' vanished with his bogus British banknotes – which in due course were proved to be value-less – but according to newspaper accounts he lived a comfortable life until his death, in Albania, some twenty years later. Now come the questions, which can best be put in series:

1 What did 'Cicero' pass to Moyzisch? The code word 'Overlord', but this was already known to the Russians at least after the Teheran conference of January 1944 and probably before to a great many persons in Britain, America and among the Western Allied forces in the Mediterranean. It was not, in any real sense, a secret, such as Ultra, that could be kept. The approximate date

of Overlord was already and obviously known to the Germans. There is no evidence that 'Cicero' gave the S.D. any firm intelligence of any more value to them than the bogus British banknotes were to be to him.

2 Why did the British ambassador, who had been in Ankara since 1939, employ an Albanian valet in 1943? In so sensitive a post, this choice is a most curious act on the part of so experienced a diplomat. British valets are, after all, known for their efficiency. Nor was Sir Hughe ever reprimanded for this strange action: on the contrary he was given important assignments after the war, such as the Brussels embassy.

3 Can Sir Hughe have been so heavy a sleeper as to permit all this pilfering to go on, in his bedroom, for some six months? Moyzisch says that some of this safe-breaking took place when Sir Hughe was out, using a duplicate key provided from Berlin. Sir Hughe, in a spectacular purple Rolls-Royce, seems to have drawn attention to these outings, and security experts from Britain were flown out to 'check' the security of his safe, rather ostentatiously.

4 What connection was there between the activities of 'Cicero' and the internecine warfare between the Abwehr and the S.D.? This might well provide the key.

5 On whose money did 'Cicero' live after April 1944? Certainly not on the forged £5 notes given him by the S.D.

One can only conclude that the whole was an elaborate hoax, mounted by the British Secret Intelligence Service to deceive the Germans – perhaps by the insertion of spurious intelligence among what was true and verifiable (i.e. R.A.F. targets in the Balkans) – designed to mislead the enemy concerning the objectives of Overlord. Another British motive would have been to exacerbate hostility between the S.D. and the Abwehr. It was certainly in the British interest to watch the destruction of the Abwehr by the far less competent S.D. If these guesses are correct, the logical conclusion can only be that 'Operation Cicero' was mounted by the S.I.S., who paid him in real banknotes. The fact that Franz von Papen believed Moyzisch's story, and has said so in print, is a form of negative confirmation: during his long career as a politician and diplomat von Papen showed his ability to believe almost anything, provided only that it was untrue.*

Far more grandiose than 'Cicero' was F.U.S.A.G., the abbreviated name of an imaginary First United States Army Group, complete with a large spectacular arm patch which at one time this writer wore. To explain F.U.S.A.G. it is first necessary to describe the Germans' intelligence appreciation of Overlord, early in 1944.

As had been the case with Operation Mincemeat and the invasion of southern Europe, the German General Staff did not base its expectations on its intelligence services – which by then were very weak indeed – but on the logic of highly experienced soldiers who ascribed the finest politico-military ability to their enemies, particularly their enemies in the West.

The O.K.W. and the O.K.H. appreciation of their enemy's point of view was that Anglo-American forces would aim for the Dutch and Belgian ports, particularly the semi-inland port of Antwerp, thence the Ruhr, thus destroying most of Germany's heavy industry, and finally Berlin. This implied the quickest and shortest invasion route, with target the Pas de Calais area. And it was this stretch of coast that was being most heavily fortified and strongly manned by the German Fifteenth Army,

* Mr Cavendish-Bentinck quite disagreed with this interpretation. He writes me: 'I knew "Cicero" when he was Horace Rumbold's valet at the Lausanne Conference in 1922–23. He was an excellent valet and of very good presence (as was required of footmen and valets). Hughe Knatchbull-Hugessen used to play the piano, at times he would leave his study to play the piano in a nearby room; Cicero would then pop in and photograph the papers on "Snatch's" desk. When the sounds of music ceased, Cicero hopped out of the study. I think that you have allowed your imagination to run riot. Operation Cicero was certainly not mounted by the S.I.S.'

Nevertheless I still feel that the very fact of Cicero having worked for so distinguished and discriminating an ambassador as Sir Horace Rumbold (who had in fact employed 'Cicero' as early as 1919, who knew Nazi Germany well and disliked it intensely), and so long before, would indicate a greater willingness on his part to work for the British than for the Germans. On the other hand his son, Sir Anthony Rumbold, believes that 'Cicero' had an anti-British bias. Despite his great eminence in Second World War intelligence, even the Director of the J.I.C. certainly did not know everything that the S.I.S. was up to, for otherwise Philby could not have survived.

264

primarily an infantry army. It all made perfect military sense, and was duly reported as such by secret and open intelligence, to the very considerable delight of the Anglo-American leaders who had anticipated this German reaction and who had therefore decided to take a more roundabout route and invade through Normandy. It was clearly in the highest interest of the Western Allies that the Germans be encouraged to reinforce, up to the limit, their defences both of men and of material in the Pas de Calais. It is possible – in the opinion of this writer probable – that the secret intelligence passed by Cicero had this purpose in view. This is guesswork: I was not there and do not know.

Now, that is to say very early in 1944, Hitler's celebrated 'intuition' came into operation. It is possible that it was nudged by his past and potentially future Soviet allies, though again this writer does not know. In any event Hitler decided that Normandy would be the Allied forces' first objective, and ordered a crash programme to reinforce that part of the French coast. Field Marshal Rommel was given command of Army Group B, with these instructions. His direct commander was Field Marshal von Rundstedt, commander of all the Western armies and Army Groups, a cynical soldier who attached little importance to Hitler's intuitive views. Nevertheless he had to carry out Hitler's orders, even though he was so senior that he might and did on occasion argue against them. He was not prepared to strip the Pas de Calais of divisions to defend Normandy, though he could not prevent reinforcements both of men and material going where Hitler's intuition said that they should. Besides, Hitler, whose attitude towards his subordinates was increasingly that of control by division of authority, was also giving direct orders to Rommel. He was not, though, prepared to give Rommel everything Rommel desired.

The main intelligence issue dividing Rommel from Rundstedt was Normandy versus the Pas de Calais; the main strategic one was the location of the counter-attack force, principally the Panzer divisions. And here Hitler backed Rundstedt, but not for Rundstedt's reasons. Runstedt wished to keep the Panzers back from the coast. Since the Allied air forces, soon to be aided by the Maquis, were systematically destroying the bridges across the Seine and other waterways between the two possible landing areas, and with the help of the Maquis were also putting the French railways out of action, we observed from London that the Panzer divisions, as they arrived, were being held further and further back from the coast. Many of them were assigned to the *Fuehrerreserve*, that is to say Hitler's reserve force, and could only be committed on his, not Rommel's or Rundstedt's, orders. This suited Hitler admirably, since it gave him a very great measure of immediate control in the battle to come. Militarily this was a folly: a battle in France cannot be satisfactorily controlled from East Prussia or the Bavarian Alps. Indeed for several vital hours the toadies around Hitler did not dare awaken him to tell him that the Allies were ashore in Normandy.

Rommel had accepted Normandy as the Allied target and he wished to have the Panzer divisions well forward, so they could counter-attack immediately, before the Anglo-American armies had time to consolidate their beach-heads. In this strategy he was obviously correct, given the assumption that Normandy was to be the major – even more if it were to prove the only – immediate Allied objective. A skilful counter-attack by half a dozen Panzer divisions on D-day, or D+1, would almost certainly have thrown the Allied armies back into the sea. And the defeat of Operation Overlord was really the last major opportunity of the Germans to win – or at least not to lose – the war. Also, with his first-hand knowledge of Allied air supremacy in Africa, Rommel knew that it would be virtually impossible to move up the Panzer divisions by day without their suffering very heavy casualties, and to move these formations only during the short summer nights meant that their commitment to battle from the areas where they were stationed before D-day must be a lengthy business. Again he was entirely correct. They arrived, mauled by air attack or too late, and in very heavy battles, particularly with the British and Canadians but also with the Americans, their counter-attack was held. It was a formidable enough counter-attack as it was: had it come in, in full force, even a couple of weeks earlier, rather than being steadily but slowly reinforced, it might well have succeeded. Once this failure became obvious to Rommel, he realized that the war was lost. He drew the conclusion that he must throw in his lot with the men of 20 July, remove Hitler though he still baulked at assassination, and surrender, unconditionally if need be, to the Western Allies at least. Unfortunately he was wounded and in hospital when Stauffenberg set off his bomb. Field Marshal von Kluge was in command of Army Group B by then. He hesitated, in part because the conspirators had had no word of encouragement of any sort from London and Washington, though a link had been established between his command and Montgomery's concerning the exchange of nurses and other medical non-combatants. Had Rommel still been in command of Army Group B it is fair to assume that he would probably and immediately have used that link to surrender his forces, and that they would, with the exception of the Waffen S.S., have obeyed him.

Such then was the background to the intelligence operation based on F.U.S.A.G. It was of supreme importance that the Germans should, first of all, believe before D-day that the Pas de Calais was the target, and after D-day that Normandy was merely a distraction, that the main attack was still to come across the Straits of Dover. The whole of the XX organization and much else was mobilized, not so much to deceive the Germans but to reinforce the opinions that Rundstedt and the General Staff already held. The fact that they did already hold these views made the task of misleading them very much more simple.

So too did the fact that we knew, from Ultra, how grossly false was their picture of the Allied Order of Battle in Britain before D-day. A great number of non-existent divisions, principally American, were created for German intelligence to report and track as they moved nominally into staging posts in the Kent area. Dummy landing craft were built in large quantities and sited, not too obviously, precisely where they would have been for a real Calais operation. Nor was that all. The whole complex signals apparatus of an American Army Group was set up. It was not too large, since the Germans would assume that while in Britain land lines would be used, but it was, I believe, slightly larger than the genuine signals network used by Field Marshal Montgomery's Army Group before D-day. Since we knew that German intelligence was not reading our X but was certainly analysing our Y, it did not really matter very much what was said by this bogus network over the air. Nevertheless just in case they should break our ciphers, credible material concerning supplies, movements, even intelligence and so on, was transmitted.

To this most complex deception plan there was one fortuitous addition. General Patton was known to the Germans as the most aggressive and successful American senior officer in Europe, both from African and from Sicilian experience, where he had commanded the American Seventh Army with great skill and dash. He was known to be in England. It was logical for the Germans to assume that he would command the major American force. But he had vanished, nor did he appear for some time in Normandy. The Germans knew, of course, of the unfortunate incident when he had slapped a hospitalized American private on the grounds that he was a malingerer, and that this had caused an uproar in the American press. They did not know, indeed could hardly be expected to believe, that this trivial incident would be used as the pretext to have him replaced by General Bradley, who had been his subordinate in Sicily and who, in Normandy, was at first only in command of the U.S. First Army under Field Marshal Montgomery. German intelligence was led to believe that Patton had in fact been moved upwards, to command the non-existent F.U.S.A.G., which would launch the major Calais attack. They did not, as did British intelligence, devote very close attention to the characters and personalities of enemy commanders. They knew that Patton was a brilliant cavalry general. They did not know that he was an extremely difficult man to work with, that he had very little interest in logistics, and that he had made no attempt to conceal either his personal dislike of Montgomery or his general anti-British bias. He was certainly not the man to handle the inevitable difficulties that arise between temperamental, often overstrained commanders of different nationalities and backgrounds at the highest level. General Bradley, soft-spoken, tactful, considerate but also with a will of iron equal to Patton's, was a far better choice – which is presumably why he was given command of the Army Group in August, with Patton under him as commander of the Third Army. None of this was known to the Germans, who continued to believe in F.U.S.A.G. commanded by General Patton and poised in southeast England.

(I myself, a member of General Bradley's rear staff that was to control 12th U.S. Army Group, was issued with a F.U.S.A.G.

patch along with several other officers and instructed to be seen wearing, and if possible be heard talking about, it in the bar of the Dorchester and other such places, just in case there should be any undetected German agents lurking about. Since I did not usually frequent such bars, and had little idea of what I was supposed to say except announce whenever possible that I was on the staff of F.U.S.A.G., and since there were no German spies lurking to hear me, I fear that my own contribution to this deception plan was nil. This is perhaps just as well. Since I speak with a pronounced British accent, a German agent hearing me might have been led to doubt the credibility of Patton's F.U.S.A.G.)

It has been frequently said that the triumph of this vast deception operation was that it kept the German Fifteenth Army tied down north of the Seine. This is not quite true. The Fifteenth Army was an infantry army, largely employed in the manning of massive fortification. When at last the Germans realized that they had been fooled, in late June or early July, they could only send a very few infantry divisions to reinforce their Seventh Army in Normandy. This was in large measure due to the destruction of the Seine bridges and the French railways. General Warlimont has maintained, on those grounds, that the O.K.W. was not deceived for so long a period and that therefore the whole, vastly expensive operation was as foolish as 'Mincemeat'. He is quite right in that the Fifteenth Army could not have been moved down to reinforce the German Seventh. He is, in my opinion, wrong in that this intelligence operation reinforced erroneous German intelligence, and above all in that it helped postpone the total commitment of the German Panzer force in France for several days – in some cases, weeks – against the Allied forces in Normandy. It may well be that the O.K.W. was quite uninfluenced by these elaborate cover plans and disposed of German forces simply in accordance with its own cool-headed military appreciation of the situation, slightly marred by Hitler's 'intuition' – which now as heretofore had not let him down. It may well be that no General Staff as competent as was that of the Germans in 1944 can be bamboozled by such tricks, even when almost deprived of its own secret intelligence service by external or internal causes, or both. It may even be that the enormous, and enormously expensive in men and equipment, cover plan to

Overlord achieved nothing that would not have occurred in any case on pure German initiative, whereas had this cover plan been detected, German intelligence would have been immediately alerted to the realities: in effect, that it was a pointless gamble. Nevertheless, that it did succeed may have been a not inconsiderable factor in the Normandy victory.

No such an intelligence operation was mounted again, with any sort of success, in the European war nor in that against the Japanese. On the other hand the somewhat exaggerated success of these operations by the Anglo-American high commands were to lead them, as will be shown, into great tactical and strategic errors when estimating enemy intentions.

Chapter Sixteen

Intelligence Among Allies

In his most informative book, *The Code Breakers*, Mr David Kahn states, without any source reference: 'By 1942 they [the Russians] had cracked messages in the Enigma, a rotor machine.' There is no reason to believe that this is correct. It is of course possible, since it is impossible to prove a negative, but there is some reason to believe that such Ultra material as the Russians were receiving was passed to them, in an exceedingly complicated manner, by the British and American intercept services.

Stalin had remarked, as early as 1917, that the Bolshevik Party should never allow itself to be provoked nor be provocative. Since, according to Marxist–Leninist dogma, history 'was on the side of' ultimate and total global Communist victory, Soviet strategy had for a long time but not necessarily for ever to be defensive and to avoid the attempts made by the Turks, Christian Europe and others to expedite an inevitable process, while of course giving 'history', that strange and non-existent force, every encouragement in the fulfilment of its aims. Since Russia was the 'fatherland of the proletariat', that is to say more accurately of the Stalinist power apparatus, it must be protected against its internal enemies – the *Yezhoushchina* and similar subsequent operations – and must continue in total distrust, combined with exploitation, of the non-Communist powers (a policy later extended to rival, foreign Communist powers, who became automatically potential enemies as soon as they shed Russian control).

Thus the frame of mind which had rejected all foreign warnings concerning Operation Barbarossa continued throughout the war, and into the post-war period.

For other reasons already outlined the Western powers dared not jeopardize their own, most important, intelligence arm by 'giving' Enigma to so unpredictable an ally as Soviet Russia. On the other hand, for reasons of the simplest national self-interest

271

neither Britain nor the United States wished to see any sort of German victory in Russia. London knew far more about German Order of Battle, and therefore about probable German intentions, not infrequently reinforced by Ultra's actual knowedge of German strategic plans, than did Moscow. However, the Russians did not believe the correct intelligence that they were receiving from their British ally, indeed regarded it as provocative and hostile in intent, and continued to lose battles. They would only accept information from their own people. Before his arrest in Tokyo, in October of 1941, the Communist agent Dr Sorge, whose earlier warnings had been ignored by Moscow, reported that the Japanese did not intend to invade Siberia. Whether he obtained this intelligence by his own espionage or whether it was fed to him by the Americans reading the Purple Machine is not known: probably a combination of both. In any event, the Soviets moved enough divisions from Siberia to the Moscow area just in time to hold the German army, the spearheads of which could already see the onion domes above the Kremlin.

In 1942 Sorge was dead, and the Russian espionage organization in occupied Europe – including occupied Russia – emasculated by the N.K.V.D. and the S.D. Nor were the Soviets accepting British (and by now American) intelligence. So, once again, the hideous series of German victories began to roll. Leningrad was besieged, while far away to the south the German armies reached the Volga, and pressed on into the Caucasus within reach of the Baku oilfields and ultimately perhaps to join hands with Rommel, whose Afrika Korps was on the Egyptian frontier. At this point the British, at least, and to lesser extent the Americans realized that they must outwit the cumbersome Soviet security system, with its stupid Marxist–Leninist credo, in order to prevent the conquest of the Soviet Union by the Wehrmacht.

It is necessary here to return to the concept of triangular warfare, before explaining the inter-Allied (with Russia one of the Allies) relationship in secret intelligence which prevailed for only three and a half years between the summer of 1941 and the winter of 1944–5. What is most relevant is the relationship between Britain and the United States on the one hand and the Soviet Union on the other during 1942.

On the day the Nazis invaded Russia in June 1941, Winston

Churchill, Prime Minister of Britain and with a long and proven hatred of the Communist ideology, informed his compatriots and the world at large that had Hitler invaded Hell he, Churchill, would have made an alliance with the Devil himself. This piece of Churchillian rhetoric, about which the theologians might have something to say, became Allied policy. It became practical policy. Enormous quantities of equipment were sent from Britain, by sea, to Murmansk, where the Germans had previously been given a U-boat base. The expense of re-equipping the Red Air Force – in so far as this could be done with Hurricanes and Spitfires urgently needed by the Royal Air Force for its own operations – was alone enormous, not only in aircraft but in ships and in the lives of skilled sailors which were lost in the convoys that rounded the North Cape. British material help was entirely acceptable, but certainly not decisive in the survival of the Soviet Union.

Help from the United States was infinitely more massive. The Soviets had a lot of very good tanks, as well as a great deal of effective artillery, though most of it was soon captured by the Germans. This they were to replace with rocket artillery in which field of weapons, as in tanks, they led the world. Their great shortage lay in the backing such weapons need, and particularly in transportation. When Hermann Goering announced that all the Americans could make was razor-blades, he had perhaps forgotten about Detroit. Billions of dollars' worth of equipment was sent to Russia, and among many other incalculable benefits to the Soviet armed forces it made the horse-drawn Red Army mobile. This vast gift, called Lend-lease, was of course never paid for, in any way save by the heroism of the Red Army soldiers which helped to hold the Wehrmacht's advance and then to drive the German army westwards. Such free material aid was entirely acceptable to the Soviet leaders, all the more so since there was no reciprocal aid involved unless self-defence can be so described. Certainly the Soviets made no direct contribution to Anglo-American victories in Africa or Western Europe, while their declaration of war against Japan only took place after the almost total defeat of the Japanese Empire and served only to increase Soviet territory at Japanese expense, and to further Communist victory in the Chinese Civil War.

To understand this strange dual standard it is necessary to return to 1942, that critical year. The British and Americans had no form of an Agitprop organization operating in their own countries, let alone inside the Soviet Union. Following on Churchill's rhetorical statement, which surely he must have come to regret, the British press gave unstinted and indeed overwhelming praise to the gallant Russian ally. There was even a ridiculous ceremony by which something called 'the Stalingrad sword' was given a form of benediction in Westminster Abbey. In America President Roosevelt, no doubt to the pleasure of his quasi-Communist wife and of his Vice-President Henry Wallace as well as to justify to the people and Congress American aid, had nothing but praise for the Soviet Union, for dear old Uncle Joe, and indeed through his wife and Vice-President for the Soviet penal system. In retrospect it is all almost incredible, were it not being repeated in other terms, by other people, today.

It was during 1942 that the Communist Agitprop organization mounted one of its major campaigns in Britain and, to a much lesser extent, in the United States, with the slogan: *Second Front Now!* The propaganda aspect was and remains obvious. Whatever was happening in the Pacific, on the mainland of Asia and in the air over Europe, the Russians alone were fighting the Germans. Winston Churchill and his government were to be discredited in the eyes of the British people because he and they did not immediately order an invasion of France. Did this propaganda, with the organized demonstrations in Trafalgar Square and elsewhere, have any influence in bringing about the extremely costly reconnaissance in force at Dieppe that summer? It is possible, and the simultaneous defeat of the British Eighth Army in Africa brought the British Government nearer to political disaster than at any other time during the war; certainly before the Battles of Midway and El Alamein in the autumn there was a genuine feeling of distress at Western military failure. The fact that the Russian armies were being systematically destroyed was, in the public mind, ascribed as much to Anglo-American as to Russian incompetence. And the fact that the ill-trained, ill-led Russians were dying while huge Anglo-American forces were being trained for future victories was paradoxically and most skilfully translated into a sense of guilt in the West.

274

At a better-informed level the Russians, like the British and American leaders and commanders, knew that a 1942 D-day could only have been a disaster for the forces involved, which would have been destroyed even as the Canadians were at Dieppe. This would by no means have displeased the Soviet leaders, since the enormous production of the British and American factories would then have had to be diverted, even more than it already was, to supplying the Red Army which would thus have emerged from the war as the solitary victor. What the Russians wanted from their Western 'allies', then as now, was technological and industrial expertise. Neither the British nor the Americans were quite so foolish as to sacrifice their manpower in order to let the Russians claim a solitary victory. Yet they did not wish the Russians to lose. With a few reservations, which will be discussed, their alliance with the Soviets was both genuine and straightforward.

In two major fields of activity only did the Western Allies attempt concealment from the Soviets: the Ultra system and the creation of a nuclear weapon, the Manhattan Project. In the first Western security was almost certainly successful, in the second not.

Nor was any attempt made to reciprocate the espionage activities of the Soviets. Indeed this would have been excessively difficult since their internal security was so tight; everything in Russia, from the production of a sock factory to the felling of timber was 'secret' at least to foreigners. An early attempt to bolster Russian resistance with R.A.F. squadrons operating from Russian airfields failed because of the obsessive secretiveness of the Red Air Force, and the squadrons were soon withdrawn, to the relief of everyone involved, British or Russian. When later the Americans were supplying planes in large numbers to the Russians, so far as was possible the Soviets saw to it that these were flown from Alaska by Russian pilots and crews. The sailors who made the perilous trip around the North Cape were treated more like dangerous aliens than friendly allies when they docked in Murmansk or Archangel.

Here two incidents should be told, the truth of which can be guaranteed. Since from this point on written resources are not always reliable or subject to test, personal memories, in particular regarding the post-war years, become selective and subject to censorship, while this writer's first-hand knowledge fades out totally after 1946.

In 1942 an extremely experienced Royal Navy submariner, the late Admiral Fawkes, was sent to the Black Sea at the request of the Soviet government, to lend technical advice in the handling and tactics of underwater craft. He told this writer that he was astonished by the technical and tactical ignorance of Soviet submariners. As part of his duties he had to acquaint himself with the nature of Soviet submarines and practice, and in so doing he was, to his very considerable astonishment, arrested by the N.K.V.D. as a spy. It took the intervention of the British ambassador to obtain his release from prison and his return to Britain. It is interesting that his experience with the Red Navy was not only, understandably, suppressed at the time, but has never to my knowledge been written about since.

A later example, again by word of mouth, was given me by the late Air Chief Marshal Sir William Elliot. It is of a later date, 1944, when the Air Marshal commanded the so-called Balkan Air Force in the Mediterranean. At the time of the Warsaw Rising, in August of that year, the Red Air Force, flying U.S. planes, was shooting down Allied planes that were supplying the embattled Poles who were fighting the Germans. Elliot was ordered to confine the Polish bomber crews, who were under his command, to their barracks, lest they engage in suicide missions in aid of their compatriots, the Allied air forces having been refused landing facilities by the Soviets in their occupied territory. Needless to say, he obeyed his orders from the Allied politicians, and in due course Poland was given by those politicians to the Soviets. Sir William, who had perhaps more political interest than had Admiral Fawkes, told me that the implementation of this order was the most tragic operational action in his life as an air force officer who had fought, ultimately in the highest commands, through two world wars. Mr Cavendish-Bentinck echoed this expression of grief when he told me of informing the Polish ambassador, count Edward Raczynski, that the airlift to Warsaw would be discontinued.

It was against this background of malice and distrust on the part of the Russians that the British and to a lesser extent the

276

Americans attempted to save the Red Army from defeat, not only in the material field but in that of secret intelligence. Since the Soviets would not believe the truth if it emanated from Western sources, and since we dared not give them Ultra direct – not primarily because we could not trust them politically but also because their own rapidly re-created General Staff, and in particular its intelligence apparatus which would have been handling the matter, was so obviously inefficient – the British invented a most ingenious method of getting the truth to the Soviets. This was the so-called Lucy Ring.[1]

Rudolf Roessler, whose code name was Lucy, was a German anti-Nazi who had settled in Switzerland in the early days of the Nazi regime. He was an ex-army officer of middle-class origin who had established a considerable reputation in theatrical circles during the Weimar period but had preserved his officer status, since he was not an actor but rather a 'power' responsible for theatrical magazines and similar activities. The theatre in Weimar Germany was largely dominated by left-wing and Communist influences – this was Bertolt Brecht's golden age. Whether or not Roessler was a Communist Party member is irrelevant. He was surrounded by *apparatchiks* both in Germany and later in Switzerland. He was also in contact with German staff officers, some quite senior, in Berlin where he had been a member of the moderately distinguished *Herrenklub*, a coarser version of White's Club in London or of the Racquet and Tennis Club in New York. He, and his Communist friends, were therefore employed by the Swiss intelligence service.

There was a joke current in neutral Ireland during the Second World War: 'We know we are neutral, but who are we neutral against?' There was no need to ask such a question in Switzerland. The Helvetian Federation was neutral against Germany. Its very competent intelligence service was in close contact with the French and, after the defeat of France, with the British, although since Switzerland was by then totally encircled by Axis powers, this co-operation was more difficult. The story can be cut short. Since the Russians would not accept military intelligence from any but their own sources, Ultra and much else was 'fed' to the Russians via the 'Lucy Ring' and undoubtedly with the help of Swiss intelligence. It was supposed to come to Roessler through his

Berlin General Staff and *Herrenklub* contacts, and since his was an essentially Communist organization it was acceptable to – and what is more important acted upon in – Moscow. How aware Roessler was that he was a tool of British intelligence in the passage of true intelligence to the Russians is of minor importance. They believed him, they moved more Siberian divisions to the Volga, and they won the Battle of Stalingrad – just.

It was indeed an extraordinary stratagem. What is at first glance almost equally astonishing is the authentification given to the story by no less a man than Allen Dulles, who had been chief of American intelligence in Switzerland, who was later head of the new American Central Intelligence Agency, and who, after his return to private life, wrote: '. . . the Soviets developed a fantastic source located in Switzerland, a certain Rudolf Roessler (code name"Lucy"). By means which have not been ascertained to this day, Roessler in Switzerland was able to get intelligence from the German High Command in Berlin on a continuous basis, often less than twenty-four hours after its daily decisions concerning the Eastern front were made'.[2]

There are two possible explanations, neither quite satisfactory, for this statement by the man who had had a long connection with top secret intelligence both military and diplomatic, whose brother was President Eisenhower's Secretary of State, and who had been personally in Switzerland, as head of American intelligence there, during the war.

The first and most obvious is that with another war, between the United States and the Soviet Union, pending or even in the balance, he had no wish to open the eyes of Soviet intelligence to what had happened; that in 1962 when the book was written there may have been other 'Lucy Rings' envisaged if not even in existence; that for so authoritative a source as Allen Dulles to have given public credence to the Roessler organization was, in fact, only a skilful ploy to deceive Soviet intelligence in its pride or at least to avoid alerting it to present or future Western intelligence methods. Certainly the Communists have continued to boast about their expertise, in this field, during the Second World War. They have heroized a rather futile, Soviet-controlled Communist espionage apparatus, *die Rote Kapelle* or the Red Orchestra which was large, achieved little and was quite rapidly

278

uncovered by the Abwehr and the S.D. in late 1941 or early 1942. (The 'Lucy Ring' was technically controlled by the same branch of the G.R.U. that ran the 'Red Choir' orchestra.) From the propaganda point of view, it was and has remained important for the Soviets to maintain the lie that their intelligence service was equal, indeed superior, to that of the Western Allies. But the late Allen Dulles cannot possibly have believed this in 1962, or indeed at a considerably earlier date.

On the other hand the security surrounding Ultra was so intense, and so successful for tactical and what the Germans called operational purposes, that the knowledge of its specific activities was concealed, so far as possible, from all who did not need to be informed. Among other restrictions, nobody with knowledge of Ultra was allowed to be in a position where he or she might fall into enemy hands. This regulation was inevitably relaxed as the war went on; but still Allen Dulles, in neutral Switzerland, was a vulnerable person. It is just possible that he was not informed of the true source of the Eastern Front intelligence that was being passed to the Soviets, under heavy camouflage, through the Lucy Ring. Possible, but not probable. Certainly as head of the C.I.A. he must later have known the truth. Therefore the first explanation of his rather astonishing statement would appear closer to the reality.

Secret intelligence, like history itself, does not stop. Only as its methods cease to be secret are they changed. During the Second World War the breaking of German ciphers was, for the British and almost equally for the Americans, the war-winning intelligence weapon. The facts of this operation must be at all costs concealed from the German enemy and the Russian 'ally'. The intensive security necessitated by our excessive reliance on this source was to boomerang, but not quite to such a disastrous extent as might have occurred. The secrecy surrounding Ultra during the triangular war was essential then, and of some value during the Western–Communist confrontation that ensued as soon as one side of the triangle had been eliminated.

What annoyed many who had kept silent was not so much the revelations in Group Captain Winterbotham's book concerning the breaking of German ciphers – here the French had anticipated him[3] – as his exposure of how this most important source of intelligence was used.

The fact that it is quite pointless to collect intelligence, as one might collect stamps, and then leave it alone in filing cabinets, is even more true in war than in peace. Not only does the 'filing cabinet' have to be extensive in many fields; it must also be properly catalogued and readily available for consultation. It is precisely this that Eric (now Professor) Birley did for British military intelligence between 1940 (when he had enough data) and 1946, when he returned to academic life. His knowledge, from his indices, was so profound, so intuitive as well, and so wide that he could almost always and immediately produce a character study of a newly appointed German army commander. He could even anticipate the numbers of new German divisions, and of such apparently unimportant formations as Fortress Battalions. In this he was greatly helped by the evaluation of Ultra, in which he was also directly involved. His most unusual capacity for analysis and deduction, often from very slender facts, was immensely superior to that of any German brain in any similar position. It is fair to assume that had he been a German military intelligence executive he would not have been confused either by Patton's F.U.S.A.G. or by the bogus Anglo-American order of battle that was being fed to the enemy in the first half of 1944, and was in part believed by *Fremde Heere West* as late as September. It is probable that the Royal Navy had an expert analyst of comparable virtuosity. The scientists on the other hand do not seem to have been quite so well served.

Order of Battle was far from being the most important value of Ultra. If the French had cracked the Enigma Machine before their 1940 defeat, they did not use this intelligence directly. If they simply filed it away, then perspicacious and brave French intelligence officers destroyed those files, or perhaps the German intelligence officers who went through the French archives stored in the Renault works did not grasp what it was that they stumbled upon, for the Germans remained arrogantly certain that their Enigma was unbreakable. Similarly the Americans do not appear to have made much use of their breaking of the Japanese Purple Machine before Pearl Harbor, and very little effective use before the Battle of Midway.

The British, on the other hand, as soon as they had complete control of their own intelligence service in June of 1940, made the speediest decisions concerning the use of Ultra and set up a most elaborate and effective organization, which remained secret until Group Captain Winterbotham saw fit to disclose most of these secrets to the world in 1974.

There were two major considerations. The Germans must not know that British intelligence had the Enigma Machine. Since it could not be known during that desperate summer how much the Germans had discovered, or might discover, from French sources, the first consideration was maximum security such as had perhaps never before been practised by any major power engaged in a major war. Had the Germans even suspected that their top secret signals were being read, if only in part to begin with, by the British it would have been comparatively easy for them to change the Enigma ciphers in such a way as to make the breaking of them far more difficult and time-consuming for British intelligence. They could even, though this would have been far more difficult, have introduced another rotor machine. Hence British security necessitated the minimum distribution of Ultra material.

However, this had to be combined with its maximum distribution. With Operation Sealion pending and always dependent, in large measure, on the aerial battle called in history the Battle of Britain, the swiftest possible dissemination of Ultra was equally vital. The German air fleets in France and the Low Countries often received their orders only a few hours before their Luftwaffe bomber and fighter squadrons were airborne. To tell the British fighter squadrons where to be, when, while still preserving maximum security, was excessively difficult, particularly as the Germans must not even guess at the source of this intelligence.

The nerve centre was Bletchley Park, where in due course many, perhaps even most, of the best brains in Britain were resident, or perhaps more often, transient visitors. It was for that reason, and that reason only, that it was a most stimulating series of offices in which to work, for it was a dreary place, where either nothing was happening, or activity was feverish. The inmates, most of whom were later on brief assignment, were too many to be housed behind the wire fences and they were billeted in gloomy pubs or private houses within a radius of many miles and with an ingenious range of reasons for being in this comparatively but deliberately obscure area of the south Midlands.

In its earliest days Bletchley was in essence a defensive force, to anticipate German attack. It had the full political backing of the British Prime Minister, Winston Churchill; apart from his First War knowledge of Room 40, it was the sort of operation that appealed to his nature. Indeed he sometimes insisted – and there were none to resist such insistence – on receiving raw, unevaluated Ultra. This form of direct transmission was always dangerous. However, Bletchley was in no position to refuse Churchill immediate access to a deciphered signal from Hitler to one of his Wehrmacht's C-in-Cs or to the Japanese Prime Minister. Such a lack of evaluation deprived Bletchley (if only very seldom) of one of its three major tasks: rapid deciphering, rapid evaluation, and very rapid dissemination to an extremely small and absolutely trustworthy group of high-level political and military commanders. (I use the word 'military' here to include naval, air and scientific personnel, and after early 1942 – if not before – to the equivalent United States organizations' leaders.)

The actual deciphering was the work of Britain's best mathematicians, assisted by the finest technological brains involved in the exploitation and creation of early computers. (Some of these, along with the physicists, chemists and their colleagues, had been, or soon were, passed on to the Manhattan Project in Chicago, Los Alamos and elsewhere.) Secondly, the broken cipher messages (and not all of them were always, immediately, broken) had to be interpreted and evaluated by an entirely different type of mind with an utterly different background. It was here that men and women, such as Eric Birley, were invaluable. German staff officers, using their most secret cipher, tended to be curt. A high proportion of what they said to one another needed an interpretation requiring a knowledge of German military affairs equivalent to their own. (The situation reports from the Japanese in Berlin to their people in Tokyo were quite simply spelled out, since the Japanese recipients knew less about German affairs than did Bletchley.) With extreme speed in these two very difficult operations, it was still necessary to get this secret intelligence to the commanders who must use it, often at once, if Bletchley were to be of any value, always remembering the intensive security involved.

The solution was rapid, and later elaborated. During the Battle of Britain the only Air Force operational headquarters in receipt of Ultra was that of the Commander-in-Chief, Fighter Command, Air Chief Marshal Dowding. The commanders of the three fighter groups involved did not receive Ultra, but just Dowding's orders which therefore those most distinguished air force commanders did not always understand, particularly as Ultra was not then, and indeed never was, 100 per cent certain, though it approached that figure in 1944. This accounted for much of the bitter criticism of Dowding, at senior Royal Air Force level, in late 1944, his removal from his command, and the failure for so long to give him the honours he deserved for his victory. He was, in fact, one of the victims of Ultra security, a security he preserved until his death.

It is not hard to see that this system needed modification, at least so far as distribution went, when it had been established that the Germans were ignorant of Ultra, when America was a total ally, and when the strategy of the Western Allies was moving from the defensive to the offensive. It was then that the S.L.U. system, as described by Group Captain Winterbotham, was invented or at least perfected.

The Special Liaison Units were manned by the most competent signals officers of the Royal Air Force. They were invisible at senior R.A.F. headquarters, hardly visible at British army headquarters, and were hidden, so far as possible physically hidden, at American headquarters. Their functon was to submit the Ultra received from Bletchley, with maximum speed, to the intelligence officer at the relevant command, so that the recipient might again evaluate it within his own sphere and submit it to his immediate Commanding General at once. When I was a recipient of German Order of Battle at 12th U.S. Army Group, there were, apart from my direct commanders in G-2 and on General Bradley's staff in 1944, perhaps three or four officers who were cognizant of Ultra. We had all been trained at Bletchley to understand the nature, and above all the secrecy, of what we were handling. I never discussed my own work with my fellow-officers, except at the very frequent Ultra conferences at which General Bradley was almost always present. I never knew the name of the Royal Air Force squadron-leader who produced the deciphered documents as they came in, during that hot summer of 1944. Nor do I know, now, how he received them from Bletchley. The probability is the 'one-time pad system', which I shall presently explain, or some variant thereof.

For the recipients of Ultra had all, I think, been trained at Bletchley, so that we might understand what it was that we were to receive together with the security implications. In order that we need not suspect that we were automata inside the intelligence machine we were shown more, but not much more, than we needed to know. So far as this writer is concerned, thirty and more years later, this psychological approach was perfect. I was honoured by the confidence given me, at no time expected promotion, and for one third of a century kept my promise not to talk or write about these matters either in public or in private. This was not a very difficult promise to keep, since I have discovered recently that most of my friends were involved, in one way or another, in this business, that they too had no particular interest in picking at what rapidly became very old bones. It all happened, as Group Captain Winterbotham remarks, a long time ago. Almost as long ago, in our time scale, lie the Napoleonic Wars. Yet those wars remain of great historical interest, and in this context.

I quote from the supplementary or New Volumes of the *Encyclopaedia Britannica*, Volume 3, approximate date, 1923: [4]

Napoleon was served by an intelligence officer of the first class – Col. Bacler d'Albe, unknown to fame save as a cartographer, but in fact the one assistant who was present when Napoleon arrived at his great decisions in the field. Lying prone on the outspread maps, compasses in hand, with d'Albe at his elbow to inform him either as to topography or as to the enemy's dispositions and order of battle,* Napoleon could handle a changing situation day by day with all the certainty that the means of communication of his day allowed. It has recently been remarked that, to a Napoleon, an intelligence staff is more indispensable than the operations staff, and the remark is historically justified by the facts. For an operations staff is the

* Bacler d'Albe kept a card index of enemy formations and units.

product of a military system – that of Germany – in which the commander-in-chief is a sovereign who may not possess the qualities of command but yet must command, and it has developed because the growing intricacy of operations detail has compelled an increase in the number of workers who collaborate with the normal commander-in-chief. A saying of Foch is illuminating in this connexion. The great French marshal, asked how Napoleon would conduct the western front campaigns, replied: 'Were he to return he would say: "You have weapons, numbers, communications, aircraft, transport such as I never possessed. Stand aside, all of you, and I will show you." But, now as then, he would have taken care to have his Bacler d'Albe at his side.'

In so intimate a union between the master of operations and the intelligence officer, it may be assumed without direct evidence that a man whose military judgment was matured by the unique experience of watching Napoleon's brain arrive at conclusions, and following his thoughts so as to be ready to supply the data on which they fed, must have added the function of 'interpretation' to those of collection and sifting.

Bletchley was the Bacler d'Albe of the Western Allies during most of the Second World War. Unfortunately it was seldom listened to at the highest political levels. This was true, in particular, in so far as the political motives of the Russians were concerned. The British were reading Russian military ciphers. They were also reading American diplomatic ciphers. (This writer, as an officer of the Army of the United States in uniform once found in his in-tray at Bletchley in 1944 a long, deciphered message from the American ambassador at the Court of St James to the President in Washington. It need not be said that I immediately took these pieces of paper to the British officer in charge of that particular section. His acute embarrassment meant either that he was a superb actor – which in 'real life' he was not – or that someone in distribution had made a slip. Such slips, however, were not allowed at Bletchley.)

To the best of my knowledge we were reading German and Japanese, but not Russian, diplomatic ciphers. The regular situation reports from the Japanese military attaché and from his ambassador in Berlin to Tokyo were of immense value, particularly to the Russians once they had been passed through the Lucy Ring. On the other hand the Russians used, and have continued to use at least until quite recently, the one-time cipher pad for most of their diplomatic and espionage communications. It is cumbersome, slow to work and even slower to break. It is therefore usually not used for operational orders but for longer-range activities, such as the Soviets have excelled at, in such fields as Agitprop and technological espionage. In this second field, though, the Western powers were only slightly more interested than they were in the first. After all, the Soviets were our allies, were they not? Gamesmanship might imply the British reading American ciphers – and even vice versa – but it was hardly worth wasting a lot of time on the gallant Soviet ally which could only mean a diminution of effort against the real enemy, Germany and Japan. This decision well suited the political viewpoints of London and Washington, at least until the Warsaw tragedy of August 1944, and so far as the Roosevelt administration went for the better part of one more year.

The one-time pad system is, like any other cipher system, not unbreakable: it just takes a long time to break, longer than it does to use. The pad itself is a series of ciphers, each of which must only be used once. It can assume the size of a small postage stamp. It can be made even smaller, in the form perhaps of a microfilm that can be inserted, as was the case with the Soviet spy named Lonsdale and others, inside a cigarette lighter or a tube of toothpaste. Once used, each of the ciphers is destroyed quickly and easily. Hence its name, and its cumbersome nature which makes it unsuitable in fluid military operations.

In the matter of intelligence collaboration, the Axis powers were seldom more trusting of one another than were their enemies. Just as we would not give our ultra top secrets to the Russians, so were the Germans distrustful, and rightly so, of the Italians. German–Japanese relations were quite different. Although they were classified as 'honorary Aryans', it was the intention, at least of Heinrich Himmler,[5] to fight them, perhaps in perpetuity, once Russia and the Western powers had been defeated and a new S.S. state, to be called Burgundia, established in control of all Europe, including European 'Russia' as far as the

Urals. Nevertheless until this happy day arrived the Japanese were reliable allies, posing no danger of surrender to the United States or to Britain.

After Midway the Japanese began to worry about their cipher security. Was the Purple Machine not, perhaps, infallible? They asked their German friends, who assured them that their own Enigma Machine was certainly unbreakable. Furthermore they offered to send a shipload of Enigma Machines to Japan, an offer which was accepted with much gratitude by the Japanese. The Germans then informed their allies when the ship would be sailing, its route, and estimated date of arrival. All this information was being read, with great satisfaction, at Bletchley.

To the annoyance of certain British and American admirals, who were not informed of the reason, a large number of warships were moved away from the route that this ship, with its cargo, was to follow. It got through safely; and the Western powers had less trouble than ever in reading Japanese ciphers. So everybody was happy, except presumably the admirals who had, inexplicably, been prevented from sinking the German ship.

Other sailors had, however, the satisfaction of sinking the *S.S. Ankara* in the Mediterranean at a slightly earlier date. The *Ankara* was a tank transporter ploughing between Italy and North Africa, loaded on the outward bound journey with German tanks for Rommel's Afrika Korps. It was regularly 'watched' by Ultra and as soon as it had landed its cargo of armoured fighting vehicles at Benghazi or Tobruk or whatever port was most convenient to the Germans, these were, with equal regularity, destroyed by the bombs of the Royal Air Force on landing. It was a sad day for the intelligence staff of the British Eighth Army when some keen submariner spotted the *Ankara* through his periscope and put a torpedo into her. He could hardly have guessed that she was of infinitely greater value to his own side than to the enemy's.

Quite apart from the chagrin of the intelligence officer who had long been involved full time in the movements of the *Ankara*, and who therefore had to adapt himself to a new routine, this incident should have aroused the Western powers to the danger of excessive reliance on Ultra. The 'cover' had been a non-existent or at best semi-existent spy in Taranto. He disappeared when the

Ankara was sunk, but it took both time and trouble to replace 'him' and the firm intelligence 'he' covered. The arrival of the then brand new German Tiger tanks in Tunisia, early in 1943, was not exactly a surprise but they might have been destroyed on landing had the *Ankara* still been afloat.

In fact Western secret intelligence was, by then, becoming reliant on Ultra to a dangerous extent. In the face of its superbly organized backing of indices and expert knowledge, almost all other forms of secret intelligence, apart from the technological, became little more than cover for Ultra. There were exceptions, often of a very simple nature, such as the counting of trains crossing through Poland. But apart from battlefield intelligence, Ultra became completely predominant. This predominance was accentuated by the immensely successful intelligence preparations for Overlord. Overlord's success and subsequent exploitation in the French campaign of 1944, combined with our thorough control of German espionage, created a form of hubris. Once the Allied armies had reached the old German frontier and the West Wall (called the Siegfried Line in Western terminology) in the autumn, it was decided by the policy-makers in London and Washington to permit a lull, until the spring, while Field Marshal Montgomery's armies cleared up the Low Countries and prepared for another massive operation across the Rhine. The V-1 (flying bomb) bases capable of bombing London had been almost entirely eliminated. The V-2 rockets were rare and did not contain the nuclear warhead that had been feared. Britain and America were moderately, though not entirely, confident that the Germans would not be able to make an atomic bomb for use in that war, while they themselves would. On the other hand they overestimated, to an almost ridiculous extent, the effect on German war productivity of the air raids. In fact such productivity was, belatedly, moving into high gear.[6] Apart from bloody battles in the area where the frontiers of Belgium, Holland and Germany meet, the Western Allies – and particularly the Americans to the south – settled down to a rather quiet winter in anticipation of a major offensive in the spring. The intelligence forces conformed. But it was not to be a quiet winter.

For the Germans had very different views. Though the Red Army was slowly advancing towards central Europe, Hitler still believed that if only he could achieve another victory in the West, he could then either defeat the Soviets or, perhaps, make another deal with Stalin. As the Red Army's always weak communications grew longer and longer, the Soviet armies became ever more ineffective. Hitler was prepared to sell space in the non-German east in order to gain time in the West. This was the ultimate logic behind the Ardennes Offensive against the U.S. First Army in December of 1944.

For the Germans, largely ignorant of the Manhattan Project, did not anticipate that the Western powers would possess an atomic weapon by the summer of 1945. This is hardly surprising. Neither the British nor the Americans were sure, in the late autumn of the previous year, when this total weapon would work, nor even if it would work at all. (In fact only three were made in wartime, the prototype and the two dropped on Japanese cities after the German surrender.) On the other hand the Germans did know that they had two war-winning weapons in production, soon to be in mass production. These were the jet plane, in which they were far ahead of their enemies, and the *Schnorkel*, which enabled their U-boats to operate without surfacing and therefore made them far less vulnerable to the Royal and the U.S. Navies. Apart from the atomic bomb, still untried, the Germans had calculated that, allowed a further six months, they could not only knock the Western air forces out of the skies, but also cut the lifeline between Europe and America. In order to achieve this, it was necessary for the Germans to inflict a bloody defeat on the Anglo-American forces and thus forestall or postpone indefinitely an invasion of Western Germany. Ostensibly, and from their point of view ideally, such an offensive would split the American and British forces, capture Antwerp, and expel their enemies from the Low Countries and France. This, however, was only a fantastical ambition. The real purpose of the German offensive was so to shake the Western Allies as to gain time for the mass production of these lethal new weapons.

Three factors contributed to the initial success of the Germans' Ardennes offensive. One was the hubris at Allied high commands, the feeling that the Germans were in effect defeated and that we could therefore kill them off at a time of our own choosing. The second was even less excusable. The topographical errors of the French in 1940 were repeated: it was thought that the Germans could not attack through the Ardennes forests, which front was therefore only lightly held with no important armoured reinforcement rapidly available. The third, and here the most relevant, was that the Germans were back in Germany, using land-lines in a static situation, and Ultra was therefore drying up. There is no evidence that the Germans had rumbled Ultra. On the other hand Western intelligence continued to rely on it, almost exclusively, and with the nonchalance of certain, impending victory. In fact, Ultra was misused.

For the Ardennes offensive should have been anticipated, even if only by the German Order of Battle as revealed from the limited amount of Ultra we were still receiving, and could then quite easily have been parried as Ludendorff had parried the Nivelle offensive of 1917, by quiet withdrawal before the battle and subsequent counter-attack. The attack was not anticipated, or at least not where it occurred. It is necessary here to refer to the deteriorating relations in Anglo-American politico-military affairs in order to explain why secret intelligence was ignored or misunderstood.

At the very highest level, and for some three years or more, the attitude of the British government towards that of the United States had been somewhat ambiguous. The almost obsequious tone of Churchill's communications with Roosevelt before the Japanese attack on Pearl Harbor reveal one of the less attractive, though perhaps politically skilful, aspects of that great English patriot's character. His attitude was to be preserved while the United States government decided whether the Pacific or the European Theatre of Operations was to receive priority. No absolute decision was ever made, nor was it necessary once Germany and Italy were so foolish as to declare war upon the United States, yet a doubt lingered on. Churchill remained, despite any cynical views he may have secretly (and later not so secretly) cherished, the leader of a client state. American power, combined with Soviet power, must defeat Nazi Germany. This was as obvious in Washington as it was in London and Moscow. However, innate American anti-colonialism, combined with the 'left-wing' sympathies of Roosevelt and his administration, were likely to sidetrack the interests of the British Empire, the leaders

290

of which thought with some justification that they deserved at least an equal share in the Western victory over Nazi Germany. Churchill stated publicly that he had not become the King's First Minister in order to preside over the dissolution of the British Empire. Nor did he wish to see the future of the Western world decided between America and Russia. In neither of these endeavours was he to succeed in the long term. In the shorter term he was more successful.

Whereas American might was and had to be ultimately of paramount importance, British skill and British experience – in no field more so than in secret intelligence – were indispensable to the Western alliance. Since the major power in any such alliance must command, an American *supremo* had to be appointed to Overlord, and this was even more true in the campaigns to follow. It was, from the British point of view, desirable that this American supreme commander of Western forces be a less rather than a more forceful figurehead. Hence the sour phrase, not infrequently heard at senior American headquarters in Europe during 1944, that Eisenhower was the best general the British had. For Ike believed his primary task to be the preservation, even the equalization, of the British army and that of the Americans, who soon vastly outnumbered their allies. In August of 1944 it should have been possible to defeat Germany rapidly by putting the total Western effort behind either the British 21st or the American 12th Army Group. However he considered that his first responsibility lay in a weird sort of 'military democracy' according to which the Americans should be held back, while the British caught up, cleared the Huertgen Forest to their north, (along with the U.S. Ninth Army), and prepared a massive offensive across the River Roer and the Lower Rhine, with ultimate, obvious objective the Ruhr and then central Germany. The Americans were starved, first of gasoline, then, when they had bogged down save for Patton's offensive far away in the Saar, of manpower. And because they had been brought to a standstill, the American formations in Europe were not receiving the best trained replacements, which were being sent to General MacArthur in the Pacific on the very sound military precept that it is always wise to reinforce success.

The quietest sector of the Western Front, the Eifel, was over one hundred miles long. It was held by General Middleton's VIIIth U.S. Army Corps, consisting of two or three divisions, badly mauled in the Huertgen battle, plus ill-trained replacements for whom this was more or less a training area.[7]

Now in October a formation called the Sixth S.S. Panzer Army was identified in Westphalia. At first it seemed to be only an administrative headquarters. It was then located, but not very satisfactorily, as having moved to a point north of Cologne. And in November the Fifth (Wehrmacht) Panzer Army was located slightly further to the north. It was believed, in so far as any credibility was attached to their reality, that these formations were either intended to launch a spoiling attack, across the River Roer, against Field Marshal Montgomery's main effort, or alternatively to counter-attack. But their very existence, as real Panzer armies, was doubted.

Our old enemy, the Wehrmacht's Fifth Panzer Army had been more or less destroyed during the summer campaign; the other, to which we had a very few tantalizing references via Ultra, was an entirely new headquarters. No S.S. formation larger than a corps had hitherto been identified. Yet it was known that since 20 July 1944 the Waffen S.S. had been rapidly expanded, and now numbered more than twenty divisions which were receiving the best and most modern equipment. Indeed Heinrich Himmler was being given command of German army groups – first in the west, opposite Patton, later on the Eastern Front, appointments incidentally for which that policeman was both untrained and unsuitable. It was all part of the long range programme whereby the Waffen S.S. should replace the Wehrmacht in a future, victorious Nazi Empire. It is notable that a high proportion of these new S.S. divisions were recruited not from Germany but from the nationals of other European states from Scandinavia to Albania. This was to be the army of 'Burgundia'. The situation had come more than full circle since the murder of Roehm ten years earlier.

Not only was the German army to be replaced, but the very German nation was to be eclipsed by the megalomaniacs in charge of the Third Reich. This basic redirection of policy was not, it seems, known – or at least not credited – by the Western powers, who still clung to the belief that what they were fighting was Nazi Germany.

292

Another basic error, to which I have earlier alluded, concerned the effects of the massive Allied air offensive against German civilians and industry. The air staffs, looking at their photographs of smashed German cities, could not believe that the production of military, naval and air weapons was in fact rapidly increasing. It was therefore assumed, erroneously, that the Germans could not effectively re-equip Fifth Panzer Army. The German defeats and withdrawals on the Eastern Front added credibility to this mis-judgment. Nor did the Russians give the West any intelligence; on the contrary they were claiming then, as they have ever since, that it was they who were fighting almost the whole German war apparatus. Thus what information they did give us was mislead-ing, probably with deliberation. British and American intelli-gence at the highest level was led to believe that the Russians, in late 1944, were tying down the Wehrmacht. This, at a slightly lower level, served to underline the belief that the Fifth Panzer Army was a paper tiger. It was not, not at all.

As for the even more formidable Sixth S.S. Panzer Army, Western intelligence was misled, for more complex reasons of its own creation, into suspecting that it did not exist at all. Here this writer can speak from personal knowledge, since I was then responsible for General Bradley's Order of Battle map at 12th U.S. Army Group headquarters, located that autumn in Luxem-bourg. I believed in the reality of Sixth S.S. Panzer Army for the following reasons:

1 It had been identified by Ultra on perhaps half a dozen occa-sions on which intelligence was passed to me.
2 Although the Russians claimed to have identified the presence of the crack S.S. Panzer divisions on their front correctly, up to and including the battle for Budapest, we had no reason other than the unreliable Russian intelligence service to think that they were still there in November. Indeed they had taken such a mauling in the Budapest battles that it was only simple military logic to assume that they would have been withdrawn, re-equipped and re-manned. The vast and rapid expansion of the Waffen S.S. at this time made such an action highly probable. At least the 1st and 2nd S.S. Panzer Divisions, as well as several others, had disappeared from our screen, though no doubt

remnants were left behind, quite deliberately, to fool the Russians and ourselves.

3 The idea, accepted at S.H.A.E.F., that the Sixth S.S. Panzer Army was perhaps a bogus formation comparable to F.U.S.A.G. made no sense. What would such a deception have achieved? The answer was, and is: nothing.

4 If it *were* bogus, then they would have drawn our attention to it. In fact, apart from a few Ultra intercepts, they almost succeeded in concealing the existence of this huge force completely. In the end they led us to believe that if it existed at all, it was facing Montgomery.

5 Whereas the O.K.W. and the O.K.H. could, had they so wished, have constructed any number of non-existent Wehrmacht formations, and had indeed unconvincingly tried to do so in the past, they could not have created an S.S. formation since the Waffen S.S. was becoming ever more insistent on its own autonomy with aim its own total power.*

These political developments remained in large measure unknown to purely military intelligence officers at my low level, and perhaps at a considerably higher level as well. However, a true appreciation of the intelligence began to percolate upwards, perhaps more than downwards but not always successfully: the identification of German bridge-building equipment opposite VIIIth Corps, for instance, should have been accepted more readily.

Why did neither S.H.A.E.F. nor London nor Washington believe entirely in the existence of Sixth S.S. Panzer Army and therefore in the strength and probable location of the coming German offensive? The answer can again be most simply tabulated.

1 The Germans lacked the ability to re-equip one Panzer army and to create, with new equipment, another.

2 Our own cover plans, such as 'Mincemeat' and F.U.S.A.G. were grossly overvalued. The Germans (whose military brains

* Churchill, in his *History of the Second World War*, omits the 'S.S.' and calls that formation simply 'Sixth Panzer Army'.

were by then under-rated) would surely copy our own allegedly successful cover methods.

3 It was more convenient to believe than to disbelieve the so-called intelligence we were receiving from the Soviets. The enormous and well nigh uncontrollable propaganda apparatus of the West had been thrown sharply into reverse in 1941 when the Germans invaded Russia. The attempts by the Communists to annihilate Anglo-American forces with their own 'Second Front Now' propaganda campaign in 1942–3 had been in large measure ignored. In 1944 it was not possible, and particularly not in the United States, once again to switch from reverse into top forward gear. The fact that the Third World War had become a shooting war, in the skies over Warsaw in August of 1944, was ignored.

4 Our air forces assured us that we had total air supremacy. This was still the case so far as bomber and fighter forces went, though it was endangered by the German production of jets. It was not true of aerial reconnaissance inside Germany, even less of espionage there. Furthermore, little attention was paid to the fact that winter weather would greatly hamper Allied air supremacy. This the Germans were relying on.

It was therefore decided, at the highest levels, that there would be no major German offensive in the West, though possibly a minor one towards the northern end of the front. Nor was there, in the purely military field, any effective espionage service inside Germany, since the men of 20 July had been ignored in their lifetime and our friends in the Abwehr had perished, with the published approval of Winston Churchill. The combination of follies was so enormous that, in retrospect, it almost seems as if the Nazis 'deserved' to win the war in late 1944.

History was set upon another course. The Ardennes offensive was defeated. In due course the American and British forces invaded Germany. In a massive operation – perhaps unnecessarily massive, since Bradley had already captured the Remagen bridge – the British crossed the Rhine. Germany was then physically occupied in so far as the political agreement with the Soviets allowed. The Germans called this *die Ueberrollung*, or steam-roller action. Secret intelligence, either as it had been used in the Second World War or as it was to be employed in the Third, played no important part in the final victory over Nazi Germany so far as the Western powers were concerned. From the Soviet point of view, on the other hand, it was quite another story. The victory celebrations in the great Soviet cities were of a very different nature from those in London or New York. For the Politburo, this was not the end of the war, but merely of a most successful campaign. Much had been gained, in territory and otherwise, from the capitalist enemy. Much still remained to be conquered, by one means or another, *so oder so* as the late Adolf Hitler used to say.

PART FOUR

THE THIRD WORLD WAR

Chapter Seventeen

The Early K.G.B.

According to Alexander Solzhenitsyn, in the Paris newspaper *Le Monde* in May of 1975, the acceptance of defeat by the United States government at the hands of the Communists in Indochina, and therefore ultimately in all Asia, marked the end of the Third World War. I do not believe that his statement is true, but rather that the Third World War will continue unless and until there is a Fourth, which must almost certainly be atomic, biochemical and perhaps even more totally destructive than other horrible forms of warfare. However, let us accept that a very novel form of global war has existed between the Western powers (in particular the United States) and the Communist powers (in particular the Soviet Union), at least since American supply planes were shot down over Warsaw in August 1944, by American and British fighters earlier given to the Red Air Force to resist defeat by the Germans.

If it be accepted that this war has been continual and global, not infrequently involving physical force – as in Korea, Indochina, Hungary, Czechoslovakia, the Middle East – and naval, air and satellite reconnaissance in peacetime, then it has to be accepted that the 'Cold War' was and remains a very real war indeed. The tune has been called by the Soviet government, the victories have almost all been theirs, but none has been decisive. And though the seeds of this war were planted in many respects in the Second World War, it has been, and is being, fought in a manner far more different from that war than the Second was from the First. More American lives have been already lost in this war than in World War II, more territory and populations occupied and captured by the Communists than by any power in any war in modern history. Yet it has been essentially an intelligence war, more so than any that has preceded it. And the rules for this new type of war have been laid down largely by the Soviets.

So far as political intelligence goes, and here it goes a very long way, Western motives and Western methods in the Third World War have been almost a repetition, in reverse, of the errors committed in the Second. These may be briefly summed up, with the inevitable over-simplification inherent in brevity, as follows.

In Britain in 1939, and in America until late 1941, the majority of the voters were pacifist or isolationist. The First World War was still a vivid memory. It seemed to have achieved nothing. Germany was once again the most powerful state in Europe and the Soviet Union was the fatherland of the proletariat, while British and American workers were subjected to the ignominy of the means test or sold apples at street intersections. So much for the war to end wars. Among Western verbalizers patriotism, in a phrase of Dr Johnson's taken out of context, became the last refuge of a scoundrel.

Therefore when the British and French honoured their guarantee to Poland on 3 September 1939, the emphasis was not on national but on ideological war, directed not against the German people but against their Nazi government. As we have seen, for more than half a year nothing happened save the dropping of British leaflets explaining all this at tedious length to uninterested German recipients, while Poland was overrun by the Nazi–Soviet alliance and Finland was attacked by the Soviets. For a moment, early in 1940, it seemed that the British and French might come to the help of the Finns. This would indeed have been an ideological war, democracy versus totalitarianism, but it did not happen, which is perhaps just as well. The Americans were only in part convinced that this was in any way an ideological war. American sympathy lay with the West, but the 'liberals' managed rapidly to forget the Hitler–Stalin pact, so great was their indoctrinated sympathy with the Workers' State, so profound their inherited dislike of British and French colonialism. The American government gave some assistance to the Western powers – and American industry made a lot of money in so doing–and President Roosevelt was re-elected, after the fall of France, largely because of his promise that no American boys would die on foreign fields.

This rather sloppy view of foreign policy was changed when Churchill became Prime Minister, when Russia was invaded, and when the Japanese bombed America into the war. In three stages, between May of 1940 and December of the following year, the Second World War became, at least for the Western Allies, a patriotic war, with objective the destruction of Germany, Italy and Japan. Even for the Russians it became, at least officially, the Great Patriotic War. When Stalin had recovered from a nervous breakdown brought about by his betrayal at the hands of his Nazi ally and had returned to Moscow, he went so far as to permit the re-opening of the Orthodox churches and the re-introduction of normal military discipline in order to unite the Russian people, who were often greeting the Wehrmacht as their liberators (erroneously for the carpetbaggers and the S.S. were following behind), and to prevent mass desertion and even enlistment in the German forces. It seemed that the Second World War was, like the First, a war between two groups of allied nation-states The Roosevelt administration believed this until the end; the Churchill administration became more and more sceptical; the Stalin administration almost certainly never believed it at all, but used the concept for immediate expediency in the first place, and after 1943 as a ploy in preparation for the Third World War.

This misappreciation of Soviet motives, particularly during the last year of the war, was not the fault of political intelligence nor even of military intelligence after the Warsaw rising. There were plenty of men in high office who saw what was going on. They did not have the ear of President Roosevelt and his immediate entourage. Premier Churchill came increasingly to see the danger, but showed a most uncharacteristic lack of courage in failing to oppose the almost omnipotent President. And Western public opinion had been gulled by endless propaganda about the gallant Soviet ally and dear old Uncle Joe. In fact the first great campaign of the Third World War was lost even before the defeat of Germany, and was duly signed at Yalta in February 1945.

This sell-out to the Soviets was inevitably a far more protracted and complex business than can be summed up in a single Crimean place-name. Its roots lay far deeper, and dated at least from the Roosevelt–Churchill conference held at Quebec in August of 1943. It was then and there that the strategy of the Western Allies for the prosecution of the war against Germany, Italy and Japan was decided upon. Plans for the immediate post-war situation, after victory, were left vague, but unfortunately not vague enough.

300

The last great German attack in Russia, the so-called Kursk Offensive, was being held by the Red Army, which was about to start its long and laborious advance westwards. According to Churchill it was then considered possible, perhaps even probable, that once the Soviets had reached their 1941 frontier (an event which clearly lay far in the future) the Soviet government would again come to terms with the National Socialists.[1] Churchill was always most conscious of security, and does not give his reasons for this presupposition. It is unlikely, though possible, that we were reading the Moscow–Stockholm–Berlin radio communications concerning a new and separate Soviet–Nazi agreement. It is possible that the British Secret Intelligence Service, the S.I.S., knew from its Stockholm agents what the Soviet ambassador there, Mme Kollontai, was passing on to her German contacts. It is probable that Bletchley Park was reading the German diplomatic cipher, Stockholm–Berlin.

In any case it was clearly in Anglo-American interests, almost a year before D-day, that the Russians be encouraged to continue as belligerents even beyond their old frontiers. Nor was it desirable that they be led to believe that we so much as suspected them of a planned duplicity. Therefore Roosevelt and Churchill drew up a very rough map for the post-war zones of occupation in a Germany that was then far from conquered. This, together with a plan of rather vague zones of global influence, was conveyed to Stalin, who in due course produced them at Yalta. Strangely enough a dying Roosevelt and an exhausted Churchill accepted these plans, remotely made in very different circumstances some eighteen months earlier, as the basis of a formal agreement. This desire, in 1943, to keep Russia in the war until final victory is in part an explanation of the cold-shouldering of German anti-Nazis in 1944, for as we will see the men about Stauffenberg were even more of an anathema to the Soviets than were the Nazis. Eastern Germany, Poland, the Baltic States, part of Finland, Eastern Austria, Czechoslovakia, Hungary, Romania, Bulgaria, Yugoslavia, Albania, Mongolia, the northern islands of Japan and, ultimately, China itself were surrendered to the Communists. Winston Churchill tried to fight for the freedom of Poland. The Americans did not support him in April of 1945; he, and the Poles, lost. This enormous victory for the Russians can in large measure

be ascribed to a crass misinterpretation by the Roosevelt administration of what was happening. The President's sources of
political intelligence were at least as poor or as ignored as President Wilson's a quarter of a century before, and with results that
have proved and must prove at least as ominous. Furthermore,
skilled politician as he was, Roosevelt was not a highly educated
man. How could a President who saw fit to inform a senior naval
British intelligence officer that Bermuda was one of the West
Indies [2] (the U.S. Navy had just leased a base in Bermuda) be
expected to find his way in the complicated maps of Eastern
Europe?

More important than such detail, save to the inhabitants of
such places, was the failure to appreciate the fact that the heady
prospect of victory, once in sight, had quite another meaning for
the Russians than it had for the Americans, or even for the British
and French.

The Americans, in 1945, intended to return to the Western
hemisphere, the Monroe Doctrine and some form of isola-
tionism just as soon as possible. The British, French and other
European powers would have to share their continent with
Russia, for ever. No one at high administrative level, save perhaps
Churchill, seems to have realized that the Russian perception of
the nature of the war had switched once more, that Stalin's
Soviet apparatus had yet again changed the party line. With victory over the Germans coming quite soon, it had ceased to be the
Great Patriotic War and was the old, ideological war. Himmler's
'Burgundian' fantasy was far closer to Soviet *Realpolitik* than
dreams being dreamed in most of the Western capitals about
democratic regimes in Africa and Asia, and world peace after
the elimination of war criminals, and eternal, increasing pros-
perity as swords were hammered into ploughshares and atomic
weapons became nuclear power stations. The Western dream was
both more sensible and more attractive, but the Marxist vision
was calling the tune. And the Russians were sufficiently cool-
headed, or sufficiently reinforced by categorical Marxist–Leninist
dogma, or sufficiently terrorized by their own secret police, to
ignore the overwhelming military and technological supremacy
of the West, in particular of the United States. This they intended,
in Krushchev's words, to 'overtake and surpass' in order to

302

'bury' us. They had plans, as the Second World War ended, for their own form of a global 'Burgundia'.

We had none for an 'anti-Burgundia', but we should have, and could have, had some such programme. Whether it could have been sold to an exhausted British and American public in 1945 is far more doubtful. Certainly Winston Churchill considered this, as he has written in the closing volume of his *History of the Second World War*.[3] However, he had been dismissed by the British electorate immediately after the war against Germany, and before the war against Japan, had been won. Major Attlee and his government were more interested – and who can say they were wrong? – in false teeth than in frontiers, in the abstraction of fair shares than in that of freedom. And though Roosevelt was dead, his heritage lingered on under a then completely inexperienced new President.

Yet an 'anti-Burgundia' had been envisaged, by Germans and particularly by Count von Stauffenberg and the men around Helmuth von Moltke, as early as 1943. At least a million Red Army prisoners of war had volunteered to fight against Stalinist Communism, under the command of the Russian general who had saved Moscow, General Vlassov. The Vlassov army did not fight for Hitler, but against Stalin. Stauffenberg, who was chief of staff of the Home Army, responsible for recruitment and training, was in a position to ensure that the Vlassov Army did not fall into the clutches of the S.S. but retained its independence. It was his intention that once Hitler and the Nazi régime had been eliminated – and he tried, more than once, to kill Hitler himself – the Vlassov Army should provide a nucleus to dispose of the Soviet dictator and his regime. This 'anti-Burgundian' movement, as has been already stated, was totally ignored by its natural allies in the West.

While Hitler, after the failure of 20 July, was exterminating several thousand of the men who should have been leaders of a post-Nazi, non-Communist Germany, Churchill made a flippant remark that to him it was all the same whether the Germans hanged together or were hanged alone, a remark he was surely to regret within less than a year. Was this attitude based on false political intelligence or merely on the desire to please the Soviets, like the British and American pretence of accepting the Soviet lie that it was the Germans who had murdered, at Katyn and else-where, the 14,000 Polish officers and members of the old govern-ing class imprisoned by the Russians in 1939 and murdered by them in April 1940? Probably a combination of both, aided by very considerable internal left-wing pressure inside the govern-ments and civil services in Washington and London.

As the Second World War merges into the Third, this book becomes considerably more difficult to write. One reason for this is subjective. I was discharged from the Army of the United States in 1946. Although a tentative and tempting offer was made me of an appointment as assistant military attaché in London, with my task liaison between the British and American military intelligence services, I did not follow this up. I had had six years in two armies, had volunteered for the British forces out of a profound dislike of Nazism, and had no wish to serve in what I then erroneously believed would be a peacetime army. Nor did the continued, public approval of the Soviet totalitarian ally appeal to me.

I had attended conferences concerning the establishment of a centralized American intelligence apparatus – we were all aware how reliant the Americans had been on the British, at least in Europe, and of the fact that this was not automatically desirable in the future. General Donovan and indeed most senior American intelligence officers knew how clumsy United States intelligence had been before and to a large measure during the war itself. His O.S.S., which was never as effective as Hollywood made out, was entirely a wartime creation and was likely to fade away as its leaders returned to civilian life. The C.I.A., as it was to become, would be able to offer these men and their successors permanent, well-paid jobs of a civil service type, in a sort of twilight zone between the established civil service, in particular the State De-partment, the armed forces and the F.B.I. I was offered such a job, but I had no wish either to be a civil servant in Washington or to be a spy, or controller of spies, abroad.

The result is that I have no direct knowledge of secret intelli-gence in any form since 1946. On the other hand, had I been en-gaged directly in secret activities during the Third World War, I obviously could not write about them at all, since the struggle for power between the Communist and non-Communist worlds

304

continues. It is only fair to explain this to the reader, to point out that almost all published material, evidence given in courts of law and before Congressional Committees and so on, is to be treated with extreme caution. It is therefore inevitable that such words as 'probably', such phrases as 'it would seem that' must recur tediously. It also, I hope, explains why the remainder of this book will be short.

Soviet strategy, since at least 1944, has been practised on three overlapping levels.

The first of these has been a determination to avoid a direct all-out war with the United States.

The second has been a determination to acquire technological, and if possible total, supremacy over the West in the event of such a war becoming desirable. Marshal Grechko, the Soviet Defence Minister, writing in *Red Star* in 1974, was bold enough to say that such a moment might arrive sooner than the West expected.

The third was a protracted and massive Agitprop operation, by which the West, and in particular the United States, were to be made to appear as the aggressors throughout this Third or 'Cold' War.

These three modes of action have been intimately intertwined. Therefore so have the activities of Soviet intelligence and the counter-activities of its Western, particularly its American, enemy. In Lenin's lapidary phrase it has been a question of: 'Who whom?' It is with this subject that the remaining pages will be concerned.

So far Russian strategy has been usually skilful. Whereas constant pressure has been exerted, on all fronts, whenever the 'Cold War' has become a Hot War, the Russians have fought it, so far as possible, by proxy and the supply of arms, while aiming at the maximum direct involvement of troops and planes by the United States and America's allies; this was true of the Chinese civil war, of the Korean War, of the Middle Eastern wars, and of the long Indochinese wars. Only when American attention was diverted, as during the Suez War of 1956 or later in the Vietnamese imbroglio, have the Soviets sent in Soviet soldiers, in the former case in Hungary, in the latter in Czechoslovakia in 1968,

305

both within their own 'sphere of influence' as defined at Yalta and Potsdam. Thus from the propaganda point of view the Soviets have, in large measure, persuaded uneducated public opinion even inside the United States that the West was not on the defensive but was an aggressive power force. No Russian soldier was sent to die 'on foreign fields' beyond the Soviet Empire. Proxy forces and – when these have been victorious – controlled, proxy Communist governments extend that empire.

It is a complicated and seldom successful strategy, since the proxy army has been subject to defeat – as in the Middle Eastern wars – while the proxy, if victorious, has usually proved restive. As with every other empire, of which that of the Russian Soviets is the last in existence, stability and obedience can only be asserted by force. No country has remained subservient to Moscow without the presence, or credibly threatened intervention, of the Red Army. It is therefore probable that this somewhat unsatisfactory strategy will be abandoned as soon as the Soviet Union has achieved the desired adequate military and naval supremacy over the United States and its faltering allies. On the other hand the very fact that these allies should falter bears obvious testimony to the success of the Agitprop concept behind this strategy during the Soviets' period of comparative weakness.

Defence-by-proxy is an even more difficult strategy when practised by successive United States governments. It implies, as Soviet aggression-by-proxy does not, the ultimate willingness of the guarantor power to use its own forces to protect its *protégés*. In the old, traditional wars the power of the defence was always stronger. In the new conditions that now prevail, the reverse is true. Whereas the Soviets can withdraw from aggression, as in Northern Persia and Greece in the late '40s, without any particular loss of face, when America abandons an ally or even a would-be ally, this is construed as betrayal and the dominoes start to fall. Yet outright intervention, as in Vietnam, is easily converted by America's enemy into 'imperialism'. Nor is it otherwise understood by much of the American people, nor always by its military and even its political leaders. The neutralist, isolationist, even pacifist part of America's heritage has created a defensive tradition. Not only Americans but foreigners tend to be bewildered when that defensive strategy is transferred beyond the Western

Hemisphere and its protective Monroe Doctrine. This inconsistency has created a fissure in American credibility into which the rulers of the Russian Empire – which neither in Czarist nor in Marxist days had subjectively accepted territorial limits – have thrust a powerful crowbar.

A second Soviet victory at Western expense has been what might be called a rationalization or assimilation of Stalin's 'change the party line' method. By blowing hot and then, suddenly, blowing cold, successive Soviet leaders have managed to bewilder Western public opinion and even, it would seem, Western leadership. At no cost to themselves the men in the Kremlin can announce 'a thaw', a period of 'co-existence', a *détente*, alternating with outbursts of violent, potential aggression against Berlin, against Israel, in Asia, Africa, the whole of the West. The pacifist West accepts the balmy zephyrs with relief, ignores the blustery gale warnings with equanimity, and thus allows the Soviets to become ever mightier while their own forces decay. This crude system of successful contradictions necessarily involves the co-operation of political intelligence operating at the highest level. The method has been simple: stupid Soviet ambassadors confirm the West in the belief that Western political intelligence is superior, while the Russian ambassador's chauffeur is at the wheel. Should this technique fail it is the ambassador, far more often than the chauffeur, who is sent to the salt mines.

The purpose behind such rigmarole is really quite simple. Revolutionary regimes have no legitimacy, unlike reformist regimes. Whereas a Kerensky, in July 1917, could claim that his government was a successor to the Czarist one, even though the Czar might abdicate, Lenin could not and indeed dared not claim, a year later, that his Bolsheviks, who had just murdered the Czar together with his children, represented any sort of continuity with the Russian past. Yet this newly established form of government, while amost simultaneously extricating itself from a world war, and fighting a civil war, could not sacrifice status or withdraw into a small-Russian isolationism while also aiming at global ideological dominance. The French had faced a similar problem during the period of Robespierre's omnipotence. The Bolsheviks had learned, from Marx, the lesson.

Lenin rebuilt, in fairly close facsimile, the Czarist model of government, even in the mercantile field including a brief resurrection of free enterprise (the N.E.P. or New Economic Policy), but also saw to it that the methods of the Okhrana were copied and immensely enlarged. The main purpose of the Cheka, the O.G.P.U. and the other but the same security services was to practise in effect security or counter-intelligence on behalf of the small Bolshevik party against the inhabitants of the U.S.S.R. and only secondly against all foreigners. A smooth glaze of legality was to disguise the realities of perpetual class warfare and conspiracy by the Bolshevik ruling clique. Hence the major importance of the chauffeur and the minor one of the ambassador. Hence, too, the fact that in 1936 Stalin promulgated what is in theory the most 'democratic' constitution ever written, precisely while creating man-made famine and preparing the Great Purges. The Soviet Constitution did not of course fool the Russians, who saw its denial in action, but did gull certain Western liberals, some of whom were quite well educated. All this was an Agitprop operation on the largest scale.

It is extremely difficult, particularly in the conditions that have prevailed in this century, to draw any clear distinction in the operational field between secret intelligence and secret counter-intelligence, between the collecting of information about the enemy and the prevention of his doing the same. The massive planting of false intelligence or disinformation has further blurred the distinction. Yet it may still be said that the whole Okhrana tradition, as inherited and perfected by its Soviet successors, has been weighted more in favour of counter-intelligence. For the Bolshevik generation between the First and Second World Wars, the target was primarily the huge Soviet diaspora, collectively known as White Russians, and their few supporters who still aimed at a Russian counter-revolution. In Paris, in the 1930s, the White Russian organizations were very successfully infiltrated and emasculated. The assassination squads of the O.G.P.U. and later of the N.K.V.D. roamed the world, principally in search of compatriots. I quote the most authoritative recent book known to me on this subject:

Consonant with the Leninist precept that whatever serves to advance Communism is moral by definition, the Soviet Union murdered and kidnapped foreigners as early as 1926, when Stalin fully consolidated his power. That year, O.G.P.U. agents gunned down the Ukrainian leader Simon Petlura in Paris. They abducted the Estonian minister to the Soviet Union, Ado Birk, off a Moscow street in broad daylight, his diplomatic immunity notwithstanding. Birk never was heard of again. On January 26, 1930, the O.G.P.U. kidnapped the White Russian leader Aleksandr Kutepov in Paris, and, on May 22, 1932, shot a former communist courier, Hans Wissengir, in Hamburg. Soviet intelligence officers who displeased their superiors were also murdered. Valentin Markin, chief of the O.G.P.U. in the United States, was liquidated in New York in 1934, and G.R.U. agent Jean Cremet was killed in Macao two years later.

To perpetrate terror abroad more efficiently and on a larger scale, the N.K.V.D. in 1936 organized the Administration of Special Tasks, which Russians in time referred to as the department of 'wet affairs' (*mokrie dela*). At first, the new administration concentrated on eliminating dissident foreign communists: Trotskyites and Trotsky himself. Among its 1937 victims were Dmitri Navachine, murdered in Paris; Juliet Stuart Poyntz, who disappeared in New York; Ignace Reiss, murdered near Lausanne; Yevgenni Miller, kidnapped in Paris; Henry Moulin, Kurt Landau, Camillo Berneri, and Andrés Nin, all killed in Spain. The Directorate probably was responsible for the disappearance in Spain that year of José Robles, Marc Rein, Erwin Wolf, and Hans Freund. In 1938, N.K.V.D. agents in Belgium abducted and killed George Arutiunov, a former O.G.P.U. officer, and blew up the Ukrainian leader Evhen Konovalec in Rotterdam. Almost certainly they murdered Rudolf Klement, an associate of Trostky's son, Leon Sedov, in Paris. Klement's decapitated corpse was found in the Seine on July 16, 1938.

The Administration of Special Tasks also may have caused the death of Sedov himself, who underwent stomach surgery in February 1938, at a small Parisian clinic staffed by Russian émigrés. The surgery was successful, and he appeared to be recovering rapidly. But on the fifth night after the operation, he was found wandering outside his room, naked and delirious, with large bruises on his abdomen. He died three days later. Without explaining what produced the bruises, an inquest attributed his death to postoperative complications.

A band of some twenty N.K.V.D. agents, armed with machine guns and led by painter David Alfaro Siqueiros, assaulted Leon Trotsky's villa in Mexico on May 24, 1940. Although Trotsky was unharmed by the more than two hundred bullets fired into his bedroom, the raiders took away and later killed one of his bodyguards, an American, Robert Sheldon Harte. (Some students of Trotsky have speculated that Harte actually was a conspirator in the attack and that the N.K.V.D. wanted to silence him.) Late in the afternoon of August 20, 1940, N.K.V.D. agent Ramon Mercader, also known as Jacques Mornard, who had worked his way into Trotsky's confidence, followed him into his study. Guards heard screams and sounds of a struggle, and Trotsky staggered out drenched with blood, fatally wounded by a blow on the head from a skiing ice ax (*piolet*). Imprisoned in comfortable style, Mercader went to Czechoslovakia upon his release in 1960.[4]

After the Second World War the White Russians as an anti-Communist element, and even the Trotskyists ceased to be a major threat to the Soviet leaders. However, the leaders of the strong Ukrainian independence movement continued to be targets. At least two were murdered, in Munich, by a certain Stashinsky in 1959. We know the facts since Stashinsky later defected. It is fair to assume that Stashinsky was but one among many. And many presumably political deaths in the West have still to be ascribed. Most of these are probably the corpses of Soviet, or quasi-Soviet, citizens. The ostentatious murder of prominent anti-Communists was a valuable form of terrorization, but *mokrie dela* had no wish to recruit unstable foreigners. Indeed when Lee Oswald wished to assassinate President Kennedy, and applied to the Soviets for help, they not only refused to help him but saw to it that he was watched by K.G.B. agents in a failed attempt to prevent such a deed.[5] (The whole crime is still swathed in mystery. Did the K.G.B. inform the F.B.I., who ignored a warning which might well have been construed as provocative? After the murder, Oswald was himself murdered before he could talk, and his killer, Ruby, was killed – or died – before he in his turn could tell much, or else what he did say has been smothered. It is unlikely that the K.G.B. officer responsible for watching Oswald, and perhaps for his and Ruby's death, is now living a healthy life anywhere, though in so strange a world as his even this is possible.) There are few hard facts about K.G.B. assassination groups that have been revealed. What is perhaps more interesting is the attempt, by America's internal and external enemy, to pin such charges on the C.I.A. The men and women engaged in this anti-C.I.A. propaganda seem to be remarkably well informed about the techniques of political assassination today in foreign countries. One wonders whence they acquire such data for their unproven and probably unprovable allegations.

During the past thirty years policy – both internal and especially external – and technology have tended increasingly to overlap. The status of super-power is not achieved by mere size, for otherwise India would be a super-power, nor by mere technological skill, since Israel would then qualify for that status. The cost of advanced modern technology, of atomic weapons for example, or satellites or even a high-grade computer industry, is so enormous that only an act of will, a deliberate act of policy, on the part of a very rich, or of an omnipotent totalitarian, government can bring such systems into being. It is obvious why the United States and the Soviet Union are the only two super-powers, with China attempting to catch up. Thus does policy affect massive high level technology and vice-versa.

This intermixture is inevitably reflected, and directly reflected, in the world of secret intelligence. Yet there is still a distinction to be drawn, particularly at the beginning of this period and particularly in the field of direct espionage. The brilliant mathematician Klaus Fuchs became an atomic spy primarily because he was a Communist and wished to strengthen the Soviet Union at the expense of the United States and the non-Communist world. He can, however, have had only the vaguest knowledge of British and American policy towards the Soviet Union and indeed towards the world as a whole, since in his time as a spy this policy was essentially pacifist and would-be friendly. Donald Maclean, on the other hand – who was in a position to watch, from the

Foreign Office, the erosion of pacifist policy under Soviet provocation, to study the complex and unstable British–Arab–Israeli triangle of his time, and to report on personalities – would probably have been unable to tell the difference between one end of a nuclear rocket and the other. If the Russian secret service is as efficient as it appears to be, neither would have known of the other's activities or perhaps even of the other's existence. (The same is true of Harry Gold and other employees of the United States government with secret knowledge.) The mosaic was in fact put together in Moscow, not always correctly.

Of these two principal forms of espionage, the technological rapidly became far the more important, though its work was increasingly taken over by machines. Yet the political, though writ on water, was and is essential for purposes of evaluation and anticipation. It takes two forms, that of direct espionage in the old-fashioned sense and that of infiltration, though again these overlap. The Communist who poses as a Labour M.P. is not always solely a Bolshevik with his primary classical purpose the destruction of alternative forms of socialism, in this case democratic socialism, in order to install dictatorship. He may also be an agent, paid or otherwise, of the Russian imperialist regime. Since the British laws are so antiquated that it is impossible to name him unless he has either admitted his Communist affiliations – in which case the M.P. in question would be a cause of acute embarrassment to his Labour Party constituency officials and would almost certainly be rejected by his constituents at the first opportunity – he can only be exposed if he is arrested on a criminal charge. A Member of Parliament will be, very properly, tainted if he accepts money from, say, a building contractor for 'services rendered'. His political career can be ruined by a comparatively trivial sexual scandal. But if he is in fact working actively but secretly to destroy his society, in the interest of a hostile social system and of a foreign power, it is extremely difficult to nail him as the traitor that he is. This applies to trade union leaders, journalists and others, who have learned how to protect themselves by means and methods designed to protect the very society they are out to destroy. Yet when it is pointed out that these persons, declared, or known but undeclared, or highly suspect (who together represent approximately 1 per cent

312

of the electorate) are what they are, shrill cries of 'McCarthyism' resound, while their fellows in the press and on television are sarcastic about those who see 'reds under the bed'.

In the United States political espionage has become even more simple. A Daniel Ellsberg can steal classified papers from the Pentagon and pass these to a respectable paper such as *The New York Times* or *The Washington Post*. Were he to pass them to a foreign power, there might be even shriller cries of 'McCarthyism', but he has no need to do so. Thus American secret material is given, free, to America's enemies through American newspapers, while the thief has also and simultaneously carried out a major Agitprop operation by making the victim of his theft, the United States government, its military forces, its police, and its judicial system, appear ridiculous and even corrupt.

No such counter-activity is of equal effect against the Soviet Empire. The certainty of English-speaking peoples in the absolute superiority of their own form of self-government is overwhelming, is usually shared with some reservations by their Western allies, but is not exportable, not even to Africa or Asia, and seldom to Latin America. The attractive concept that truth must prevail has led the Americans in particular to attach great importance and to expend vast treasure on attempts to get the truth, as Americans see it, to the Russian people. We know that the radio networks, such as Radio Free Europe and Radio Liberty, have helped and encouraged a handful of dissidents within the Soviet Union, much as the British Broadcasting Corporation helped and encouraged anti-Nazi Germans during the Hitler period. But for the vast Soviet majority such activity would seem to be of little more value than was the dropping of leaflets over Germany during the 'phoney war' period. Only one major triumph can be openly ascribed, in this field, to the American Central Intelligence Agency, and this was the procurement and publication of Krushchev's 'secret speech' to the 20th Congress of the C.P.U. S.S.R. on 25 February 1956, denouncing the crimes of the Stalin period. Had the C.I.A. not obtained the text of this speech it would have remained, as it was intended to be, secret.

In fact in this world of intelligence activity, political espionage and political propaganda, the U.S.S.R. holds two trump cards or more exactly, to use a poker term, two jokers. The first of these is inherent in a 'closed' society in conflict with an 'open' one. Only in wartime can an open society become closed to the enemy. And the second joker is that the Soviet leaders, together with their friends and agents in the West, have almost always been able to persuade the peoples of the West that the Third World War is not a war at all.

How was this extraordinary situation brought about? How much credit can be given to Communist intelligence, how much blame to that of its Western enemies? The answer lies partly in technological intelligence, dating back now more than thirty years, and partly in the pro-Soviet propaganda, already referred to, with which the Western governments had saturated their own people during the last half of the Second World War, while scarcely believing it themselves. Such disingenuous behaviour can boomerang, particularly in a free society.

British and American security had been arranged, during the Second World War, almost entirely to outwit German and Japanese secret intelligence, and to a lesser extent that of the Italians before 1943. Soviet intelligence was an altogether different story.

That allied powers do not invariably share their secrets has been shown, in the case of Room 40 for instance; yet Yardley's information-gathering mission to Europe in 1918, however unsuccessful, was openly diplomatic and far from clandestine. This policy of straightforwardness was invalidated by Stalin's *renversement d'alliances* and the fear of its repetition. Hence the concealment of Ultra from the Soviets, the creation of the Lucy Ring, and much else. In the military-naval-air world, and to a lesser degree in the diplomatic field, British security was superb, that of the Americans in the Pacific only a little less so. In the scientific and technological spheres, however, there was very little precedent.

Yet for obvious reasons the Manhattan Project had to be kept as secret from Russian as from German intelligence. Since at its height some 200,000 persons were employed in the creation of the nuclear weapon, total security would have been extremely difficult to preserve in so novel a situation. It was preserved, and quite adequately, from the enemy belligerents, but not from the Soviet ally. Immensely complicated plots and operations were

314

mounted to mislead the German scientists into believing that heavy water would provide the key to nuclear fission. Indeed, a series of air, sabotage, submarine and commando raids, with Allied casualties of about one hundred, took place against such a heavy water laboratory-factory in Norway, and the transportation of the heavy water to Germany, with the sole purpose of convincing the Germans that their research was correct and that their enemies were prepared to sacrifice highly trained men's lives in order to foil their experiments with heavy water.[6]

In this complicated scientific field, simplification is inevitable and, let us hope, excusable. The material needed was not heavy water but uranium, in very short supply in 1942–3.* This was certainly known to the great Soviet physicist, Peter Leonidorich Kapitza (who had worked with Lord Rutherford on the splitting of the atom at the Cavendish Institute of Magnetic Research, attached to Cambridge University, in the 1920s and '30s), and to half a dozen or more highgrade Soviet physicists who had survived the Purges. How they, or Soviet intelligence, knew that the Manhattan Project was in operation in 1942 is still a matter of speculation. Direct espionage, at least to begin with, is a not altogether satisfactory answer. Some variant of what might be called scientific freemasonry (this is no reflection on the Free Masons) in the search for pure knowledge is more probable. In any event the Soviets were obtaining, under Lend-lease, uranium from the United States at least as early as 1943. The Russians therefore must have known of the Manhattan Project, and the Americans must have known that the Russians knew, since they first refused to supply this rare element to their ally. The Soviets then buried their request for uranium-235 deep in

* 'A fission bomb of superlatively destructive power will result from bringing quickly together a sufficient mass of element U-235. This seems as sure as any untried prediction based upon theory can be.' This report, ascribed probably correctly to a secret committee of the National Academy of Science, Washington, and dated 6 November 1941, is quoted by Walter Millis in his book entitled *This is Pearl!* and published by William Morrow, New York, 1947. It is noteworthy that this report is dated just over a month before the Japanese attack on Pearl Harbor; and also that Mr Millis's book must have been written at least two, and more probably three, years before the Soviets first exploded their own atomic bomb.

requests for medical supplies, and duly received it via American transport or bomber planes given to the Soviets and flown by Soviet crews. By this same route they also received a steady progress report on the Manhattan Project provided by top scientists. When, at the Potsdam Conference in July of 1945, President Truman informed Premier Stalin that the atomic bomb had been tested and worked, Stalin showed no surprise. This was then ascribed to ignorance on Stalin's part; it is now accepted that he knew more about the atomic bomb at that time than did Truman.

Why was the Western scientific élite so vulnerable to Communist espionage in the 1940s and, perhaps, later? Since these brilliant men, a few dozen perhaps out of the two hundred thousand employed, were usually a-political many did not see that they were, in W. H. Auden's phrase, 'fingering the levers that control eternity'. In effect they were the heirs to nineteenth-century materialistic science – though this simple concept they had themselves disproved – and therefore felt a certain, usually unrecognized, sympathy with the materialism of Marx and his heirs. Being very busy men they did not often translate their own scientific reappraisals of reality into political terms, save when these were totally obvious. Einstein urged Roosevelt to build an atomic bomb against Nazism, yet a few years later he urged that a hydrogen bomb should *not* be built against Communist imperialism. Robert Oppenheimer followed in his master's footsteps, with disastrous personal consequences; and many others, though by no means all, suffered from a similar confusion. Very few of these, and certainly not Oppenheimer and Einstein, were Communists or Soviet agents. Yet their uneasy belief in 'pure science' mixed with an awareness of its amoral applications made them quite easy prey for the enemies of the Western society that had treated them with such material lavishness and intellectual respect. It is not impossible that the exaggerated rewards that scientists enjoyed had tended to bewilder even the more percipient among them.

In a world of 'abstract' science, where morality as understood by Christians and Jews and the believers in some other great religions played no part whatsoever, very eminent scientists found themselves embroiled in practical politics. The Max Planck Institut in Berlin was one of the greatest centres, if not the greatest, of scientific research into nuclear energy. Its Jewish scientists fled, of course, when Hitler came to power, many to follow Einstein's advice and work in the Manhattan Project. Those who remained, in particular Professor Dr Werner Heisenberg (director of the Kaiser Wilhelm Institute for Physics, Berlin, 1941–5) quietly sabotaged the creation of a Nazi-controlled nuclear bomb.[7]

Thus when it came to an attack by Soviet secret intelligence upon the American scientific establishment, the K.G.B. (which incidentally did not officially exist until 13 March 1954, but which was at an earlier date busily swallowing the N.K.V.D. and the army's G.R.U. and was in effect only a rationalization of these) had two prongs to its fork, espionage being one, propaganda linked with sabotage the other.

Direct espionage quite rapidly assumed the minor role, simply because it was no longer needed. The Russians had acquired all the information they immediately needed: slave labour was digging uranium out of the mines in Siberia, the Erzgebirge and elsewhere; even in the Congo the vast reserves were being rapidly exhausted. The Russians built their bomb, with the witting or unwitting help of British, American, Canadian scientists. Only the delivery systems (a typical euphemism) remained inferior to those of the Americans for a few more years. And in some measure to rectify this, the budget of the K.G.B. was vastly increased in 1961.

While one part of the Soviet secret intelligence apparatus was busy stealing Western atomic technology, another was simultaneously engaged, with some success, in harming that very technology, in particular those branches concerned directly with military power. To tilt an adverse balance in one's own favour the quickest way is to weight one's own side while simultaneously depriving the other's. Soviet atomic policy, at home and abroad, between 1943 and, say, 1963 is a classic example of this technique. Perhaps the first exposed case was that of Igor Gousenko, in September of 1945, that is to say in the month following the Japanese surrender. In the interests of preserving the Western-Soviet 'alliance' his tale was smothered for nearly six months, despite the fact that Gousenko's defection was well known to the Soviets.

The Gousenko story is so well documented, from so many sources, that it need only be briefly summarized. In May 1943 a Soviet military attaché, Colonel Nikolai Sabotin, had arrived in Ottawa together with a staff that included, among its cipher clerks, Igor Gousenko. Sabotin's main, perhaps his only, function was to use his diplomatic immunity to pass information concerning the research into, and development of, the atomic bomb. Among his principal sources were the British physicist, Allan Nunn May, and the Italian, Bruno Pontecorvo. It was a very successful operation. Sabotin's deputy, a certain Colonel Motinov, personally flew the espionage material to G. M. Malenkov, who was Stalin's closest associate and immediate successor and who had himself briefed Sabotin before sending him to Ottawa.

Gousenko, realizing the advantages of Western society over that of his native country and aware through his sensitive position of what was happening, contacted the Canadian police. They did not believe him, and told him to go home. This he did not do, and the N.K.V.D. then made a severe blunder. Aware of Gousenko's absence, which was correctly construed as defection with a considerable amount of espionage material, they made a clumsy attempt to burgle his house in the hopes of retrieving that material. The Canadians thus had no choice but to take Gousenko seriously, and he was given asylum, while the material the Russians had obtained from their atomic spies was passed to the highest levels in Ottawa, thence to Washington and London.

None of the Western governments concerned wished to take action. Yet the security services uncovered more and more of this widespread operation. In the spring of 1946 arrests were, reluctantly, made. Pontecorvo was allowed to disappear. Some of the British and American traitors were sent to prison; the Rosenbergs to the electric chair. No very highly classified documents were produced in court, for evident reasons. It was now that the Soviets most skilfully turned their espionage defeat into something not unlike an Agitprop victory.

The fundamental concepts behind the vast campaign which Soviet intelligence now loosed upon the Western world are hard to understand by those who do not accept the dialectical principle, whether Hegelian or Marxist. Allowing, please, for gross oversimplification – since this book is not a philosophical survey –

318

Hegel taught that truth is not an absolute, but rather a synthesis, which becomes a thesis to be opposed by an antithesis from which a further synthesis will be made, and so *ad infinitum*. Marx claimed that he found Hegelian dialectic standing on its head and turned it the right way up. The way he achieved this was, in his mind and in that of his successors, to proclaim the eventual existence of a perfect and permanent synthesis. While this was a denial of Hegelian thought, for what that is worth, it was a re-statement in other terms of Judaeo-Christian eschatology. Marx, however, applied the concept of the 'final judgement' to social forms. The Communist dogma has therefore been based on two, contradictory ideas: that all history is working towards a pre-destined end, and that until this end is reached there can be no absolute truth, but only the flux of the Marxist dialectic. This was coarsened, especially by Lenin, into the concept of 'the dictatorship of the proletariat'. When the proletarians showed a marked lack of enthusiasm for dictatorship being exercised by a tiny minority of dedicated Bolsheviks (far smaller than their Czarist predecessors), Lenin, in 1918 and in the most brutal terms, advocated mass terrorism against the reluctant workers whom he was supposed to represent. In fact truth, both in practice and in theory, was ruled out of all calculations in Soviet Russia. The truth, according again to Lenin, was what expedited the Marxist eschatological end.

It is extremely difficult for anyone trained in modern Western intellectual disciplines to understand the near-suicidal impulses behind Soviet behaviour. It grew even more difficult when these strange ideas became an export product, after 1945. The enor-mous Agitprop operation following the Gousenko case showed how bewildering this policy was, perhaps more to the political and intellectual leaders of the West – who were constantly trying to rationalize Soviet irrationality – than to the mass public who steadfastly voted against the *olla podrida* of Marxist–Leninism whenever they were allowed so to do. So, of course, would the vast majority of Soviet citizens had they ever been given the opportunity of any credible choice.

It was this ideological amalgam of historical materialism, Talmudic eschatology, internal terror, and Marxist ideology that the Soviet leaders now, in 1946, intended to export with redoubled

319

energy to the rest of the world, with primary targets the United States of America and what was still then called Great Britain. It was as full of holes as a shrimping net, but it caught quite a number of shrimps as well as a few larger fish. To adopt a sub-Hegelian methodology, the theses and antitheses can be summed up as follows. Soviet thesis:

1 This atomic bomb was an Anglo-American invention which threatened the whole globe.
2 The bomb had been used against Asiatics. It therefore proved a continuing (Nazi) belief in racism as well as in colonialism.
3 The bomb had not been given to the Soviets. Therefore it was of anti-Soviet intent.
4 Monopoly-capitalism was bent on world domination, by any means, no matter how ferocious.
5 The Soviet Union, and the other Communist states it protected, could alone save the whole world from the impending horrors.
6 It was therefore quite correct for the Soviet Union to recruit, or send spies into, the West, since increased power to the Bolshevik élite must be interpreted as part of an ineluctible process called '*Histmat*' (historical materialism). Contrary activities by non-Communists would only postpone the day when history must cease, and should therefore be treated with the utmost rigour. In the West Roosevelt's ex-ambassador to the Soviet Union, a Mr Davis, declared in *The Times* of 4 March 1946: 'In self-defence, Russia has an absolute moral right to obtain atomic secrets by military espionage.' In 1947 the pro-Communist or Communist politician, Professor Harold Laski, head of the London School of Economics and speaking, rather curiously, on behalf of a body called the Association of British Scientists, described the ten-year sentence passed on the convicted Soviet spy Nunn May as 'unusually harsh' since it bore 'no relation to what had happened'. This person was neither a scientist, an authority on jurisprudence, nor an acknowledged expert on intelligence or counter-intelligence matters. Yet such voices echoed round the world. The campaign goes on today, particularly in regard to the executed Rosenberg spies. Like so much Marxist propaganda it is contradictory. The Rosenbergs were either innocent, in which case they should not have been sentenced to

320

death, or they were guilty, in which case they were martyrs to American 'fascism', since their crime was only one in 'fascist' eyes, and in either case their deaths were concrete proof of American brutality.

There is little point in debunking this Agitprop action, in pointing out that while the United States, in the late 1940s, was dismantling its atomic capability as fast as ever it could, the Soviets were building theirs; that the Russians decided on making a hydrogen bomb before the Americans; that while the British were withdrawing from empire, the Russians were extending theirs; that the main islands of Japan were rapidly handed back to the Japanese, while the Russians still cling to their booty in the northern Kuriles; that American monopoly-capitalism could not even withstand the policies of General de Gaulle in weak, impoverished France, while Soviet economic domination has been and is being backed by Soviet tanks, and now by Soviet warships, wherever these can reach; that it is the Soviets, not the Americans, who have tested 100-megaton bombs. Why go on? When the Russians realized, in Korea in 1951, that sheer brute strength was not enough, they turned increasingly to subversion. The outcome remains undecided, and the Soviet leaders may yet revert to naked aggression if they decide they cannot win either by proxy or by subversion.

In which case it may be assumed that they will have learned their Chinese lesson, that their objective will not be a Communist United States remotely controlled from Moscow but rather the physical destruction not only of the American educated classes (as in Poland) but of America as a whole. Such a suggestion will be dismissed as 'hysterical anti-Communism': would a prognosis of Auschwitz, Treblinka and the other Nazi extermination camps have been dismissed, in 1938, as 'hysterical anti-Nazism'? Probably. Unfortunately, the precedent has been set. And the Third World War is now being waged on intelligence-propaganda lines, technological espionage and secret political infiltration being the most obvious, active weapons. If there is to be a Fourth it will be very different.

Who were the Soviet agents throughout the period between 1945

321

and (to fix an arbitrary date) 1961, when even more massive support was given to the K.G.B. by the Krushchev administration? Apart from normal, usually low-level, espionage and propaganda persons, male and female, inside and outside the U.S.S.R., the Soviets seem to have relied largely on the awakening of their 'sleepers'. Since then this reliance has, apparently, given way to a greater reliance upon trained Soviet agents than upon foreign traitors. Such a trend would accord not only with normal Russian xenophobia but also with the political and military failures (Azerbaijan, the Berlin blockade of 1948, the Korean War) that resulted in large measure from a faulty appraisal of Western, particularly American, will. The success of the Marshall Plan in the rebuilding of Europe, the breach with China, and finally the near-collapse of the Cuban offensive marked the end of the so-called Cold War, the loss by the Russians of a long and protracted campaign in the undeclared Third World War, but not of the war itself. In that campaign they had committed a great part of their espionage organization overseas. Some of the British and American traitors were eliminated, some fled to the Soviet Union, others no doubt remain undiscovered and perhaps inactive.

Who were these men of the 1940s and 1950s, men of high intelligence and not infrequently of great political education, who desired to see Soviet supremacy over their own countries and peoples? They were, of course, utterly different from one another and any form of generalization is both dangerous and suspect. Their roots were deeply implanted in the so-called left-wing liberalism of the 1930s, but few such liberals were prepared to betray their own society in clandestine fashion no matter how much they might denigrate it in public. Nor were the more important traitors open to bribes, for they were generally far better off in the West. Well aware of what had happened, and was happening, in the Soviet Union these men were yet willing to sacrifice their careers, usually in early middle age, for what?

One answer is the naked attraction of power. This appeal to the members of a governing class can be great, and has been exercised before, in particular during the French Revolution. Some men are so preoccupied with power that they will go where they believe it lies – regardless.

A second answer is blackmail. A young man may be so compromised and so easily that when it is time, years later, to awaken the sleeper he has, or thinks he has, little choice but to obey. Then the first, solitary act of treacherous obedience seals his destiny. In the German phrase, a man who says A will also say B, and at last find himself saying X, Y and Z.

A third, but perhaps rather specious, explanation is a psychological one. Many of these traitors had habits which were regarded as anti-social, less so in the West than in the Eastern bloc, but nevertheless officially frowned upon: sexual perversions, drunkenness, drugs, an addiction to physical violence, financial instability. Such weaknesses, however, are far from rare, and in the period in question were usually ignored, even when flaunted, amidst a permissive governing class; and only a minor proportion of those so afflicted became traitors. Nor could they have expected to be so tolerated by the Soviet authorities.

The most plausible answer would seem to be hatred. Lenin had long ago advocated 'merciless mass terror' against the Russian people who refused to accept his Bolshevik panacea. From various motives the Western traitors hated their own society. They wished to see the utmost brutality exercised against their own people. Across the generations the voice of Count Esterhazy can once again be heard. And Zola? Some listened to George Orwell.

Chapter Eighteen

Some Comments on the C.I.A.

Since the United States had never had any co-ordinated secret intelligence service, save briefly and not too happily in time of war, and since well-informed men foresaw the duration of U.S.S.R.–U.S.A. hostility at least as early as 1945, it was clear that an efficient, peacetime secret intelligence service was both essential and of high priority. As has been shown, such intelligence services are usually traditional, or to be more exact are based on earlier models. The Americans really had no such preceding organizations that could be modernized to participate actively in what might become, in itself, an imponderable situation. Added to this was a basic, public dislike of 'secrecy' as such. The United States authorities were faced with a dual problem. A secret service was needed, but an American secret service was almost an innate contradiction.

The Americans looked first, and obviously, to the British model, then to the German (about which almost everything was now known) and only belatedly at what the Russians were up to in this murky world. The result was, for some years and perhaps today, moderately successful (save in monetary expenditure). There were however some built-in errors in the original structure of the C.I.A.

In theory, and to some extent in practice, the British drew an organizational distinction between secret intelligence and counter-intelligence, somewhat loosely referred to as security. Espionage is usually and incorrectly referred to as M.I.6, or D.I.6, counter-espionage being called, in public, M.I.5, the first operating abroad, the second within what is now called the Commonwealth. That these designations of two complementary intelligence organizations became obsolete long ago is of small importance. The fundamental theory remains, though this has become extremely blurred, particularly in the political climate of the late twentieth century, in this Third World War that is not a war as previous generations understood that word. And to this out-of-date dichotomy of functions must be added the increasingly powerful weapons of subversion, up to and including physical sabotage, and propaganda.

Since the Americans did not wish for any extension of a secret police within the United States, the C.I.A. was explicitly forbidden to operate domestically. This was left amost entirely to the F.B.I., a police force trained to capture domestic criminals and with limited experience in the neutralization of political traitors or of foreign agents. It learned, rather slowly, for the necessary techniques are not easily or quickly acquired.

Since the F.B.I. was assigned, among its other duties, those of 'M.I.5', it meant that the C.I.A. had to fulfil, among its other duties, those of 'M.I.6'. And those other duties have become, in the Third World War, far more complicated than those which faced 'M.I.6' half a century ago. It is here that the Nazi–German parallel enters into the calculation.

The British division between external and internal intelligence probably made good sense in the nineteenth century, for a self-contained and very homogeneous island priding itself on its 'splendid isolation' from the European mainland. Yet even then the system had to be supplemented by the secret police force known, originally, as the Irish Special Branch and now simply called the Special Branch. When all Ireland was still part of the United Kingdom, until 1922, the Special Branch was in effect an espionage service directed against an internal enemy, against persons who in theory at least were subjects of the Crown. During the Anglo-Irish War of 1918–21 the Special Branch worked ever more closely with military intelligence in Ireland. It was never a very satisfactory arrangement, which the much inferior forces under Michael Collins could and did outwit, first by superior espionage and finally by assassination.

In the Second World War altogether new forces emerged. The British Special Operations Executive (S.O.E.) functioned in a twilight zone between direct military activity, political activity in the German-occupied countries in assisting some of the resistance movements, and sabotage or commando-type operations usually but not always against 'intelligence' targets. Their processing of captured enemy documents and the interrogation of enemy prisoners further blurred the distinctions among various forms of intelligence and para-intelligence activity. So too did the immensely complicated operations based in Bletchley. The Joint Intelligence Committee, which had immediate access to the British cabinet and thus to British supreme command, both political and military, co-ordinated the material and the tasks to be assigned, with varying success. Subordinate committees controlled such activities as disinformation, propaganda and specialized operations, for example the study of the V-1 and V-2, of German atomic potentiality, and many more. The rigid division between external intelligence and internal security virtually ceased to exist.

Yet with an illusion of peacetime intelligence, it was precisely this distinction that the Americans adopted as basic policy. The C.I.A. was officially constituted on the basis that it might *only* operate overseas. This has caused, and at the time of writing is causing, much confusion in the minds of the American public. In theory an enemy agent inside the United States is the target of the F.B.I. When he crosses the border into Mexico, he comes under the supervision of the C.I.A. If he comes back, he is once again the F.B.I.'s meat. This oversimplified example is given to show the fallacy inherent in the C.I.A.'s constitution. Based on outmoded, legalistic concepts, that constitution has inevitably been frequently ignored.

If the C.I.A. was not given enough power (in theory none) to act within the U.S.A., it was lumbered with far too much abroad. A secret espionage agency, which is what it was intended to be, should not be directly responsible at the same time for S.O.E./ O.S.S. types of active operation. In an advisory capacity, yes; in a direct military capacity, no. Yet here the C.I.A. was forced to copy the not very happy experiences of the old German Abwehr, which had at its disposal the Brandenburg units – originally the 'Instructional Building Battalion for Special Purposes 800', then a regiment but later much expanded – which were used for all sorts of skulduggery, such as the wearing of enemy uniforms, deep infiltration, the kidnapping of enemy or hostile persons and similar activities. When the C.I.A. was ordered to carry out such operations, it had very few 'Brandenburg' armed men, and had to

326

borrow them from the army, navy or air force, since its own armed force, the Special Operations Division (S.O.D.) had been repeatedly proved inadequate. The most spectacular fiasco of this sort was the Cuban operation known as the Bay of Pigs. The C.I.A. lacked both the trained leaders and the men, as well as the experience, to carry out an action of this sort – nor should Presidents Eisenhower and Kennedy ever have made such a demand on the organization.

As an intelligence organization it would appear to have been similarly frustrated by an almost unbelievable and clumsy structure, also based on ancient, legalistic modes. The United States made the grave error of creating an independent air force, precisely at the time when most intelligent persons in Britain were accepting the fact that an autonomous air force was a mistake. The Canadians were going a step further and creating one armed force to operate on land, sea and in the air. The Russians, for quite other reasons, were creating a central intelligence agency, the K.G.B., with real power everywhere. The United States acted in a precisely opposite manner. On the one hand the Central Intelligence Agency was supposed to be what its name implies. On the other, such vital intelligence as might be described as electronic, that in to say cipher-breaking and other forms of high-level espionage, was assigned to another agency; counter-espionage in almost every sense to yet a third; while aerial reconnaissance, whether by plane or satellite, became more and more the perquisite of the new United States Air Force.

The C.I.A. built itself an ostentatious, indeed a palatial, plate-glass building at Langley, Virginia, in which, we may assume, some considerable attempt was made – amidst maximum publicity – to evaluate intelligence material. The almost incredible clumsiness which permitted the Soviet government nearly to install nuclear weapons on Cuban soil, the folly of American policy in the Middle East in 1956, the American defeat in Southeast Asia, all these show how deplorably inadequate the C.I.A. must have been as a centre of evaluation. It was left with its own subversive role. Unattractive and not very competent, it became an obvious Aunt Sally for America's enemies even before it was found to have broken its constitutional rights by internal espionage. From the American point of view it is to be hoped that this lame duck is a decoy and that a real secret intelligence service exists.

Certainly huge sections of American secret intelligence were not under the control of the C.I.A. One of these was the enormous and enormously expensive code and cipher-breaking apparatus, the National Security Agency or N.S.A. In 1967 it was collecting huge quantities of 'enemy' material, too much in fact for it to cope with, and only a portion was being evaluated. Partial evaluation is extremely dangerous, since it can produce a lopsided and misleading picture of enemy intentions and provides the perfect breeding ground for disinformation. Bad intelligence is probably worse than no intelligence.

Aerial reconnaissance was, as I have stated, under the control of the Air Force. This applied not only to the old-fashioned type of reconnaissance, the U-2 being the most famous model, but to the ever-increasing, and increasingly important, satellite intelligence. Miles Copeland, who was a member of the C.I.A., has reckoned that an American satellite, cameras and television transmitters whirring, is passing over sensitive areas of the globe every twenty minutes, a Soviet equivalent every forty.[1] The amount of visual and aural material (for lasers in satellites can report conversations on earth) being constantly transmitted is so enormous that most of this also remains, probably correctly, unprocessed and unevaluated, save at critical times and in critical areas. To this huge expense was added that of the Manned Orbiting Laboratories (M.O.L.), rather thinly disguised as elaborate instruments of scientific research but actually intended to perfect the intelligence work of the unmanned satellites. They, it seems, were a failure.[2] Nor is it conceivable that the United States could have spent so many billions of dollars in landing men on the moon simply for the prestige of planting the stars and stripes in lunar dust and bringing back some moon rock for geologists and astronomers to study. The fact that these expeditions were repeated would indicate that the U.S. Air Force was hoping to establish a permanent base or bases for espionage and possibly for the launching of nuclear weapons. The fact that these expeditions seem to have been discontinued would in turn imply that these attempts, like the M.O.L.'s, were a failure. On the other hand there seems no reasonable explanation for the

328

sending, by the U.S.A. and the U.S.S.R., of unmanned space vehicles to explore the other planets. That this was not just done for fun (scientific research is the more respectable term) seems obvious. Yet what military significance a jaunt to, say, Jupiter, can have escapes this writer.

The vitally important intelligence task of watching the new, huge Red Fleet – and above all its nuclear submarines, their potential and their deployment – was of course a duty of naval intelligence, working primarily in collaboration with the N.S.A.

Propaganda, in particular the huge radio propaganda of Radio Free Europe and Radio Liberty (originally called Radio Liberation) were subsidized by the C.I.A., to the tune of some $35 million per annum, peanuts of course compared to the space programme but still a sizeable whack of the taxpayers' money. Of course it cost the Soviets a certain amount of time, money and trouble to jam these, not always successfully. But Congress decided in 1971 that the C.I.A. should cease to finance open propaganda. 'Black' propaganda remained a C.I.A. activity, but the promulgation of spurious news, intended to disinform the Russians, Chinese and others, was not infrequently picked up by quite reputable American journalists and thus served to disinform the American people without reaching the Russian or Chinese people at all. The resultant confusion in Southeast Asia (was there or was there not a war going on in Laos and/or Cambodia? What was really happening in Vietnam?) became a matter of increasing distress to the American public, indeed to the whole Western world, which distress was most skilfully exploited by the Communists' own Agitprop organization, infinitely more experienced and better led. Abroad, and even inside the United States, the C.I.A. has most certainly not won the propaganda war and is probably still losing it, everywhere, save perhaps now in the U.S.A.

Clandestine operations have been discussed. So what is there left for the C.I.A. to do? The answer is simple; espionage and counter-espionage outside the borders of the United States. But espionage in Russia and China is almost impossible, so tight is security in the first, so difficult the role of a spy in the other. Besides, the work of espionage has become increasingly the work of machines, particularly satellites, radio intercepts and cipher-breaking computers. This does not mean that there are no spies working for the C.I.A. inside Russia and even inside the Kremlin. But they cannot be many. Espionage in some of the Soviet-occupied countries is slightly less perilous, but then there is not a great deal to be found out in most of them. Furthermore, the Americans 'inherited' the Gehlen Institute in 1945, with its invaluable files concerning Eastern Europe and the Soviet Union. For some years it has been part of the West German intelligence service, and it proved very effective until the Soviets built the Berlin Wall. Willy-nilly the C.I.A. has had to entrust its espionage spearhead to Gehlen and his successors.

This leaves – what? The Americans of course spy on their allies and quasi-allies, but this is a highly delicate operation. The Soviet Agitprop organization consistently and usually accurately blames the C.I.A. for all sorts of activities, from attempted strike-control in Britain to counter-revolution in Chile. Their success in creating anti-American feeling almost throughout the world has helped them to paint the C.I.A. as an extremely sinister force, which unfortunately it is not. Since the public has an almost insatiable love of spy stories, and since few concerning the K.G.B. are released, the C.I.A. enjoys what might be described as a near monopoly in the popular press. And since no one likes the idea of foreign spies or agitators being active in his own country, this also feeds Agitprop anti-Americanism. What tends to be forgotten is that the poor old C.I.A. exists to preserve the freedom not only of Americans but of the Western world from conquest for a foul and permanent tyranny.

One of the misfortunes of any secret intelligence service is that its failures are trumpeted abroad; its successes remain, almost invariably, secret. The C.I.A. has been most particularly hampered in this way. Apart from obtaining and publishing Krushchev's 'secret' speech, the most spectacular American intelligence triumphs have concerned defectors, yet even these, with few exceptions, have acted on their own initiative and have not been suborned by the C.I.A. Indeed the logic of the situation implies that a Russian with important knowledge of Soviet technology, military affairs or policy, and who was in touch with C.I.A. operatives, would be encouraged on no account to defect, unless aware of imminent arrest and personal destruction by the K.G.B. Needless to say, we do not hear of those who remain. It is, however, possible to deduce from the arrest of K.G.B. spies in the West that there have been, and almost certainly still are, a small number of men holding confidential posts within the espionage branch of the K.G.B. who are passing the necessary information to the C.I.A. and, perhaps more often, to the British S.I.S. Their identity and methods must remain secret, obviously.

What we get, then, are bungled operations, unexplained arrests such as those of 'Abel' in America or 'Lonsdale' in London, and also deliberately publicized defections. Of these the most recent spectaculars were, eastwards, that of the British intelligence officer, 'Kim' Philby in 1963 and, westwards, that of the G.R.U. operator Penkovsky in 1960. Both had been, for many years, double agents. Both, after defection, wrote their memoirs; both books are highly suspect in form as well as in content, and were obviously and drastically edited, if not actually written, by their new masters. In the early 1960s *The Penkovsky Papers* attracted much attention; so too did Philby's book some years later.

Penkovsky worked for the British S.I.S. When he attempted to seek refuge with the C.I.A. in Turkey, in 1960, he was at first refused asylum and refuge for this very reason. The defection of Donald Maclean and of Guy Burgess from the British to the Russians had recently blown, in American eyes, a great hole in British security. It was known that they were not alone in their treachery, that they had been warned by a person or persons inside British security. This was certainly Philby, perhaps among others so far unnamed, who was then still at large as a correspondent of London's moderately left-wing paper, *The Observer*, in the Middle East. All this was of course known to the C.I.A., which therefore hesitated to accept the S.I.S.'s affidavits concerning the reliability of Penkovsky, fearing that he might be a K.G.B. infiltrator, and having themselves suffered from several such in the recent past. Nor does Penkovsky seem to have given much information to the C.I.A. that was not already available, save names, procedures and personalities. (He contributed nothing, for instance, about the installation of Soviet nuclear rockets in Cuba.) Strangely enough the same must have been true of Philby, who had been sidetracked into *The Observer* for some years. It is an odd mirror image, and one that is characteristic of publicized espionage in our time. It is almost certain that history would have remained entirely unaffected if these two men had remained true to their first allegiances.

It has been suggested that in the mid-1960s, as Henry Kissinger assumed ever-increasing power in the American intelligence world with ultimate power in American foreign policy, and while Leonid Brezhnev was reaching the apex of power in the Soviet Union, the plot of a Soviet–U.S. global condominium (theoretically to avoid war) was being hatched under the code-name *détente*, and, like the SALT agreements, involved a measure of co-operation, in this case between the secret intelligence services of the two super-powers. Possible, but in the opinion of this writer, an improbable example of global-political paranoia.

Yet equally strange 'arrangements' of a temporary sort have marked all Soviet history, while American pacifism has remained a constant save in times of declared war. To enlist American pacifism against the Chinese threat would seem obvious from a Muscovite point of view. To flirt with Peking in order to strengthen Washington's hand would seem an equally obvious stratagem for so keen an admirer of Metternich as is Mr Kissinger. Certain odd events give the apparent paranoia referred to a measure of verisimilitude. Why did Soviet intelligence, well aware of the Israeli pre-emptive strike in 1967, not then inform their Egyptian protégés of what was about to hit them? Why does the American government allow and even encourage the run-down of American military power?

Only one certainty remains. The American and Russian intelligence services have not decreased their mutual investigations. And an outside observer can only assume that this is, and will remain, normal.

Chapter Nineteen

Conclusions

There can be no conclusion to this book, save in the improbable Marxist theory that somehow and at some time history will cease. Since this ending is most certainly not even a possibility at this time: since in the year that must elapse before this book is published much will be divulged and more enacted: any conclusion is suspect. When Julius Caesar dictated his *De Bello Gallico*, to his slave-scribe, he ended, in rough translation, with the words: 'That's all, there isn't any more,' which of course the slave also wrote down and included in the book. Julians were far too busy to read proofs of their dictated works, so Caesar's perfect culmination remains.

The slave-scribe did not become an emperor, and though this scribe may in certain circumstances become a slave of the Soviets, it is highly unlikely that he will be otherwise too busy to read proofs. Besides, Julius Caesar's Gallic Wars *were* ended, for a long time, while our wars are not.

Conclusions are another matter, as are apologies. The apologies, first, deal with the obvious, gaping omissions, and in particular those concerning recent events. To take but a few glaring examples, the intensely complex intelligence war between Israel and its Arab neighbours has hardly been touched upon, save marginally. The role of secret intelligence in the Asiatic wars of the 1960s has not been mentioned, yet has obviously been of the greatest importance. The actions of the British Secret Intelligence Service, since its earliest days, have not been stressed, nor have those of the huge contemporary American Defense Intelligence Agency. There are many other omissions. The slave-scribe's excuse is that he lacked the knowledge to write about these important matters; others have done so, more will. I have limited myself to what I knew or what, explicitly, I might surmise. That there must be errors is obvious; that these will be pounced upon, even more so.

333

Conclusions? Knowledge is power, as we all know. In no century more than our own has power, or the search for power, been the essence of history. In retrospect nationalisms, religious convictions, ideologies, morality and standards of conduct have all been in a state of periodic flux dictated by the will for power as foreseen in philosophic terms by Nietzsche and others longer ago. Materialism and its apprentice, technology, have made this lust justifiable to quite honourable men even though it takes the form of rape. Whether we choose to call ourselves democrats or not, we remain responsible for our governors, and since it is they who exercise power it is for them that knowledge is essential. In political terms such knowledge, among the powers, consists of intelligence and counter-intelligence. Wisdom may be invoked, but it remains a minor element in a highly complex, essentially futile, equation.

Futility may sound a strong word when applied to current secret intelligence, upon which vast resources of every kind are being expended. Yet assuming that that expense is, voluntarily or otherwise, being met by the states concerned, then it may also be assumed that their knowledge of one another's tactical or operational intentions will have been obtained. As for their ultimate, strategic intentions, these have usually been written down (as in *Mein Kampf*, or the writings of Lenin and his successors) or publicly asserted, as by the Western leaders of all countries during and since the Second World War. These are underlined. These strategic intentions are made abundantly clear by pacts, treaties and the physical distribution of military, air and naval forces. With the existence of satellites, together with sophisticated cipher-breaking, deception has become almost impossible, even strategic deception, except in so far as we cannot see into the mind of the potential enemy's leader, let alone into the mind of his unknown successor. Yet we do, or at least should, know the weapons that will be at his disposal and therefore, if we are on the defensive, how these can and should be countered. Provided only that our secret and open intelligence are adequate, and that our defensive or counter-offensive potential is also adequate, we are quite capable of dealing with any enemy. It is at this point that intelligence, by its very perfection, becomes futile. Eventually, or to be more precise temporarily, there is nothing more to know.

This was realized by President Eisenhower, when he advocated an 'open skies' policy nearly twenty years ago. The Soviets, of course, did not accept this simplistic view of American–Soviet intelligence relations. Why should they? They had quite other plans to further their aim of global dominance. One element of this was the destruction of Western intelligence. And since the officers of only moderately sophisticated secret intelligence services tend to the fallacy that the enemy's service approximates to their own, Agitprop was diverted against the C.I.A. even as if it were the K.G.B. They have been remarkably successful in this endeavour. It is to be hoped that what they are so skilfully demolishing is in effect a paper tiger, and even more that the real tiger is burning, not too brightly, in the jungles of the night.

Notes

Chapter One
1 Sir Denis Brogan, *Development of Modern France 1870–1939*, Hamish Hamilton, London, 1940. (Revised edition, 1967.) Published in America as *France under the Republic*, Harper and Brothers, New York, 1940.

Chapter Two
1 Ronald Hingley, *The Russian Secret Police*, Hutchinson, London, 1970; Simon and Schuster, New York, 1971.
2 Ibid.

Chapter Three
1 Winfried Ludecke, *Behind the Scenes of Espionage*, Harrap, London, 1929. Published in America as *Secrets of Espionage: Tales of the Secret Service*, J. B. Lippincott, Philadelphia, 1929.
2 Robin Bruce Lockhart, *Ace of Spies*, Hodder and Stoughton, London, 1967; Stein and Day, New York, 1968.
3 Donald McLachlan, *Room 39*, Weidenfeld and Nicolson, London, 1968; Atheneum, New York, 1968.

Chapter Four
1 Dr Wilhelm Steiber, *Denkwürdigkeiten des Geheimen Regierungsrathes*, Berlin, 1884.
2 Paul Lanoir, *The German Spy System in France*, Mills and Boon, London, 1910.

Chapter Five
1 Herbert O. Yardley, *The American Black Chamber*, published by Bobbs Merrill in June 1931 after part serialization in the *Saturday Evening Post*. (The English edition was published by Faber and Faber in the same year.)
2 David Kahn, *The Codebreakers*, Collier-Macmillan London, 1974; The New American Library, New York, 1973.

Chapter Seven
1 Admiral Sir William James, *The Eyes of the Navy*, Methuen, London, 1955.
2 Burton H. Hendrick, *The Life and Letters of Walter H. Page*, vol. III, Doubleday, Page & Co, New York, 1925.

Chapter Eight
1 The need for foreign knowledge, foreign money and even recently for foreign corn has been a Russian constant since at least the time of Peter the Great in the late seventeenth century. A slightly ex-

336

aggerated account of this demand, from building technology to nuclear fission, is to be found in Dr Werner Keller's *Ost Minus West = Null*,* Droemersche Verlagsanstalt, Zurich, 1960, and translated by myself for Thames and Hudson, London, 1961, a translation to which the publisher gave the somewhat distasteful title of *Are the Russians Ten Feet Tall?* It shows, with very considerable documentation, the intensity with which the Russians have always culled and used information from abroad and therefore by derivation their extreme secrecy concerning their own affairs.

* Published in America as *East minus West = Zero; Russia's Debt to the Western World*, G. P. Putnam's, New York, 1962.

2 For this tale of Pinkus Urwicz, and indeed for much else not only in this chapter the reader is referred to *Der Deutsche Geheimdienst* by Dr Gert Buchheit, List Verlag, Munich, 1966. It is extraordinary that, at least to this writer's knowledge, so important a study has not as yet appeared in an English translation.

3 For an extremely sensitive and militarily acute account of this operation, see Alexander Solzhenitsyn's *August 1914*, The Bodley Head, London, 1973; Farrer, Straus & Giroux, New York, 1972, one of the very few Russian accounts not tainted by subsequent political events.

4 The extreme complexity of Jewish communities, as opposed to 'assimilated' Jews, in European history is only marginally relevant to this study. For a magisterial analysis, the reader is referred to Leon Poliakov's *Histoire de l'Antisémitisme*, Calmann-Lévy, Paris, of which the first of a projected four volumes appeared in 1961. It will be for many years the authoritative work.

5 Yardley, op. cit.

6 The best account of this still mysterious business known to this writer is to be found in Barbara W. Tuchman, *The Zimmermann Telegram*, Constable, London, 1959; Viking, New York, 1959.

Chapter Nine

1 *Die Nachhut*, no. 8, 15 September 1969.

2 George Katkov, *Russia 1917: The February Revolution*, Longman, Green, London, 1967.

3 *The Wiener Library Bulletin*, 1973–4, vol. XXVII.

4 Z. A. B. Zeman, *Germany and the Revolution in Russia 1915–18* Oxford University Press, New York, 1958.

5 See Joel Carmichael, 'German Money and Bolshevik Honour', *Encounter*, vol. XLII, no. 3, March 1974.

6 See Z. A. B. Zeman and W. B. Scharlav, *The Merchant of Revolution, The Life of Alexander Helphand 1867–1924*, Oxford University Press, New York, London, 1965. This book is entirely reliable on the later facts, culled from German documents.

Chapter Ten

1 Yardley, op. cit.

2 Tuchman, op. cit.

3 James, op. cit.

4 Kahn, op. cit.

Chapter Eleven

1 Georges Clemenceau, *Grandeur and Misery of Victory*, Harrap, London, 1930; Harcourt, Brace & Co, New York, 1930.

2 See McLachlan, op. cit., 'Room 39' was intended to be a reincarnation, in the Second World War, of what Room 40 had been in the First.

3 David Neligan, *The Spy in the Castle*, MacGibbon and Kee, London, 1968. This is an autobiographical work.

4 Herbert Hoover, *The Ordeal of Woodrow Wilson*, Museum Press, London, 1958; McGraw-Hill, New York, 1958. Few men have had so many advantages in writing a historical study: a vast mass of unpublished material and a highly skilled research staff; great personal knowledge of the events and the principal characters; above all first-hand experience of a Presidency that also failed; finally a profound sympathy with, and understanding of, American ideals.

5 Yardley, op. cit., p. 142.

Chapter Twelve

1 Fritz Fischer, *Germany's Aims in the First World War*, Chatto & Windus, London, 1967; W. W. Norton, New York, 1967.

2 The unpublished papers of Colonel House, Yale University Library.

3 Ray Stannard Baker, *Woodrow Wilson, Life & Letters*, 8 vols, Doubleday, New York, 1939.

4 *Decrety Sovetskoy Vlast*, vol. III, Moscow, 1964, p. 291.

5 Martin Gilbert, *The Life of Winston Churchill 1917–1922*, vol. IV, Heinemann, London, 1975; Houghton Mifflin, Boston, 1975.

6 Robert Conquest, *The Great Terror*, Macmillan, London, New York, 1968.

7 Boris Souvarine, *Stalin: A Critical Survey of Bolshevism*, Secker and Warburg, London, 1939; Octagon Books, New York, 1972.

8 Conquest, op. cit.

9 Hoover, op. cit.

10 Alexander Weissberg, *Conspiracy of Silence*, Hamish Hamilton, London, 1952. Published in America as *Accused*, Simon and Schuster, New York, 1951.

11 Robert Bruce Lockhart, *Memoirs of a British Agent*, G. P. Putnam's, New York, London, 1934, is among the very best personal records.

Chapter Thirteen

1 Sir John Wheeler-Bennett, *The Neurosis of Power*, Macmillan, London, 1953; published in America as *Nemesis of Power; The German Army in Politics, 1918–1945*, St Martin's Press, New York, 1954. In the opinion of this writer still the authoritative general history of the German army between 1918 and 1945.

2 Yardley, op. cit.

Chapter Fourteen

1 Kahn, op. cit.

2 F. W. Winterbotham, *The Ultra Secret*, Weidenfeld and Nicolson, London, 1974; Harper and Row, New York, 1975.
3 Gustave Bertrand, *Enigma*, Plon, Paris, 1973.
4 See Barton Whaley, *Codeword Barbarossa*, M.I.T. Press, Cambridge, Mass., 1973.
5 Ibid.
6 F. W. Deakin and G. R. Storry, *The Case of Richard Sorge*, Chatto and Windus, London, 1966; Harper and Row, New York, 1966.
7 Hingley, op. cit.
8 See Sir Basil Liddell Hart, *Memoirs*, Cassell, London, 1965; G. P. Putnam's, New York, 1966.
9 Weissberg, op. cit.
10 For its detailed organization, which went far beyond secret intelligence, see André Brissaud, *The Nazi Secret Service*, English translation, The Bodley Head, London, 1972; W. W. Norton, New York, 1974.
11 *Master of Spies, The Memoirs of General Frantisek Moravec* (then a senior officer in, and later head of, the Czechoslovak intelligence apparatus), The Bodley Head, London, 1975; Doubleday, New York, 1975.
12 See this writer's *The Shirt of Nessus*, Cassell, London, 1956, later republished by Tom Stacey Ltd as *To Kill Hitler*. (Published in America as *20 July*, Norton, New York, 1956.)
13 Heinz Guderian, *Panzer Leader*, Michael Joseph, London, 1952; E. P. Dutton, New York, 1952.
14 Ibid.

Chapter Fifteen
1 J. C. Masterman, *The Double-Cross System*, Yale University Press, New Haven, Conn., 1972.
2 Sefton Delmer, *The Counterfeit Spy*, Harper and Row, New York, 1971; Hutchinson, London, 1973.
3 Ewen Montagu, *The Man Who Never Was*, Evans, London, 1953; J. P. Lippincott, New York, 1967.
4 For the 'official' British version see Masterman, op. cit., a cool, brief but still enthusiastic account.
5 L. C. Moyzisch, *Operation Cicero*, Wingate, London, undated but I believe published in 1951; Universal Publishing and Distributing Corp. (Award Books), Hauppage, New York, 1969. It was filmed with the title *Five Fingers*.

Chapter Sixteen
1 Pierre Accocae and Pierre Quet, *The Lucy Ring*, English translation, W. H. Allen, London, 1967. Published in America as *A Man Called Lucy*, Coward-McCann, New York, 1967. It must not be accepted as factually correct. Even names are misspelled and ranks as well as appointments misattributed.
2 Allen Dulles, *The Craft of Intelligence*, Weidenfeld and Nicolson, London, 1964; Harper and Row, New York, 1963.
3 Apart from Bertrand's book, already referred to, see Michel

Garder, *La Guerre Secréte des Services Speciaux Français 1934–45*, Plon, Paris, 1967.

4 *The Encyclopaedia Britannica*, eleventh edition with supplement. The article on 'Intelligence, military' is attributed to Major Charles Atkinson and Captain Frederick Haphold.

5 Felix Kersten, *The Kersten Memoirs*, Hutchinson, London, 1956.

6 Albert Speer, *Inside the Third Reich*, Weidenfeld and Nicolson, London, 1970: Macmillan, New York, 1970.

7 Omar N. Bradley, *A Soldier's Story*, Eyre and Spottiswoode, London, 1951; Greenwood Press, Westport, Conn., 1975.

Chapter Seventeen

1 Winston Churchill, *The Second World War*, vol. VI: *Triumph and Tragedy*, Cassell, London, 1954; Houghton Mifflin, Boston, 1953.

2 McLachlan, op. cit.

3 Churchill, op. cit.

4 John Barron, *K.G.B.*, Hodder and Stoughton, London, 1974; Bantam Books, Inc., New York, 1974.

5 Ibid., p. 335.

6 Max Manus, *Underwater Saboteur*, William Kimber, London, 1953.

7 Dr Heisenberg's book, *Physics and Philosophy*, Harper and Row, New York, 1958; Allen and Unwin, London, 1959, is indicative of change by its title alone, although even more so by its content.

Chapter Eighteen

1 Miles Copeland, *The Real Spy World*, Weidenfeld and Nicolson, London, 1974. Published in America as *Without Cloak or Dagger*, Simon and Schuster, New York, 1974.

2 Victor Marchetti and John D. Marks, *The C.I.A. and the Cult of Intelligence*, Jonathan Cape, London, 1974; Alfred A. Knopf, New York, 1974.

INDEX

'Abel', arrest in U.S. 331

Abteilung (Department) IIIb, German Army High Command 115, 116; administration and activities under Nicolai 118; most spectacular victory 147; memorandum by Helphand, read 146; policy towards French deserters 133–4; Helphand's contacts useful to 145

Abwehr 55 and n., 214, 215, 246, 258, 262, 263; controlled by O.K.W. 238; expanded after 1933 238; preserved considerable independence 238; supplied explosive to Stauffenberg 243

Ace of Spies (Robin Bruce Lockhart) 48

Administration of Special Tasks 309

Aerial reconnaissance in U.S. 327; controlled by Air Force 328

Agadir 48

Agents, breaking of 80, 81

Agitprop 234, 305, 308, 318, 319; controlled by Comintern 234; help to Russian infiltration 248, 252; 'Second Front Now!' slogan, 1942 274

American Black Chamber, The (Herbert O. Yardley) 72

American Central Intelligence

Agency *see* C.I.A.

American secret intelligence, neglected and negligible pre-First World War 79; perhaps exists outside C.I.A. 328; reading some Japanese ciphers by 1940 229. *See also* C.I.A. *and* Yardley

Anglo-Irish War, 1918–22 43, 172; became intelligence war 173

Anglo-Japanese Treaty of Alliance 77, 99; renewed 181

Ankara, S.S. 287, 288

Ashenden (Somerset Maugham) 112

Assembly of Russian Working Men 37

Azev, Yezno (police spy) 38, 39; arranges assassination of Plehve 39; concerned with assassination of Grand Duke Sergei 39

Baden Powell, Robert 48

Balfour, Arthur James (later Lord) 190, 191

Barbarossa, Operation 233, 246, 271

Bay of Pigs 53; spectacular fiasco 327

Bell, Bishop of Chichester 250 n.

Bell, Edward 166, 183

Benckendorff, General von 37

Beria, Lavrenti 237

Bernstorff, Count 153, 160

341

Bertrand, Gustave 230 and n.
Bethmann-Hollweg, German
   Chancellor 160, 162, 163
Birley, Professor Eric 9, 280, 282
Bismarck, Prince von 56–8, 59,
   60
Black-and-Tans (regiment) 172
'Black Chamber' (U.S.A.) *see*
   Yardley, Herbert; closed in
   1929 158
Bletchley (Park) 228, 281–5, 321;
   and Churchill 282; probably
   reading German diplomatic
   cipher 301
Blockade and counter-blockade
   100
'Bloody Sunday' (Russia), 1905
   37, 38; Ireland, 21 November
   1920 174
Bolshevism 40
Bonhoeffer, Dietrich 250 n.
Boy-Ed, Captain 152
Bradley, General 268, 294, 295
Brezhnev, Leonid 237; Doctrine
   150
'Brinkmanship' 16
British ('English') Secret Service,
   reputation for efficiency 43;
   collapse of legend 43; decay
   in India 46; incompetence in
   Boer War 48; increasingly
   imperialist in later 19th
   century 45; invention and
   nature of 43–4; international
   esteem scarcely warranted 46;
   centred in Admiralty in First
   World War 26
Brogan, Sir Denis, quoted 30
Brusilov, General 139, 140, 146
Buchan, John 48
Bugging 93
Burgess, Guy 50, 248, 331
'Burgundia' 292, 302, 303

Canaris, Admiral 219, 242, 243;

and Operation Mincemeat
   258, 262
Carmichael, Joel 144, 145, 147
Casement, Sir Roger 108
Cavell, Nurse 86
Cavendish-Bentinck, V. 9,
   255 n.; on 'Cicero' 264, 276
Central Intelligence Bureau
   (Germany) 62
Cheka 54, 196, 197, 216, 308
Chernomazov, *Pravda* editor and
   Okhrana agent 40
Childers, Erskine 64
Churchill, Winston 35, 97, 98,
   272, 273, 294 n.; caused
   drastic change in British
   attitude to secret intelligence
   231; full backing for
   Bletchley 282
C.I.A. (correctly American
   Central Intelligence Agency)
   52, 53; anti-C.I.A.
   propaganda 311; built-in
   errors in original structure
   324; forbidden to operate
   domestically 325; espionage
   and counter-espionage outside
   U.S. 331; has not won
   propaganda war 329; perhaps
   a decoy 328; inadequacy as
   centre of evaluation 327;
   limitations of its scope 327;
   obtained Krushchev's 'secret'
   speech 313; Nazi-German
   parallel 325; only to operate
   abroad 326
Ciano, Count 244
Cipher 81, 223–4
Clemenceau, Georges 33, 159,
   163, 169, 171, 183
'Cicero', Albanian spy 261 and
   n., 262–4, 265
Codebreakers, The (David
   Kahn) 80, 271
Codes and ciphers 80 n.

House, Colonel 153, 158, 187, 188, 191

Ideal spy, the 247, 248
India 47, 48
Ignatyev, Count 37
Invisible or secret ink 80, 81
Irish Nationalism 27; and breaking of British secret intelligence 107
Irish Republican Army 172, 173
Irish Republican Brotherhood 46, 108
Irish Special Branch 46, 47. *See also* Special Branch
Italian intelligence service 231

James, Admiral William 163 and n.
Japan 76; climactic year of 1905 77; reading American naval cipher 232; technical preparation against another war 227. *See also* Anglo-Japanese Treaty of Alliance
Japanese–American relations, ambiguity of 74; feelers out to, 1914–15 160–1
Japanese intelligence 79, 161, 165
Jellicoe, Admiral John 100
Jews, in Western Russia and Eastern Poland, treated as potential German agents 122; played important part on Russo-German front 125, 126
Jewish Committee for the Aid of War Victims (Russia) 140
Journalists, in intelligence 253
Joyce, William ('Lord Haw-Haw') 52, 53, 254
Jutland, Battle of 100

Kaganovich, Lazar 198–9
Kaltenbrunner, Ernst 262

Kameyan, Kazuji, chief of signals, Japan, 1941 72
Kapitza, Peter, Soviet physicist 315
Kapp Putsch, 13 March 1920 213, 214
Katkov, George, difficulties of establishing truth about The February and Bolshevik Revolutions 135, 147, 307
Kennedy, John F. 310
Kennedy, Joseph 244
Kerensky, Alexander 135, 307
K.G.B. (previously M.V.D., N.K.V.D., O.G.P.U., Cheka) 54, 68, 201, 310, 311, 327; officially in existence, 13 March 1954 317; budget vastly increased 317
Kipling, Rudyard 48
Kissinger, Henry 332
Kluge, Field Marshal von 267
Knatchbull-Hugessen, Sir Hughe 262, 264 n., 265
Koestler, Arthur 252
Kollontai, Alexandra, Soviet Ambassador in Stockholm 257, 301

Langridge, Commander Sir Hercules 111
Lanoir, Paul, French writer on German secret intelligence 64–71
Lenin 40, 42, 76, 144, 145, 147, 192, 193, 194, 195, 196, 200, 204; journey to the Finland Station 116; exile in Zurich 143; his definition of Bolshevism 143; unimportant to Okhrana 143; rebuilt Czarist model of government 307–8
Liddell Hart, Captain (later Sir Basil) 21, 97

Nunn May, Allan 318, 320

Oberquartiermeister III, German army intelligence 62
O.G.P.U. 54; murders by assassination squads 308–9
Okhrana the, reasons for 34; duties of 37; alliance with Lenin's Bolsheviks 39; dissolved by 1919 195; inefficient and corrupt over internal enemies 121; infiltration of Social Democrats 143; harassed foreign spies 121; ran most successful trade unions 144; withdrawn in 1914 from peacetime army 86; weighted more in favour of counter-intelligence 308
O.K.W. 264, 269
One-time pad system 284, 286
Open intelligence 13–17
Oppenheimer, Robert 316
Oprichnina, the, *see* Okhrana
Orwell, George 323
Oster, Colonel 242, 243
Oswald, Lee Harvey 310, 311
O.V.H. 264, 294

Page, Walter H. 104, 105, 117, 165, 170; resignation from London Embassy 187
Papen, Franz von 152
Parrott (German spy) 112
Patton, General George 268, 269, 280
Patzig, Captain 219
Pearl Harbor 116, 255
Penkovsky, worked for British S.I.S. 331
Persian oilfields 48
Perry, Commodore Matthew 74
Pershing, General John 150, 161, 179, 180

Pétain, Marshal 133
Peter the Great 34, 35, 37
Philby, Harold 'Kim' 50, 248, 331
Pontecorvo, Bruno 318
Portes, Madame de (Paul Reynaud's mistress) 69
Potemkin, battleship, seizing of 41
Propaganda, in intelligence 253; in psychological warfare 51
Psychological warfare and intelligence service 50–3
Purple Machine (Japan) 226, 272, 280, 287; probably known to Yardley 226; essence predicted by Yardley 228; built in Washington by working backwards 229; outdated by computers 228

Raczynski, Count Edward 276
Radek, Karl 216
Radio ciphers 247
Radio Free Europe 313
Radio Liberty 313
Railway sabotage in Soviet Russia 198
Rakovsky, Christo 145
Rasputin, Gregori 121
Rathenau, Walter 119
Red Army 277
'Reds under the bed' 313
Reichssicherheitshauptdienst 239
Reith, Sir John (later Lord) 254
Roosevelt, Franklin D. 73, 86, 274
Roosevelt, Theodore 25, 78, 149, 151, 156
Ribbentrop, Joachim von 233, 243, 244
Rintelen, Captain Franz von 152
Rodzianko, M. V. 138
Roeder, Captain von 124
Roessler, Rudolf 278. *See also* Lucy Ring